"No other guide has as much to offer . . . these books are a pleasure to read."   Gene Shalit on the *Today Show*

". . . Excellently organized for the casual traveler who is looking for a mix of recreation and cultural insight."
Washington Post

★ ★ ★ ★ ★ (5-star rating) "Crisply written and remarkably personable. Cleverly organized so you can pluck out the minutest fact in a moment. Satisfyingly thorough."
Réalités

"The information they offer is up-to-date, crisply presented but far from exhaustive, the judgments knowledgeable but not opinionated."   *New York Times*

"The individual volumes are compact, the prose succinct, and the coverage up-to-date and knowledgeable . . . The format is portable and the index admirably detailed."
John Barkham Syndicate

". . . An abundance of excellent directions, diversions, and facts, including perspectives and getting-ready-to-go advice — succinct, detailed, and well organized in an easy-to-follow style."   *Los Angeles Times*

"They contain an amount of information that is truly staggering, besides being surprisingly current."
Detroit News

"These guides address themselves to the needs of the modern traveler demanding precise, qualitative information . . . Upbeat, slick, and well put together."
Dallas Morning News

". . . Attractive to look at, refreshingly easy to read, and generously packed with information."   *Miami Herald*

"These guides are as good as any published, and much better than most."   *Louisville* (Kentucky) *Times*

Stephen Birnbaum Travel Guides

Acapulco
Bahamas, and Turks & Caicos
Barcelona
Bermuda
Boston
Canada
Cancun, Cozumel, & Isla Mujeres
Caribbean
Chicago
Disneyland
Eastern Europe
Europe
Europe for Business Travelers
Florence
France
Great Britain
Hawaii
Honolulu
Ireland
Italy
Ixtapa & Zihuatanejo
Las Vegas
London
Los Angeles
Mexico
Miami & Ft. Lauderdale
Montreal & Quebec City
New Orleans
New York
Paris
Portugal
Puerto Vallarta
Rome
San Francisco
South America
Spain
Toronto
United States
USA for Business Travelers
Vancouver
Venice
Walt Disney World
Washington, DC
Western Europe

CONTRIBUTING EDITORS

Kevin Causey
Julith Jedamus
Stephen Mills
Eileen Morin
David P. Schulz
Melinda Tang

MAPS B. Andrew Mudryk

SYMBOLS Gloria McKeown

A Stephen Birnbaum Travel Guide

Birnbaum's BAHAMAS, AND TURKS & CAICOS 1993

Alexandra Mayes Birnbaum
EDITOR

Lois Spritzer
EXECUTIVE EDITOR

Laura L. Brengelman
Managing Editor

Mary Callahan
Jill Kadetsky
Susan McClung
Beth Schlau
Dana Margaret Schwartz
Associate Editors

Gene Gold
Assistant Editor

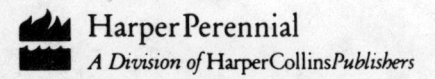

HarperPerennial
A Division of HarperCollins*Publishers*

To Stephen, who merely made all this possible.

BIRNBAUM'S BAHAMAS, TURKS & CAICOS 1993. Copyright © 1992 by HarperCollins Publishers. All rights reserved. Printed in the United States of America. No part of this book may be used or reproduced in any manner whatsoever without written permission except in the case of brief quotations embodied in critical articles and reviews. For information address HarperCollins*Publishers,* 10 East 53rd Street, New York, NY 10022.

FIRST EDITION

ISSN 0749-2561 (Stephen Birnbaum Travel Guides)
ISSN 1055-5625 (Bahamas)
ISBN 0-06-278042-5 (pbk.)

92 93 94 95 96 CC/WP 10 9 8 7 6 5 4 3 2 1

Contents

ix   **A Word from the Editor**

1   **How to Use This Guide**

GETTING READY TO GO

Practical information for planning your trip.

When and How to Go

- 9   What's Where
- 9   When to Go
- 11   Traveling by Plane
- 27   Traveling by Cruise Ship
- 31   Traveling by Chartered Boat
- 32   Touring by Car
- 36   Package Tours

Preparing

- 41   Calculating Costs
- 42   Planning a Trip
- 44   How to Use a Travel Agent
- 45   Entry Requirements and Documents
- 46   Insurance
- 50   Hints for Handicapped Travelers
- 56   Hints for Single Travelers
- 58   Hints for Older Travelers
- 60   Hints for Traveling with Children

On the Islands

- 65   Credit and Currency
- 68   Hotels and Guesthouses
- 68   Rental Homes and Vacation Apartments
- 71   All-Inclusive Resorts: Couples' and Club Med
- 72   Time Zones, Business Hours, and Holidays
- 72   Mail, Telephone, and Electricity
- 74   Staying Healthy
- 77   Legal Aid and Consular Services

vi CONTENTS

- 79 Drinking and Drugs
- 79 Tipping
- 80 Religion in the Islands
- 81 Customs and Returning to the US

Sources and Resources

- 85 Island Tourist Offices
- 86 Books and Newletters
- 87 Cameras and Equipment

PERSPECTIVES

A cultural and historical survey of the islands, their history, people, food, music, religions, folk life, and environment.

- 91 History
- 97 Music and Dance
- 102 Religion and Religious Heritages
- 105 Island Food and Drink
- 109 Flora, Fauna, and Fertile Lands
- 118 Folk Legends and Lore, and Crafts

THE ISLANDS

Thorough, qualitative guides to the Bahamas and the Turks & Caicos. Each section offers a comprehensive report on the islands' most compelling attractions and amenities, designed to be used on the spot. Directions and recommendations are immediately accessible.

- 121 Bahamas
- 151 Turks & Caicos

DIVERSIONS

A selective guide to more than a dozen active and/or cerebral vacation themes, including the best places to pursue them.

For the Experience

- 167 Quintessential Bahamas
- 173 Special Havens
- 174 Private Islands
- 175 Natural Wonderlands
- 176 Shopping

CONTENTS

176 Casino Countdown
177 A Shutterbug's View

For the Body

182 Dream Beaches
182 Best Depths: Snorkeling and Scuba
184 Lots of Yachts: Sailing
185 Top Tennis
185 Golf
186 Sport Fishing
187 Hunting
187 Sunken and Buried Treasure

DIRECTIONS

A dozen of the most delightful walks and drives through the Bahamas and the Turks & Caicos.

191 Introduction

193 Nassau
198 New Providence
204 Paradise Island
209 Grand Bahama
215 Bimini
221 Abacos
228 Andros
234 Eleuthera
240 Cat Island
245 Exumas
251 San Salvador
258 Turks & Caicos

265 **Index**

A Word from the Editor

To tell the truth, neither my husband Stephen Birnbaum nor I started out as fans of the Bahamas. Our first Bahamian travel experience began a couple of decades ago on Grand Bahama Island, arguably the least attractive of all the 700 or so Bahamian islands. It wasn't so much that Grand Bahama was any less attractive physically than its sister islands, but that it was cursed by the kind of cynical development that had no regard for Bahamas culture or island values, and the island looked like a kind of poor man's Las Vegas with the emphasis on bad taste and indifferent management. It wasn't the kind of place to which you'd willingly return.

Things weren't improved much by the prevalent attitude of native Bahamians to visitors. Independence had recently been achieved, and the resentment exhibited by Bahamians for folks from the mainland was clear and near-constant. Very few kind words were spoken, and returning travelers were full of stories of hassles and harassment.

But attitudes in the Bahamas have changed significantly over the last generation, and while Grand Bahama Island hasn't improved much, it is no more representative of the broad scope of the Bahamas than New York City is an example of the United States as a whole. Bahamians have come to recognize that a pleasant relationship with visitors is essential to their own economic health, and the pendulum has swung back to permit a newly welcoming demeanor.

At least as important is the discovery by travelers that such popular stops as Nassau/Paradise Island and Grand Bahama are not the real lure of the Bahamas. The Bahamian places where the appeal of authentic island life is most often discovered are on Eleuthera and Spanish Wells, on Great Abaco and the Exumas, and on the Berry Islands and the Turks & Caicos. And at a time when true get-away-from-it-all escapes are harder and harder to find in our modern world, the Bahamas represent a nearby destination that can produce serenity and solitude in abundance. As a matter of fact, peace and quiet may turn out to be the Bahamas' most valuable natural resource.

The new accessibility and appeal of the Bahamas are the spur to the creation of this guide (now in only its second but completely revised year) to these numerous, diverse islands. Development has slowed (blissfully), allowing the native population to evaluate the desirability of unchecked hotel and resort building, and thereby retain a full measure of island ambience. Though all members of the same island group, the individual atolls that make up the Bahamas have very different flavors and atmospheres, and we have tried to isolate and explain these very varied attitudes that prevail within a single nation.

Obviously, any guidebook to the Bahamas must keep pace with and answer

x A WORD FROM THE EDITOR

the real needs of today's travelers. That's why we've tried to create a guide that's specifically organized, written, and edited for the more demanding modern traveler, one for whom qualitative information is infinitely more desirable than mere quantities of unappraised data. We think that this book, along with all the other guides in our series, represents a new generation of travel guides — one that is especially responsive to modern needs and interests.

For years, dating back as far as Herr Baedeker, travel guides have tended to be encyclopedic, seemingly much more concerned with demonstrating expertise in geography and history than with a real analysis of the sorts of things that actually concern a typical modern tourist. But today, when it is hardly necessary to tell a traveler where New Providence is (in many cases, the traveler has been there nearly as often as the guidebook editors), it becomes the responsibility of those editors to provide new perspectives and to suggest new directions in order to make the guide genuinely valuable.

That's exactly what we've tried to do in this series. I think you'll notice a different, more contemporary tone to the text, as well as an organization and focus that are distinctive and more functional. And even a random reading of what follows will demonstrate a substantial departure from the standard guidebook orientation, for we've not only attempted to provide information of a more compelling sort, but we also have tried to present the data in a format that makes it particularly accessible.

Needless to say, it's difficult to decide just what to include in a guidebook of this size — and what to omit. Early on, we realized that giving up the encyclopedic approach precluded our listing every single route and restaurant, a realization that helped define our overall editorial focus. Similarly, when we discussed the possibility of presenting certain information in other than strict geographic order, we found that the new format enabled us to arrange data in a way that we feel best answers the questions travelers typically ask.

Large numbers of specific questions have provided the real editorial skeleton for this book. The volume of mail we regularly receive emphasizes that modern travelers want very precise information, so we've tried to organize our material in the most responsive way possible. Readers who want to know the best restaurant in the Bahamas or the best beach will have no trouble extracting that data from this guide.

Travel guides are, understandably, reflections of personal taste, and putting one's name on a title page obviously puts one's preferences on the line. But I think I ought to amplify just what "personal" means. Like Steve, I don't believe in the sort of personal guidebook that's a palpable misrepresentation on its face. It is, for example, hardly possible for any single travel writer to visit thousands of restaurants (and nearly as many hotels) in any given year and provide accurate appraisals of each. And even if it were physically possible for one human being to survive such an itinerary, it would of necessity have to be done at a dead sprint, and the perceptions derived therefrom would probably be less valid than those of any other intelligent individual visiting the same establishments. It is, therefore, impossible (especially in a large, annually revised and updated guidebook *series* such as we offer) to have only one person provide all the data on the entire world.

I also happen to think that such individual orientation is of substantially less value to readers. Visiting a single hotel for just one night or eating one hasty meal in a random restaurant hardly equips anyone to provide appraisals that are of more than passing interest. No amount of doggedly alliterative or oppressively onomatopoeic text can camouflage a technique that is essentially specious. We have, therefore, chosen what I like to describe as the "thee and me" approach to restaurant and hotel evaluation and, to a somewhat more limited degree, to the sites and sights we have included in the other sections of our text. What this really reflects is personal sampling tempered by intelligent counsel from informed local sources, and these additional friends-of-the-editors are almost always residents of the island and/or area about which they are consulted.

Despite the presence of several editors, writers, researchers, and local contributors, very precise editing and tailoring keep our text fiercely subjective. So what follows is the gospel according to Birnbaum, and represents as much of our own taste and instincts as we can manage. It is probable, therefore, that if you like your beaches largely unpopulated, prefer small hotels with personality to huge high-rise anonymities, and can't tolerate fresh fish that's been relentlessly overcooked, we're likely to have a long and meaningful relationship. Readers with dissimilar tastes may be less enraptured.

I should also point out something about the person to whom this guidebook is directed. Above all, he or she is a "visitor." This means that such elements as restaurants have been specifically picked to provide the visitor with a representative, enlightening, stimulating, and above all pleasant experience. Since so many extraneous considerations can affect the reception and service accorded a regular restaurant patron, our choices can in no way be construed as an exhaustive guide to resident dining. We think we've listed all the best places, in various price ranges, but they were chosen with a visitor's enjoyment in mind.

Other evidence of how we've tried to tailor our text to reflect modern travel habits is most apparent in the section we call DIVERSIONS. Where once it was common for travelers to spend an island visit nailed to a single spot, the emphasis today is more likely to be directed toward pursuing some sport or special interest while seeing the surrounding countryside. So we've organized every activity we could reasonably evaluate and arranged the material in a way that is especially accessible to activists of either athletic or cerebral bent. It is no longer necessary, therefore, to wade through a pound or two of superfluous prose just to find the most challenging golf course within a reasonable distance of your destination.

If there is one single thing that best characterizes the revolution in and evolution of current holiday habits, it is that most travelers now consider travel a right rather than a privilege. No longer is a family trip to the far corners of the world necessarily a once-in-a-lifetime thing; nor is the idea of visiting exotic, faraway places in the least worrisome. Travel today translates as the enthusiastic desire to sample all of the world's opportunities, to find that elusive quality of experience that is not only enriching but comfortable. For that reason, we've tried to make what follows not only helpful and enlightening, but the sort of welcome companion of which every traveler dreams.

Finally, I also should point out that every good travel guide is a living enterprise; that is, no part of this text is carved in stone. In our annual revisions, we refine, expand, and further hone all our material to serve your travel needs better. To this end, no contribution is of greater value to us than your personal reaction to what we have written, as well as information reflecting your own experiences while using the book. We earnestly and enthusiastically solicit your comments about this guide *and* your opinions and perceptions about places you have recently visited. In this way, we will be able to provide the most current information — including the actual experiences of recent travelers — and to make those experiences more readily available to others. Please write to us at 10 E. 53rd St., New York, NY 10022.

We sincerely hope to hear from you.

ALEXANDRA MAYES BIRNBAUM

How to Use This Guide

A great deal of care has gone into the special organization of this guidebook, and we believe it represents a real breakthrough in the presentation of travel material. Our aim is to create a new, more modern generation of travel books, and to make this guide the most useful and practical travel tool available today.

Our text is divided into five basic sections, in order to present information in the best way on every possible aspect of a Bahamas vacation. This organization itself should alert you to the vast and varied opportunities available, as well as indicate all the specific data necessary to plan a successful visit. You won't find much of the conventional "swaying palms and shimmering sands" text here; we've chosen instead to deliver more useful and practical information. Prospective itineraries tend to speak for themselves, and with so many diverse travel opportunities, we feel our main job is to highlight what's where and to provide basic information — how, when, where, how much, and what's best — to assist you in making the most intelligent choices possible.

Here is a brief summary of the five sections of this book, and what you can expect to find in each. We believe that you will find both your travel planning and on-island enjoyment enhanced by having this book at your side.

GETTING READY TO GO

This mini-encyclopedia of practical travel facts is a sort of know-it-all companion, with all the precise information necessary to create a successful Bahamas holiday. There are entries on more than 20 separate topics, including how to get where you're going, what preparations to make before leaving, what to expect, what your trip is likely to cost, and how to avoid prospective problems. The individual entries are specific, realistic, and, where appropriate, cost-oriented.

We expect you to use this section most in the course of planning your trip, for its ideas and suggestions are intended to simplify this often confusing period. Entries are intentionally concise, in an effort to get to the meat of the matter with the least extraneous prose. These entries are augmented by extensive lists of specific sources from which to obtain even more specialized data, plus some suggestions for obtaining special-interest travel information on your own.

PERSPECTIVES

Any visit to an unfamiliar destination is enhanced and enriched by understanding the cultural and historical heritage of that area. We have, therefore, provided just such an introduction to the Bahamas and Turks & Caicos, their history, people, food, music, religion, and other pertinent subjects.

THE ISLANDS

These individual reports on the Bahamas and the Turks & Caicos have been created with the assistance of researchers, contributors, professional journalists, and experts who live on the islands. Although useful at the planning stage, THE ISLANDS are really designed to be taken along and used on the spot. Each report offers a short-stay guide, including an essay introducing the island as a contemporary place to visit. *At-a-Glance* material is actually a site-by-site survey of the most important, interesting, and sometimes most eclectic sights to see and things to do. *Sources and Resources* is a concise listing of pertinent tourist information, meant to answer myriad potentially pressing questions as they arise — from simple things such as the address of the local tourism office, how to get around, which sightseeing tours to take, and when special events occur to something more difficult like where to find the best nightspot, to play golf, to rent scuba equipment, to find the best beach, or to get a taxi. *Best on the Islands* lists our collection of cost-and-quality choices of the best places to eat and sleep on a variety of budgets.

DIVERSIONS

This section is designed to help travelers find the best places in which to engage in a wide range of physical and cerebral activities, without having to wade through endless pages of unrelated text. This very selective guide lists the broadest possible range of vacation activities, including all the best places to pursue them.

We start with a list of special places to stay and eat, and move to activities that require some perspiration — sports preferences and other rigorous pursuits. In every case, our suggestion of a particular location — and often our recommendation of a specific resort — is intended to guide you to that special place where the quality of experience is likely to be highest. Whether you seek great golf or tennis, scuba or snorkeling, or the Bahamas' most luxurious resorts, each category is the equivalent of a comprehensive checklist of the absolute best of the island.

DIRECTIONS

Here are 12 itineraries that follow the most beautiful routes and roads, past the most spectacular diving spots, and through the most serene and quaint little towns. DIRECTIONS is the only section of this book that is organized geographically; walks, bike tours, and drives can be connected for longer trips or used individually for short, intensive explorations.

Each entry includes a guide to sightseeing highlights, a qualitative guide to food along the road, and suggestions for activities.

Although each of the book's sections has a distinct format and a special function, they have all been designed to be used together to provide a complete inventory of travel information. To use this book to full advantage, take a few minutes to read the table of contents and random entries in each section to get a firsthand feel for how it all fits together.

In other words, the sections of this book are building blocks designed to help you put together the best possible trip. Use them selectively as a tool, a source of ideas, a reference work for accurate facts, and a guidebook to the best buys, the most exciting sights, the most pleasant accommodations, and the tastiest foods — *the best travel experience* that you can possibly have.

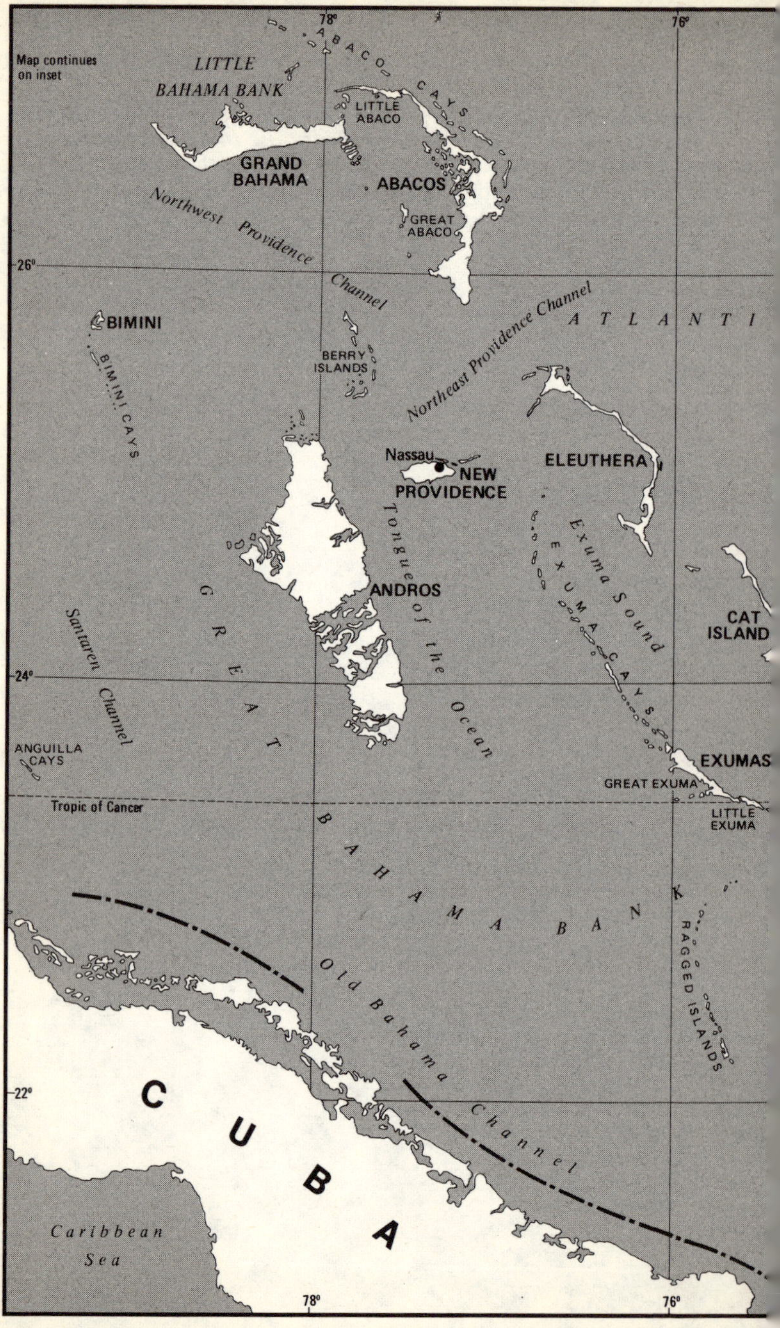

Map continues on inset
78°
76°
LITTLE BAHAMA BANK
ABACO CAYS
LITTLE ABACO
GRAND BAHAMA
ABACOS
GREAT ABACO
Northwest Providence Channel
26°
BIMINI
BIMINI CAYS
BERRY ISLANDS
Northeast Providence Channel
ATLANTI
Nassau
NEW PROVIDENCE
ELEUTHERA
Tongue of the Ocean
ANDROS
Exuma Sound
EXUMA CAYS
CAT ISLAND
Santaren Channel
GREAT
24°
ANGUILLA CAYS
EXUMAS
GREAT EXUMA
LITTLE EXUMA
Tropic of Cancer
BAHAMA BANK
RAGGED ISLANDS
Old Bahama Channel
22°
CUBA
Caribbean Sea

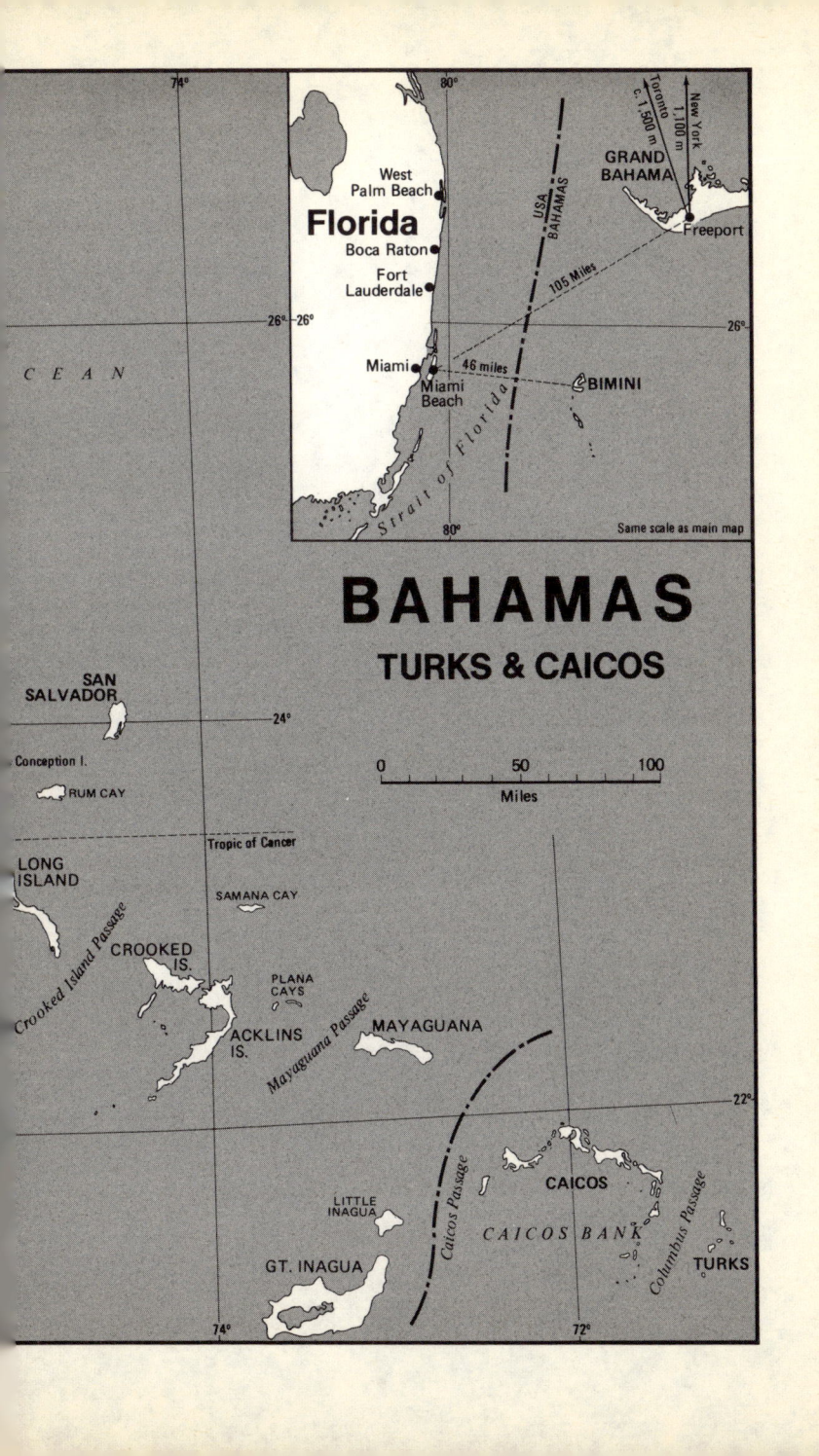

BAHAMAS

TURKS & CAICOS

GETTING READY TO GO

When and How to Go

What's Where

Starting just 50 miles east of central Florida, the Bahamas spread in a gentle arc for 700 miles to the southeast. They comprise a maze of 700 islands, innumerable cays (pronounced *keys*), and myriad coral reefs.

The most popular tourist centers are Nassau, the capital, on the island of New Providence, and Freeport, on Grand Bahama, which is barely 30 minutes by plane from Palm Beach. A number of well-known destinations, equally popular with yachtsmen, fishermen, and determined escapists, are in the outlying islands. These include Bimini, only about 50 miles east of Miami, famous for its deep-sea fishing; the Berry Islands, once frequented by pirate vessels cruising between Florida and Nassau; Andros, the largest island in the Bahamas, a few miles northeast of the Great Bahama Bank, the world's third-largest barrier reef; Eleuthera, the most developed of the outlying islands (also known as the Family Islands or Out Islands); Harbour Island, noted for its pink sand beach; the Exuma chain, the site of the annual *Family Island Regatta;* and San Salvador, the first landfall — according to Bahamian tradition — claimed by Columbus in 1492. Others with facilities for visitors are the Abacos, Cat Island, Long Island, and Spanish Wells.

Since 1973, the Bahamas have been an independent nation affiliated with the British Commonwealth. Their chief natural attributes are an appealing subtropical climate, with temperatures averaging between 60F and 90F year-round, and an extensive range of islands and well-charted sailing waters scattered over almost 100,000 square miles.

Geographically, the Turks & Caicos Islands fit within the orbit of the Bahamas and are at the southern tip of that island group, 90 miles north of the island of Hispaniola. A British Crown Colony, the Turks & Caicos (the plural is always used) Islands consist of eight major islands and a number of cays surrounded by warm currents. As in the Bahamas, average temperatures here range from 60F to 90F throughout the year. The islands of most interest are Grand Turk (the site of Cockburn Town, the capital), Salt Cay, South Caicos, Middle (or Grand) Caicos, North Caicos, Providenciales ("Provo"), and Pine Cay.

When to Go

The lures of the Bahamas are essentially natural: sun, sand, and sea in a climate that virtually begs you to relax. But the elements do vary; logically, the best weather is to be enjoyed for the highest prices during the peak (winter) season.

GETTING READY / When to Go

The Bahamas, in a subtropical zone, offer warmer temperatures throughout much of the year, although the midsummer months can be enervating; December through April are the most pleasant, and, therefore, are the most popular months.

It is important to emphasize, however, that more and more travelers are enjoying the advantages of off-season travel to the Bahamas. Though the weather may be slightly less desirable, major attractions, shops, beaches, and other facilities tend to be less crowded, as are the islands in general. During the off-season, Bahamian life proceeds at its most natural pace, and a lively social and cultural calendar flourishes. What's more, travel generally is less expensive, with hotel rates running 30% to 60% lower. Although some establishments may close during the off-season in response to reduced demand, there still are plenty of alternatives, and cut-rate "mini-break" packages — discounts for stays of more than 1 night, particularly over a weekend — are more common.

An additional bonus to visiting during the off-season is that even the most basic services are performed more efficiently. In theory, off-season service is identical to that offered during high season, but the fact is that the absence of demanding crowds inevitably begets much more thoughtful and personal attention. The very same staff that barely can manage to get fresh towels onto the racks during December and January has the time to chat pleasantly during July and August.

It is not only hotel service that benefits from the absence of the high-season mobs. Fine restaurants, filled to capacity during peak travel times, pay rapt attention to their guests during the off-season. And the food preparation and service are also likely to be best when the chef is required to create only a reasonable number of meals.

CLIMATE AND CLOTHES: In winter months, the Gulf Stream warms the Bahamas to a balmy average of 70F (21C). From June through October, the average thermometer reading is about 80F (27C), and in November it's about 75F (24C). September is the riskiest month as far as storms are concerned, although the actual hurricane season can stretch from June through October.

Travelers can get current readings and extended forecasts through the *Weather Channel Connection*, the worldwide weather report number of the *Weather Channel*, a cable TV station. By dialing 900-WEATHER and punching in either the first four letters of the city name or the area code for over 600 cities in the US (including Puerto Rico and the US Virgin Islands), an up-to-date recording will provide weather information, as well as (for some locations) beach, boating, and highway reports. To obtain weather information for over 225 international destinations, callers can punch in the first four letters of the city — or, in some cases, the island. (To find out which cities in a given country are covered, enter the first four letters of the country's name.) To hear the weather in the Bahamas, punch in BAHA. This 24-hour service can be accessed from any touch-tone phone in the US, and costs 95¢ per minute. The charge will show up on your phone bill.

Casual, lightweight resortwear is the rule, with some dressing up in the evenings (long dresses, skirts, or evening tops and pants for women; jackets or long-sleeve shirts for men), particularly for dining, dancing, or the casinos in Nassau, Cable Beach, Paradise Island, or Freeport. Women should bring a scarf, stole, or evening sweater for occasional cool nights. As a rule, the farther from Nassau and Freeport you get, the more casual it is, although at resorts like *Cotton Bay* or *Treasure Cay*, there's still a tendency to dress up at night. Bathing suits are *never* worn in town, on any island. Be cautious about the sun; take cover-ups to the beach. When cycling, use a sunscreen or wear long-sleeve shirts and slacks to prevent burn on the back of your neck, arms, and knees.

Traveling by Plane

Air travel is most often the choice of vacationers to the Bahamas. As an efficient means of transportation to a single destination, air travel is far faster and more direct; it is rare to have to spend more than a day getting to the Bahamas by air, even from the most inaccessible part of the US. The less time spent in transit, the more time spent on the islands. And that is even truer as conveniently scheduled connecting flights to the Bahamas are becoming available from an increasing number of US gateways.

Despite recent attempts at price simplification by a number of major US carriers, the airlines offering flights to the Bahamas continue to sell seats at a variety of prices under a vast spectrum of requirements and restrictions. Since you probably will spend more for your airfare than for any other single item in your travel budget, try to take advantage of the lowest available fare. You should know what kinds of flights are available, the rules and regulations pertaining to air travel, and all the special package options.

SCHEDULED FLIGHTS: Airlines that schedule direct (one-plane or nonstop) flights from North American cities to Nassau and/or Freeport include *Air Canada* from Montreal and Toronto; *American* from New York; *Bahamasair* from Miami; *Delta* from Atlanta, Ft. Lauderdale, New York, and Orlando; *Laker Airways* from Miami and Ft. Lauderdale; and *USAir* from Baltimore and Charlotte.

Getting to the outlying islands used to be iffy, but various smaller, commuter or regional airlines, including some linked to the major scheduled carriers, now fly to a variety of Family Island airports from Florida gateways. *American's American Eagle Commuter Service* flies to Freeport, Treasure Cay, and Marsh Harbour from Miami. *Comair,* the Bahamas-bound link in the *Delta Connection,* flies to Nassau and Freeport from Ft. Lauderdale, Melbourne, Orlando, and West Palm Beach. *USAir Express (Henson Airlines)* serves Nassau, Treasure Cay, Marsh Harbour, Governor's Harbour, and North Eleuthera with flights from Ft. Lauderdale, Orlando, and West Palm Beach. *Chalk's International* offers 30-minute seaplane service to Nassau and Bimini from either its hometown, Ft. Lauderdale, or Miami; an affiliate, *Paradise Island Airlines,* flies Dash 7s to Paradise Island from Ft. Lauderdale, Miami, Orlando, and West Palm Beach. *Bahamasair* serves the greatest number of destinations in the outlying islands, but the airline's flights from the US land in Nassau or Freeport — the Family Islands are reached via connections in Nassau.

Bahamasair departs from Nassau to South Caicos. *Turks and Caicos National Airline (TCNA)* makes inter-island connections. *Carnival Air Lines* flies from Miami to the Turks & Caicos.

Tickets – When traveling on one of the many regularly scheduled flights, a full-fare ticket provides maximum travel flexibility (although at considerable expense) because there are no advance booking requirements. A prospective passenger can buy a ticket for a flight right up to the minute of takeoff — if a seat is available. The Bahamian government's immigration policy, however, requires that you have a return or forwarding flight ticket upon your arrival in the Bahamas. (Tickets are generally good for a year and can be renewed if not used.) On some airlines, you may be able to cancel your flight at any time without penalty; on others, cancellation — even of a full-fare ticket — may be subject to a variety of restrictions. It pays to check *before* booking your flight. In addition, while it is true that this category of ticket can be purchased at the last minute, it is advisable to reserve well in advance during popular vacation periods and around holiday times.

12 GETTING READY / Traveling by Plane

Fares – Airfares continue to change so rapidly that even the experts find it difficult to keep up with them. This ever-changing situation is due to a number of factors, including airline deregulation, volatile labor relations, increasing fuel costs, and vastly increased competition.

Perhaps the most common misconception about fares on scheduled airlines is that the cost of the ticket determines how much service will be provided on the flight. This is true to only a certain extent. A far more realistic rule of thumb is that the less you pay for your ticket, the more restrictions and qualifications are likely to come into play before you board the plane (as well as after you get off). These qualifying aspects relate to the months (and the days of the week) during which you must travel, how far in advance you must purchase your ticket, and the minimum and maximum amount of time you may or must remain away, your willingness to decide on a return date at the time of booking — and your ability to stick to that date. It is not uncommon for passengers sitting side by side on the same wide-body jet to have paid fares varying by hundreds of dollars, and all too often the traveler paying more would have been equally willing (and able) to accept the terms of the far less expensive ticket.

In general, the great variety of airfares to the Bahamas can be reduced to four basic categories, including first class, coach (also called economy or tourist class), and excursion or discount fares. A fourth category, called business class, has been added by many airlines in recent years. In addition, Advance Purchase Excursion (APEX) fares offer savings under certain conditions.

A **first class** ticket is your admission to the special section of the aircraft, with larger seats, more legroom, sleeperette seating on some wide-body aircraft, better (or more elaborately served) food, free drinks and headsets for movies and music channels, and, above all, personal attention. First class fares are about twice those of full-fare economy, although both first class passengers and those paying full-fare economy fares are entitled to reserve seats and are sold tickets on an open reservation system. An additional advantage of a first class ticket is that you may be able to include one or two stops en route to or from your final destination in the Bahamas free of charge, provided that certain set, but generous, maximum permitted mileage limits are respected.

The terms of the **coach** or **economy** fare may vary slightly from airline to airline, and, in fact, from time to time airlines may be selling more than one type of economy fare. Coach or economy passengers sit more snugly, as many as 10 in a single row on a wide-body jet, behind the first class and business class sections. Normally alcoholic drinks are not free, nor are the headsets. If there are two economy fares on the books, one (often called "regular economy") still may include a number of free stopovers. The other, less expensive fare (often called "special economy") may limit stopovers to one or two, with a charge (typically $25) for each one. Like first class passengers, travelers paying the full coach fare are subject to none of the restrictions that are usually attached to less expensive excursion and discount fares. There are no advance booking requirements, no minimum stay requirements, and (often) no cancellation penalties — but beware, the rules regarding cancellation vary from carrier to carrier. Tickets are sold on an open reservation system: They can be bought for a flight right up to the minute of takeoff (if seats are available), but in the case of the Bahamas, the return ticket must be purchased *before* departure. Both first class and coach tickets are generally good for a year, after which they can be renewed if not used, and if you ultimately decide not to fly at all, your money may be refunded (again, policies vary).

Excursion and other **discount** fares are the airlines' equivalent of a special sale and apply to round-trip bookings only. These fares generally differ according to the season and the number of travel days permitted. They are only a bit less flexible than full-fare economy tickets, and are, therefore, often useful for both business and holiday travelers. Most round-trip excursion tickets include strict minimum and maximum stay require-

GETTING READY / Traveling by Plane 13

ments, and reservations can be changed only within the specified time limits. So don't count on extending a ticket beyond the prescribed time of return or staying less time than required. Different airlines may have different regulations concerning the number of stopovers permitted, and sometimes excursion fares are less expensive during midweek. The availability of these reduced-rate seats is most limited at busy times, such as holidays. Discount or excursion fare ticket holders sit with the coach passengers and, for all intents and purposes, are indistinguishable from them. They receive all the same basic services, even though they may have paid anywhere between 30% and 55% less for the trip. Obviously, it's wise to make plans early enough to qualify for this less expensive transportation, if possible.

These discount or excursion fares may masquerade under a variety of names, they may vary from city to city (from the East Coast to the West Coast, especially), but they invariably have strings attached. A common requirement is that the ticket be purchased a certain number of days — usually between 7 and 21 days — in advance of departure, though it may be booked weeks or months in advance (it has to be "ticketed," or paid for, shortly after booking, however). The return reservation usually has to be made at the time of the original ticketing and often cannot be changed later than a certain number of days (again, usually 7 to 21 days) before the return flight. If events force a change in the return reservation after the date allowed, the passenger may have to pay the difference between the round-trip excursion rate and the round-trip coach rate although some carriers permit such scheduling changes for a nominal fee. In addition, some airlines may allow passengers to use their discounted fares by standing by for an empty seat, even if they don't otherwise have standby fares. Another common condition is a minimum and maximum stay requirement; for example, 1 to 6 days, or 6 to 14 days (but including at least a Saturday night). Last, cancellation penalties of up to 50% of the full price of the ticket have been assessed — check the specific penalty in effect when you purchase your discount/excursion ticket — so careful planning is imperative.

On some airlines, the ticket bearing the lowest price of all the current discount fares is the ticket where no change at all in departure and/or return flights is permitted, and where the ticket price is totally nonrefundable. If you do buy such a nonrefundable ticket, you should be aware of a policy followed by some airlines, regarding international flights, that may make it easier to change your plans if necessary. For a fee — set by each airline and payable at the airport when checking in — you *may* be able to change the time or date of a return flight on a nonrefundable ticket. However, if the nonrefundable ticket price for the replacement flight is higher than that of the original (as is often the case when trading in a weekday for a weekend flight), you will have to pay the difference. Any such change must be made a certain number of days in advance — in some cases as little as 2 days — of either the original or the replacement flight, whichever is earlier; restrictions are set by the individual carrier. (Travelers holding a nonrefundable or other restricted ticket who must change their plans due to a family emergency should know that some carriers may make special allowance in such situations; for further information, see *Legal Aid and Consular Services,* in this section.)

■ **Note:** Due to recent changes in many US airlines' policies, nonrefundable tickets are now available that carry none of the above restrictions. Although passengers still may *not* be able to obtain a refund for the price paid, the time or date of a departing or return flight may be changed at any time (assuming seats are available) for a nominal service charge.

There also is a newer, often less expensive type of excursion fare, the **APEX**, or **Advanced Purchase Excursion** fare. As with traditional excursion fares, passengers paying an APEX fare sit with and receive the same basic services as any other coach or economy passengers, even though they may have paid up to 50% less for their seats. In return, they are subject to certain restrictions. In the case of flights to the Bahamas, the ticket is usually good for a minimum of 2 days in the islands and a maximum, currently, of 45 days; and as its name implies, it must be "ticketed," or paid for in its entirety a certain period of time before departure — usually 21 days.

The drawback to some APEX fares is that they penalize travelers who change their minds — and travel plans. Usually the return reservation must be made at the time of the original ticketing, and if for some reason you change your schedule, you will have to pay a penalty of up to $100 or 10% of the ticket value, whichever is greater, as long as you travel within the validity period of your ticket. More flexible APEX fares recently have been introduced, which allow travelers to make changes in the date or time of their flights for a nominal charge (as low as $25).

With either type of APEX fare, if you change your return to a date less than the minimum stay or more than the maximum stay, the difference between the round-trip APEX fare and the full round-trip coach rate will have to be paid. There is also a penalty of anywhere from $50 to $100 or more for canceling or changing a reservation *before* travel begins — check the specific penalty in effect when you purchase your ticket.

Travelers looking for the least expensive possible airfares should, finally, scan the pages of their hometown newspapers (especially the Sunday travel section) for announcements of special promotional fares. Most airlines offer their most attractive special fares to encourage travel during slow seasons, and to inaugurate and publicize new routes. Even if none of these factors applies, prospective passengers can be fairly sure that the number of discount seats per flight at the lowest price is strictly limited, or that the fare offering includes a set expiration date — which means it's absolutely necessary to move fast to enjoy the lowest possible price.

Among other special airline promotional deals for which you should be on the lookout are discount or upgrade coupons sometimes offered by the major carriers and found in mail-order merchandise catalogues. For instance, airlines sometimes issue coupons that typically cost around $25 each and are good for a percentage discount or an upgrade on an international airline ticket — including flights to the Bahamas. The only requirement beyond the fee generally is that a coupon purchaser must buy at least one item from the catalogue. There are usually some minimum airfare restrictions before the coupon is redeemable, but in general these are worthwhile offers. Restrictions often include certain blackout days (when the coupon cannot be used at all), usually imposed during peak travel periods. These coupons are particularly valuable to business travelers who tend to buy full-fare tickets, and while the coupons are issued in the buyer's name, they can be used by others who are traveling on the same itinerary.

It's always wise to ask about discount or promotional fares and about any conditions that might restrict booking, payment, cancellation, or changes in plans. Check the prices from neighboring cities. A special rate may be offered in a nearby city but not in yours, and it may be enough of a bargain to warrant your leaving from that city. Ask if there is a difference in price for midweek versus weekend travel, or if there is a further discount for traveling early in the morning or late at night. Also be sure to investigate package deals, which are offered by virtually every airline. These may include accommodations and dining and/or sightseeing features, in addition to the basic airfare, and the combined cost of packaged elements usually is considerably less than the cost of the exact same elements when purchased separately.

If in the course of your research you come across a deal that seems too good to be true, keep in mind that logic may not be a component of deeply discounted airfares — there's not always any sane relationship between miles to be flown and the price to get

GETTING READY / Traveling by Plane 15

there. More often than not, the level of competition on a given route dictates the degree of discount, and don't be dissuaded from accepting an offer that sounds irresistible just because it also sounds illogical. Better to buy that inexpensive fare while it's being offered and worry about the sense — or absence thereof — while you're flying to your desired destination.

When you're satisfied that you've found the lowest possible price for which you can conveniently qualify (you may have to call the airline more than once, because different airline reservations clerks have been known to quote different prices), make your booking. Then, to protect yourself against fare increases, purchase and pay for your ticket as soon as possible after you've received a confirmed reservation. Airlines generally will honor their tickets, even if the operative price at the time of your flight is higher than the price you paid; if fares go up between the time you *reserve* a flight and the time you *pay* for it, you likely will be out of luck. Finally, with excursion or discount fares, it is important to remember that when a reservation clerk says that you must purchase a ticket by a specific date, this is an absolute deadline. Miss it and the airline may automatically cancel your reservation without telling you.

■ **Note:** Another wrinkle in the airfare scene is that if the fares go *down* after you purchase your ticket, you *may* be entitled to a refund of the difference. However, this is only possible in certain situations — availability and advance purchase restrictions pertaining to the lower rate are set by the airline. If you suspect that you may be able to qualify for such a refund, check with your travel agent or the airline.

Frequent Flyers – Most of the leading carriers serving the Bahamas offer a bonus system to frequent travelers. After the first 10,000 miles, for example, a passenger might be eligible for a first class seat for the coach fare; after another 10,000 miles, he or she might receive a discount on his or her next ticket purchase. The value of the bonuses continues to increase as more miles are logged.

Bonus miles also may be earned by patronizing affiliated hotel chains and car rental companies, or by using one of the credit cards that now offer this reward. In deciding whether to accept such a credit card from one of the issuing organizations that tempt you with frequent flyer mileage bonuses on a specific airline, first determine whether the interest rate charged on the unpaid balance is the same as (or less than) possible alternate credit cards, and whether the annual "membership" fee is also equal or lower. If these charges are slightly higher than those of competing cards, weigh the difference against the potential value in airfare savings. Also ask about any bonus miles awarded just for signing up — 1,000 is common, 5,000 generally the maximum.

For the most up-to-date information on frequent flyer bonus options, you may want to send for the monthly newsletter *Frequent*. Issued by Frequent Publications, it provides current information about frequent flyer plans in general, as well as specific data about promotions, awards, and combination deals to help you keep track of the profusion — and confusion — of current and upcoming availabilities. For a year's subscription, send $33 to Frequent Publications, 4715-C Town Center Dr., Colorado Springs, CO 80916 (phone: 800-333-5937).

There also is a monthly magazine called *Frequent Flyer,* but unlike the newsletter mentioned above, its focus is primarily on newsy articles of interest to business travelers and other frequent flyers. Published by Official Airline Guides (PO Box 58543, Boulder, CO 80322-8543; phone: 800-323-3537), *Frequent Flyer* is available for $24 for a 1-year subscription.

Taxes and Other Fees – Travelers who have shopped for the best possible flight at the lowest possible price should be warned that a number of extras will be added

16 GETTING READY / Traveling by Plane

to that price and collected by the airline or travel agent who issues the ticket. There is also a $6 International Air Transportation Tax, a departure tax paid by all passengers flying from the US to a foreign destination.

Still another fee is charged by some airlines to cover more stringent security procedures, prompted by recent terrorist incidents. The 10% federal US Transportation Tax applies to travel within the US or US territories (such as the US Virgin Islands or Puerto Rico) en route to a foreign destination, unless the trip includes a stopover of more than 12 hours at a US point. It does not apply to passengers flying between US cities or territories en route to a foreign destination, unless the trip includes a stopover of more than 12 hours at a US point. Someone flying from Chicago to Ft. Lauderdale and stopping in Ft. Lauderdale for more than 12 hours before boarding a flight to the Bahamas, for instance, would pay the 10% tax on the domestic portion of the trip. Note that these taxes *usually* (but not always) are included in advertised fares and in the prices quoted by airline reservation clerks.

Reservations – For those who don't have the time or patience to investigate personally all possible air departures and connections for a proposed trip, a travel agent can be of inestimable help. A good agent should have all the information on which flights go where and when, and which categories of tickets are available on each. Most have computerized reservation links with the major carriers, so that a seat can be reserved and confirmed in minutes. An increasing number of agents also possess fare-comparison computer programs, so they often are very reliable sources of detailed competitive price data. (For more information, see *How to Use a Travel Agent,* in this section.)

When making plane reservations through a travel agent, ask the agent to give the airline your home phone number, as well as your daytime business phone number. All too often the agent uses the agency number as the official contact for changes in flight plans. Especially during the winter — prime time for a Bahamas escape — weather conditions hundreds or even thousands of miles away can wreak havoc with flight schedules. Aircraft are constantly in use, and a plane delayed in the Orient or on the West Coast can miss its scheduled flight from the East Coast the next morning. The airlines are fairly reliable about getting this sort of information to passengers if they can reach them; diligence does little good at 10 PM if the airline has only the agency's or an office number.

Reconfirmation is strongly recommended for all international flights (though it is not usually required on domestic flights), and in the case of flights to the Bahamas, it is essential that you confirm your round-trip reservations — *especially the return leg.* Some (though increasingly fewer) reservations to and from international destinations are automatically canceled after a required reconfirmation period (typically 72 hours) has passed — even if you have a confirmed, fully paid ticket in hand. It is always wise to call ahead to make sure that the airline did not slip up in entering your original reservation, or in registering any changes you may have made since, and that it has your seat reservation and/or special meal request in the computer. Although policies vary from carrier to carrier, some recommend that you confirm your return flight 48 or 72 hours in advance. If you look at the printed information on your ticket, you'll see the airline's reconfirmation policy stated explicitly.

Don't be lulled into a false sense of security by the "OK" on your ticket next to the number and time of the flight. This only means that a reservation has been entered; a reconfirmation may still be necessary. If in doubt — call.

If you plan not to take a flight on which you hold a confirmed reservation, by all means inform the airline. Because the problem of "no-shows" is a constant expense for airlines, they are allowed to overbook flights, a practice that often contributes to the threat of denied boarding for a certain number of passengers (see "Getting Bumped," below).

Seating – For most types of tickets, airline seats are usually assigned on a first-come,

GETTING READY / Traveling by Plane 17

first-served basis at check-in, although some airlines make it possible to reserve a seat at the time of ticket purchase. Always check in early for your flight, even with advance seat assignments. A good rule of thumb for international flights is to arrive at the airport *at least* 2 hours before the scheduled departure to give yourself plenty of time in case there are long lines.

Most airlines furnish seating charts, which make choosing a seat much easier, but, in general, there are a few basics to consider. You must decide whether you prefer a window, aisle, or middle seat. On flights where smoking is permitted, you should also indicate if you prefer the smoking or nonsmoking section.

The amount of legroom provided (as well as chest room, especially when the seat in front of you is in a reclining position) is determined by something called "pitch," a measure of the distance between the back of the seat in front of you and the front of the back of your seat. The amount of pitch is a matter of airline policy, not the type of plane you fly. First class and business class seats have the greatest pitch, a fact that figures prominently in airline advertising. In economy class or coach, the standard pitch ranges from 33 to as little as 31 inches — downright cramped.

The number of seats abreast, another factor determining comfort, depends on a combination of airline policy and airplane dimensions. First class and business class have the fewest seats per row. Economy generally has 5 seats per row on a DC-9, 6 seats per row on a 727 and a 737.

Airline representatives claim that most aircraft are more stable toward the front and midsection, while seats farthest from the engines are quietest. Passengers who have long legs and are traveling on a wide-body aircraft might request a seat directly behind a door or emergency exit, since these seats often have greater than average pitch, or a seat in the first row of a given section, which offer extra legroom — although these seats are increasingly being reserved for passengers who are willing (and able) to perform certain tasks in the event of emergency evacuation. Be aware that the first row of the economy section (called a "bulkhead" seat) on a conventional aircraft (not a widebody) does *not* offer extra legroom, since the fixed partition will not permit passengers to slide their feet under it. These bulkhead seats do, however, provide ample room to use a bassinet or safety seat and often are reserved for families traveling with children.

A window seat protects you from aisle traffic and clumsy serving carts and also provides a view, while an aisle seat enables you to get up and stretch your legs without disturbing your fellow travelers. Middle seats are the least desirable, and seats in the last row are the worst of all, since they seldom recline fully. If you wish to avoid children on your flight or if you find that you are sitting in an especially noisy section, you are usually free to move to any unoccupied seat — if there is one.

Despite all these rules of thumb, finding out which specific rows are near emergency exits or at the front of a wide-body cabin can be difficult because seating arrangements on two otherwise identical planes vary from airline to airline. There is, however, a quarterly publication called the *Airline Seating Guide* that publishes seating charts for most major US airlines and many foreign carriers as well. Your travel agent should have a copy, or you can buy the US edition for $39.95 per year and the overseas edition for $44.95. Order from Carlson Publishing Co., Box 888, Los Alamitos, CA 90720 (phone: 800-728-4877 or 213-493-4877).

Simply reserving an airline seat in advance, however, may actually guarantee very little. Most airlines require that passengers arrive at the departure gate at least 45 minutes (sometimes more) ahead of time to hold a seat reservation. Some, for example, may cancel seat assignments and may not honor reservations of passengers who have not checked in some period of time — usually around 45 minutes, depending on the airline — before the scheduled departure time, and they *ask* travelers to check in at least 1 hour before all domestic flights and 2 hours before international flights. It pays to read the fine print on your ticket carefully and plan ahead.

18 GETTING READY / Traveling by Plane

A far better strategy is to visit an airline ticket office (or one of a select group of travel agents) to secure an actual boarding pass for your specific flight. Once this has been issued, airline computers show you as checked in, and you effectively own the seat you have selected (although some carriers may not honor boarding passes of passengers arriving at the gate less than 10 minutes before departure). This is also good — but not foolproof — insurance against getting bumped from an overbooked flight and is, therefore, an especially valuable tactic at peak travel times.

Smoking – One decision regarding choosing a seat has been taken out of the hands of many travelers who smoke. Effective February 25, 1990, the US government imposed a ban that prohibits smoking on all flights scheduled for 6 hours or less within the US and its territories. The regulation applies to both domestic and international carriers serving these routes.

In the case of flights to the Bahamas, these rules do not apply to nonstop flights from the US or those with a continuous flight time of over 6 hours between stops in the US or its territories. Although smoking is permitted on most flights to the Bahamas, certain airlines — *Delta, USAir,* and *Air Canada,* at press time — offer only nonsmoking flights.

On those flights that do permit smoking, the US Department of Transportation has determined that nonsmoking sections must be enlarged to accommodate all passengers who wish to sit in one. The airline does not, however, have to shift seating to accommodate nonsmokers who arrive late for a flight. Cigar and pipe smoking are prohibited on all flights, even in the smoking sections.

For a wallet-size guide, which notes in detail the rights of nonsmokers according to these regulations, send a self-addressed, stamped envelope to *ASH (Action on Smoking and Health),* Airline Card, 2013 H St. NW, Washington, DC 20006 (phone: 202-659-4310).

Meals – If you have specific dietary requirements, be sure to let the airline know well before departure time. The available meals include vegetarian, seafood, kosher, Muslim, Hindu, high-protein, low-calorie, low-cholesterol, low-fat, low-sodium, diabetic, bland, and children's menus (not all of these may be available on every carrier). There is no extra charge for this option. It is usually necessary to request special meals when you make your reservations — check-in time is too late. It's also wise to reconfirm that your request for a special meal has made its way into the airline's computer — the time to do this is 24 hours before departure.

Baggage – Travelers from the US face two different kinds of rules. When you fly on a US airline or on a major international carrier, US baggage regulations will be in effect. Though airline baggage allowances vary slightly, in general all passengers are allowed to carry on board, without charge, one piece of luggage that will fit easily under a seat of the plane or in an overhead bin, and whose combined dimensions (length, width, and depth) do not exceed 45 inches. (If you prefer not to carry it with you, most airlines will allow you to check this bag in the hold.) A reasonable amount of reading material, camera equipment, and a handbag are also allowed. In addition, all passengers are allowed to check two bags in the cargo hold: one usually not to exceed 62 inches when length, width, and depth are combined, the other not to exceed 55 inches in combined dimensions. Generally, no single bag may weigh more than 70 pounds.

Charges for additional, oversize, or overweight bags usually are made at a flat rate; the actual dollar amount varies from carrier to carrier. If you plan to travel with any special equipment or sporting gear, be sure to check with the airline beforehand. Most have specific procedures for handling such baggage, and you may have to pay for transportation regardless of how much other baggage you have checked. Golf clubs may be checked through as luggage (most airlines are accustomed to handling them), but tennis rackets should be carried onto the plane. Aqualung tanks, depressurized and appropriately packed with padding, and surfboards (minus the fin and padded) also

GETTING READY / Traveling by Plane 19

may go as baggage. Snorkeling gear should be packed in a suitcase, duffel, or tote bag. Some airlines require that bicycles be partially dismantled and packaged.

Airline policies regarding baggage allowances for children vary and usually are based on the percentage of full adult fare paid. On most US carriers, children who are ticket holders are entitled to the same baggage allowance as a full-fare passenger. Often there is no luggage allowance for a child traveling on an adult's lap or in a bassinet. Particularly for international carriers, it's always wise to check ahead. (For more information on flying with children, see *Hints for Traveling with Children,* in this section.)

To reduce the chances of your luggage going astray, remove all airline tags from previous trips, then label each bag inside and out — with your business address rather than your home address on the outside, to prevent thieves from knowing whose house might be unguarded. Lock everything and double-check the tag that the airline attaches to make sure that it is coded correctly for your destination: BAH for Bahamas, for instance.

If your bags are not in the baggage claim area after your flight, or if they're damaged, report the problem to airline personnel immediately. Keep in mind that policies regarding the specific time limit within which you have to make your claim vary from carrier to carrier. Fill out a report form on your lost or damaged luggage and keep a copy of it and your original baggage claim check. If you must surrender the check to claim a damaged bag, get a receipt for it to prove that you did, indeed, check your baggage on the flight. If luggage is missing, be sure to give the airline your destination and/or a telephone number where you can be reached. Also, take the name and number of the person in charge of recovering lost luggage.

Most airlines have emergency funds for passengers stranded away from home without their luggage, but if it turns out that your bags are truly lost and not simply delayed, do not then and there sign any paper indicating you'll accept an offered settlement. Since the airline is responsible for the value of your bags within certain statutory limits ($1,250 per passenger for lost baggage on a US domestic flight; $640 for checked baggage and up to $400 per passenger for unchecked baggage on an international flight), you should take some time to assess the extent of your loss (see *Insurance,* in this section). It's a good idea to keep records indicating the value of the contents of your luggage. A wise alternative is to take a Polaroid picture of the most valuable of your packed items just after putting them in your suitcase.

Considering the increased incidence of damage to baggage, it's now more than ever a good idea to keep the sales slips that confirm how much you paid for your bags. These are invaluable in establishing the value of damaged luggage and eliminate any arguments. A better way to protect your precious gear from the luggage-eating conveyers is to try to carry it on board wherever possible.

Be aware that airport security is increasingly an issue worldwide, including the Bahamas, and is taken very seriously. Police patrol the airports, and unattended luggage of any description may be confiscated and quickly destroyed. Passengers checking in at an airport may undergo at least two separate inspections of their tickets, passports, and luggage by courteous, but serious, airline personnel — who ask passengers if their baggage has been out of their possession between packing and the airport, or if they have been given gifts or other items to transport — before checked items are accepted.

Airline Clubs – Some US and foreign carriers often have clubs for travelers who pay for membership. These clubs are not solely for first class passengers, although a first class ticket *may* entitle a passenger to lounge privileges. Membership entitles the traveler to use the private lounges at airports along their route, to refreshments served in these lounges, and to check-cashing privileges at most of their counters. Extras include special telephone numbers for individual reservations, embossed luggage tags, and a membership card for identification. One airline that offers membership in such clubs is *American* — the *Admiral's Club,* single membership $225 for the first year;

$225 yearly thereafter; spouse an additional $70; lifetime memberships also available.

Note that such companies do not have club facilities in all airports. Other airlines also offer a variety of special services in many airports.

Getting Bumped – A special air travel problem is the possibility that an airline will accept more reservations (and sell more tickets) than there are seats on a given flight. This is entirely legal and is done to make up for "no-shows," passengers who don't show up for a flight for which they have made reservations and bought tickets. If the airline has oversold the flight and everyone does show up, there simply won't be enough seats. When this happens, the airline is subject to stringent rules designed to protect travelers.

In such cases, the airline first seeks ticket holders willing to give up their seats voluntarily in return for a negotiable sum of money or some other inducement, such as an offer of upgraded seating on the next flight or a voucher for a free trip at some other time. If there are not enough volunteers, the airline may bump passengers against their wishes.

Anyone inconvenienced in this way, however, is entitled to an explanation of the criteria used to determine who does and does not get on the flight, as well as compensation if the resulting delay exceeds certain limits. If the airline can put the bumped passengers on an alternate flight that is *scheduled to arrive* at their original destination within 1 hour of their originally scheduled arrival time, no compensation is owed. If the delay is more than 1 hour, but less than 2 hours on a domestic US flight, they must be paid denied-boarding compensation equivalent to the one-way fare to their destination (but not more than $200). If the delay is more than 2 hours after the original arrival time on a domestic flight or more than 4 hours on an international flight, the compensation must be doubled (not more than $400). The airline may also offer bumped travelers a voucher for a free flight instead of the denied-boarding compensation. Each passenger may be given the choice of either the money or the voucher, the dollar value of which may be no less than the monetary compensation to which the passenger would be entitled. The voucher is not a substitute for the bumped passenger's original ticket; the airline continues to honor that as well. Keep in mind that the above regulations and policies are only for flights leaving the US, and do *not* apply to inbound flights originating abroad, even on US carriers.

To protect yourself as best you can against getting bumped, arrive at the airport early, allowing plenty of time to check in and get to the gate. If the flight is oversold, ask immediately for the written statement explaining the airline's policy on denied-boarding compensation and its boarding priorities. If the airline refuses to give you this information, or if you feel they have not handled the situation properly, file a complaint with both the airline and the appropriate government agency (see "Consumer Protection," below).

Delays and Cancellations – The above compensation rules also do not apply if the flight is canceled or delayed, or if a smaller aircraft is substituted due to mechanical problems. Each airline has its own policy for assisting passengers whose flights are delayed or canceled or who must wait for another flight because their original one was overbooked. Most airline personnel will make new travel arrangements if necessary. If the delay is longer than 4 hours, the airline may pay for a phone call or telegram, a meal, and, in some cases, a hotel room and transportation to it.

■ **Caution:** If you are bumped or miss a flight, be sure to ask the airline to notify other airlines on which you have reservations or connecting flights. When your name is taken off the passenger list of your initial flight, the computer usually cancels all of your reservations automatically, unless *you* take steps to preserve them.

CHARTER FLIGHTS: By booking a block of seats on a specially arranged flight, charter operators offer travelers air transportation for a substantial reduction over the full coach or economy fare. These operators may offer air-only charters (selling transportation alone) or charter packages (the flight plus a combination of land arrangements such as accommodations, meals, tours, or car rental). Charters are especially attractive to people living in smaller cities or out-of-the-way places, because they frequently leave from nearby airports, saving travelers the inconvenience and expense of getting to a major gateway.

From the consumer's standpoint, charters differ from scheduled airlines in two main respects: You generally need to book and pay in advance, and you can't change the itinerary or the departure and return dates once you've booked the flight. In practice, however, these restrictions don't always apply. Today, most of the charter flights to the Bahamas have the most popular resort areas as their prime destinations, and although most still require advance reservations, some permit last-minute bookings (when there are unsold seats available), and some even offer seats on a standby basis.

Though charters almost always are round-trip, and it is unlikely that you would be sold a one-way seat on a round-trip flight, on rare occasions one-way tickets on charters are offered. Although it may be possible to book a one-way charter in the US, giving you more flexibility in scheduling your return, note that US regulations pertaining to charters may be more permissive than the charter laws of other countries. For example, if you want to book a one-way charter back to the US, you may find advance booking rules in force.

Some things to keep in mind about the charter game:

1. It cannot be repeated often enough that if you are forced to cancel your trip, you can lose much (and possibly all) of your money unless you have cancellation insurance, which is a *must* (see *Insurance,* in this section). Frequently, if the cancellation occurs far enough in advance (often 6 weeks or more), you may forfeit only a $25 or $50 penalty. If you cancel only 2 or 3 weeks before the flight, there may be no refund at all unless you or the operator can provide a substitute passenger.
2. Charter flights may be canceled by the operator up to 10 days before departure for any reason, usually underbooking. Your money is returned in this event, but there may be too little time for you to make new arrangements.
3. Most charters have little of the flexibility of regularly scheduled flights regarding refunds and the changing of flight dates; if you book a return flight, you must be on it or lose your money.
4. Charter operators are permitted to assess a surcharge, if fuel or other costs warrant it, of up to 10% of the airfare up to 10 days before departure.
5. Because of the economics of charter flights, your plane almost always will be full, so you will be crowded, though not necessarily uncomfortable. (There is, however, a new movement among charter airlines to provide flight accommodations that are more comfort-oriented, so this situation may change in the near future.)

To avoid problems, *always* choose charter flights with care. When you consider a charter, ask your travel agent who runs it and carefully check the company. The Better Business Bureau in the company's home city can report on how many complaints, if any, have been lodged against it in the past. Protect yourself with trip cancellation and interruption insurance, which can help safeguard your investment if you or a traveling companion is unable to make the trip and must cancel too late to receive a full refund from the company providing your travel services. (This is advisable whether you're buying a charter flight alone or a tour package for which the airfare is provided by charter or scheduled flight.)

Bookings – If you do fly on a charter, read the contract's fine print carefully and pay particular attention to the following:

Instructions concerning the payment of the deposit and its balance and to whom the

check is to be made payable. Ordinarily, checks are made out to an escrow account, which means the charter company can't spend your money until your flight has safely returned. This provides some protection for you. To ensure the safe handling of your money, make out your check to the escrow account, the number of which must appear by law on the brochure, though all too often it is on the back in fine print. Write the details of the charter, including the destination and dates, on the face of the check; on the back, print "For Deposit Only." Your travel agent may prefer that you make out your check to the agency, saying that it will then pay the tour operator the fee minus commission. It is perfectly legal to write the check as we suggest, however, and if your agent objects too vociferously (he or she should trust the tour operator to send the proper commission), consider taking your business elsewhere. If you don't make your check out to the escrow account, you lose the protection of that escrow should the trip be canceled. Furthermore, recent bankruptcies in the travel industry have served to point out that even the protection of escrow may not be enough to safeguard a traveler's investment. More and more, insurance is becoming a necessity. The charter company should be bonded (usually by an insurance company), and if you want to file a claim against it, the claim should be sent to the bonding agent. The contract will set a time limit within which a claim must be filed.

Specific stipulations and penalties for cancellations. Most charters allow you to cancel up to 45 days in advance without major penalty, but some cancellation dates are 50 to 60 days before departure.

Stipulations regarding cancellation and major changes made by the charterer. US rules say that charter flights may not be canceled within 10 days of departure except when circumstances — such as natural disasters or political upheavals — make it physically impossible to fly. Charterers may make "major changes," however, such as in the date or place of departure or return, but you are entitled to cancel and receive a full refund if you don't wish to accept these changes. A price increase of more than 10% at any time up to 10 days before departure is considered a major change; no price increase at all is allowed during the last 10 days immediately before departure.

At the time of this writing, the following companies regularly offer charter flights to the Bahamas and the Turks & Caicos:

Apple Vacations East (PO Box 6500, Newtown Sq., PA 19073; phone: 800-727-3400). This agency is a wholesaler, so you'll have to buy a seat on their charters through a travel agent.

Carnival Airline (1815 Griffin Rd., Suite 205, Dania, FL 33004; phone: 305-923-8672). Offers trips to the general public.

Paradise Island Express (545 Eighth Ave., Suite 16N, New York, NY 10018; phone: 212-947-3440). Offers trips to the general public.

Trans National Travel (2 Charlesgate West, Boston, MA 02215; phone: 800-262-0123). This agency is a wholesaler, so you'll have to buy a seat on their charters through a travel agent.

For the most current information on charter flight options, the travel newsletter *Jax Fax* regularly features a list of charter companies and packagers offering seats on charter flights. For a year's subscription send a check or money order for $12 to *Jax Fax,* 397 Post Rd., Darien, CT 06820 (phone: 203-655-8746).

DISCOUNTS ON SCHEDULED FLIGHTS: Promotional fares often are called discount fares because they cost less than what used to be the standard airline fare — full-fare economy. Nevertheless, they cost the traveler the same whether they are bought through a travel agent or directly from the airline. Tickets that cost less if bought from some outlet other than the airline do exist, however. While it is likely that the vast majority of travelers flying to the Bahamas in the near future will be doing so on a promotional fare or charter rather than on a "discount" air ticket of this sort, it still is a good idea for cost-conscious consumers to be aware of the latest developments in the budget airfare scene. Note that the following discussion makes clear-cut distinctions among the types of discounts available based on how they reach the consumer; in actual practice, the distinctions are not nearly so precise.

Net Fare Sources – The newest notion for reducing the costs of travel services comes from travel agents who offer individual travelers "net" fares. Defined simply, a net fare is the bare minimum amount at which an airline or tour operator will carry a prospective traveler. It doesn't include the amount that would normally be paid to the travel agent as a commission. Traditionally, such commissions amount to about 10% on domestic fares and 10% to 20% on international fares — not counting significant additions to these commission levels that are paid retroactively when agents sell more than a specific volume of tickets or trips for a single supplier. At press time, at least one travel agency in the US was offering travelers the opportunity to purchase tickets and/or tours for a net price. Instead of earning its income from individual commissions, this agency assesses a fixed fee that may or may not provide a bargain for travelers; it requires a little arithmetic to determine whether to use the services of a net travel agent or those of one who accepts conventional commissions. One of the potential drawbacks of buying from agencies selling travel services at net fares is that some airlines refuse to do business with them, thus possibly limiting your flight options.

Travel Avenue is a fee-based agency that rebates its ordinary agency commission to the customer. For domestic flights, they will find the lowest retail fare, then rebate 7% to 10% (depending on the airline selected) of that price minus a $10 ticket-writing charge. The rebate percentage for international flights varies from 5% to 16% (again depending on the airline), and the ticket-writing fee is $25. The ticket-writing charge is imposed per ticket; if the ticket includes more than eight separate flights, an additional $10 or $25 fee is charged. Customers using free flight coupons pay the ticket-writing charge, plus an additional $5 coupon processing fee.

Travel Avenue will rebate its commissions on all tickets, including heavily discounted fares and senior citizen passes. Available 7 days a week, reservations should be made far enough in advance to allow the tickets to be sent by first class mail, since extra charges accrue for special handling. It's possible to economize further by making your own airline reservation, then asking *Travel Avenue* only to write/issue your ticket. For travelers outside the Chicago area, business may be transacted by phone and purchases charged to a credit card. For information, contact *Travel Avenue* at 641 W. Lake St., Suite 201, Chicago, IL 60606-1012 (phone: 312-876-1116 in Illinois; 800-333-3335 elsewhere in the US).

Consolidators and Bucket Shops – Other vendors of travel services can afford to sell tickets to their customers at an even greater discount because the airline has sold the tickets to them at a substantial discount (usually accomplished by sharply increasing commissions to that vendor), a practice in which many airlines indulge, albeit discreetly, preferring that the general public not know they are undercutting their own "list" prices. Airlines anticipating a slow period on a particular route sometimes sell off a certain portion of their capacity at a very great discount to a wholesaler, or consolidator. The wholesaler sometimes is a charter operator who resells the seats to the public as though they were charter seats, which is why prospective travelers perusing the brochures of charter operators with large programs frequently see a number of flights designated as "scheduled service." As often as not, however, the consolidator, in turn, sells the seats to a travel agency specializing in discounting. Airlines can also sell seats directly to such an agency, which thus acts as its own consolidator. The airline offers the seats either at a net wholesale price, but without the volume-purchase requirement that would be difficult for a modest retail travel agency to fulfill, or at the standard price, but with a commission override large enough (as high as 50%) to allow both a profit and a price reduction to the public.

Travel agencies specializing in discounting sometimes are called "bucket shops," a term once fraught with connotations of unreliability in this country. But in today's highly competitive travel marketplace, more and more conventional travel agencies are selling consolidator-supplied tickets, and the old bucket shop's image is becoming respectable. Agencies that specialize in discounted tickets exist in most large cities, and usually can be found by studying the smaller ads in the travel sections of Sunday newspapers.

Before buying a discounted ticket, whether from a bucket shop or a conventional, full-service travel agency, keep the following considerations in mind: To be in a position to judge how much you'll be saving, first find out the "list" prices of tickets to your destination. Then do some comparison shopping among agencies. Also bear in mind that a ticket that may not differ much in price from one available directly from the airline may, however, allow the circumvention of such things as the advance purchase requirement. If your plans are less than final, be sure to find out about any other restrictions, such as penalties for canceling a flight or changing a reservation. Most discount tickets are non-endorsable, meaning that they can be used only on the airline that issued them, and they usually are marked "nonrefundable" to prevent their being cashed in for a list price refund.

A great many bucket shops are small businesses operating on a thin margin, so it's a good idea to check the local Better Business Bureau for any complaints registered against the one with which you're dealing — before parting with any money. If you still do not feel reassured, consider buying discounted tickets only through a conventional travel agency, which can be expected to have found its own reliable source of consolidator tickets — some of the largest consolidators, in fact, sell only to travel agencies.

A few bucket shops require payment in cash or by certified check or money order, but if credit cards are accepted, use that option. Note, however, if buying from a charter operator selling both scheduled and charter flights, that the scheduled seats are not protected by the regulations — including the use of escrow accounts — governing the charter seats. Well-established charter operators, nevertheless, may extend the same protections to their scheduled flights, and when this is the case, consumers should be sure that the payment option selected directs their money into the escrow account.

At press time, the only consolidator regularly offering discount fares to the Bahamas was *TFI Tours International* (34 W. 32nd St., 12th Floor, New York, NY 10001; phone: 212-736-1140). Check with your own travel agent for other sources of consolidator tickets to the Bahamas.

■**Note:** Although rebating and discounting are becoming increasingly common, there is some legal ambiguity concerning them. Strictly speaking, it is legal to discount domestic tickets but not international tickets. On the other hand, the law that prohibits discounting, the Federal Aviation Act of 1958, is consistently ignored these days, in part because consumers benefit from the practice and in part because many illegal arrangements are indistinguishable from legal ones. Since the line separating the two is so fine that even the authorities can't always tell the difference, it is unlikely that most consumers would be able to do so, and in fact it is not illegal to *buy* a discounted ticket. If the issue of legality bothers you, ask the agency whether any ticket you're about to buy would be permissible under the above-mentioned act.

Other Discount Travel Sources – An excellent source of information on economical travel opportunities is the *Consumer Reports Travel Letter,* published monthly by Consumers Union. It keeps abreast of the scene on a wide variety of fronts, including package tours, insurance, and more, but it is especially helpful for its comprehensive coverage of airfares, offering guidance on all the options from scheduled flights on major or low-fare airlines to discount sources. For a year's subscription, send $37 to

GETTING READY / Traveling by Plane

Consumer Reports Travel Letter (PO Box 2886, Boulder, CO 80322; phone: 800-234-1970 or 303-447-9330). For information on other travel newsletters, see *Books and Newsletters*, in this section.

Last-Minute Travel Clubs – Still another way to take advantage of bargain airfares is open to those who have a flexible schedule. A number of organizations, usually set up as last-minute travel clubs and functioning on a membership basis, routinely keep in touch with travel suppliers to help them dispose of unsold inventory at discounts of between 15% and 60%. A great deal of the inventory consists of complete package tours and cruises, but some clubs offer air-only charter seats and, occasionally, seats on scheduled flights.

Members pay an annual fee and receive a toll-free hotline telephone number to call for information on imminent trips. In some cases, they also receive periodic mailings with information on bargain travel opportunities for which there is more advance notice. Despite the suggestive names of the clubs providing these services, last-minute travel does not necessarily mean that you cannot make plans until literally the last minute. Trips can be announced as little as a few days or as much as 2 months before departure, but the average is from 1 to 4 weeks' notice.

Among the organizations regularly offering such discounted travel opportunities to the Bahamas are the following:

Discount Travel International (Ives Building, 114 Forrest Ave., Suite 205, Narberth, PA 19072; phone: 800-334-9294). Annual fee: $45 per household.

Encore Short Notice (4501 Forbes Blvd., Lanham, MD 20706; phone: 301-459-8020; 800-638-0930 for customer service). Annual fee: $48 per family.

Last Minute Travel Club (1249 Boylston St., Boston, MA 02215; phone: 800-LAST-MIN or 617-267-9800). No fee.

Moment's Notice (425 Madison Ave., New York, NY 10017; phone: 212-486-0503). Annual fee: $45 per family.

Spur-of-the-Moment Tours and Cruises (10780 Jefferson Blvd., Culver City, CA 90230; phone: 213-839-2418 in California; 800-343-1991 elsewhere in the US). No fee.

Traveler's Advantage (3033 S. Parker Rd., Suite 1000, Aurora, CO 80014; phone: 800-548-1116 or 303-337-3247). Annual fee: $49 per family.

Vacations to Go (2411 Fountain View, Suite 201, Houston, TX 77057; phone: 713-974-2121 in Texas; 800-338-4962 elsewhere in the US). Annual fee: $19.95 per family.

Worldwide Discount Travel Club (1674 Meridian Ave., Miami Beach, FL 33139; phone: 305-534-2082). Annual fee: $40 per person; $50 per family.

Generic Air Travel – Organizations that apply the same flexible-schedule idea to air travel only and sell tickets at literally the last minute also exist. The service they provide sometimes is known as "generic" air travel, and it operates somewhat like an ordinary airline standby service except that the organizations running it offer seats on not one but several scheduled and charter airlines.

One pioneer of generic flights is *Airhitch* (2790 Broadway, Suite 100, New York, NY 10025; phone: 212-864-2000), which arranges flights to the Bahamas from various US cities at relatively low prices. Prospective travelers register by paying a fee (applicable toward the fare) and stipulate a range of acceptable departure dates and their desired destination, along with alternate choices. The week before the date range begins, they are notified of at least two flights that will be available during the time period, agree on one, and remit the balance of the fare to the company. If they do not accept any of the suggested flights, they lose their deposit; if, through no fault of their own, they do not ultimately get on any agreed-on flight, all of their money is refunded. Return flights are arranged the same way. The company's Sunhitch program, which operates only during the peak season from December through April, is available for week-long stays in the Bahamas. Their slightly more expensive Target program offers greater certainty regarding destinations and is available year-round.

Bartered Travel Sources – Suppose a hotel buys advertising space in a newspaper. As payment, the hotel gives the publishing company the use of a number of hotel rooms in lieu of cash. This is barter, a common means of exchange among hotels, airlines, car rental companies, cruise lines, tour operators, restaurants, and other travel service companies. When a bartering company finds itself with empty airline seats (or excess hotel rooms or cruise ship cabin space, and so on) and offers them to the public, considerable savings can be enjoyed.

Bartered-travel clubs often offer discounts of up to 50% to members who pay an annual fee (approximately $50 at press time), which entitles them to select the flights, cruises, hotel rooms, or other travel services that the club obtained by barter. Members usually present a voucher, club credit card, or scrip (a dollar-denomination voucher negotiable only for the bartered product) to the hotel, which in turn subtracts the dollar amount from the bartering company's account.

Selling bartered travel is a perfectly legitimate means of retailing. One advantage to club members is that they don't have to wait until the last minute to obtain flight or room reservations.

Among the companies specializing in bartered service, two frequently offer members travel services to the Bahamas:

IGT (In Good Taste) Services (1111 Lincoln Rd., 4th Floor, Miami Beach, FL 33139; phone: 800-444-8872 or 305-534-7900). Annual fee: $48 per family.

Travel World Leisure Club (225 W. 34th St., Suite 2203, New York, NY 10122; phone: 800-444-TWLC or 212-239-4855). Annual fee: $50 per family.

CONSUMER PROTECTION: Consumers who feel that they have not been dealt with fairly by an airline should make their complaints known. Begin with the customer service representative at the airport where the problem occurs. If he or she cannot resolve your complaint to your satisfaction, write to the airline's consumer office. In a businesslike, typed letter, explain what reservations you held, what happened, the names of the employees involved, and what you expect the airline to do to remedy the situation. Send copies (never the originals) of the tickets, receipts, and other documents that back your claims. Ideally, all correspondence should be sent via certified mail, return receipt requested. This provides proof that your complaint was received.

Passengers with consumer complaints — lost baggage, compensation for getting bumped, violations of smoking and nonsmoking rules, deceptive practices by an airline, charter regulations — who are not satisfied with the airline's response should contact the US Department of Transportation (DOT), Consumer Affairs Division (400 Seventh St. SW, Washington, DC 20590; phone: 202-366-2220). DOT personnel stress, however, that consumers should initially direct their complaints to the airline that provoked them.

Travelers with an unresolved complaint involving a foreign carrier can also contact the US Department of Transportation. DOT personnel will do what they can to help resolve all such complaints, although their influence may be limited.

Although the Bahamas do not have a specific government bureau that deals with airline complaints, consumers with complaints against other travel-related services can contact the Ministry of Tourism, PO Box N3701, Nassau, Bahamas (phone: 809-322-7500).

Remember, too, that the federal Fair Credit Billing Act permits purchasers to refuse to pay for credit card charges for services that have not been delivered, so the onus of dealing with the receiver for a bankrupt airline falls on the credit card company. Do not rely on another airline to honor the ticket you're holding, since the days when virtually all major carriers subscribed to a default protection program that bound them to do so are long gone. Some airlines may voluntarily step forward to accommodate the stranded passengers of a fellow carrier, but this is now an entirely altruistic act.

The deregulation of US airlines has meant that travelers must find out for themselves what they are entitled to receive. The US Department of Transportation's informative consumer booklet *Fly Rights* is a good place to start. To receive a copy, send $1 to the Superintendent of Documents (US Government Printing Office, Washington, DC 20402-9325; phone: 202-783-3238). Specify its stock number, 050-000-000513-5, and allow 3 to 4 weeks for delivery.

■ **Note:** Those who tend to experience discomfort due to the change in air pressure while flying may be interested in the free pamphlet *Ears, Altitude and Airplane Travel;* for a copy send a self-addressed, stamped, business-size envelope to the *American Academy of Otolaryngology* (One Prince St., Alexandria, VA 22314; phone: 703-836-4444). And for when you land, *Overcoming Jet Lag* offers some helpful tips on minimizing post-flight stress; it is available from Berkeley Publishing Group (PO Box 506, Mail Order Dept., East Rutherford, NJ 07073; phone: 800-631-8571) for $6.95, plus shipping and handling.

Traveling by Cruise Ship

There was a time when traveling by ship was extraordinarily expensive, time consuming, utterly elegant, and utilized almost exclusively for getting from one point to another. No longer primarily pure transportation, cruising currently is riding a wave of popularity as a leisure activity in its own right, and the host of new ships (and dozens of rebuilt old ones) testifies dramatically to the attraction of vacationing on the high seas.

The only thing that's lacking from the cruising scene today is much of that old elegance — ships like *Cunard*'s *Sea Goddess I* and *Sea Goddess II* and the *Seabourn Cruise Line*'s *Seabourn Pride* and *Seabourn Spirit* are notable exceptions — though modern-day passengers don't seem to notice. Many modern-day cruise ships seem much more like motels-at-sea than the classic liners of a couple of generations ago, but they are consistently comfortable and passengers are often quite well cared for. Cruise prices can be quite reasonable, and since the single cruise price covers all the major items in a typical vacation — transportation, accommodations, all meals and entertainment, and a full range of social activities, sports, and recreation — a traveler need not fear any unexpected assaults on the family travel budget.

When selecting a cruise to the Bahamas, your basic criteria should be the time you have available, how much you want to spend, and the kind of environment that best suits your style and taste (in which case price is an important determinant). Rely on the suggestions of a travel agent — preferably one specializing in cruises (see "A final note on picking a cruise," below) — but be honest with the agent (and with yourself) in describing the type of atmosphere you're seeking. Ask suggestions from friends who have been on cruises; if you trust their judgment, they should be able to suggest a ship on which you'll feel comfortable.

There are a number of moments in the cruise-planning process when discounts are available from the major cruise lines, so it may be possible to enjoy some diminution of the list price almost anytime you book passage on a cruise ship. For those willing to commit early — say 4 to 6 months before sailing — most of the major cruise lines routinely offer a 10% reduction off posted prices, in addition to the widest selection of cabins. For those who decide to sail rather late in the game — say 4 to 6 weeks before departure — savings often are even greater — an average of 20% — as steamship lines try to fill up their ships. The only negative aspect is that the choice of cabins tends to be limited, although it is possible that a fare upgrade will be offered to make this limited selection more palatable. In addition, there's the option of buying from a discount travel club or a travel agency that specializes in last-minute bargains; these discounters and other discount travel sources are discussed at the end of *Traveling by Plane,* above.

Although there are less expensive ways to see the Bahamas, the romance and enjoyment of a sea voyage remain irresistible for some, so a few points should be considered by such sojourners before they sign on for a seagoing vacation (after all, it's hard to get off in mid-ocean). Herewith, a rundown on what to expect from a cruise, and a few suggestions on what to look for and arrange when purchasing passage on one.

CABINS: The most important factor in determining the price of a cruise is the cabin. Cabin prices are set according to size and location. The size can vary considerably on older ships, less so on newer or more recently modernized ones, and may be entirely uniform on the very newest vessels.

Shipboard accommodations utilize the same pricing pattern as hotels. Suites, which consist of a sitting room–bedroom combination and occasionally a small private deck that could be compared to a patio, cost the most. Prices for other cabins (interchangeably called staterooms) are usually more expensive on the upper passenger decks, less expensive on lower decks; if the cabin has a bathtub instead of a shower, the price probably will be higher. The outside cabins with portholes cost more than inside cabins without views and are generally preferred — although many experienced cruise passengers eschew the more expensive accommodations for they know they will spend very few waking hours in their cabins. As in all forms of travel, accommodations are more expensive for single travelers. If you are traveling on your own but want to share a double cabin to reduce the cost, some ship lines will attempt to find someone of the same sex willing to share quarters (also see *Hints for Single Travelers,* in this section).

FACILITIES AND ACTIVITIES: You may not use your cabin very much — organized shipboard activities are geared to keep you busy. A standard schedule might consist of swimming, sunbathing, and numerous other outdoor recreations. Evenings are devoted to leisurely dining, lounge shows or movies, bingo and other organized games, gambling, dancing, and a midnight buffet. Your cruise fare normally includes all of these activities — except the cost of drinks.

Most cruise ships have at least one major social lounge, a main dining room, several bars, an entertainment room that may double as a discotheque for late dancing, an exercise room, indoor games facilities, at least one pool, and shopping facilities, which can range from a single boutique to an arcade. Still others have gambling casinos and/or slot machines, card rooms, libraries, children's recreation centers, indoor pools (as well as one or more on open decks), separate movie theaters, and private meeting rooms. Open deck space should be ample, because this is where most passengers spend their days at sea.

Usually there is a social director and staff to organize and coordinate activities. Evening entertainment is provided by professionals. Movies are mostly first-run and drinks are moderate in price (or should be) because a ship is exempt from local taxes when at sea.

■ **Note:** To be prepared for possible illnesses at sea, travelers should get a prescription from their doctor for medicine to counteract motion sickness. All ships with more than 12 passengers have a doctor on board, plus facilities for handling sickness or medical emergencies.

Shore Excursions – These side trips are almost always optional and available at extra cost. Before you leave, do a little basic research about the Bahamas and decide what sights will interest you. If several of the most compelling of these are some distance from the pier where your ship docks, the chances are that paying for a shore excursion will be worth the money.

Shore excursions usually can be booked through your travel agent at the same time you make your cruise booking, but this is worthwhile only if you can get complete details on the nature of each excursion being offered. If you can't get these details, better opt to purchase your shore arrangements after you're on board. Your enthusiasm for an excursion may be higher once you are on board because you will have met other passengers with whom to share the excitement of "shore leave." And depending on your time in port, you may decide to eschew the guided tour and venture out on your own.

Meals – All meals on board almost always are included in the basic price of a cruise, and the food generally is abundant and quite palatable. Evening meals are taken in the main dining room, where tables are assigned according to the passengers' preferences. Tables usually accommodate from 2 to 10; specify your preference when you book your cruise. If there are two sittings, you also can specify which one you want at the time you book or, at the latest, when you first board the ship. Later sittings usually are more leisurely. Breakfast frequently is available in your cabin, as well as in the main dining room. For lunch, many passengers prefer the buffet offered on deck, usually at or near the pool, but again, the main dining room is available.

DRESS: Most people pack too much for a cruise on the assumption that their daily wardrobe should be chic and every night is a big event. Comfort is a more realistic criterion. Daytime wear on most ships is decidedly casual. Evening wear for most cruises is dressy-casual. Formal attire probably is not necessary for 1-week cruises, optional for longer ones.

TIPS: Tips are a strictly personal expense, and you *are* expected to tip — in particular, your cabin and dining room stewards. The general rule of thumb (or palm) is to expect to pay from 10% to 20% of your total cruise budget for gratuities — the actual amount within this range is based on the length of the cruise and the extent of personalized services provided. Allow $2 to $5 a day for each cabin and dining room steward (more if you wish) and additional sums for very good service. (*Note:* Tips should be paid by and for each individual in a cabin, whether there are one, two, or more.) Others who may merit tips are the deck steward who sets up your chair at the pool or elsewhere, the wine steward in the dining room, porters who handle your luggage (tip them individually at the time they assist you), and any others who provide personal service. On some ships you can charge your bar tab to your cabin; throw in the tip when you pay it at the end of the cruise. Smart travelers tip twice during the trip: about midway through the cruise and at the end; even wiser travelers tip a bit at the start of the trip to ensure better service throughout.

Although some cruise lines do have a no-tipping policy and you are not penalized by the crew for not tipping, naturally, you aren't penalized for tipping, either. If you can restrain yourself, it is better not to tip on those few ships that discourage it. However, never make the mistake of not tipping on the majority of ships, where it is a common, expected practice. (For further information on calculating gratuities, see *Tipping,* in this section.)

SHIP SANITATION: The US Public Health Service (PHS) currently inspects all passenger vessels calling at US ports, so very precise information is available on which ships meet its requirements and which do not. The further requirement that ships immediately report any illness that occurs on board adds to the available data.

The problem for a prospective cruise passenger is to determine whether the ship on which he or she plans to sail has met the official sanitary standard. US regulations require the PHS to publish actual grades for the ships inspected (rather than the old pass or fail designation), so it's now easy to determine any cruise ship's status. Nearly 4,000 travel agents, public health organizations, and doctors receive a copy of each monthly ship sanitation summary, but be aware that not all travel agents fully understand what this ship inspection program is all about. The best advice is to deal with a travel agent who specializes in cruise bookings, for he or she is most likely to have the latest information on the sanitary conditions of all cruise ships (see "A final note on picking a cruise," below). To receive a copy of the most recent summary or a particular inspection report, write to Chief, Vessel Sanitation Program, Center for Environmental Health and Injury Control, 1015 N. America Way, Room 107, Miami, FL 33132 (phone: 305-536-4307; note that the center requests that all inquiries be made in writing).

CRUISES TO THE BAHAMAS: Many cruise lines include Freeport and Nassau as regular stops, including overnight stays that allow passengers to disembark and enjoy the casinos, cabarets, golf courses, and shops. Visitors to Ft. Lauderdale or Miami, Florida, interested in a day of sightseeing or shopping in the Bahamas can take day trips to Freeport or Bimini aboard *SeaEscape* ships (phone: 800-327-7400 or 305-377-0900). *Crown Cruise Line* (phone: 800-841-7447 or 407-845-7447) offers similar 1-day "getaway" trips to Freeport from the port of Palm Beach. *Premier Cruise Lines* packages 3- or 4-night sailings to the Abaco Islands or to Nassau and one Family Island with a 3- or 4-day stay at *Walt Disney World;* both cruises sail from Port Canaveral, about 45 minutes away. Check with a travel agent for current cruise schedules or call 800-327-7113.

Below is a list of cruise lines and ships that offer 3-night to 2-week (and longer) sailings to the Bahamas from the US.

Carnival Cruises: Offers 3- and 4-day cruises on the *Mardi Gras, Carnivale,* and *Fantasy* from Miami or Port Canaveral to Freeport and Nassau. Contact *Carnival Cruises,* 3655 Northwest 87th Ave., Miami, FL 33178 (phone: 800-327-9501).

Chandris Celebrity Cruises: The *Meridian* sails on 7-day cruises from Ft. Lauderdale to San Juan, St. Martin, Nassau, and St. Thomas. Contact *Chandris Celebrity Cruises,* 5200 Blue Lagoon Dr., Miami, FL 33126 (phone: 800-437-3111).

Cunard: The *Sagafjord* offers 14-day cruises from Ft. Lauderdale to Bermuda, Charleston, Key West, Nassau, Norfolk, and Savannah. Contact *Cunard,* 555 Fifth Ave., New York, NY 10017 (phone: 800-221-4770).

Dolphin Cruise Line: Offers 3- to 14-day cruises aboard the *Dolphin IV* from Miami/Key West to Nassau. Contact *Dolphin Cruise Line,* 901 S. America Way, Miami, FL 33132 (phone: 800-222-1003).

Holland America Line: The *Westerdam* offers 7-day cruises to Nassau and several Caribbean islands from Ft. Lauderdale. Contact *Holland America Line,* 300 Elliot Ave. W., Seattle, WA 98119 (phone: 800-426-0327).

Norwegian Cruise Line: The *Sunward II* offers 3- or 4-day cruises from Miami to Freeport and Nassau. Contact *Norwegian Cruise Line,* 95 Merrick Way, Coral Gables, FL 33134 (phone: 800-327-7030).

Premier Cruise Lines: Offers 3- to 4-day cruises on the *Star/Ship Atlantic* and *Star/Ship Oceanic* from Port Canaveral to Nassau. Contact *Premier Cruise Lines,* PO Box 656, Cape Canaveral, FL 32920 (phone: 800-327-7113).

Royal Caribbean Cruise Line: The *Emerald Seas* and *Nordic Empress* sail on 3- to 4-day cruises from Ft. Lauderdale/Miami to Freeport and Nassau. Contact *Royal Caribbean Cruise Line,* 1050 Caribbean Way, Miami FL 33132 (phone: 800-327-2055).

Some outfits specialize in long-term cruises from central points in the Bahamas to exotic, out-of-the-way destinations like Mayaguana and Hogsty Reef Atoll. *Coral Bay Cruises,* for example, offers a variety of 7- and 12-day excursions on the *Coral Star* luxury yacht. For information, write to *Coral Bay Cruises,* 17 Fort Royal Isle, Fort Lauderdale, FL 33308, or call 800-433-7262.

■ **A final note on picking a cruise:** A "cruise-only" travel agency can best help you choose a cruise ship and itinerary. Cruise-only agents are best equipped to tell you about a particular ship's "personality," the kind of person with whom you'll likely be traveling on a particular ship, what dress is appropriate (it varies from ship to ship), and much more. Travel agencies that specialize in booking cruises usually are members of the *National Association of Cruise Only Agencies (NACOA).* For a listing of the agencies in your area (requests are limited to three states), send a self-addressed, stamped envelope to *NACOA,* PO Box 7209, Freeport, NY 11520, or call 516-378-8006.

Traveling by Chartered Boat

Once you are in the Bahamas, few travel experiences are more exhilarating than sailing on your own, or with a crew, among the islands. An immense variety of private vessels may be chartered (rented) by anyone seeking an authentic sea experience. Vessels are available for couples, groups (usually up to a maximum of 6 or 8), and sometimes for individuals willing to book on a single basis and share with whoever books the same way.

CREWED BOATS: Don't shy away because you're a neophyte. The majority of travelers booking sailing holidays are inexperienced or have never been on yachts before. Most vessels can be rented with full crews, as well as with sleeping accommodations, water sports and fishing equipment, meal provisions, a fully equipped bar, and other features.

There are numerous advantages to chartering a vessel with a crew. The most important is that professional sailors run the ship while the chartering group decides the itinerary (where to stop, and so on). In addition, a crewed vessel can pick up and drop off the chartering group at any island with air service — although the group must allow for the cost of the ship's getting from and back to its home port.

Vessels accepting individual bookings are referred to as head boats because they take passengers on a head (one-by-one) basis. The number on board can range from a half dozen to 100 or more, and the cost usually is reasonable. Itineraries normally will include islands within a week's sailing distance from the home port. Again, the vessels are well stocked with provisions and water sports equipment.

BAREBOAT CHARTERS: Experienced sea hands, for whom the operation and sailing of a vessel are the most important allures, normally opt for a bareboat (without crew) charter, which are readily available, again in all sizes and types.

Bareboating is for experts. Parties chartering without crews should check in advance with the rental agents to learn what specific experience and qualifications are required.

The cost of either a fully manned or bareboat charter varies depending upon size and accommodations, as well as upon season. Most charter parties average from four to six persons, and the per-person daily cost for a crewed boat (including meals) usually ranges from about two to three times the cost of a bareboat charter (without provisions). Charters rarely are available for less than a week. Head boat sailings — particularly on larger, less private cruises — are likely to be the least expensive of the three options and may be more flexible regarding the minimum booking period.

The Bahamas, by virtue of possessing excellent sailing waters, also have a plentiful collection of charter craft. Among the best-known locations for rentals are Marsh Harbour in the Abacos and Nassau on New Providence island.

A number of companies in the US specialize in chartering yachts in the Bahamas. Among the best known are the following:

32 GETTING READY / Touring by Car

Lynn Jachney Charters (1 Townhouse Sq., Marblehead, MA 09145; phone: 617-639-0787 in Massachusetts; 800-223-2050 elsewhere in the US).
SailAway Yacht Charter Consultants (15605 S.W. 92nd Ave., Miami, FL 33157; phone: 305-232-2800 in Florida; 800-872-9224 elsewhere in the US).
Sunsail (2 Prospect Park, 3347 N.W. 55th St., Fort Lauderdale, FL 33309; phone: 800-327-2276).
Whitney Yacht Charters (750 North Dearborn, Suite 1411, Chicago, IL 60610; phone: 312-929-8989 in Illinois; 800-223-1426 elsewhere in the US).
Worldwide Yacht Charters (145 King St. W., Toronto, Ontario M5H 1J8; phone: 416-365-1950).

Touring by Car

Although it may seem that a car is unnecessary for an island stay, even where a car is not essential, driving still is a highly desirable way to explore. On a number of islands, a car provides the flexibility to venture a distance from your hotel, to see more than the sights included on the traditional organized sightseeing excursion, and to leave with a broader view of the people and cultures of the Bahamas. It will allow you to take the scenic stretches at your own pace, satisfy your curiosity about some out-of-the-way corner, and stop for snack, a swim, or a photograph at will.

DRIVING: Before setting out, make certain that everything you need is in order. If possible, discuss the island with someone who knows it to find out about road conditions and available services. If you can't speak to someone personally, try to read about others' experiences.

Tourist offices in the Bahamas can be a good source of driving information. When requesting brochures and maps from bureaus that cover several islands, be sure to specify the areas you are planning to visit. (See *Island Tourist Offices,* in this section, for addresses in the US and Canada.)

In the Bahamas, a US or Canadian driver's license is required. When renting a car you should always bring along proof of citizenship, which is also required for entering the Bahamas (see *Entry Requirements and Documents,* in this section); for other requirements, see "Renting a Car," below.

Another wrinkle involved in driving in the Bahamas is that — unlike the US — driving is on the left side of the road rather than the right. Adjusting to this variation is further complicated by the fact that rental cars may be either US imports with the steering wheel on the left or foreign models with the wheel on the right. If you are given a choice, the reversed wheel on the right will help US drivers to adjust to the switch. Either way, it generally pays to practice for a few minutes in the parking lot of the rental agency before heading out on the road. And when in doubt, *slow down.* Your automatic reaction when faced with head-on traffic most likely will be to veer to the right — particularly dangerous on the narrow, winding roads to be found on a number of islands. Before you go, read the information given in the *Sources and Resources* section of THE ISLANDS chapters, and contact the island tourist board, which can provide specific information on requirements and local laws.

You occasionally will encounter one-lane bridges on two-lane highways. Your best bet is to back off and yield the right-of-way. Obey speed limits and traffic regulations, especially when driving through towns. As the only road often goes through the middle of the town or resort area, slow down as you pass through busy, populated centers.

As a result of the British influence, the Bahamas follow the British system of

GETTING READY / Touring by Car 33

measurement, and gasoline is sold by the British or "imperial" gallon (equal to 1.2 US gallons). Road signs showing the distance from point to point are in miles. The speed limit is 30 to 35 mph on most roads, 45 mph on major highways.

Although it is difficult to say exactly how much fuel will cost when you travel, it is probably safe to assume that gas prices will be considerably higher in the Bahamas than you are accustomed to paying in the US. The number of miles per gallon is also increased by driving smoothly. Accelerate gently, anticipate stops, get into high gear quickly, and maintain a steady speed.

Most roads are well surfaced, but you will find few of the multi-lane highways found in the US, except around Nassau and Freeport. In general, secondary and lesser roads also are kept in reasonably good condition, although in more remote areas and on the smaller islands, particularly during the rainy season, this may not be the case. If you are planning to explore off the beaten track, we strongly suggest your renting a four-wheel-drive vehicle. Either way, there is plenty to see en route.

RENTING A CAR: Visitors who want to drive in the Bahamas can rent a car through a travel agent or an international rental firm before leaving home or from a local company once they are in the islands. Another possibility, also arranged before departure, is to rent the car as part of a larger travel package.

Renting a car in the Bahamas is not inexpensive, but it is possible to economize by determining your own needs and then shopping around among the car rental companies until you find the best deal. As you comparison shop, keep in mind that rates vary considerably from location to location on the same island. For instance, it might be less expensive to rent a car from an office near the center of town rather than at the airport. Ask about special rates or promotional deals, such as weekend or weekly rates, bonus coupons for airline tickets, or 24-hour rates that include gas and unlimited mileage.

Rental car companies operating in the Bahamas can be divided into two basic categories: large international companies, and small locals that operate only on the island where they are located. Because of aggressive local competition, the cost of renting a car can be less expensive once a traveler arrives in the Bahamas, compared to the prices quoted in advance in the US. Local companies usually are less expensive than the international giants.

Given this situation, it's tempting to wait until arriving to scout out the lowest-priced rental from the company located the farthest from the airport high-rent district and offering no pick-up services. But if your arrival coincides with a holiday or a peak travel period, you may be disappointed to find that even the most expensive car in town was spoken for months ago. Whenever possible, it is best to reserve in advance, anywhere from a few days in slack periods to a month or more during the busier seasons.

If you do decide to wait until after you arrive and let your fingers do the walking through the local island phone books, you'll often find a surprising number of small companies listed — particularly on the more developed islands, but some on the smaller islands too. The best guide to sorting through the options is usually to contact one of the tourist offices in the US and Canada (see *Sources and Resources*), which usually can provide recommendations and a list of reputable firms.

Even if you do rent in advance, be aware that some Bahamas car rental experiences bear little resemblance to the normally efficient process found almost everywhere in the US. It is not at all uncommon, for example, to arrive at an airport rental counter — even that of a giant international company — and have your confirmed reservation greeted with a shrug: No cars available. (If you use a car rental firm's toll-free number to reserve a vehicle, it *may* make a difference if you arrive with written confirmation of your reservation in hand — leave enough time for the rental company to mail it to you before you leave home. Also be sure you get a receipt for any deposit.) It is similarly common that the class and make of car you ordered will be notable by its absence. More

34 GETTING READY / Touring by Car

shrugs. And even when you do get a car, and even when it is precisely the brand and type you want, chances are that its physical appearance and mechanical condition will be substantially inferior to similar rental cars you are used to driving in the US. Caveat renter.

Travel agents can arrange rentals for clients, but it is just as easy to call and rent a car yourself. Listed below are the major international rental companies represented in the Bahamas that have information and reservations numbers that can be dialed toll-free from the US (note that these numbers are all for the companies' international divisions, which cover Bahamian rentals):

Avis Rent-a-Car (phone: 800-331-1084).
Budget Rent-A-Car (phone: 800-472-3325).
Hertz (phone: 800-654-3001).
National Car Rental (phone: 800-CAR-EUROPE).

The following is a sampling of the local car rental companies:

Griffin Rent-a-Car (Governor's Harbour, PO Box 40, Eleuthera, Bahamas; phone: 809-332-2077).
Johnson's Rental (PO Box 153, Harbour Island, Bahamas; phone: 809-333-2376).
Wallace Rent-a-Car (Marathon Estate, PO Box SS6147, Nassau, Bahamas; phone: 809-393-0650).
Yvette Rent-a-Car (North Palmetto Point, PO Box 12, Eleuthera, Bahamas; phone: 809-332-2256).

Car rentals from these and other firms are available on the following islands in the Bahamas: Eleuthera, Grand Bahama, New Providence (Nassau), and Paradise Island; in the Turks & Caicos: Grand Turk and Providenciales.

Visitors should be aware, however, that some of the islands in the Bahamas *are* too small to require a car for exploration; others prohibit visitors from driving. (The larger islands generally do offer some form of public transportation and/or taxi service.) On islands where driving a car is not an option, some companies specialize in alternative types of rented transport such as mopeds, motorbikes, and a variety of all-terrain jeeps and mini-jeep–type vehicles, and — for those who are particularly energetic — bicycles. Information on local car rental companies, as well as sources for the more unusual types of motorized transport, can be found in the *Sources and Resources* section of THE ISLANDS chapters.

Requirements – Whether you decide to rent a car in advance from a large international rental company with Bahamian branches or wait to rent from a local company, you should know that renting a car is rarely as simple as signing on the dotted line and roaring off into the night. If you are renting for personal use, you must have a valid driver's license and will have to convince the renting agency that (1) you are personally creditworthy, and (2) you will bring the car back at the stated time. This will be easy if you have a major credit card; most rental companies accept credit cards in lieu of a cash deposit, as well as for payment of your final bill. If you prefer to pay in cash, leave your credit card imprint as a "deposit," then pay your bill in cash when you return the car.

If you are planning to rent a car once in the islands, *Avis, Budget, Hertz,* and other US rental companies usually *will* rent to travelers paying in cash and leaving either a credit card imprint or a substantial amount of cash as a deposit. This is not necessarily standard policy, however, as other international chains and a number of local island companies will *not* rent to an individual who doesn't have a valid credit card. In this case, you may have to call around to find a company that accepts cash.

Also keep in mind that although the minimum age to drive a car in the Bahamas is 18 years, the minimum age to rent a car is set by the company. (Restrictions vary from company to company, as well as at different locations.) Many firms have a minimum age requirement of 21 years, some raise that to 23 or 25 years, and for some models of cars it rises to 30 years. The upper age limit at many companies is between 69 and 75; others have no upper limit or may make drivers above a certain age subject to special conditions.

Costs – Finding the most economical car rental will require some telephone shopping on your part. As a *general* rule, expect to hear lower prices quoted by the smaller, strictly local companies than by the well-known international names.

Comparison shopping always is advisable, however, because the company that has the least expensive rentals on one island may not have the least expensive cars on another, and even the international giants offer discount plans whose conditions are easy for most travelers to fulfill. For instance, *Budget* and *National* offer discounts of anywhere from 10% to 30% off their usual rates (according to the size of the car and the duration of the rental), provided that the car is reserved a certain number of days before departure (usually 7 to 14 days, but it can be less), is rented for a minimum period (5 days or, more often, a week), is paid for at the time of booking, and in most cases, is returned to the same location that supplied it or to another in the same country. Similar discount plans include *Hertz*'s Affordable Rates and *Avis*'s Supervalue Rates.

If driving short distances for only a day or two, the best deal may be a per-day, per-mile (or per-kilometer) rate: You pay a flat fee for each day you keep the car, plus a per-mile (or per-kilometer) charge. An increasingly common alternative is to be granted a certain number of free miles or kilometers each day and then be charged on a per-mile or per-kilometer basis over that number.

Most companies also offer a flat per-day rate with unlimited free mileage. Make sure that the low, flat daily rate that catches your eye, however, is indeed a per-day rate: Often the lowest price advertised by a company turns out to be available only with a minimum 3-day rental — fine if you want the car that long, but not the bargain it appears if you really intend to use it no more than 24 hours. Flat weekly rates also are available, and some flat monthly rates that represent a further saving over the daily rate.

Other factors influencing cost include the type of car you rent. Rentals are based on a tiered price system, with different sizes of cars — variations of budget, economy, regular, and luxury — often listed as A (the smallest and least expensive) through F, G, or H, and sometimes even higher. Charges may increase by only a few dollars a day through several categories of subcompact and compact cars — where most of the competition is — then increase by great leaps through the remaining classes of full-size and luxury cars and passenger vans. The larger the car, the more it costs to rent and the more gas it consumes, but for some people the greater comfort and extra luggage space of a larger car (in which bags and sporting gear can be safely locked out of sight) may make it worth the additional expense. Also more expensive are sleek sports cars, but, again, for some people the thrill of driving such a car — for a week or a day — may be worth it. In the Bahamas, models with standard stick shifts may cost less than those with automatic transmissions.

Electing to pay for collision damage waiver (CDW) protection will add considerably to the cost of renting a car. You may be responsible for the *full value* of the vehicle being rented, but you can dispense with the possible obligation by buying the offered waiver at a cost of around $10 a day for rentals in the Bahamas. Before making any decisions about optional collision damage waivers, check with your own insurance agent and determine whether your personal automobile insurance policy covers rented vehicles; if it does, you probably won't need to pay for the waiver. Be aware, too, that increasing numbers of credit cards automatically provide CDW coverage if the car rental is charged to the appropriate credit card. However, the specific terms of such coverage differ sharply among individual credit card companies, so check with the credit card company for information on the nature and amount of coverage provided. Business travelers also should be aware that, at the time of this writing, *American Express* had withdrawn its automatic CDW coverage from some corporate *Green* card accounts — watch for similar cutbacks by other credit card companies.

When inquiring about CDW coverage and costs, you should be aware that a number of the major international car rental companies now are automatically including the cost of this waiver in their quoted prices. This does not mean that they are absorbing this cost and you are receiving free coverage — total rental prices have increased to include the former CDW charge. The disadvantage of this inclusion is that you probably will not have the option to refuse this coverage, and will end up paying the added charge — even if you already are adequately covered by your own insurance policy or through a credit card company.

Additional costs to be added to the price tag include drop-off charges or one-way service fees. The lowest price quoted by any given company may apply only to a car that is returned to the same location from which it was rented. A slightly higher rate may be charged if the car is to be returned to a different location on the island.

A further consideration: Don't forget that car rentals are subject to local sales taxes, or that the price of gas, on the whole, is higher in the Bahamas than in the US. Rental cars usually are delivered with a full tank of gas. (This is not always the case, however, so check the gas gauge when picking up the car, and have the amount of gas noted on your rental agreement if the tank is not full.) Remember to fill the tank before you return the car or you will have to pay to refill it, and gasoline at the car rental company's pump always is much more expensive than at a service station. This policy may vary for smaller, local companies; ask when picking up the vehicle. Before leaving the lot, also check that the rental car has a spare tire and jack in the trunk. (For further information on gasoline economy, see "Driving," above.)

Fly/Drive Packages – Airlines, charter companies, car rental companies, and tour operators have been offering fly/drive packages for years, and even though the basic components of the package have changed somewhat — return airfare, a car waiting at the airport, and perhaps a night's lodging all for one inclusive price used to be the rule — the idea remains the same. You rent a car *here* for use *there* by booking it along with other arrangements for the trip. These days, the very minimum arrangement possible is the result of a tie-in between a car rental company and an airline, which entitles customers to a rental car for less than the company's usual rates, provided they show proof of having booked a flight on that airline. For information on available packages, check with the airline or your travel agent.

Package Tours

If the mere thought of buying a package for travel to and through the Bahamas and the Turks & Caicos conjures up visions of a trip spent marching in lockstep with a horde of frazzled fellow travelers, remember that packages have come a long way. For one thing, not all packages are necessarily escorted tours, and the one you buy does not have to include any organized touring at all — nor will it necessarily include traveling companions. If it does, however, you'll find that people of all sorts — many just like yourself — are taking advantage of packages today because they are economical and convenient, save you an immense amount of planning time, and exist in such variety that it's virtually impossible not to find one that fits at least the majority of your travel preferences. Given the high cost of travel these days, packages have emerged as a particularly wise buy.

GETTING READY / Package Tours 37

In essence, a package is just an amalgam of travel services that can be purchased in a single transaction. A package (tour or otherwise) to and around the Bahamas may include any or all of the following: round-trip transportation from your home to the islands, local transportation (and/or car rentals), accommodations, some or all meals, sightseeing, entertainment, transfers to and from the hotel, taxes, tips, escort service, and a variety of incidental features that might be offered as options at additional cost. In other words, a package can be any combination of travel elements, from a fully escorted tour offered at an all-inclusive price to a simple booking allowing you to move about totally on your own. Its principal advantage is that it saves money: The cost of the combined arrangements invariably is well below the price of all of the same elements if bought separately. A package provides more than economy and convenience: It releases the traveler from having to make individual arrangements for each separate element of a trip.

Tour programs generally can be divided into two categories — "escorted" (or locally hosted) and independent. An escorted tour means that a guide will accompany the group from the beginning of the tour through to the return flight; a locally hosted tour means that the group will be met upon arrival by a local host. On independent tours, there is generally a choice of hotels, meal plans, and sightseeing trips, as well as a variety of special excursions. The independent plan is for travelers who do not want a totally set itinerary, but who do prefer confirmed hotel reservations. Whether choosing an escorted or independent tour, always bring along complete contact information for your tour operator in case a problem arises, although US tour operators often have local affiliates who can give additional assistance or make other arrangements on the spot.

To determine whether a package — or more specifically, *which* package — fits your travel plans, start by evaluating your interests and needs, deciding how much and what you want to spend, see, and do. Gather whatever package tour information is available for your schedule. Be sure that you take the time to read the brochure *carefully* to determine precisely what is included. Keep in mind that travel brochures are written to entice you into signing up for a package tour. Often the language is deceptive and devious. For example, a brochure may quote the lowest prices for a package tour based on facilities that are unavailable during the off-season, undesirable at any season, or just plain nonexistent. Information such as "breakfast included" or "plus tax" (which can add up) should be taken into account. Note, too, that the prices quoted in brochures are almost always based on double occupancy: The rate listed is for each of two people sharing a double room, and if you travel alone, the supplement for single accommodations can raise the price considerably (see *Hints for Single Travelers,* in this section).

In this age of erratic airfares, the brochure will most often *not* include the price of an airline ticket in the price of the package, though sample fares from various gateway cities usually will be listed separately as extras to be added to the price of the ground arrangements. Before figuring your actual cost, check the latest fares with the airlines, because the samples are invariably out of date by the time you read them. If the brochure gives more than one category of sample fares per gateway city — such as an individual tour-basing fare, a group fare, an excursion, APEX or other discount ticket — your travel agent or airline tour desk will be able to tell you which one applies to the package you choose, depending on when you travel, how far in advance you book, and other factors. (An individual tour-basing fare is a fare computed as part of a package that includes land arrangements, thereby entitling a carrier to reduce the air portion almost to the absolute minimum. Though it always represents a saving over full-fare coach or economy, lately the individual tour-basing fare has not been as inexpensive as the excursion and other discount fares that are also available to individuals. The group fare is usually the least expensive fare, and it is the tour operator, not you, who makes up the group.) When the brochure does include round-trip transportation in the package price, don't forget to add the cost of round-trip

GETTING READY / Package Tours

transportation from your home to the departure city to come up with the total cost of the package.

▪**Note:** Finding the most economical package tour can be a laborious and time-consuming task. A new service that takes some of the effort out of the selection process is *TourScan, Inc.* (PO Box 2367, Darien, CT 06820; phone: 800-962-2080 or 203-655-8091). Focused exclusively on the Caribbean, the Bahamas, and Bermuda, *TourScan* provides travelers with a computerized listing of hotel and airfare packages offered by numerous tour operators, wholesalers, hotels, and airlines. These are organized and presented twice a year in the form of the *Island Vacation Catalog,* which lists packages in a variety of categories (deluxe, all-inclusive, family) to each island destination in order of increasing price, with separate columns detailing each tour's amenities and features. Catalogues are available by mail for $4 each, and the price of the catalogue will be credited to any tour booked directly through *TourScan,* although travelers are free to book tours through any agency they wish.

Finally, read the general information regarding terms and conditions and the responsibility clause (usually in fine print at the end of the descriptive literature) to determine the precise elements for which the tour operator is — and is not — liable. Here the tour operator frequently expresses the right to change services or schedules as long as equivalent arrangements are offered. This clause also absolves the operator of responsibility for circumstances beyond human control, such as hurricanes or floods, or injury to you or your property. While reading, ask the following questions:

1. Does the tour include airfare or other transportation, sightseeing, meals, transfers, taxes, baggage handling, tips, or any other services? Do you want all these services?
2. If the brochure indicates that "some meals" are included, does this mean a welcoming and farewell dinner, two breakfasts, or every evening meal?
3. What classes of hotels are offered? If you will be traveling alone, what is the single supplement?
4. Does the tour itinerary or price vary according to the season?
5. Are the prices guaranteed; that is, if costs increase between the time you book and the time you depart, can surcharges unilaterally be added?
6. Do you get a full refund if you cancel? If not, be sure to obtain cancellation insurance.
7. Can the operator cancel if too few people join? At what point?

One of the consumer's biggest problems is finding enough information to judge the reliability of a tour packager, since individual travelers seldom have direct contact with the firm putting the package together. Usually, a retail travel agent is interposed between customer and tour operator, and much depends on his or her candor and cooperation. So ask a number of questions about the tour you are considering. For example:

- Has the agent ever used a package provided by this tour operator?
- How long has the tour operator been in business? Check the Better Business Bureau in the area where the tour operator is based to see if any complaints have been filed against it.
- Is the tour operator a member of the *United States Tour Operators Association* (*USTOA,* 211 E. 51st St., Suite 12B, New York, NY 10022; phone: 212-944-5727)? The *USTOA* will provide a list of its members on request; it also offers a useful brochure, *How to Select a Package Tour.*
- How many and which companies are involved in the package?

GETTING READY / Package Tours

■ **A word of advice:** Purchasers of vacation packages who feel they're not getting their money's worth are more likely to get a refund if they complain in writing to the operator — and bail out of the whole package immediately. Alert the tour operator or resort manager to the fact that you are dissatisfied, that you will be leaving for home as soon as transportation can be arranged, and that you expect a refund. They may have forms to fill out detailing your complaint; otherwise, state your case in a letter. Even if difficulty in arranging immediate transportation home detains you, your dated, written complaint should help in procuring a refund from the operator.

SAMPLE PACKAGES TO THE BAHAMAS: As discussed above, a typical package tour to the Bahamas might include transportation to and from the islands, accommodations for the duration of a stay, a sightseeing tour of the area, and several meals.

Although some packages just cover arrangements at a specific hotel, others offer more extensive arrangements and may be built around activities such as golf, tennis, or scuba diving or may provide special features such as a day of sailing, a sightseeing tour, a book of discount coupons for shopping, or a free cocktail party. Special getaway weekend packages and honeymoon packages are essentially organized by hotels or resorts (sometimes in conjunction with airlines) and may include any number of special features that might be termed extras.

For example, a 3-night honeymoon package at the *Princess Tower* (phone: 809-352-9661) in Freeport, Grand Bahama, includes Tower or Country Club accommodations with champagne, souvenir photo, welcoming rum punch, $100 discount booklet, cable television, admission to health club facilities, sightseeing tour of the *Princess* estate, transportation to a private beach, and taxes and tips. On Paradise Island, several resorts offer honeymoon packages, with 3- and 7-night options. The estate-like *Ocean Club* has packages that feature admission to a Las Vegas–style show, a champagne and cocktail reception, and champagne breakfast in bed (10% hotel room tax and tips not included; phone: 800-321-3000). For the athletically inclined couple, *Paradise Paradise,* also run by Merv Griffin's Resorts International, offers packages that include admission to a Las Vegas–style show, free water sports — including sailing, waterskiing, windsurfing, and snorkeling — golf at the *Paradise Island Golf Club* (for an additional charge), and complimentary tennis, bicycling, and volleyball (tax and tips not included; phone: 800-321-3000). *Club Med* is on Eleuthera, San Salvador, and Paradise Island in the Bahamas, and *Club Med Turkoise* is in the Turks & Caicos. Most week-long package prices include airfare from major gateway cities, as well as all sports activities, land features (except bar drinks and sundries), and meals with wine. Accommodations are in simple, colorful, air conditioned rooms with private baths. The Caribbean "villages" have space for about 600 guests. *Club Med*s are erroneously considered exclusively swinging singles places; in fact, they're also geared to couples, families, and easygoing singles looking for an extremely friendly, casual holiday atmosphere. Prices vary with the place and season. Check with your travel agent or call the *Club*'s information number: 800-CLUB-MED. Packages vary seasonally, and are subject to revision by the package organizer. They can be booked through any travel agent or tour operator, although in many cases the resort may be contacted directly.

The following is a list of some of the major US tour operators specializing in package tours to the Bahamas. Contact them directly or through a travel agent — however, as noted, some operators are wholesalers only, and in those cases you must use a travel agent to make reservations.

American Express Travel Related Services (300 Pinnacle Way, Norcross, GA 30071; phone: 800-327-7737 or 404-368-5100). Offers a full range of escorted

GETTING READY / Package Tours

tours in the Bahamas, as well as "free-lance" programs for independent travelers. The tour operator is a wholesaler, so use a travel agent.

GoGo Tours (contact the central office for the nearest location: 69 Spring St., Ramsey, NJ 07446-0507; phone: 201-934-3500). Serving the Bahamas through major carriers from most US gateways, their packages range from budget to deluxe, and include airfare, accommodations at large resort hotels, transfers, and US departure tax. A wholesaler, so have your travel agent contact the nearest branch office.

Liberty Travel (contact the central office for the nearest location: 69 Spring St., Ramsey, NJ 07446; phone: 201-934-3500). Offers air/hotel packages to the Bahamas.

Trans National Travel (2 Charlesgate West, Boston, MA 02215; phone: 800-262-0123). Offers a range of different packages to the Bahamas.

Travel Impressions (465 Smith St., Farmingdale, NY 11735; phone: 800-284-0077 in the Southeast, Midwest, and western US; 800-284-0044 or 800-284-0055 in the Northeast and elsewhere in the US). Offers packages to the Bahamas including round-trip airfare and transfers, hotel accommodations, US departure tax, hotel gratuities and taxes, and discounts on sightseeing, shopping, and water sports (where available). Before you go they will provide a customized hints and tips booklet, and *Travel Impressions* representatives are available for on-the-spot assistance in the Bahamas. The tour operator is a wholesaler, so use a travel agent.

Preparing

Calculating Costs

A realistic appraisal of travel expenses is the most crucial bit of planning required before any trip. It is also, unfortunately, one for which it is most difficult to give precise, practical advice.

In the Bahamas, estimating travel expenses depends on the mode of transportation you choose, how long you will stay, the level of luxury to which you aspire, and in some cases, what time of year you plan to travel. In addition to the basics of transportation, hotels, meals, and sightseeing, you have to take into account seasonal price changes.

DETERMINING A BUDGET: When calculating costs, start with the basics, the major expenses being transportation, accommodations, and food. However, don't forget such extras as local transportation, shopping, and such miscellaneous items as laundry and tips. The reasonable cost of these items usually is a positive surprise to your budget; such extras as drinks served with imported liquors and airport departure taxes are definite negatives.

Additional expenses, such as the cost of local sightseeing and other excursions, will vary depending on the tour and the guide you select. The tourist information office and most of the better hotels will have someone to provide a rundown on the costs of local tours and full-day excursions on the islands. Travel agents also can provide this information.

A double room at one of the best Nassau, Cable Beach, or Paradise Island hotels runs from about $135 and up a day European Plan (without meals) from mid-December to May, but breakfasts and dinners add $35 to $50 per person a day. There are many more moderately priced places — especially on the outlying islands, where much of the Bahamas' charm lies these days. There you'll find all the creature comforts, but no show-off chic, at rates that run from about $130 and up a day for two — including two, and sometimes three, meals. From May to mid-December, prices drop 30% to 50% across the board. Package tours, offered year-round, are especially popular in summer to Nassau/Paradise and Freeport/Lucaya. Prices for 8-day/7-night packaged stays on the outlying islands run from about $310 (per person) and up in winter, about $190 and up in summer; a number of water sport features are usually included, but airfare is usually extra. An 8-day/7-night stay in a top-rated Nassau hotel, including sightseeing tour, aquarium admission, and transfers, is priced at about $375 and up per person in winter, about $225 and up per person in summer, with airfare extra. Individual hotels and resorts also offer specialized tennis, golf, diving, and honeymoon packages that include special extras at considerable savings. Several operators offer weekend and week-long casino packages combined with charter flights, designed to attract high rollers at very low prices.

A government room tax of 4% of the EP (room only) rate and a resort levy of 4% are added to hotel bills. There is also an airport departure tax of $13 (children under 2 years free). A 15% service charge usually is charged on hotel and restaurant bills in the Bahamas. Nevertheless, there still are many situations not covered by the service charge — or where an additional gratuity is appropriate. For more on these matters, see *Tipping,* in this section.

Lunch at one of the better Nassau restaurants runs about $30 for two; dinner, about $50 and up, with drinks and tip extra. Breakfasts costing $7 to $10 per person are not unusual in the better hotels.

Budget-minded families also can take advantage of some of the more economical accommodations options to be found in the Bahamas. For information on other alternatives, such as renting a condominium, a housekeeping apartment, or a cottage, see the discussions of accommodations in *On the Islands,* in this section.

Picnicking is another way to cut costs, and the Bahamas abound with beaches and idyllic tropical settings. A stop at a local market can provide an island feast at a surprisingly economical price than a restaurant lunch.

In planning any travel budget, it also is wise to allow a realistic amount for both entertainment and recreation. Are you planning to spend time sightseeing and visiting local tourist attractions? Do you intend to rent scuba equipment or a sailboat or take windsurfing lessons? Is daily golf or tennis a part of your plan? Will your children be disappointed if they don't take a trip in a glass-bottom boat? Finally, don't forget that if haunting discotheques or other nightspots is an essential part of your vacation, or you feel that one dinner show or one visit to a casino may not be enough, allow for the extra cost of nightlife. This one item alone can add a great deal to your daily expenditures.

If at any point in the planning process it appears impossible to estimate expenses, consider this suggestion: The easiest way to put a ceiling on the price of all these elements is to buy a package tour. A totally planned and escorted one, with almost all transportation, rooms, meals, sightseeing, local travel, tips, and a dinner show or two included and prepaid, provides a pretty exact total of what the trip will cost beforehand, and the only surprise will be the one you spring on yourself by succumbing to some irresistible, expensive souvenir.

Planning a Trip

Travelers fall into two categories: those who make lists and those who do not. Some people prefer to plot the course of their trip to the finest detail, with contingency plans and alternatives at the ready. For others, the joy of a voyage is its spontaneity; exhaustive planning only lessens the thrill of anticipation and the sense of freedom.

For most travelers, however, any week-plus trip to the Bahamas can be too expensive for an "I'll take my chances" type of attitude. Even perennial gypsies and anarchistic wanderers have to take into account the time-consuming logistics of getting around, and even with minimal baggage, they need to think about packing. Hence, at least some planning is crucial.

This is not to suggest that you work out your itinerary in minute detail before you go; but it's still wise to decide certain basics at the very start: where to go, what to do, and how much to spend. These decisions require a certain amount of consideration. So

GETTING READY / Planning a Trip 43

before rigorously planning specific details, you might want to establish your general travel objectives:

1. How much time will you have for the entire trip, and how much of it are you willing to spend getting where you're going?
2. What interests and/or activities do you want to pursue while on vacation? Do you want to visit one, a few, or several different places?
3. At what time of year do you want to go?
4. Do you want peace and privacy or lots of activity and company?
5. How much money can you afford to spend for the entire trip?

You now can make almost all of your own travel arrangements if you have time to follow through with hotels, airlines, tour operators, and so on. But you'll probably save considerable time and energy if you have a travel agent make arrangements for you. The agent also should be able to advise you of alternate arrangements of which you may not be aware. Only rarely will a travel agent's services cost a traveler any money, and they may even save you some (see *How to Use a Travel Agent,* below).

Pay particular attention to the dates when off-season rates go into effect. For instance, if you don't mind warmer temperatures, a trip after mid-April and before mid-December may reduce the cost of your hotel accommodations in the Bahamas by 30% to 60%, compared to the rates during high season. In general, it is a good idea to beware of holiday weeks, as rates at hotels generally are higher during these periods and rooms normally are heavily booked. (In addition, service is apt to be under par unless more staff people are employed for the holidays, since the regular bellhops, maids, dining room personnel, and others will be trying to cope with a full house instead of being able to provide personal attention to individual guests.)

If you are traveling by plane and want to benefit from savings offered to the Bahamas (see *Traveling by Plane,* in this section), you may need reservations as much as 3 months ahead. In the high season, hotel reservations are required months in advance. Many hotels in the Bahamas require deposits before they will guarantee reservations, and this most often is the case during peak travel periods. (Be sure to request a receipt for any deposit.) Travel to the Bahamas during *Easter Week,* the *Christmas/New Year* period, and local festival and holiday times also requires reservations well in advance.

Make a list of any valuable items you are carrying with you, including credit card numbers and the serial numbers of your traveler's checks. Put copies in your purse or pocket and leave other copies at home. Put a label with your name and home address on the inside of your luggage for identification in case of loss. Put your name and business address — *never your home address* — on a label on the outside of your luggage. (Those who run businesses from home should use the office address of a friend or relative.)

Review your travel documents. If you are traveling by air, check that your ticket has been filled in correctly. The left side of the ticket should have a list of each stop you will make (even if you are stopping only to change planes), beginning with your departure point. Be sure that the list is correct, and count the number of copies to see that you have one for each plane you will take. If you have confirmed reservations, be sure that the column marked "status" says "OK" beside each flight. Have in hand vouchers or proof of payment for any reservation for which you've paid in advance; this includes hotels, transfers to and from the airport, sightseeing tours, car rentals, and tickets to special events.

Although policies vary from carrier to carrier, it's still smart to reconfirm your flight 48 to 72 hours before departure, both going and returning.

Finally, you always should bear in mind that despite the most careful plans, things do not always occur on schedule. If you maintain a flexible attitude and try to accept minor disruptions as less than cataclysmic, you will enjoy yourself a lot more.

How to Use a Travel Agent

A reliable travel agent remains the best source of service and information for planning a trip, whether you have a specific itinerary and require an agent only to make reservations or you need extensive help in sorting through the maze of airfares, tour offerings, hotel packages, and the scores of other arrangements that may be involved in a trip to the Bahamas.

Know what you want from a travel agent so that you can evaluate what you are getting. It is perfectly reasonable to expect your agent to be a thoroughly knowledgeable travel specialist, with information about your destination and, even more crucial, a command of current airfares, ground arrangements, and other wrinkles in the travel scene.

Most travel agents work through computer reservations systems (CRS). These are used to assess the availability and cost of flights, hotels, and car rental firms, and through them they can book reservations. Despite reports of "computer bias," in which a computer may favor one airline over another, the CRS should provide agents with the entire spectrum of flights available to a given destination and the complete range of fares in considerably less time than it takes to telephone the airlines individually — and at no extra cost to the traveler.

Make the most intelligent use of a travel agent's time and expertise; understand the economics of the industry. As a client, traditionally you pay nothing for the agent's services; with few exceptions, it's all free, from hotel bookings to advice on package tours. Any money the travel agent makes on the time spent arranging your itinerary — booking hotels, resorts, or flights, or suggesting activities — comes from commissions paid by the suppliers of these services — the airlines, hotels, and so on. These commissions generally run from 10% to 15% of the total cost of the service, although suppliers often reward agencies that sell their services in volume with an increased commission, called an override. In most instances, you'll find that travel agents make their time and experience available to you at no charge, and you do not pay more for an airline ticket, package tour, or other product bought from a travel agent than you would for the same one bought directly from the supplier.

Exceptions to the general rule of free service by a travel agency are the agencies that practice net pricing. In essence, such agencies return their commissions and overrides to their customers and make their income by charging a flat fee per transaction instead (thus adding a charge after a reduction for the commission has been made). Net fares and fees are a growing practice, though hardly widespread (see *Traveling by Air,* in this section).

Even a conventional travel agent sometimes may charge a fee for special services. These chargeable items may include long-distance telephone or cable costs incurred in making a booking, for reserving a room in a place that does not pay a commission (such as a small, out-of-the way hotel), or for a special attention such as planning a highly personalized itinerary. A fee also may be assessed in instances of deeply discounted airfares.

Choose a travel agent with the same care with which you would choose a doctor or lawyer. You will be spending a good deal of money on the basis of the agent's judgment, so you have a right to expect that judgment to be mature, informed, and interested. At the moment, unfortunately, there aren't many standards within the travel agent industry to help you gauge competence, and the quality of individual agents varies enormously.

At present, only nine states have registration, licensing, or some other forms of travel agent–related legislation on their books. Rhode Island licenses travel agents; Florida, Hawaii, Iowa, and Ohio register them; and California, Illinois, Oregon, and Washington have laws governing the sale of transportation or related services. While state licensing of agents cannot absolutely guarantee competence, it can at least ensure that an agent has met some minimum requirements.

Perhaps the best-prepared agents are those who have completed the CTC Travel Management program offered by the *Institute of Certified Travel Agents* (*ICTA*) and carry the initials CTC (Certified Travel Counselor) after their names. This indicates a relatively high level of expertise. For a free list of CTCs in your area, send a self-addressed, stamped, #10 envelope to *ICTA,* 148 Linden St., Box 82-56, Wellesley, MA 02181 (phone: 617-237-0280 in Massachusetts; 800-542-4282 elsewhere in the US).

An agent's membership in the *American Society of Travel Agents (ASTA)* can be a useful guideline in making a selection. But keep in mind that *ASTA* is an industry organization, requiring only that its members be licensed in those states where required; be accredited to represent the suppliers whose products they sell, including airline and cruise tickets; and adhere to its Principles of Professional Conduct and Ethics code. *ASTA* does not guarantee the competence, ethics, or financial soundness of its members, but it does offer some recourse if you feel you have been dealt with unfairly. Complaints may be registered with *ASTA* (Consumer Affairs Dept., 1101 King St., Alexandria, VA 22314; phone: 703-739-2782). First try to resolve the complaint directly with the supplier. You may call the above number for a list of *ASTA* members in your area. If you require a detailed printed list, there is a variable charge.

There also is the *Association of Retail Travel Agents (ARTA),* a smaller but highly respected trade organization similar to *ASTA.* Its member agencies and agents similarly agree to abide by a code of ethics, and complaints about a member can be made to *ARTA*'s Grievance Committee, 1745 Jeff Davis Hwy., Arlington, VA 22202-3402 (phone: 800-969-6069 or 703-553-7777).

Perhaps the best way to find a travel agent is by word of mouth. If the agent (or agency) has done a good job for your friends over a period of time, it probably indicates a certain level of commitment and competence. Always ask not only for the name of the company, but also for the name of the specific agent with whom your friends dealt, for it is that individual who will serve you, and quality can vary widely within a single agency. There are some superb travel agents in the business, and they can facilitate vacation or business arrangements.

Entry Requirements and Documents

US and Canadian citizens need only proof of citizenship (passport, birth certificate, or *certified* copy of a birth certificate, plus an additional positive photo identification) and an ongoing or return ticket to gain entry to the Bahamas. Maximum stay for US and Canadian citizens is 8 months. To extend the stay, or to apply for a work permit, contact the Ministry of Employment and Immigration, Clarence Bain Bldg., PO Box N3002, Nassau, Bahamas.

Insurance

It is unfortunate that most decisions to buy travel insurance are impulsive and usually are made without any real consideration of the traveler's existing policies. Therefore, the first person with whom you should discuss travel insurance is your own insurance broker, not a travel agent or the clerk behind the airport insurance counter. You may discover that the insurance you already carry — homeowner's policies and/or accident, health, and life insurance — protects you adequately while you travel and that your real needs are in the more mundane areas of excess value insurance for baggage or trip cancellation insurance.

TYPES OF INSURANCE: To make insurance decisions intelligently, however, you first should understand the basic categories of travel insurance and what they cover. Then you can decide what you should have in the broader context of your personal insurance needs, and you can choose the most economical way of getting the desired protection: through riders on existing policies; with onetime short-term policies; through a special program put together for the frequent traveler; through coverage that's part of a travel club's benefits; or with a combination policy sold by insurance companies through brokers, automobile clubs, tour operators, and travel agents.

There are seven basic categories of travel insurance:

1. Baggage and personal effects insurance
2. Personal accident and sickness insurance
3. Trip cancellation and interruption insurance
4. Default and/or bankruptcy insurance
5. Flight insurance (to cover injury or death)
6. Automobile insurance (for driving a rented car)
7. Combination policies

Baggage and Personal Effects Insurance – Ask your insurance agent if baggage and personal effects are included in your current homeowner's policy, or if you will need a special floater to cover you for the duration of a trip. The object is to protect your bags and their contents in case of damage or theft anytime during your travels, not just while you're in flight and covered by the airline's policy. Furthermore, only limited protection is provided by the airline. Baggage liability varies from carrier to carrier, but generally speaking, on domestic flights, luggage usually is insured to $1,250 — that's per passenger, not per bag. For most international flights, including domestic portions of international flights, the airline's liability limit is approximately $640 for each checked bag. This limit should be specified on your airline ticket, but to be awarded any amount, you'll have to provide an itemized list of lost property, and if you're including new and/or expensive items, be prepared for a request that you back up your claim with sales receipts or other proof of purchase.

If you are carrying goods worth more than the maximum protection offered by the airline, consider excess value insurance. Additional coverage is available from airlines at an average, currently, of $1 to $2 per $100 worth of coverage, up to a maximum of $5,000. This insurance can be purchased at the airline counter when you check in, though you should arrive early to fill out the necessary forms and to avoid holding up other passengers.

Major credit card companies also provide coverage for lost or delayed baggage — and this coverage often also is over and above what the airline will pay. The basic coverage is automatic for all cardholders who use the credit card to purchase tickets, but to qualify for additional coverage, cardholders generally must enroll in advance.

American Express: Provides $500 coverage for checked baggage; $1,250 for carry-on baggage; and $250 for valuables, such as cameras and jewelry.

Carte Blanche and Diners Club: Each provides $1,250 worth of free insurance for checked or carry-on baggage that's lost or damaged.

Discover Card: Offers $500 insurance for checked baggage and $1,250 for carry-on baggage — but to qualify for this coverage cardholders first must purchase additional flight insurance (see "Flight Insurance," below).

MasterCard and Visa: Baggage insurance coverage is set by the issuing institution.

Additional baggage and personal effects insurance also is included in certain of the combination travel insurance policies discussed below.

■ **A note of warning:** Be sure to read the fine print of any excess value insurance policy; there often are specific exclusions, such as cash, tickets, furs, gold and silver objects, art, and antiques. And remember that insurance companies ordinarily will pay only the depreciated value of the goods rather than their replacement value. The best way to protect the items you're carrying in your luggage is to take photos of your valuables and keep a record of the serial numbers of such items as cameras, laptops, radios, and so on. This will establish that you do, indeed, own the objects. If your luggage disappears or is damaged en route, deal with the situation immediately. If an airline loses your luggage, you will be asked to fill out a Property Irregularity Report before you leave the airport. If your property disappears at other transportation centers, tell the local company, but also report it to the police (since the insurance company will check with the police when processing your claim).

Personal Accident and Sickness Insurance – This covers you in case of illness during your trip or death in an accident. Most policies insure you for hospital and doctor's expenses, lost income, and so on. In most cases, it is a standard part of existing health insurance policies, though you should check with your insurance broker to be sure that your policy will pay for any medical expenses incurred abroad. If not, take out a separate vacation accident policy or an entire vacation insurance policy that includes health and life coverage.

Two examples of such comprehensive health and life insurance coverage are the travel insurance packages offered by *Wallach & Co:*

HealthCare Global: This insurance package, which can be purchased for periods of 10 to 180 days, is offered for two age groups: Men and women up to age 75 receive $25,000 medical insurance and $50,000 death benefit; those from age 76 to 84 are eligible for $12,500 medical insurance and $25,000 death benefit. For either policy, the cost for a 10-day period is $25, with decreasing rates up to 75 days, after which the rate is $1.50 per day.

HealthCare Abroad: This program is available to individuals up to age 75. For $3 per day (minimum 10 days, maximum 90 days), policy holders receive $100,000 medical insurance and $25,000 death benefit.

Both of these basic programs also may be bought in combination with trip cancellation and baggage insurance at extra cost. For further information, write to *Wallach & Co.,* 107 West Federal St., Box 480, Middleburg, VA 22117-0480 (phone: 703-687-3166 in Virginia; 800-237-6615 elsewhere in the US).

48 GETTING READY / Insurance

Trip Cancellation and Interruption Insurance – Most charter and package tour passengers pay for their travel well before departure. The disappointment of having to miss a vacation because of illness or any other reason pales before the awful prospect that not all (and sometimes none) of the money paid in advance might be returned. So cancellation insurance for any package tour is a must.

Although cancellation penalties vary (they are listed in the fine print of every tour brochure, and before you purchase a package tour you should know exactly what they are), rarely will a passenger get more than 50% of this money back if forced to cancel within a few weeks of scheduled departure. Therefore, if you book a package tour or charter flight, you should have trip cancellation insurance to guarantee full reimbursement or refund should you, a traveling companion, or a member of your immediate family get sick, forcing you to cancel your trip or *return home early*.

The key here is *not* to buy just enough insurance to guarantee full reimbursement for the cost of the package or charter in case of cancellation. The proper amount of coverage should be sufficient to reimburse you for the cost of having to catch up with a tour after its departure or having to travel home at the full economy airfare if you have to forgo your return flight of your charter. There usually is quite a discrepancy between a charter airfare and the amount charged to travel the same distance on a regularly scheduled flight at full economy fare.

Trip cancellation insurance is available from travel agents and tour operators in two forms: as part of a short-term, all-purpose travel insurance package (sold by the travel agent); or as specific cancellation insurance designed by the tour operator for a specific charter tour. Generally, tour operators' policies are less expensive, but also less inclusive. Cancellation insurance also is available directly from insurance companies or their agents as part of a short-term, all-inclusive travel insurance policy.

Before you decide on a policy, read each one carefully. (Either type can be purchased from a travel agent when you book the charter or package tour.) Be certain that your policy includes enough coverage to pay your fare from the farthest destination on your itinerary should you have to miss the flight. Also, be sure to check the fine print for stipulations concerning "family members" and "pre-existing medical conditions," as well as allowances for living expenses if you must delay your return due to bodily injury or illness.

Default and/or Bankruptcy Insurance – Although trip cancellation insurance usually protects you if *you* are unable to complete — or begin — your trip, a fairly recent innovation is coverage in the event of default and/or bankruptcy on the part of the tour operator, airline, or other travel supplier. In some travel insurance packages, this contingency is included in the trip cancellation portion of the coverage; in others, it is a separate feature. Either way, it is becoming increasingly important. Whereas sophisticated travelers have long known to beware of the possibility of default or bankruptcy when buying a charter flight or tour package, in recent years more than a few respected airlines have unexpectedly revealed their shaky financial condition, sometimes leaving hordes of stranded ticket holders in their wake. While default/bankruptcy insurance will not ordinarily result in reimbursement in time to pay for new arrangements, it can ensure that you will get your money back, and even independent travelers buying no more than an airplane ticket may want to consider it.

Flight Insurance – Airlines have carefully established limits of liability for injury to or the death of passengers for international flights. For international flights to, from, or with a stopover in the US, all carriers are liable for up to $75,000 per passenger. For all other international flights, the liability is based on where you purchase the ticket: If booked in advance in the US, the maximum liability is $75,000; if arrangements are made abroad, the liability is between $10,000 and $20,000. But remember,

GETTING READY / Insurance

these liabilities are not the same thing as insurance policies; every penny that an airline eventually pays in the case of injury or death will likely be subject to a legal battle.

But before you buy last-minute flight insurance from an airport vending machine, consider the purchase in light of your total existing insurance coverage. A careful review of your current policies may reveal that you already are amply covered for accidental death, sometimes up to three times the amount provided for by the flight insurance you're buying at the airport.

Be aware that airport insurance, the kind typically bought at a counter or from a vending machine, is among the most expensive forms of life insurance coverage, and that even within a single airport, rates for approximately the same coverage vary widely. Often policies sold in vending machines are more expensive than those sold over the counter, even when they are with the same national company.

If you buy your plane ticket with a major credit card, you generally receive automatic insurance coverage at no extra cost. Additional coverage usually can be obtained at extremely reasonable prices, but a cardholder must sign up for it in advance. (Note that rates vary slightly for residents of some states.) As we went to press, the travel accident and life insurance policies of these major credit cards were as follows:

American Express: Automatically provides $100,000 in insurance to its *Green, Gold,* and *Optima* cardholders, and $500,000 to *Platinum* cardholders. With *American Express,* $4.50 per ticket buys an additional $250,000 worth of flight insurance; $7.50 buys $500,000 worth; and $14 provides an added $1 million worth of coverage.

Carte Blanche: Automatically provides $150,000 flight insurance.

Diners Club: Provides $350,000 free flight insurance. An additional $250,000 worth of insurance is available for $4; $500,000 costs $6.50.

Discover Card: Provides $500,000 free flight insurance. An additional $250,000 worth of insurance is available for $4.50; $500,000 costs $6.50.

MasterCard and Visa: Insurance coverage for each is set by the issuing institution.

Automobile Insurance – If you are renting a car in the islands, automobile insurance *is* a necessity, but the required coverage will be included as part of the rental contract. In some instances, an existing car insurance policy at home may partially or completely cover a rental car abroad. Check with your travel agent. When you rent a car, the rental company is required to offer you collision protection. In your car rental contract, you'll see that for about $10 a day, you may buy optional collision damage waiver (CDW) protection.

If you do not accept the CDW coverage, you may be liable for as much as the full retail cost of the rental car, and by paying for the CDW you are relieved of all responsibility for any damage to the car. Before agreeing to this coverage, however, check with your own broker about your own existing personal auto insurance policy. It very well may cover your entire liability exposure without any additional cost, or you automatically may be covered by the credit card company to which you are charging the cost of your rental. To find out the amount of rental car insurance provided by major credit cards, contact the issuing institutions.

You also should know that an increasing number of the major international car rental companies automatically are including the cost of the CDW in their basic rates. Car rental prices have increased to include this coverage, although rental company ad campaigns may promote this as a new, improved rental package feature. The disadvantage of this inclusion is that you may not have the option to turn down the CDW — even if you already are adequately covered by your own insurance policy or through a credit card company.

50 GETTING READY / Handicapped Travelers

Combination Policies – Short-term insurance policies, which may include a combination of any or all of the types of insurance discussed above, are available through retail insurance agencies and many travel agents. These combination policies are designed to cover you for the duration of a single trip.

Policies of this type include the following:

Access America: A subsidiary of the Blue Cross/Blue Shield plans of New York and Washington, DC, now available nationwide. Contact *Access America,* 600 Third Ave., PO Box 807, New York, NY 10016 (phone: 800-424-3391 or 212-949-5960).

Carefree: Underwritten by The Hartford. Contact *Carefree Travel Insurance,* Arm Coverage, PO Box 310, Mineola, NY 11501 (phone: 800-645-2424 or 516-294-0220).

NEAR Services: In addition to a full range of travel services, this organization offers a comprehensive travel insurance package. An added feature is coverage for lost or stolen airline tickets. Contact *NEAR Services,* 450 Prairie Ave., Suite 101, Calumet City, IL 60409 (phone: 708-868-6700 in the Chicago area; 800-654-6700 elsewhere in the US and Canada).

Tele-Trip: Underwritten by the Mutual of Omaha Companies. Contact *Tele-Trip Co.,* PO Box 31685, 3201 Farnam St., Omaha, NE 68131 (phone: 800-228-9792 or 402-345-2400).

Travel Assistance International: Provided by Europ Assistance Worldwide Services, and underwritten by Transamerica Occidental Life Insurance Company. Contact *Travel Assistance International,* 1133 15th St. NW, Suite 400, Washington, DC 20005 (phone: 202-331-1609 in Washington, DC; 800-821-2828 elsewhere in the US).

Travel Guard International: Underwritten by the Insurance Company of North America, it is available through authorized travel agents, or contact *Travel Guard International,* 1145 Clark St., Stevens Point, WI 54481 (phone: 715-345-0505 in Wisconsin; 800-826-1300 elsewhere in the US.

Travel Insurance PAK: Underwritten by The Travelers. Contact *The Travelers Companies,* Ticket and Travel Plans, One Tower Sq., Hartford, CT 06183-5040 (phone: 203-277-2318 in Connecticut; 800-243-3174 elsewhere in the US).

Hints for Handicapped Travelers

From 40 to 50 million people in the US alone have some sort of disability, and over half this number are physically handicapped. Like everyone else today, they — and the uncounted disabled millions around the world — are on the move. More than ever before, they are demanding facilities they can use comfortably, and they are being heard.

PLANNING: Collect as much information as you can about your specific disability and facilities for the disabled in the Bahamas. Make your travel arrangements well in advance and specify to all services involved the exact nature of your condition or restricted mobility, as your trip will be much more comfortable if you know that there are accommodations and facilities to suit your needs.

The best way to find out if your intended destination can accommodate a handicapped traveler is to write or call the local tourist authority or hotel and ask specific questions. If you require a corridor of a certain width to maneuver a wheelchair or if you need handles on the bathroom walls for support, ask the hotel manager. A travel

GETTING READY / Handicapped Travelers 51

agent or the local chapter or national office of the organization that deals with your particular disability — for example, the *American Foundation for the Blind* or the *American Heart Association* — will supply the most up-to-date information on the subject. The following organizations offer general information on access:

- *ACCENT on Living* (PO Box 700, Bloomington, IL 61702; phone: 309-378-2961). This information service for persons with disabilities provides a free list of travel agencies specializing in arranging trips for the disabled; for a copy send a self-addressed, stamped envelope. Also offers a wide range of publications, including a quarterly magazine ($10 per year; $17.50 for 2 years), for persons with disabilities.

- *Information Center for Individuals with Disabilities* (Fort Point Pl., 1st Floor, 27-43 Wormwood St., Boston, MA 02210; phone: 800-462-5015 in Massachusetts; 617-727-5540/1 elsewhere in the US; both numbers provide voice and TDD — telecommunications device for the deaf). The center offers information and referral services on disability-related issues, publishes fact sheets on travel agents, tour operators, and other travel resources, and can help you research your trip.

- *Mobility International USA* (*MIUSA;* PO Box 3551, Eugene, OR 97403; phone: 503-343-1284; both voice and TDD). This US branch of *Mobility International* (the main office is at 228 Borough High St., London SE1 1JX, England; phone: 44-71-403-5688), a nonprofit British organization with affiliates worldwide, offers members advice and assistance — including information on accommodations and other travel services, and publications applicable to the traveler's disability. *Mobility International* also offers a quarterly newsletter and a comprehensive sourcebook, *A World of Options for the 90s: A Guide to International Education Exchange, Community Service and Travel for Persons with Disabilities.* Individual membership is $20 a year, and includes the newsletter; subscription to the newsletter alone is $10 annually.

- *National Rehabilitation Information Center* (8455 Colesville Rd., Suite 935, Silver Spring, MD 20910; phone: 301-588-9284). A general information, resource, research, and referral service.

- *Paralyzed Veterans of America* (*PVA;* PVA/ATTS Program, 801 18th St. NW, Washington, DC 20006; phone: 202-872-1300 in Washington, DC; 800-424-8200 elsewhere in the US). The members of this national service organization all are veterans who have suffered spinal cord injuries, but it offers advocacy services and information to all persons with a disability. *PVA* also sponsors *Access to the Skies* (*ATTS*), a program that coordinates the efforts of the national and international air travel industry in providing airport and airplane access for the disabled. Members receive several helpful publications, as well as regular notification of conferences on subjects of interest to the disabled traveler.

- *Society for the Advancement of Travel for the Handicapped* (*SATH;* 347 Fifth Ave., Ste. 610, New York, NY 10016; phone: 212-447-7284). To keep abreast of developments in travel for the handicapped as they occur, you may want to join *SATH,* a nonprofit organization whose members include consumers, as well as travel service professionals who have experience (or an interest) in travel for the handicapped. For an annual fee of $45 ($25 for students and travelers who are 65 and older) members receive a quarterly newsletter and have access to extensive information and referral services. *SATH* also offers two useful publications: *Travel Tips for the Handicapped* (a series of informative fact sheets) and *The United States Welcomes Handicapped Visitors* (a 48-page guide covering domestic transportation and accommodations that includes useful hints for

52 GETTING READY / Handicapped Travelers

travelers with disabilities abroad); to order, send a self-addressed, #10 envelope and $1 per title for postage.

Travel Information Service (Moss Rehabilitation Hospital, 1200 W. Tabor Rd., Philadelphia, PA 19141-3099; phone: 215-456-9600 for voice; 215-456-9602 for TDD). This service assists physically handicapped people in planning trips and supplies detailed information on accessibility for a nominal fee.

Blind travelers should contact the *American Foundation for the Blind* (15 W. 16th St., New York, NY 10011; phone: 212-620-2147 or 800-829-0500 in New York State; 800-232-5463 elsewhere in the US) and *The Seeing Eye* (Box 375, Morristown, NJ 07963-0375; phone: 201-539-4425); both provide useful information on resources for the visually impaired. *Note:* All dogs arriving in the Bahamas must have a permit issued by the Ministry of Agriculture, a certificate of inoculation against rabies, and a health certificate issued by a veterinarian within 10 days prior to arrival. To obtain an application form for the permit, contact one of the Department of Tourism offices in the US (see *Sources and Resources,* in this section).

In addition, there are a number of publications — from travel guides to magazines — of interest to handicapped travelers. Among these are the following:

Access to the World, by Louise Weiss, offers sound tips for the disabled traveler. Information about the Bahamas is included in several sections. Published by Facts on File (460 Park Ave. S., New York, NY 10016; phone: 212-683-2244 in New York State; 800-322-8755 elsewhere in the US; 800-443-8323 in Canada), it costs $16.95. Check with your local bookstore; it also can be ordered by phone with a credit card.

The Diabetic Traveler (PO Box 8223 RW, Stamford, CT 06905; phone: 203-327-5832) is a useful quarterly newsletter. Each issue highlights a single destination or type of travel and includes information on general resources and hints for diabetics. A 1-year subscription costs $19.95. When subscribing, ask for the free fact sheet including an index of special articles; back issues are available for $4 each.

Guide to Traveling with Arthritis, a free brochure available by writing to the Upjohn Company (PO Box 307-B, Coventry, CT 06238), provides lots of good, commonsense tips on planning your trip and how to be as comfortable as possible when traveling by car, bus, cruise ship, or plane.

Handicapped Travel Newsletter is regarded as one of the best sources of information for the disabled traveler. It is edited by wheelchair-bound Vietnam veteran Michael Quigley, who has traveled to 93 countries around the world. Issued every 2 months (plus special issues), a subscription is $10 per year. Write to *Handicapped Travel Newsletter,* PO Box 269, Athens, TX 75751 (phone: 903-677-1260).

Handi-Travel: A Resource Book for Disabled and Elderly Travellers, by Cinnie Noble, is a comprehensive travel guide full of practical tips for those with disabilities affecting mobility, hearing, or sight. To order this book, send $12.95, plus shipping and handling, to the *Canadian Rehabilitation Council for the Disabled,* 45 Sheppard Ave. East, Suite 801, Toronto, Ontario M2N 5W9, Canada (phone: 416-250-7490; both voice and TDD).

The Itinerary (PO Box 2012, Bayonne, NJ 07002-2012; phone: 201-858-3400). This bimonthly travel magazine for people with disabilities includes information on accessibility, listings of tours, news of adaptive devices, travel aids, and special services, as well as numerous general travel hints. A subscription costs $10 a year.

The Physically Disabled Traveler's Guide, by Rod W. Durgin and Norene Lindsay, rates accessibility of a number of travel services and includes a list of organizations specializing in travel for the disabled. It is available for $9.95, plus shipping and handling, from *Resource Directories,* 3361 Executive Pkwy., Suite 302, Toledo, OH 43606 (phone: 419-536-5353 in the Toledo area; 800-274-8515 elsewhere in the US).

Ticket to Safe Travel offers useful information for travelers with diabetes. A reprint of this article is available free from local chapters of the *American Diabetes Association.* For the nearest branch, contact the central office at 505 Eighth Ave., 21st Floor, New York, NY 10018 (phone: 212-947-9707; elsewhere in the US, 800-232-3472).

Travel for the Patient with Chronic Obstructive Pulmonary Disease, a publication of the George Washington University Medical Center, provides some sound practical suggestions for those with emphysema, chronic bronchitis, asthma, or other lung ailments. To order, send $2 to Dr. Harold Silver, 1601 18th St. NW, Washington, DC 20009 (phone: 202-667-0134).

Traveling Like Everybody Else: A Practical Guide for Disabled Travelers, by Jacqueline Freedman and Susan Gersten, offers the disabled tips on traveling by car, cruise ship, and plane, as well as lists of accessible accommodations, tour operators specializing in tours for disabled travelers, and other resources. It is available for $11.95 plus shipping and handling from Modan Publishing, PO Box 1202, Bellmore, NY 11710 (phone: 516-679-1380).

Travel Tips for Hearing-Impaired People, a free pamphlet for deaf and hearing-impaired travelers, is available from the *American Academy of Otolaryngology* (One Prince St., Alexandria, VA 22314; phone: 703-836-4444). For a copy, send a self-addressed, stamped, business-size envelope to the academy.

Travel Tips for People with Arthritis, a 31-page booklet published by the *Arthritis Foundation,* provides helpful information regarding travel by plane, bus, car, and cruise ship, planning your trip, medical considerations, and ways to save your energy while traveling. It also includes listings of helpful resources, such as associations and travel agencies that operate tours for disabled travelers. For a copy, contact your local *Arthritis Foundation* chapter, or send $1 to the national office, PO Box 19000, Atlanta, GA 30326 (phone: 404-872-7100).

The Wheelchair Traveler, by Douglass R. Annand, lists accessible hotels, motels, restaurants, and other information on accommodations in the Bahamas. This valuable resource is available directly from the author. For the price of the most recent edition, contact Douglass R. Annand, 123 Ball Hill Rd., Milford, NH 03055 (phone: 603-673-4539).

A few more basic resources to look for are *Travel for the Disabled,* by Helen Hecker ($19.95), and by the same author, *Directory of Travel Agencies for the Disabled* ($19.95). *Wheelchair Vagabond,* by John G. Nelson, is another useful guide for travelers confined to a wheelchair (hardcover, $14.95; paperback, $9.95). All three titles are published by Twin Peaks Press (PO Box 129, Vancouver, WA 98666; phone: 800-637-CALM or 206-694-2462 to order).

PLANE: The US Department of Transportation (DOT) has ruled that US airlines must accept all passengers with disabilities. As a matter of course, US airlines were pretty good about accommodating handicapped passengers even before the ruling, although each airline has somewhat different procedures.

Disabled passengers should always make reservations well in advance, and should provide the airline with all relevant details of their condition. These details include information on mobility and equipment that you will need the airline to supply — such as a wheelchair for boarding or portable oxygen for in-flight use. Be sure that the person to whom you speak fully understands the degree of your disability — the more details provided, the more effective help the airline can give you.

On the day before the flight, call back to make sure that all arrangements have been prepared, and arrive early on the day of the flight so that you can board before the rest of the passengers. It's a good idea to bring a medical certificate with you, stating your specific disability or the need to carry particular medicine.

Because most airports have jetways (corridors connecting the terminal with the door of the plane), a disabled passenger usually can be taken as far as the plane, and sometimes right onto it, in a wheelchair. If not, a narrow boarding chair may be used to take you to your seat. Your own wheelchair, which will be folded and put in the baggage compartment, should be tagged as escort luggage to assure that it's available at planeside upon landing rather than in the baggage claim area. Travel is not quite as simple if your wheelchair is battery-operated: Unless it has non-spillable batteries, it might not be accepted on board, and you will have to check with the airline ahead of time to find out how the batteries and the chair should be packaged for the flight. Usually people in wheelchairs are asked to wait until other passengers have disembarked. If you are making a tight connection, be sure to tell the attendant.

Passengers who use oxygen may not use their personal supply in the cabin, though it may be carried on the plane as cargo (the tank must be emptied) when properly packed and labeled. If you will need oxygen during the flight, the airline will supply it to you (there is a charge) provided you have given advance notice — 24 hours to a few days, depending on the carrier.

Among the major US carriers flying to the Bahamas, the following airlines have TDD toll-free lines for the hearing-impaired:

American (phone: 800-582-1573 in Ohio; 800-543-1586 elsewhere in the US).

Delta (phone: 800-831-4488).

USAir (phone: 800-242-1713 in Pennsylvania; 800-245-2966 elsewhere in the US).

The free booklet *Air Transportation of Handicapped Persons* explains the general guidelines that govern air carrier policies. For a copy, write to the US Department of Transportation (Distribution Unit, Publications Section, M-443-2, Washington, DC 20590) and ask for "Free Advisory Circular #AC-120-32."

SHIP: Check with your travel agent or cruise line when making reservations, as some cruise ships cannot accommodate handicapped travelers because of their many sets of narrow steps, which are less convenient than wide ramps.

For those in wheelchairs or with limited mobility, one of the best sources for evaluating a ship's accessibility is the free chart issued by the *Cruise Lines International Association* (500 Fifth Ave., Suite 1407, New York, NY 10110; phone: 212-921-0066). The chart lists accessible ships and indicates whether they accommodate standard-size or only narrow wheelchairs, have ramps, wide doors, low or no doorsills, handrails in the rooms, and so on. (For information on ships cruising Bahamian waters, see *Traveling by Cruise Ship*, in this section.)

GROUND TRANSPORTATION: Perhaps the simplest solution to getting around is to travel with an able-bodied companion who can drive. Competition is fierce among rental car companies, and prices are relatively reasonable. Hand-controlled cars are virtually nonexistent in the Bahamas. If you plan far enough ahead, you may be able to bring your own hand controls and have them installed, but for a short vacation it is probably not worth the trouble. The manager of your hotel generally is your best source of advice on the possibility of making such arrangements. On the whole, you'd be better advised to ask him to line up a reliable car and driver for you if you are traveling alone. On many islands, public transportation also is available, but accessibility for the disabled varies; check with a travel agent or the island tourist board for information.

GETTING READY / Handicapped Travelers 55

The *American Automobile Association (AAA)* publishes a useful book, *The Handicapped Driver's Mobility Guide*. Contact the central office of your local *AAA* club for availability and pricing, which may vary in different branch offices.

TOURS: Programs designed for the physically impaired are run by specialists who have researched hotels, restaurants, and sites to be sure they present no insurmountable obstacles. The following travel agencies and tour operators specialize in making group and individual arrangements for travelers with physical or other disabilities:

Access: The Foundation for Accessibility by the Disabled (PO Box 356, Malverne, NY 11565; phone: 516-887-5798). A travelers' referral service that acts as an intermediary with tour operators and agents worldwide, and provides information on accessibility at various locations.

Accessible Journeys (412 S. 45th St., Philadelphia, PA 19104; phone: 215-747-0171). Arranges for traveling companions who are medical professionals — registered or licensed practical nurses, therapists, or doctors (all are experienced travelers). Several prospective companions' profiles and photos are sent to the client for perusal, and if one is acceptable, the "match" is made. The client usually pays all travel expenses for the companion, plus a certain amount in "earnings" to replace wages the companion would be making at his or her usual job. This company also offers tours and cruises for people with special needs, although you don't have to take one of their tours to hire a companion through them.

Accessible Tours/Directions Unlimited (720 N. Bedford Rd., Bedford Hills, NY 10507; phone: 914-241-1700 in New York State; 800-533-5343 elsewhere in the continental US). Arranges group or individual tours for disabled persons traveling in the company of able-bodied friends or family members. Accepts the unaccompanied traveler if completely self-sufficient.

Dialysis at Sea Cruises (611 Barry Place, Indian Rocks Beach, FL 34635; phone: 800-544-7604 or 813-596-7604). Offers cruises that include the medical services of a nephrologist (a specialist in kidney disease) and a staff of dialysis nurses. Family, friends, and companions are welcome to travel on these cruises, but the number of dialysis patients usually is limited to roughly ten travelers per trip.

Evergreen Travel Service (4114-198th St. SW, Suite 13, Lynnwood, WA 98036-6742; phone: 800-435-2288 or 206-776-1184). Offers worldwide tours and cruises for the disabled (Wings on Wheels Tours), sight-impaired/blind (White Cane Tours), and hearing-impaired/deaf (Flying Fingers Tours). Most programs are first class or deluxe, and include a trained escort.

First National Travel Limited (Thornhill Sq., 300 John St., Suite 405, Thornhill, Ontario L3T 5W4, Canada; phone: 416-731-4714). Handles tours and individual arrangements.

Flying Wheels Travel (143 W. Bridge St., Box 382, Owatonna, MN 55060; phone: 800-535-6790 or 507-451-5005). Handles both tours and individual arrangements.

The Guided Tour (613 W. Cheltenham Ave., Suite 200, Melrose Park, PA 19126-2414; phone: 215-782-1370). Arranges tours for people with developmental and learning disabilities and sponsors separate tours for members of the same population who also are physically disabled or who simply need a slower pace.

Sprout (893 Amsterdam Ave., New York, NY 10025; phone: 212-222-9575). Arranges travel programs for mildly and moderately developmentally disabled teens and adults.

USTS Travel Horizons (11 E. 44th St., New York, NY 10017; phone: 212-687-5121; 800-487-8787). Travel agent and registered nurse Mary Ann Hamm designs trips for individual travelers requiring any type of kidney dialysis and handles arrangements for the dialysis.

Whole Person Tours (PO Box 1084, Bayonne, NJ 07002-1084; phone: 201-858-3400). Handicapped owner Bob Zywicki travels the world with his wheelchair and offers a lineup of escorted tours (many conducted by him) for the disabled. *Whole Person Tours* also publishes *The Itinerary,* a bimonthly newsletter for disabled travelers (see the publication source list above).

Travelers who would benefit from being accompanied by a nurse or physical therapist also can hire a companion through *Traveling Nurses' Network,* a service provided by Twin Peaks Press (PO Box 129, Vancouver, WA 98666; phone: 800-637-CALM or 206-694-2462). For a $10 fee, clients receive the names of three nurses, whom they can then contact directly; for a $125 fee, the agency will make all the hiring arrangements for the client. Travel arrangements also may be made in some cases — the fee for this further service is determined on an individual basis.

A similar service is offered by *MedEscort International* (ABE International Airport, PO Box 8766, Allentown, PA 18105; phone: 800-255-7182 in the continental US; elsewhere call 215-791-3111). Clients can arrange to be accompanied by a nurse, paramedic, respiratory therapist, or physician through *MedEscort.* The fees are based on the disabled traveler's needs. This service also can assist in making travel arrangements.

Hints for Single Travelers

Just about the last trip in human history on which the participants were neatly paired was the voyage of Noah's Ark. Ever since, passenger lists and tour groups have reflected the same kind of asymmetry that occurs in real life, as countless individuals set forth to see the world unaccompanied (or unencumbered, depending on your outlook) by spouse, lover, friend, or relative. Unfortunately, traveling alone can turn a traveler into a second class citizen.

The truth is that the travel industry is not very fair to people who vacation by themselves. People traveling alone almost invariably end up paying more than individuals traveling in pairs. Most travel bargains, including package tours, accommodations, resort packages, and cruises, are based on *double occupancy* rates. This means that the per-person price is offered on the basis of two people traveling together and sharing a double room (which means they each will spend a good deal more on meals and extras). The single traveler will have to pay a surcharge, called a single supplement, for exactly the same package. In extreme cases, this can add as much as 35% to the basic per-person rate.

Don't despair, however. Throughout the Bahamas, there are scores of smaller hotels and other hostelries where, in addition to a cozier atmosphere, prices still are quite reasonable for the single traveler. And some ship lines have begun to offer special cruises for singles.

The obvious, most effective alternative is to find a traveling companion. Even special "singles' tours" that promise no supplements are usually based on people sharing double rooms. Perhaps the most recent innovation along these lines is the creation of organizations that "introduce" the single traveler to other single travelers, somewhat like a dating service. Some charge fees, others are free, but the basic service offered by all is the same: to match an unattached person with a compatible travel mate, often as part of the company's own package tours. Among the better established of these organizations are the following:

GETTING READY / Single Travelers

Partners-in-Travel (PO Box 491145, Los Angeles, CA 90049; phone: 213-476-4869). Members receive a list of singles seeking traveling companions; prospective companions make contact through the agency. The membership fee is $40 per year and includes a chatty newsletter (6 issues per year).

Singleworld (401 Theodore Fremd Ave., Rye, NY 10580; phone: 914-967-3334 or 800-223-6490 in the continental US). For a yearly fee of $25, this club books members on tours and cruises, and arranges shared accommodations, allowing individual travelers to avoid the single supplement charge; members also receive a quarterly newsletter. *Singleworld* also offers its own package tours for singles, with departures categorized by age group.

Travel Companion Exchange (PO Box 833, Amityville, NY 11701; phone: 516-454-0880). This group publishes a newsletter for singles and a directory of individuals looking for travel companions. On joining, members fill out a lengthy questionnaire and write a small listing (much like an ad in a personal column). Based on these listings, members can request copies of profiles and contact prospective traveling companions. It is wise to join well in advance of your planned vacation so that there's enough time to determine compatibility and plan a joint trip. Membership fees, including the newsletter, are $30 for 6 months ($60 a year) for a single-sex listing; $66 for 6 months ($120 a year) for a complete listing.

Also note that certain cruise lines offer guaranteed shared rates for single travelers, whereby cabin mates are selected on request. Two cruise lines that provide such rates are *Cunard* (phone: 800-221-4770) and *Royal Cruise Line* (phone: 800-622-0538 or 415-956-7200 in California; 800-227-4534 elsewhere in the US).

In addition, a number of tour packagers cater to single travelers. These companies offer packages designed for individuals interested in vacationing with a group of single travelers or in being matched with a traveling companion. Among the better established of these agencies are the following:

Grand Circle Travel (347 Congress St., Boston, MA 02210; phone: 800-221-2610 or 617-350-7500). Arranges extended vacations, escorted tours and cruises for the over-50 traveler, including singles. Membership, which is automatic when you book a trip through *Grand Circle,* includes travel discounts and other extras, such as a Pen Pals service for singles seeking traveling companions.

Singles in Motion (545 W. 236th St., Suite 1D, Riverdale, NY 10463; phone: 718-884-4464). Offers a number of packages for single travelers, including tours, cruises, and excursions focusing on outdoor activities such as hiking and biking.

Travel in Two's (239 N. Broadway, Suite 3, N. Tarrytown, NY 10591; phone: 914-631-8409). This company books solo travelers on packages offered by a number of companies (at no extra cost to clients), offers its own tours, and matches singles with traveling companions. Many offerings are listed in their quarterly *Singles Vacation Newsletter,* which costs $7.50 per issue or $20 per year.

A good book for single travelers is *Traveling On Your Own,* by Eleanor Berman, which offers tips on traveling solo and includes information on trips for singles, ranging from outdoor adventures to educational programs. Available in bookstores, it also can be ordered by sending $12.95, plus postage and handling, to Random House, Order Dept., 400 Hahn Rd., Westminster, MD 21157 (phone: 800-733-3000).

Single travelers also may want to subscribe to *Going Solo,* a newsletter that offers helpful information on going on your own. Issued eight times a year, a subscription costs $36. Contact Doerfer Communications, PO Box 1035, Cambridge, MA 02238 (phone: 617-876-2764).

Hints for Older Travelers

Special discounts and more free time are just two factors that have given Americans over age 65 a chance to see the world at affordable prices. Senior citizens make up an ever-growing segment of the travel population, and the trend among them is to travel more frequently and for longer periods of time.

PLANNING: When planning a vacation, prepare your itinerary with one eye on your own physical condition and the other on a topographical map. Keep in mind variations in climate, terrain, and altitudes, which may pose some danger for anyone with heart or breathing problems.

Older travelers may find the following publications of interest:

Going Abroad: 101 Tips for Mature Travelers offers tips on preparing for your trip, commonsense precautions en route, and some basic travel terminology. This concise, free booklet is available from *Grand Circle Travel* (347 Congress St., Boston, MA 02210; phone: 800-221-2610 or 617-350-7500).

The International Health Guide for Senior Citizen Travelers, by Dr. W. Robert Lange, covers such topics as trip preparations, food and water precautions, adjusting to weather and climate conditions, finding a doctor, motion sickness, jet lag, and so on. Also includes a list of resource organizations that provide medical assistance for travelers. It is available for $4.95 plus postage from Pilot Books, 103 Cooper St., Babylon, NY 11702 (phone: 516-422-2225).

The Mature Traveler is a monthly newsletter that provides information on travel discounts, places of interest, useful tips, and other topics of interest for travelers 49 and up. To subscribe, send $24.50 to GEM Publishing Group, PO Box 50820, Reno, NV 89513 (phone: 702-786-7419).

Take a Camel to Lunch and Other Adventures for Mature Travelers, by Nancy O'Connell, offers offbeat and unusual adventures for travelers over 50. Available for $8.95 at bookstores or directly from Bristol Publishing Enterprises (include $2.75 for shipping and handling), PO Box 1737, San Leandro, CA 94577 (phone: 800-346-4889 or 510-895-4461).

Travel Tips for Older Americans is a useful booklet that provides good, basic advice. This US State Department publication (stock number: 044-000-02270-2) can be ordered by sending a check or money order for $1 to the Superintendent of Documents (US Government Printing Office, Washington, DC 20402) or by calling 202-783-3238 and charging the order to a credit card.

Unbelievably Good Deals & Great Adventures That You Absolutely Can't Get Unless You're Over 50, by Joan Rattner Heilman, offers travel tips for older travelers, including discounts on accommodations and transportation, as well as a list of organizations for seniors. It is available for $7.95, plus shipping and handling, from Contemporary Books, 180 N. Michigan Ave., Chicago, IL 60601 (phone: 312-782-9181).

HEALTH: Health facilities in the Bahamas are generally good. A number of organizations help travelers avoid or deal with a medical emergency abroad. For more information on these services, see *Medical and Legal Aid and Consular Services,* in this section.

Most doctors and hospitals in the Bahamas will routinely honor Blue Cross and Blue Shield. Before you go, check the applicability of your current insurance coverage while traveling abroad, and if you are not fully covered look into one of the comprehensive insurance packages offered to travelers (see *Insurance,* in this section).

Pre-trip medical and dental checkups are strongly recommended. In addition, be sure to take along any prescription medication you need, enough to last *without a new*

GETTING READY / Older Travelers

prescription for the duration of your trip; pack all medications with a note from your doctor for the benefit of airport authorities. If you have specific medical problems, bring duplicate prescriptions and a "medical file" composed of the following:

1. A summary of medical history and current diagnosis.
2. A list of drugs to which you are allergic.
3. Your most recent electrocardiogram, if you have heart problems.
4. Your doctor's name, address, and telephone number.

DISCOUNTS AND PACKAGES: Although guidelines change from place to place, many hotel chains, airlines, and other travel suppliers offer discounts to older travelers. Some US airlines offer those age 62 and over (and often one traveling companion per qualifying senior citizen) discounts on flights to the Bahamas. For information on current prices and applicable restrictions, contact the individual carriers. Some discounts, however, are extended only to bona fide members of certain senior citizens organizations. For instance, although *Sheraton* offers a 25% discount to any senior citizen, participating *Holiday Inn* hotels offer 10% discounts to *AARP* members. Be aware, however, that these discounts may not apply during certain "blackout" periods. (See listings below for more information on *AARP* benefits.) Because the same organizations frequently offer package tours to both domestic and international destinations, the benefits of membership are twofold: Those who join can take advantage of discounts as individual travelers and also reap the savings that group travel affords. In addition, because the age requirements for some of these organizations are quite low (or nonexistent), the benefits can begin to accrue early.

Among the organizations dedicated to helping older travelers see the world are the following:

American Association of Retired Persons (AARP; 601 E St. NW, Washington, DC 20049; phone: 202-434-2277). The largest and best known of these organizations. Membership is open to anyone 50 or over, whether retired or not; dues are $8 a year, $20 for 3 years, or $45 for 10 years, and include spouse. The *AARP* Travel Worldwide Experience program, available through *American Express Travel Related Services,* offers members tours, cruises, and other travel programs worldwide, designed exclusively for older travelers. Members can book these services by calling *American Express* at 800-927-0111 for land and air travel, or 800-745-4567 for cruises.

Mature Outlook (Customer Service Center, 6001 N. Clark St., Chicago, IL 60660; phone: 800-336-6330). Through its *Travel Alert,* tours, cruises, and other vacation packages are available to members at special savings. Hotel and car rental discounts and travel accident insurance also are available. Membership is open to anyone 50 years of age or older, costs $9.95 a year, and includes a bimonthly newsletter and magazine, as well as information on package tours.

National Council of Senior Citizens (1331 F St. NW, Washington, DC 20005; phone: 202-347-8800). Here, too, the emphasis is on keeping costs low. This nonprofit organization offers members a different roster of package tours each year, as well as individual arrangements through its affiliated travel service *(Vantage Travel Service).* Although most members are over 50, membership is open to anyone (regardless of age) for an annual fee of $12 per person or couple. Lifetime membership costs $150.

Certain travel agencies and tour operators offer special trips geared to older travelers. Among them are the following:

Elderhostel, a nonprofit organization, offers programs at educational institutions worldwide. The foreign programs generally last about 2 weeks, and include double occupancy accommodations in hotels or student residence halls and all meals. Travel to the programs usually is by designated scheduled flights, and participants can arrange to extend their stay at the end of the program. Elderhostelers must be at least 60 years old (younger if a spouse or companion qualifies), in good health, and not in need of special diets. For a free catalogue describing the program and current offerings, write to *Elderhostel* (75 Federal St., Boston, MA 02110; phone: 617-426-7788). Those interested may purchase an informational videotape for $5.

Evergreen Travel Service (4114-198th St. SW, Suite 13, Lynnwood, WA 98036-6742; phone: 206-776-1184 or 800-435-2288 throughout the continental US and Canada). This specialist in trips for persons with disabilities recently introduced Lazybones Tours, a program offering leisurely tours for older travelers. Most programs are first class or deluxe, and include an escort.

Grand Circle Travel (347 Congress St., Boston, MA 02210; phone: 800-221-2610 or 617-350-7500). Caters exclusively to the over-50 traveler and packages a large variety of escorted tours, cruises, and extended vacations. Membership, which is automatic when you book a trip through *Grand Circle,* includes discount certificates on future trips and other extras, such as a matching service for single travelers and a helpful free booklet, *Going Abroad: 101 Tips for Mature Travelers* (see the source list above).

Insight International Tours (745 Atlantic Ave., Suite 720, Boston, MA 02111; phone: 800-582-8380 or 617-482-2000). Offers a matching service for single travelers. It also caters to many mature travelers.

Many travel agencies, particularly the larger ones, are delighted to make presentations to help a group of senior citizens select destinations. A local chamber of commerce should be able to provide the names of such agencies. Once a time and place are determined, an organization member or travel agent can obtain group quotations for transportation, accommodations, meal plans, and sightseeing. Larger groups usually get the best breaks.

Hints for Traveling with Children

What better way to encounter the world's variety than in the company of the young, wide-eyed members of your family? Their presence does not have to be a burden or an excessive expense. The current generation of discounts for children and family package deals can make a trip together quite reasonable.

A family trip will be an investment in your children's future, making geography and history come alive for them, and leaving a sure memory that will be among the fondest you will share with them someday. Their insights will be refreshing to you; their impulses may take you to unexpected places with unexpected dividends.

PLANNING: Here are several hints for making a trip with children easy and fun.

1. Children, like everyone else, will derive more pleasure from a trip if they know something about their destination before they arrive. Begin their education about a month before you leave. Using maps, travel magazines, and books gives children a clear idea of where you are going and how far away it is.
2. Children should help to plan the itinerary, and where you go and what you do should reflect some of their ideas. If they already know something about the sites they'll visit, they will have the excitement of recognition when they arrive.

GETTING READY / Traveling with Children 61

3. Give children specific responsibilities: The job of carrying their own flight bags and looking after their personal things, along with some other light chores, will give them a stake in the journey.
4. Give each child a travel diary or scrapbook to take along.

Children's books that cover the Bahamas include the following:

The Caribbean: The Land and its Peoples, by Eintou Springer, is available for $16.95, plus shipping and handling, from Silver Burdett Press, PO Box 2649, Columbus, OH 43216 (phone: 800-843-3464).

People and Places: The Caribbean, by Antony Mason, for children ages 9 to 11, is available for $14.98, plus shipping and handling, from Silver Burdett Press, PO Box 2649, Columbus, OH 43216 (phone: 800-843-3464).

Bookstores specializing in children's books include the following:

Books of Wonder (132 7th Ave., New York, NY 10011; phone: 212-989-3270; or 464 Hudson St., New York, NY 10014; phone: 212-645-8006). Carries both new and used books for children.

Cheshire Cat (5512 Connecticut Ave. NW, Washington, DC 20015; phone: 202-244-3956). Specializes in books for children of all ages.

Eeyore's Books for Children (2212 Broadway, New York, NY 10024; phone: 212-362-0634; or 25 E. 83rd St., New York, NY 10028; phone: 212-988-3404). Carries an extensive selection of children's books; features a special travel section.

Reading Reptile, Books and Toys for Young Mammals (4120 Pennsylvania, Kansas City, MO 64111; phone: 816-753-0441). Carries books for children and teens to age 15.

Red Balloon Bookshop (891 Grand Ave., St. Paul, MN 55105; phone: 612-224-8320). Carries both new and used books for children.

White Rabbit Children's Books (7755 Girard Ave., La Jolla, CA 92037; phone: 619-454-3518). Carrries books and music for children (and parents).

And for parents, *Travel With Your Children* (*TWYCH;* 80 Eighth Ave., New York, NY 10011; phone: 212-206-0688) publishes a newsletter, *Family Travel Times,* that focuses on families with young travelers and offers helpful hints. An annual subscription (10 issues) is $35 and includes a copy of the "Airline Guide" issue (updated every other year), which focuses on the subject of flying with children. This special issue is available separately for $10.

Another newsletter devoted to family travel is *Getaways.* This quarterly publication provides reviews of family-oriented literature, activities, and useful travel tips. To subscribe, send $25 to *Getaways,* att. Ms. Brooke Kane, PO Box 8282, McLean, VA 22107 (phone: 703-534-8747).

Also of interest to parents traveling with their children is *How to Take Great Trips With Your Kids,* by psychologist Sanford Portnoy and his wife, Joan Flynn Portnoy. The book includes helpful tips from fellow family travelers, a chapter on child development relating to travel, tips on economical accommodations and touring by car, recreational vehicle, and train, as well as over 50 games to play with your children en route. It is available for $8.95, plus shipping and handling, from Harvard Common Press, 535 Albany St., Boston, MA 02118 (phone: 617-423-5803). Another title worth looking for is *Great Vacations with Your Kids,* by Dorothy Jordan (Dutton: $12.95).

Finally, parents arranging a trip with their children may want to deal with an agency specializing in family travel such as *Let's Take the Kids* (2560 Barrington Ave., Suite 107, Los Angeles, CA 90064; phone: 800-726-4349 or 213-472-4449). In addition to arranging and booking trips for individual families, this group occasionally organizes

62 GETTING READY / Traveling with Children

trips for single-parent families traveling together. They also offer a parent travel network, whereby parents who have been to a particular destination can evaluate it for others.

GETTING THERE AND GETTING AROUND: Begin early to investigate all available discount and charter flights, as well as any package deals and special rates offered by the major airlines. If traveling by ship, note that children under 12 usually travel at a considerably reduced fare on cruise lines.

PLANE: When you make your reservations, tell the airline that you are traveling with a child. Children ages 2 through 11 generally travel at about half to two-thirds of the regular full-fare adult ticket price on most international flights. This children's fare, however, usually is much higher than an excursion fare (which also may be even further reduced for children). On many international flights, children under 2 travel at about 10% of the adult fare if they sit on an adult's lap. A second infant without a second adult would pay the fare applicable to children ages 2 through 11.

Although some airlines will, on request, supply bassinets for infants, most carriers encourage parents to bring their own safety seat on board, which then is strapped into the airline seat with a regular seat belt. This is much safer — and certainly more comfortable — than holding the child in your lap. If you do not purchase a seat for your baby, you have the option of bringing the infant restraint along on the off-chance that there might be an empty seat next to yours — in which case some airlines will let you use that seat at no charge for your baby and infant seat. However, if there is no empty seat available, the infant seat no doubt will have to be checked as baggage (and you may have to pay an additional charge), since it generally does not fit under the airplane seats or in the overhead racks. The safest bet is to pay for a seat.

Be forewarned: Some safety seats designed primarily for use in cars do not fit into plane seats properly. Although nearly all seats manufactured since 1985 carry labels indicating whether they meet federal standards for use aboard planes, actual seat sizes may vary from carrier to carrier. At the time of this writing, the FAA was in the process of reviewing and revising the federal regulations regarding infant travel and safety devices — it was still to be determined if children should be *required* to sit in safety seats and whether the airlines will have to provide them.

If using one of these infant restraints, you should try to get bulkhead seats, which will provide extra room to care for your child during the flight. You also should request a bulkhead seat when using a bassinet — again, this is not as safe as strapping the child in. On some planes bassinets hook into a bulkhead wall; on others they are placed on the floor in front of you. (Note that bulkhead seats often are reserved for families traveling with children.) As a general rule, babies should be held during takeoff and landing.

Request seats on the aisle if you have a toddler or if you think you will need to use the bathroom frequently. Carry onto the plane all you will need to care for and occupy your children during the flight — formula, diapers, a sweater, books, favorite stuffed animals, and so on. Dress your baby simply, with a minimum of buttons and snaps, because the only place you may have to change a diaper is at your seat or in a small lavatory. The flight attendant can warm a bottle for you.

On most US carriers, you also can ask for a hot dog or hamburger instead of the airline's regular dinner if you give at least 24 hours' notice. Some, but not all, airlines have baby food aboard. While you should bring along toys from home, also ask about children's diversions. Some carriers have terrific free packages of games, coloring books, and puzzles.

When the plane takes off and lands, make sure your baby is nursing or has a bottle, pacifier, or thumb in its mouth. This sucking will make the child swallow and help to clear stopped ears. A piece of hard candy will do the same thing for an older child.

Parents traveling by plane with toddlers, children, or young teenagers may want to consult *When Kids Fly,* a free booklet published by Massport (Public Affairs Department, 10 Park Plaza, Boston, MA 02116-3971; phone: 617-973-5600), which includes helpful information on airfares for children, infant seats, what to do in the event of overbooked or canceled flights, and so on.

■ **Note:** Newborn babies, whose lungs may not be able to adjust to the altitude, should not be taken aboard an airplane. And some airlines may refuse to allow a pregnant woman in her 8th or 9th month to fly.

SHIP: Some shipping lines offer cruises that feature special activities for children, particularly during periods that coincide with major school holidays like *Christmas, Easter,* and the summer months. On such cruises, children may be charged special cut-rate fares, and there are youth counselors to organize activities. Occasionally, a shipping line even offers free passage during the summer months for children under age 16 occupying a stateroom with two (full-fare) adult passengers. Your travel agent should know which cruise lines offer such programs. For further information, see *Traveling by Cruise Ship,* in this section.

ACCOMMODATIONS AND MEALS: Often a cot for a child will be placed in a hotel room at little or no extra charge. If you wish to sleep in separate rooms, special rates sometimes are available for families; some places do not charge for children under a certain age. In many of the larger chain hotels, the staffs are more used to children. These hotels also are likely to have swimming pools or gamerooms — both popular with most youngsters.

Housekeeping apartments and cottages available for rent in the Bahamas provide excellent accommodations for families. The apartment or cottage becomes a "home away from home," and a considerable sum can be saved by preparing meals yourself rather than taking the entire crew out to restaurants three times a day. In addition, many of these do not charge for children under 12 years old, and a few permit anyone under 18 to stay with their families free. (On the other hand, some properties don't allow children, so before you set your heart on a particular one, find out all the details of its rental policy.) Most condominiums are available for rent through real estate agents only.

In addition, a few hotels offer special youth activities programs, particularly during summer months. Detailed information can be obtained from a travel agent. A few hotels offer day camp programs during school holiday periods.

Hotels and condominium complexes also often recommend baby-sitters (whether the sitter is hired directly or through an agency, ask for and check references).

At mealtime, don't deny yourself or your children the delights of a new style of cooking. Encourage them to try new things. Children like to know what kind of food to expect, so it will be interesting to look up Bahamian dishes before leaving. And don't forget about picnics.

Things to Remember
1. If you are spending your vacation touring, pace the days with children in mind. Break the trip into half-day segments, with running around or "doing" time built in.
2. Don't forget that a child's attention span is far shorter than an adult's. Children don't have to see every sight or all of any sight to learn something from their trip; watching, playing with, and talking to other children can be equally enlightening.
3. Let your children lead the way sometimes; their perspective is different from yours, and they may lead you to things you would never have noticed on your own.

4. Remember the places that children love to visit: aquariums, zoos, beaches, nature trails, and so on. Among the attractions that may pique their interest are the following:
    - A surrey ride in Nassau.
    - Watching a cricket or a soccer game.
    - Swimming with dolphins in the Atlantic.
    - A tour of Fort Charlotte on New Providence.
    - Taking scuba lessons.
    - Watching the flamingos parade at Ardastra Gardens near Cable Beach.
    - A ride on a glass-bottom boat.

On the Islands

Credit and Currency

It may seem hard to believe, but one of the greatest (and least understood) costs of travel is money itself. Your one single objective in relation to the care and retention of your travel funds is to make them stretch as far as possible. When you do spend money, it should be on things that expand and enhance your travel experience, with no buying power lost due to carelessness or lack of knowledge. This requires more than merely ferreting out the best airfare or the most charming budget hotel. It means being canny about the management of money itself. Herewith, a primer on making money go as far as possible while traveling.

CURRENCY: The Bahamian dollar has parity with the US dollar. US and Canadian dollars are accepted throughout the islands, as are traveler's checks. Credit cards are more widely honored in Nassau and Freeport than on the outlying islands. Banks are open Mondays through Thursdays from 9 AM to 3 PM, and from 9 AM to 5 PM on Fridays.

In the Turks & Caicos, the US dollar is legal tender. Full international banking facilities are available on Grand Turk, South Caicos, and Providenciales. Hours are from 9 AM to 4:30 PM every weekday. On Fridays, some banks close at noon and reopen at 2:30 PM and stay open until 5 PM. Traveler's checks are accepted at most hotels, the larger stores, and at the banks. Be aware that few places take credit cards in the Turks & Caicos.

TRAVELER'S CHECKS: It's wise to carry traveler's checks while on the road instead of (or in addition to) cash, since it's possible to replace them if they are stolen or lost; you usually can receive partial or full replacement funds the same day if you have your purchase receipt and proper identification. Issued in various denominations, with adequate proof of identification (credit cards, driver's license, passport), traveler's checks are as good as cash in most hotels, restaurants, stores, and banks. However, don't assume that restaurants, small shops, and other establishments are going to be able to change checks of large denominations. Worldwide, more and more establishments are beginning to restrict the amount of traveler's checks they will accept or cash, so it is wise to purchase at least some of your checks in small denominations — say, $10 and $20.

Every type of traveler's check is legal tender in banks around the world, and each company guarantees full replacement if checks are lost or stolen. After that the similarity ends. Some charge a fee for purchase, others are free; you can buy traveler's checks at almost any bank, and some are available by mail. Most important, each traveler's check issuer differs slightly in its refund policy — the amount refunded immediately, the accessibility of refund locations, the availability of a 24-hour refund service, and the time it will take for you to receive replacement checks. For instance,

American Express guarantees replacement of lost or stolen traveler's checks in under 3 hours at any *American Express* office — other companies may not be as prompt. (Note that *American Express*'s 3-hour policy is based on a traveler's being able to provide the serial numbers of the lost checks. Without these numbers, refunds can take much longer.)

We cannot overemphasize the importance of knowing how to replace lost or stolen checks. All of the traveler's check companies have agents around the world, both in their own name and at associated agencies (usually, but not necessarily, banks), where refunds can be obtained during business hours. Most of them also have 24-hour toll-free telephone lines, and some even will provide emergency funds to tide you over on a Sunday.

Be sure to make a photocopy of the refund instructions that will be given to you by the issuing institution at the time of purchase. To avoid complications should you need to redeem lost checks (and to speed up the replacement process), keep the purchase receipt and an accurate list, by serial number, of the checks that have been spent or cashed. You may want to incorporate this information in an "emergency packet," also including the numbers of the credit cards you are carrying and any other bits of information you shouldn't be without. Always keep these records separate from the checks and the original records themselves (you may want to give them to a traveling companion to hold).

Several of the major traveler's check companies charge 1% for the acquisition of their checks. To receive fee-free traveler's checks you may have to meet certain qualifications — for instance, *Thomas Cook*'s checks issued in US currency are free if you make your travel arrangements through its travel agency. *American Express* traveler's checks are available without charge to members of the *American Automobile Association (AAA)*. Holders of some credit cards (such as the *American Express Platinum* card) also may be entitled to free traveler's checks. The issuing institution (e.g., the particular bank at which you purchase them) may itself charge a fee. If you purchase traveler's checks at a bank in which you or your company maintains significant accounts (especially commercial accounts of some size), the bank may absorb the 1% fee as a courtesy.

American Express, Bank of America, Citicorp, MasterCard, Thomas Cook, and *Visa* all offer traveler's checks. Here is a list of the major companies issuing traveler's checks and the numbers to call in the event that loss or theft makes replacement necessary:

American Express: To report lost or stolen checks in the US and Canada, and in the Bahamas, call 800-221-7282. To report lost or stolen checks in the Turks & Caicos, call 801-964-6665, collect.

Bank of America: To report lost or stolen checks throughout the US, call 800-227-3460. In the Bahamas, call 415-624-5400 or 415-622-3800, collect.

Citicorp: To report lost or stolen checks in the continental US and Hawaii, call 800-645-6556. In the Bahamas, call 813-623-1709, collect.

MasterCard: Note that *Thomas Cook MasterCard* is now handling all *MasterCard* traveler's checks inquiries and refunds.

Thomas Cook MasterCard: To report lost or stolen checks in the US, call 800-223-7373. In the Bahamas, call 609-987-7300, collect.

Visa: To report lost or stolen checks in the continental US and Canada, call 800-227-6811. In the Bahamas, call 415-574-7111, collect.

CREDIT CARDS: Some establishments you may encounter during the course of your travels may not honor any credit cards and some may not honor all cards, so there is

GETTING READY / Credit and Currency 67

a practical reason to carry more than one. The following is a list of credit cards that enjoy wide domestic and international acceptance:

American Express: Cardholders can cash personal checks for traveler's checks and cash at *American Express* or its representative's offices up to the following limits (within any 21-day period): $1,000 for *Green* and *Optima* cardholders, $5,000 for *Gold* cardholders, and $10,000 for *Platinum* cardholders. Check cashing also is available to cardholders who are guests at participating hotels (up to $250) and for holders of airline tickets at participating airlines (up to $50). Free travel accident, baggage, and car rental insurance if ticket or rental is charged to card; additional insurance also is available for additional cost. For further information or to report a lost or stolen *American Express* card, call 800-528-4800 throughout the continental US; elsewhere, call 212-477-5700, collect.

Carte Blanche: Free travel accident, baggage, and car rental insurance if ticket or rental is charged to card; additional insurance also is available at additional cost. For medical, legal, and travel assistance available worldwide, call 800-356-3448 throughout the US; elsewhere, call 214-680-6480, collect. For further information or to report a lost or stolen *Carte Blanche* card, call 800-525-9135 or 303-790-2433, collect.

Diners Club: Emergency personal check cashing for cardholders staying at participating hotels and motels (up to $250 per stay). Free travel accident, baggage, and car rental insurance if ticket or rental is charged to card; additional insurance also is available for an additional fee. For medical, legal, and travel assistance worldwide, call 800-356-3448 throughout the US; elsewhere, call 214-680-6480, collect. For further information or to report a lost or stolen *Diners Club* card, call 800-525-9135 or 303-790-2433, collect.

Discover Card: Offered by a subsidiary of Sears, Roebuck & Co., it provides cardholders with cash advances at numerous automatic teller machines and *Sears* stores throughout the US. Note that *Discover* is not accepted in the Bahamas or the Turks & Caicos. For further information or to report a lost or stolen *Discover* card, call 800-DISCOVER.

MasterCard: Cash advances are available at participating banks worldwide. Check with your issuing bank for information. *MasterCard* also offers a 24-hour emergency lost card service; call 800-826-2181 throughout the US; in the Bahamas, call 314-275-6690, collect.

Visa: Cash advances are available at participating banks worldwide. Check with your issuing bank for information. *Visa* also offers a 24-hour emergency lost card service; call 800-336-8472 throughout the US; elsewhere, call 415-574-7700, collect.

SENDING MONEY TO THE BAHAMAS: If you have used up your traveler's checks, cashed as many emergency personal checks as your credit card allows, drawn on your cash advance line to the fullest extent, and still need money, it is possible to have it sent to you via *Western Union Telegraph Company* (phone: 800-325-4176 throughout the US). A friend or relative can go, cash in hand, to any *Western Union* office in the US, where, for a *minimum* charge of $13 (it rises with the amount of the transaction), the funds will be transferred to a centralized *Western Union* account. When the transaction is fully processed — in the case of the Bahamas within 15 minutes — you can go to any *Western Union* branch office or correspondent bank (with a picture ID, for example, a driver's license or passport) to pick up the transferred funds. For a higher fee, the sender may call Western Union with a *MasterCard* or *Visa* number to send up to $2,000.

Hotels and Guesthouses

In the Bahamas, accommodations range from large, modern, luxury hotels to small, simply furnished, but quite comfortable guesthouses. What you get, therefore, should be not just a question of what you're paying, but, more important, what you're seeking.

Most of the larger hotels, for instance, offer a wide range of sports, recreation, and entertainment facilities, in addition to a larger staff for service. Invariably, they have swimming pools, but this shouldn't be a major criterion; most areas have excellent sand beaches and swimming waters nearby. If tennis or golf is a major consideration, you'll find that some hotels have their own courts and courses right on the grounds; others may provide transportation to nearby facilities.

Most of the refurbished hotels fit into a category now commonly known as "international standard." Rooms are sizable and frequently have two oversize beds, ocean-view balconies, conventional modern facilities, and full room service. They feature a variety of restaurants, poolside bars, and nightclubs. *Holiday Inn* (phone: 800-HOLIDAY) and *Sheraton* (phone: 800-325-3535) are among the major US hotel groups represented in the Bahamas.

Some of the smaller establishments in the Bahamas are often even more elegant than the chains. Word of mouth among the social set is a mainstay of their reputations, and how good — and well patronized — they usually is reflected in their prices. To find out, stop by for a look or ask for a brochure with a tariff sheet.

The majority of the Bahamas' hotels are medium-size, are equally modern — or at least modernized — and are more likely to offer local ambience and charm than their high-rise counterparts. But though they may lack the arcades and coffee shops, extensive facilities, or the fashionable guests of the super-resorts, they are not necessarily more reasonably priced.

Rental Homes and Vacation Apartments

The range of possible accommodations in the Bahamas is not limited to hotels. These days, several other alternatives offer various levels of luxury and convenience at the price you want to pay.

One of the charms of staying in a home, housekeeping apartment, or cottage rather than a hotel is that you will feel much more like a traveler than a tourist. This type of accommodation provides the ordinary traveler with the extraordinary opportunity to live for a while as a Bahamian does. You can buy fresh produce from the local market and prepare your own meals. You may hear of small, out-of-the-way beaches and restaurants about which only locals know. Most important, you live in the environment you choose to visit, not in a mini-US that's been decorated with palm trees and blue seas.

The main charms are probably economic: For a family of four, or two or more couples, the price per night can work out up to 60% less than the cost of comparable hotel accommodations. (For one or two people the *economic* advantages do not amount to quite as much.) Don't expect these savings to extend to food, however, as groceries in the Bahamas are notoriously expensive — as much as 50% higher than in metropoli-

GETTING READY / Rental Homes and Vacation Apartments

tan areas of the US — although eating in will still be less expensive than dining out. Also to be considered is the added bonus of space, usually far more than is offered in any but the most extravagant hotel suite.

Housekeeping accommodations fall into four main categories: houses, condominiums (available through real estate agents only), housekeeping apartments, and cottages. All provide cooking utensils, flatware, and linen, but some differences are noted below:

HOUSES: These are the Brahmins of island real estate rentals. Most have maid service 3 or 4 hours a day; some even have a private swimming pool. Some of the more luxurious places arrange pick-up service at the airport and supply provisions for the first day — eggs, milk, bread, butter, fruit, as well as soap, toothpaste, and other toilet essentials.

CONDOMINIUMS: Not very prevalent in the Bahamas, and available through US representatives and local real estate agents, these usually have daily maid service. Most have a living room, dining area, and kitchen or kitchenette; almost all have swimming pools. Transportation may be necessary for sightseeing and, depending on location, for purchasing provisions.

HOUSEKEEPING APARTMENTS: These can be rented through US representatives or local real estate agents. Maid service usually is optional. They are generally close to shopping, but transportation may be necessary if the property is not close to town.

COTTAGES: Beachcombing, romance, roughing it . . . well, not necessarily. They can be attached to a fully staffed hotel that has complete dining room facilities, a small home with kitchen and maid service, or more often, something that resemble cabañas on wealthy US estates. They snuggle around a swimming pool, and the means for preparing a daiquiri are more evident than the utensils for a five-course meal. Equally often they are what they say: simple cottages with a kitchen and bath, and the ocean for swimming and fishing. Open-air fruit-and-vegetable stands and supermarkets may be a taxi or car ride away.

Rental Property Discounts and Agents – Several discount travel organizations provide a substantial savings — up to 50% off list prices — on rental accommodations (and some hotels) in the Bahamas. Reservations are handled by the central office of the organization, or members may deal directly with the rental agencies or individual property owners. To take advantage of the full selection of properties, these organizations often require that reservations be made as much as 6 months in advance — particularly for stays during peak travel periods.

Concierge (1600 Wynkoop St., Suite 102, Denver, CO 80202; phone: 303-623-6775 in Colorado; 800-346-1022 elsewhere in the US). Offers up to 50% discounts on stays in the Bahamas. Annual membership fee is $69.95 per couple.

Entry Unlimited (6970 Miramar Rd., San Diego, CA 92121; phone: 619-621-2795). Up to 50% discounts offered on condominium rentals in the Bahamas; rentals from 1 night to 1 week, depending on availability. Annual membership fee $39.95 per family.

IntlTravel Card (6001 N. Clark St., Chicago, IL 60660; phone: 312-465-8891). Discounts on rental accommodations throughout the islands. The $36 annual membership fee includes a spouse.

Privilege Card (PO Box 629, Duluth, GA 30136; phone: 800-359-0066 or 404-623-0066). Up to 50% discounts available on accommodations in the Bahamas; minimum length of stay depends on availability. Annual membership fee is $49.95 per family.

In addition to these discounters, a number of companies specialize in rental vacations. Their plans typically include rental of the property (usually for a minimum 2- or 3-day stay), to which can be applied an excursion, individual tour-basing, or group airfare (whichever is least expensive when and from where you travel), just as it could be applied to any other package. If your travel agent doesn't have the brochures of these specialists, contact one of the companies listed below or the island's US tourist office (also see "For Further Information," below).

While perusing the brochures from these companies, look for answers to the following questions:
- How do you get from the airport to the property?
- How far is the nearest beach?
- Is it sandy or rocky and is it safe for swimming?
- What size and number of beds are provided?
- How far is the property from whatever else is important to you, such as a golf course or nightlife?
- If there is no grocery store on the premises (which may be comparatively expensive, anyway), how far is the nearest market?
- Are baby-sitters, cribs, bicycles, or anything else you may need for your children available?
- Is maid service provided daily?
- Is air conditioning and/or a phone provided?

Before deciding which accommodation is for you, make sure you have satisfactory answers to all your questions. Ask your travel agent to find out, or call the company involved directly. Below are some US rental agencies offering properties in the Bahamas:

Bahamas Reservation Service (362 Minorca Ave, Suite 101, Coral Gables, FL 33134; phone: 800-327-0787). This agency specializes exclusively in accommodations in the Bahamas. It represents a large number of hotels on the islands as well as some villas, condominiums, and cottages.

Bed & Breakfast USA (PO Box 418, Old Sheffield Rd., S. Egremont, MA 01258; phone: 800-255-7213). This bed and breakfast reservation service represents one B&B in the Bahamas, and one in the Turks & Caicos.

Condo World (4301 Orchard Lake Rd., Suite 209-217, West Bloomfield, MI 48323 (phone: 800-521-2980 or 313-683-02022). A typical condominium rental in the Bahamas comes with maid service.

Hideaways International (PO Box 1270, Littleton, MA 01460; phone: 800-843-4433 or 508-486-8955). Rents properties in the Bahamas and the Turks & Caicos. Weekly villa rentals are available for 4 to 10 people. Many come with maid service, although this may be optional. For $79, subscribers receive two issues per year of their guide to current listings, as well as a quarterly newsletter and discounts on a variety of travel services.

La Cure Villas (116611 San Vincente Blvd., Suite 1010, Los Angeles, CA 90049; phone: 213-877-4930, 800-387-2726, or 800-387-2715). Lists condominiums in the Bahamas; most have maid service. Daily, as well as weekly, rates can be arranged.

Rent a Home International (7200 34th Ave. NW, Seattle, WA 98117; phone: 206-789-9377). Rents condominiums in the Bahamas. All rentals include a full housekeeping staff.

VHR, Worldwide (235 Kensington Ave., Norwood, NJ 07648; phone: 800-NEED-A-VILLA or 201-767-9393). Handles private islands, estates, houseboats, condominiums, and villas in the Bahamas and the Turks & Caicos. Most rentals include maid service; some come with a cook.

Villas International Ltd. (605 Market St., Suite 510, San Francisco, CA 94105; phone: 415-281-0919 in California, 800-221-2260 elsewhere in the US). Rents houses and condominiums in the Bahamas. Many rentals include maid service. Minimum 1-week stay.

You may also want to send for the *Worldwide Home Rental Guide,* which lists cottages in the Bahamas, along with the managing agencies. Issued twice annually, single copies may be available at newsstands for $10 an issue. For a year's subscription (two issues), send $18 to *Worldwide Home Rental Guide,* PO Box 2842, Sante Fe, NM 87504 (phone: 505-988-5188).

FOR FURTHER INFORMATION: For additional information on sources for rentals in the Bahamas, contact the Bahamas Tourist Office in New York (150 E. 52nd St., New York, NY 10022; phone: 212-758-2777) and ask for the *Nassau, Paradise Island, Cable Beach Newsletter* and the *Hotel Rate Book* (a listing of condominiums, villas, hotels, and guesthouses), which is issued twice a year.

Self-catering accommodations, ranging from 1-bedroom cottages to 5-bedroom, air conditioned villas, are available throughout the Bahamas. Take your pick.

All-Inclusive Resorts: Couples' and Club Med

COUPLES' RESORTS: While the Bahamas always have been a special magnet for honeymooners and other lovers, it's only recently that resorts catering exclusively to couples — both married and unmarried — have emerged in depth. Some quite explicitly bar singles and children; at others, the atmosphere alone is probably enough to make the unattached feel uncomfortable — if not expressly unwelcome. Despite the common bond between these resorts, their tone varies considerably, from frantically active to get-away-from-it all peaceful. Most are all-inclusive, although some features (such as airfare or a full meal plan) may be extra.

One such resort for couples is *Paradise, Paradise* (c/o *Resorts International Ltd.,* 915 NE 125th St., N. Miami, FL 33161; phone: 800-321-3000 or 809-363-3000). Located on Paradise Island in the Bahamas, this resort on Paradise Beach offers access to the large local casino and a host of restaurants and related diversions. Nearby Nassau adds the option of sightseeing. The price includes all water sports; drinks are not included.

CLUB MED: A special breed of destination that has been described as "summer camp for adults," *Club Med,* founded in 1950, now has nearly 100 locations worldwide. The self-contained resorts, or "villages," all share the one-price-covers-everything policy (accommodations, meals, wine, sports), and each has its own distinct personality, now seldom consistent with the old swinging-singles image that gave the clubs their flying start. For general information and reservations, contact *Club Med* (3 E. 54th St., New York, NY 10022; phone: 800-CLUB-MED).

Club Med, Eleuthera, Bahamas – A family-oriented resort on the Bahamian island of the same name, it offers a Mini-Club with special facilities for children ages 2 to 12. Scuba programs for divers of all levels of ability are a special lure. Deep-sea fishing excursions are extra.

Club Med, Paradise Island, Bahamas – Atypically close to civilization, it offers easy access to the Paradise Island casinos and Nassau shopping. Tennis is king here, with 20 courts, and a weekly tournament. This club has perhaps the greatest variety of activity in all the Caribbean "villages." Ask about the golf and tennis festivals. Offers a Mini-Club for children.

Club Med, San Salvador, Bahamas – Located on the shores of Bonefish Bay, this

72 GETTING READY / Mail

latest facility opened on October 12, 1992, to coincide with the Columbus quincentennial celebration. The "Columbus Isle" luxury village features 300 large rooms equipped with TV sets and telephones. At the Intensive Diver Center, guests can earn certification within a week. Also available are snorkeling, sailing, water skiing, windsurfing, and deep-sea fishing. For landlubbers there are 12 tennis courts, and plenty of fitness programs from which to choose.

Club Med Turkoise, Turks & Caicos – Among the newest of the operations, it's on the lonely island of Providenciales, or "Provo." Facilities — including an abundance of fitness equipment and two Jacuzzis — cater to the "pressured executive." Sailing, snorkeling, bicycling, and tennis are available. Deep-sea fishing excursions and diving certification courses are also offered for an additional charge.

Time Zones and Business Hours

TIME: The Bahamas run on eastern standard time from the last Sunday in October to the last Sunday in April, on daylight saving time the rest of the year. This means it has the same time as eastern US cities throughout the year.

BUSINESS HOURS: In the Bahamas, business hours are similar to those in the United States. Establishments open at 9 AM and stay open until 5 or 6 PM. Stores are also open Saturdays from 9 AM to 6 PM.

Holidays and festivals in the Bahamas and the Turks & Caicos are listed in detail under *Special Events* in THE ISLANDS chapters.

Mail, Telephone, and Electricity

MAIL: Always use airmail, and unless advised otherwise locally, allow from 3 to 7 days for delivery to and from the United States. Stamps are available at most hotel desks as well as at post offices.

There are several places that will receive and hold mail for travelers in the Bahamas. Mail sent to you at a hotel and clearly marked "Guest Mail, Hold for Arrival" is a safe approach. If you want to receive your mail but do not know what your address will be, have your mail addressed to the nearest post office in care of "General Delivery." In areas with more than one post office, the letter will have to be addressed to the specific branch with the corresponding street address — and, under the best of conditions, this is very risky. Most foreign post offices have a time limit for holding such mail — 30 days is a common limit. To claim this mail, you must go in person to the post office, ask for General Delivery, and present identification (driver's license, credit card, birth certificate, or passport).

If you are an *American Express* customer (a cardholder, a carrier of *American Express* traveler's checks, or on an *American Express Travel Related Services* tour) you can have mail sent to the *American Express* branch office in the Bahamas. Letters are held free of charge — registered mail and packages are not accepted. You must be able to show an *American Express* card, traveler's checks, or a voucher proving you are on one of the company's tours to qualify for mail privileges. Those who aren't clients cannot use the service. There also is a forwarding fee of $15. Mail should be addressed to you, care of *American Express,* and should be marked "Client Mail Service." Additional information on this mail service is listed in the pamphlet *American Express Travelers Companion,* available from any US branch of *American Express.*

While the US Embassy and Consulate in the Bahamas (Mosmar Bldg., Queen St., Nassau, Bahamas; phone: 809-322-1181 or 809-322-4753) will not under ordinary circumstances accept mail for tourists, it *may* hold mail for US citizens in an emergency. In such instances it is best to inform them either by separate letter or cable, or by phone (particularly if you are in the islands already), that you will be using their address for this purpose.

TELEPHONE: The area code for the Bahamas is 809, and you can dial direct from the US. To call a number in the Bahamas dial: 1 + 809 + (the local number); to call a number in the Turks & Caicos, dial: 1 + 809 + 94 + (the local number). To make a call within the 809 area code, simply dial the local number; to make a call in the Turks & Caicos, dial 94 + the local number. To call a number in the US from the Bahamas, dial: 1 + (the area code) + the local number.

To reach a local or international operator in the Bahamas; dial 0. For information on calling for help in the event of an emergency, see *Legal Aid and Consular Services,* in this section.

Calls between the US and the Bahamas can be expensive, but avoiding operator-assisted calls can cut costs considerably and bring rates into a somewhat more reasonable range — except for calls made through hotel switchboards. One of the most unpleasant surprises travelers encounter in many foreign countries is the amount they find tacked on to their hotel bill for telephone calls, because foreign hotels routinely add on astronomical surcharges. (It's not at all uncommon to find 300% or 400% added to the actual telephone charges.)

Until recently, the only recourse against this unconscionable overcharging was to call collect from abroad or to use a telephone credit card — available through a simple procedure from any local US phone company. (Note, however, that even if you use a telephone credit card, some hotels still may charge a fee for line usage.) Now *American Telephone and Telegraph (AT&T)* offers *USA Direct,* a service that connects users, via a toll-free number, with an *AT&T* operator in the US, who then will put a call through at the standard international rate. A new feature of this service is that travelers abroad can reach US toll-free (800) numbers by calling a *USA Direct* operator, who will connect them. Charges for all calls made through *USA Direct* appear on the calling card or the caller's regular US phone bill. To access this service from the Bahamas, dial 800-872-2881. For a brochure and wallet card listing toll-free numbers by country, contact International Information Service, *AT&T Communications,* 635 Grand St., Pittsburgh, PA 15219 (phone: 800-874-4000).

It's wise to ask about the surcharge rates *before* calling from a hotel. If the rate is high, it's best to use a telephone credit card, the direct-dial service described above, make a collect call, or place the call and ask the party to call right back. If none of these choices is possible, to avoid surcharges, make international calls from the local post office or special telephone center to avoid surcharges. Another way to keep down the cost of telephoning from the Bahamas is to leave a copy of your itinerary and telephone numbers with people in the US so that they can call you instead.

ELECTRICITY: The Bahamas have the same electrical current system as that in the US — 110 volts, 60 cycles, alternating current (AC). Appliances running on standard current can be used throughout the islands without adapters or convertors.

Staying Healthy

The surest way to return home in good health is to be prepared for medical problems that might occur on vacation. Below, we've outlined some things you need to think about before your trip begins.

BEFORE YOU GO: Older travelers or anyone suffering from a chronic medical condition, such as diabetes, high blood pressure, cardiopulmonary disease, asthma, or ear, eye, or sinus trouble, should consult a physician before leaving home. Those with conditions requiring special consideration when traveling should consider seeing, in addition to their regular physician, a specialist in travel medicine. For a referral in a particular community, contact the nearest medical school or ask a local doctor to recommend such a specialist. Dr. Leonard Marcus, a member of the *American Committee on Clinical Tropical Medicine and Travelers' Health,* provides a directory of more than 100 travel doctors across the country. For a copy, send a 9-by-12-inch, self-addressed, stamped envelope to Dr. Marcus at 148 Highland Ave., Newton, MA 02165 (phone: 617-527-4003).

Also be sure to check with your insurance company ahead of time about the applicability of your hospitalization and major medical policies away from home; many policies do not apply, and others are not accepted in the Bahamas. Older travelers should know that Medicare does not make payments outside the US and its territories. If your medical policy does not protect you while you're traveling, there are comprehensive combination policies specifically designed to fill the gap. (For a discussion of medical insurance and a list of inclusive combination policies, see *Insurance,* in this section.)

First Aid – Put together a compact, personal medical kit including Band-Aids, first-aid cream, antiseptic, nose drops, insect repellent, aspirin, an extra pair of prescription glasses or contact lenses (and a copy of your prescription for glasses or contact lenses), sunglasses, over-the-counter remedies for diarrhea, indigestion, and motion sickness, a thermometer, and a supply of those prescription medicines you take regularly.

In a corner of your kit, keep a list of all the drugs you have brought and their purpose, as well as duplicate copies of your doctor's prescriptions (or a note from your doctor). As brand names may vary in different countries, it's a good idea to ask your doctor for the generic name of any drugs you use so that you can ask for their equivalent should you need a refill.

It also is a good idea to ask your doctor to prepare a medical identification card that includes such information as your blood type, your social security number, any allergies or chronic health problems you have, and your medical insurance information. Considering the essential contents of your kit, keep it with you, rather than in your checked luggage.

MINIMIZING THE RISKS: Tourists usually suffer one major health problem in the Bahamas: sunburn. Neither this nor any other health problems nor illnesses are inevitable, however, and with suitable precautions, your trip to the Bahamas can proceed untroubled by ill health.

Sunburn – The burning power of the sun can quickly cause severe sunburn or sunstroke. This is especially important to remember when traveling in the Bahamas, where much time may be spent out of doors and on the beach. To protect yourself against these ills, wear sunglasses, take along a broad-brimmed hat and cover-up, and, most importantly, use a sunscreen lotion. When riding a bicycle or a moped, long pants and long sleeves will protect against painful sunburn of knees and arms.

GETTING READY / Staying Healthy 75

Water Safety – The Bahamas' beaches are so beautiful, with sands so caressing and waters so crystalline, that it's hard to remember that the waters of the Atlantic also can be treacherous. A few precautions are necessary. Beware of the undertow, that current of water running back down the beach after a wave has washed ashore; it can knock you off your feet and into the surf. Even more dangerous is the riptide, a strong current of water running against the tide, which can pull you out to sea. If you get caught offshore, don't panic or try to fight the current, because it will only exhaust you; instead, ride it out while waiting for it to subside, which usually happens not too far from shore, or try swimming away parallel to the beach.

Sharks are sometimes sighted, but they usually don't come in close to shore, and they are well fed on fish. Should you meet up with one, just swim away as quietly and smoothly as you can, without shouting or splashing. Although not aggressive, eels can be dangerous when threatened. If snorkeling or diving, beware of crevices where these creatures may be lurking. The tentacled Portuguese man-of-war and other jellyfish may drift in quiet salt waters for food and often wash up onto the beach; the long tentacles of these creatures sting whatever they touch — a paste made of household vinegar and unseasoned meat tenderizer is the recommended treatment.

The Bahamas' coral reefs are extensive and razor sharp. Treat all coral cuts with an antiseptic, and then watch carefully since coral is a living organism with bacteria on the coral surface which may cause an infection. If you step on a sea urchin, you'll find that the spines are very sharp, pierce the skin, and break off easily. Like splinters, the tips left embedded in the skin are difficult to remove, but they will dissolve in a week or two; rinsing with vinegar may help to dissolve them more quickly. To avoid these hazards, keep your feet covered whenever possible.

If complications, allergic reactions (such as breathlessness, fever, or cramps), or signs of serious infection result from any of the above circumstances, *see a doctor.*

Following all these precautions will not guarantee an illness-free trip, but should minimize the risk. For more information regarding preventive health care for travelers, contact the *International Association for Medical Assistance to Travelers (IAMAT;* 417 Center St., Lewiston, NY 14092; phone: 716-754-4883). This organization also assists travelers in obtaining emergency medical assistance while abroad (see list of such organizations below).

MEDICAL ASSISTANCE IN THE BAHAMAS: Fortunately, should you need medical attention, competent, professional doctors, surgeons, and specialists perfectly equipped to handle any medical problem can be found in the Bahamas.

In an Emergency – If a bona fide emergency occurs, the fastest way to get attention may be to take a taxi to the emergency room of the nearest hospital. An alternative is to dial 919, the emergency number for police, or 322-2221 for ambulance; or dial "0" (for operator) and immediately state the nature of your problem and your location. In the Turks & Caicos, the emergency number for police, fire, or ambulance is 999.

Non-Emergency Care – If a doctor is needed for something less than an emergency, there are several ways to find one. If you are staying in a hotel or resort, ask for help in reaching a doctor or other emergency services, or for the house physician, who may visit you in your room or ask you to visit an office. When you register at a hotel, it's not a bad idea to include your home address and telephone number; this will facilitate the process of notifying relatives and/or friends in case of an emergency.

The US Embassy and Consulate in the Bahamas (Mosmar Bldg., Queen St., Nassau; phone: 809-322-1181 or 809-322-4753) also can provide a list of doctors and dentists.

76 GETTING READY / Staying Healthy

Pharmacies and Prescription Drugs – There should be no problem finding a drugstore in the Bahamas. Unlike in the US, none are open around the clock, although some will open after hours in an emergency situation — such as for a diabetic needing insulin — for a fee. Contact a local hospital or medical clinic for information on these on-call pharmacists.

Again, bring along a copy of any prescription you may have from your doctor in case you should need a refill. In the case of minor complaints, pharmacists in the Bahamas *may* agree to fill a foreign prescription if the drug needed is readily available; however, do not count on this. In most cases, you probably will need a local doctor to rewrite the prescription. Even in an emergency, a traveler will more than likely be given only enough of a drug to last a few days or until a local prescription can be obtained.

Travelers will find that pharmacies throughout the Bahamas stock a range of over-the-counter drugs that astonishes most first-time visitors from the US. In addition, as previously mentioned, some drugs sold only by prescription in the US are sold over the counter in the Bahamas (and vice versa). Although this can be quite handy, be aware that common cold medicines and aspirin that contain codeine or other controlled substances will not be allowed back into the US.

Despite the general availability of these medications in the Bahamas, it is advisable to bring a small medical kit with you. (See "First Aid" above.)

ADDITIONAL RESOURCES: Medical assistance also is available from various organizations and programs designed for travelers who have chronic ailments or whose illness requires them to return home:

International Association of Medical Assistance to Travelers (*IAMAT;* 417 Center St., Lewiston, NY 14092; phone: 716-754-4883). Entitles members to the services of participating doctors around the world, as well as clinics and hospitals in various locations. Participating physicians agree to adhere to a basic charge of around $40 to see a patient referred by *IAMAT.* To join, simply write to *IAMAT;* in about 3 weeks you will receive a membership card, the booklet of members, and an inoculation chart. A nonprofit organization, *IAMAT* appreciates donations; with a donation of $25 or more, you will receive a set of worldwide climate charts detailing weather and sanitary conditions. (Delivery can take up to 5 weeks, so plan ahead.)

International SOS Assistance (PO Box 11568, Philadelphia, PA 19116; phone: 800-523-8930 or 215-244-1500). Subscribers are provided with telephone access — 24 hours a day, 365 days a year — to a worldwide, monitored, multilingual network of medical centers. A phone call brings assistance ranging from a telephone consultation to transportation home by ambulance or aircraft, or, in some cases, transportation of a family member to wherever you are hospitalized. Individual rates are $35 for 2 weeks of coverage ($3.50 for each additional day), $70 for 1 month, or $240 for 1 year; couple and family rates also are available.

Medic Alert Foundation (2323 N. Colorado, Turlock, CA 95380; phone: 800-ID-ALERT or 209-668-3333). If you have a health condition that may not be readily perceptible to the casual observer — one that might result in a tragic error in an emergency situation — this organization offers identification emblems specifying such conditions. The foundation also maintains a computerized central file from which your complete medical history is available 24 hours a day by phone (the telephone number is clearly inscribed on the emblem). The onetime membership fee (between $25 and $45) is based on the type of metal from which the emblem is made — the choices range from stainless steel to 10K gold-filled.

TravMed (PO Box 10623, Baltimore, MD 21204; phone: 800-732-5309 or 301-296-5225). For $3 per day, subscribers receive comprehensive medical assistance while abroad. Major medical expenses are covered up to $100,000, and special transportation home or of a family member to wherever you are hospitalized is provided at no additional cost.

Practically every phase of health care — before, during, and after a trip — is covered in *The New Traveler's Health Guide,* by Drs. Patrick J. Doyle and James E. Banta. It is available for $4.95, plus postage and handling, from Acropolis Books Ltd., 13950 Park Center Rd., Herndon, VA 22071 (phone: 800-451-7771 or 703-709-0006).

■**Note:** Those who are unable to take a reserved flight due to personal illness or who must fly home unexpectedly due to a family emergency should be aware that airlines may offer a discounted airfare (or arrange a partial refund) if the traveler can demonstrate that his or her situation is indeed a legitimate emergency. Your inability to fly or the illness or death of an immediate family member usually must be substantiated by a doctor's note or by the name, relationship, and funeral home from which the deceased will be buried. In such cases, airlines often will waive certain advance purchase restrictions or you may receive a refund check or voucher for future travel at a later date. Be aware, however, that this bereavement fare may not necessarily be the least expensive fare available and, if possible, it is best to have a travel agent check all possible flights through a computer reservations system (CRS).

Legal Aid and Consular Services

There is one crucial place to keep in mind when outside the US, namely, the American Services section of the US Consulate. If you are injured or become seriously ill, the consulate will direct you to medical assistance and notify your relatives. If, while abroad, you become involved in a dispute that could lead to legal action, the consulate, once again, is the place to turn.

It usually is far more alarming to be arrested abroad than at home. Not only are you alone among strangers, but the punishment can be worse. Granted, the US Consulate can advise you of your rights and provide a list of English-speaking lawyers, but it cannot interfere with the local legal process. Except for minor infractions of the local traffic code, there is no reason for any law-abiding traveler to run afoul of immigration, customs, or any other law enforcement authority.

The best advice is to be honest and law-abiding. If you get a traffic ticket, pay it. If you are approached by drug hawkers, ignore them. The penalties for possession of marijuana, cocaine, and other narcotics are even more severe abroad than in the US. (If you are picked up for any drug-related offense, do not expect US foreign service officials to be sympathetic. Chances are they will notify a lawyer and your family and that's about all. See "Drugs," below.)

In the case of minor traffic accidents (such as a fender bender), it often is most expedient to settle the matter before the police get involved. For other routine traffic

GETTING READY / Legal Aid and Consular Services

violations — a standing or moving violation or other car-related incident — police generally are very lenient with tourists. If, however, you are involved in a serious accident, where an injury or fatality results, the first step is to contact the nearest US Consulate (address below) and ask the consul to locate a lawyer to assist you. If you have a traveling companion, ask him or her to call the consulate (unless either of you has a local contact who can help you quickly).

The US Department of State in Washington, DC, insists that any US citizen who is arrested abroad has the right to contact the US Embassy or Consulate "immediately," but it may be a while before you are given permission to use a phone. Do not labor under the illusion, however, that in a scrape with foreign officialdom, the consulate can act as an arbitrator or ombudsman on a US citizen's behalf. Nothing could be farther from the truth. Consuls have no power, authorized or otherwise, to subvert, alter, or contravene the legal processes, however unfair, of the foreign country in which they serve. Nor can a consul oil the machinery of a foreign bureaucracy or provide legal advice. The consul's responsibilities do encompass "welfare duties," including providing a list of lawyers and information on local sources of legal aid, informing relatives in the US, and organizing and administering any defense monies sent from home. If a case is tried unfairly or the punishment seems unusually severe, the consul can make a formal complaint to the authorities. For questions about US citizens arrested abroad, how to get money to them, and other useful information, call the *Citizens' Emergency Center* of the Office of Special Consular Services in Washington, DC, at 202-647-5225. (For further information about this invaluable hotline, see below.)

Other welfare duties, not involving legal hassles, cover cases of both illness and destitution. If you should get sick, the US consul can provide names of doctors and dentists, as well as the names of the local hospital; the consul also will contact family members in the US and help arrange special ambulance service for a flight home. In a situation involving "legitimate and proven poverty" of a US citizen stranded abroad without funds, the consul will contact sources of money (such as family or friends in the US), apply for aid to agencies in foreign countries, and in a last resort — which is *rarely* — arrange for repatriation at government expense, although this is a loan that must be repaid. And in case of natural disasters or civil unrest, consulates around the world handle the evacuation of US citizens if it becomes necessary.

The consulate is not occupied solely with emergencies and is certainly not there to aid in trivial situations, such as canceled reservations or lost baggage, no matter how important these matters may seem to the victimized tourist. The main duties of any consulate are administering statutory services, such as the issuance of passports and visas; providing notarial services; distributing VA, social security, and civil service benefits to US citizens; taking depositions; handling extradition cases; and reporting to Washington the births, deaths, and marriages of US citizens living within the consulate's domain.

We hope that none of the information in this section will be necessary during your stay in the Bahamas. If you can avoid legal hassles altogether, you will have a much more pleasant trip. If you become involved in an imbroglio, the local authorities may spare you legal complicatons if you make clear your tourist status. And if you run into a confrontation that might lead to legal complications developing with a citizen or with local authorities, the best tactic is to apologize and try to leave as gracefully as possible. The Bermuda government impresses upon its citizens the importance of the tourist industry to the island's future. It may give your opponent a moment's pause, which is just enough time for you to leave. When traveling in a foreign country it is important to remember that some things are best left unsettled.

The US Embassy and Consulate in the Bahamas (the Turks & Caicos are within its jurisdiction) are in Mosmar Building, Queen St., Nassau, New Providence, Bahamas (phone: 809-322-1181 or 809-322-4753).

Drinking and Drugs

In general, the laws concerning alcohol and drugs in the Bahamas are quite strict.

DRINKING: In the Bahamas, the legal drinking age is 18. Most bars close around 1 AM. Nightclubs and hotel bars usually close between 2 and 4 AM. Liquor stores are closed on Sundays.

DRUGS: Though illegal narcotics are perhaps as prevalent in the Bahamas as in the US, don't be deluded into believing that this means easy access to them. The moderate legal penalties and vague social acceptance that marijuana has gained in the US have no equivalents in the Bahamas. Due to the international war on drugs, enforcement of drug laws is becoming as increasingly strict on this island as it is throughout the world.

In the Bahamas, marijuana is often called "herb." It is just as illegal in the Bahamas as it is in the US. Anyone in possession of even a small amount of marijuana could be sentenced to a fine of up to thousands of dollars — or even life imprisonment. Bahamian authorities also notify US authorities of any arrests and/or convictions of US citizens. Opiates and barbiturates, and other increasingly popular drugs — "white powder" substances like cocaine, and "crack," a cocaine derivative — also continue to be of major concern to narcotics officials.

The important things to bear in mind are that (1) the quantity of drugs involved is of very minor importance, and (2) there isn't much that the US Embassy or Consulate can do for drug offenders beyond providing a list of lawyers. Persons arrested are subject to the laws of the country they are visiting, and these laws and their procedures are often very harsh.

Those who carry medicines that contain a controlled drug should be sure to have a current doctor's prescription with them. Ironically, travelers can get into almost as much trouble coming through US Customs with over-the-counter drugs picked up abroad that contain substances that are controlled in the US. Cold medicines, pain relievers, and the like often have codeine or codeine derivatives that are illegal, except by prescription, in the US. Throw them out before leaving for home.

■ **Be forewarned:** US narcotics agents warn travelers of the increasingly common ploy of drug dealers asking travelers to transport a "gift" or other package back to the US. Don't be fooled into thinking that the protection of US law applies abroad — if accused of illegal drug trafficking, you will be considered guilty until you prove your innocence. In other words, do not, under any circumstances, agree to take anything across the border for a stranger.

Tipping

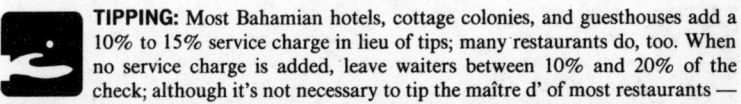

TIPPING: Most Bahamian hotels, cottage colonies, and guesthouses add a 10% to 15% service charge in lieu of tips; many restaurants do, too. When no service charge is added, leave waiters between 10% and 20% of the check; although it's not necessary to tip the maître d' of most restaurants — unless he has been especially helpful in arranging a special party or providing a table (slipping him something *may,* however, get you seated sooner or procure a preferred table) — when tipping is desirable or appropriate, the least amount should be $5. In the finest restaurants, where a multiplicity of servers are present, plan to tip 5% to the captain. The sommelier (wine waiter) is entitled to a gratuity of approximately 10% of the price of the bottle of wine.

In allocating gratuities at a restaurant, pay particular attention to what has become the standard credit card charge form, which now includes separate places for gratuities for waiters and/or captains. If these separate boxes are not on the charge slip, simply ask the waiter or captain how these separate tips should be indicated. Be aware, too, of the increasingly common — and devious — practice of placing the amount of an entire restaurant bill (in which service already has been included) in the top box of a charge slip, leaving the "tip" and "total" boxes ominously empty. Don't be intimidated: Leave the "tip" box blank and just repeat the total amount next to "total" before signing. In some establishments, tips indicated on credit card receipts may not be given to the help, so you may want to leave tips in cash.

If no service charge has been added to your hotel bill, leave the hotel maid at least $1 a day. Tip the concierge for specific services only, with the amount of such gratuities dependent on the level of service provided. For any special service you receive in a hotel, a tip is expected — $1 being the minimum for a small service.

Bellhops, doormen, and porters at hotels and transportation centers generally are tipped at the rate of $1 per piece of luggage, along with a small additional amount if a doorman helps with a cab. Taxi drivers should get about 15% of the total fare.

Miscellaneous tips: Sightseeing tour guides should be tipped. If you are traveling in a group, decide together what you want to give the guide and present it from the group at the end of the tour. If you have been individually escorted, the percentage of the tour price should depend on the degree of your satisfaction, but it should not be less than 10%. Museum and monument guides also are usually tipped a few dollars. Coat checks are worth about 50¢ to $1 a coat, and washroom attendants are tipped — there usually is a little plate with a coin already in it suggesting the expected amount. In barbershops and beauty salons, tips also are expected, but the percentages vary — 10% in the most expensive salons; 15% to 20% in less expensive establishments. (As a general rule, the person who washes your hair should get a small additional tip.) For information on tipping aboard ships, see *Traveling by Cruise Ship*, in this section.

Tipping always is a matter of personal preference. In the situations covered above, as well as in any others that arise where you feel a tip is expected or due, feel free to express your pleasure or displeasure. Again, never hesitate to reward excellent and efficient attention or to penalize poor service. Give an extra gratuity and a word of thanks when someone has gone out of his or her way for you. Either way, the more personal the act of tipping, the more appropriate it seems. And if you didn't like the service — or the attitude — don't tip.

Religion in the Islands

Bahamian churches, though not numerous, represent the standard Christian sects. Three houses of worship of note (all on Nassau) are Christ Church Cathedral (Anglican); St. Matthew's Church (Roman Catholic); and St. John's Baptist Church.

The surest source of information on religious services in an unfamiliar area is the desk clerk of the hotel or guesthouse in which you are staying; the local tourist information office, the American consul, or a church of another religious affiliation also may be able to provide this information. If there aren't any services held in your own denomination, you might find it interesting to attend the service of another religion. There are a number of charming churches in the Bahamas, and visitors are welcome.

Customs and Returning to the US

Whether you return to the United States by air or sea, you must declare to the US Customs official at the customs checking point everything you have bought or acquired while in the islands (see "Clearing Customs," below). The customs check can go smoothly, lasting only a few minutes, or can take hours, depending on the officer's instinct. To speed up the process, keep all your receipts handy and try to pack your purchases together in an accessible part of your suitcase. It might save you from unpacking all your belongings or even from dismantling your entire car.

DUTY-FREE ARTICLES: In general, the duty-free allowance for US citizens returning from abroad is $400, provided your purchases accompany you and are for personal use. This limit includes items used or worn while abroad, souvenirs for friends, and gifts received during the trip. A flat 10% duty based on the "fair retail value in country of acquisition" is assessed on the next $1,000 worth of merchandise brought in for personal use or gifts. Amounts over $1,400 are dutiable at a variety of rates. The average rate for typical tourist purchases is about 12%, but you can find out rates on specific items by consulting *Tariff Schedules of the United States* in a library or any US Customs Service office.

Families traveling together may make a joint declaration to US Customs, which permits one member to exceed his or her duty-free exemption to the extent that another falls short. Families also may pool purchases dutiable under the flat rate. A family of three, for example, would be eligible for up to a total of $3,000 at the 10% flat duty rate (after each member had used up his or her $400 duty-free exemption) rather than three separate $1,000 allowances. This grouping of purchases is extremely useful when considering the duty on a high-tariff item, such as jewelry.

Personal exemptions can be used once every 30 days; in order to be eligible, an individual must have been out of the country for more than 48 hours. If any portion of the exemption has been used once within any 30-day period or if your trip is less than 48 hours long, the duty-free allowance is cut to $25.

There are certain articles, however, that are duty-free only up to certain limits. The $25 allowance includes the following: 10 cigars (not Cuban), 50 cigarettes, and four ounces of perfume. Individuals eligible for the full $400 duty-free limit are allowed 1 carton of cigarettes (200), 100 cigars, and 1 quart of liquor or wine if over 21. Alcohol above this allowance is liable for both duty and an Internal Revenue Service tax. Antiques, if they are 100 or more years old and you have proof from the seller of that fact, are duty-free, as are paintings and drawings if done entirely by hand.

To avoid paying duty twice, register the serial numbers of computers, watches, and expensive electronic equipment with the nearest US Customs bureau before departure; receipts of insurance policies also should be carried for other foreign-made items. (Also see the note at the end of *Entry Requirements and Documents,* in this section.)

Gold, gold medals, bullion, and up to $10,000 in currency or negotiable instruments may be brought into the US without being declared. Sums over $10,000 must be declared in writing.

Personal exemptions can be used once every 30 days; in order to be eligible, an individual must have been out of the country for more than 48 hours. If any portion of the exemption has been used once within any 30-day period or if your trip is less than 48 hours long, the duty-free allowance is cut to $25. The allotment for individual "unsolicited" gifts *mailed* from abroad (no more than one per day per recipient) has been raised to $50 retail value per gift. These gifts do not have to be declared and are not included in your duty-free exemption (see below).

DUTY-FREE CRAFT ITEMS: In January 1976, the United States approved a Generalized System of Preferences (GSP) to help developing nations improve their economies through exports. The GSP, which recognizes dozens of developing nations, including the Bahamas, allows Americans to bring certain kinds of goods into the US duty-free, and has designated some 2,800 items as eligible for duty-free treatment.

This system entitles you to exceed the $400 exemption as long as the purchases are eligible for GSP status. The list of eligible goods includes the following categories: baskets and woven bags; cameras and other photographic equipment; candy; china and silverware; cigarette lighters; earthenware; some furniture; games and toys; golf and ski equipment; some jewelry, unset precious or semi-precious stones, and pearls; jewelry and music boxes; musical instruments, radios, tape recorders, records, and tapes; paper goods and printed matter; perfume and toilet preparations; electric shavers; items made of cork, jade, or shell; wigs; and woodcarvings. Note that, depending on the country of origin, some items may not always be included, and other items not in these categories also may be eligible.

If you have any questions about the GSP status of a particular item, check with your nearest customs office or at the nearest US Embassy or Consulate (see "Legal Aid and Consular Services," above, for the location in the Bahamas). A useful pamphlet identifying GSP beneficiary nations is the *GSP and the Traveler;* to order ask for "US Customs Publication No. 515," from the US Customs Service, Customs Information, 6 World Trade Center, Rm. 201, New York, NY 10048 (phone: 212-466-5550).

CLEARING CUSTOMS: This is a simple procedure. There are pre-clearance customs offices at both the Nassau and Freeport international airports. US Customs officers are on staff to clear US citizens before they leave the Bahamas. They do not have to go through customs again once they arrive in the US. Forms are distributed by airline at the airport. If your purchases total no more than the duty-free $400 limit, you need only fill out the identification part of the form and make an oral declaration to the customs inspector. If departing the Bahamas with more than $400 worth of goods, you must submit a written declaration.

For US citizens returning to the US from the Turks & Caicos, all of the above regulations apply. But unlike the Bahamas, departing passengers from the Turks & Caicos must go through customs at their port of entry.

It is illegal not to declare dutiable items; not to do so, in fact, constitutes smuggling, and the penalty can be anything from stiff fines and seizure of the goods to prison sentences. It simply isn't worth doing. Nor should you go along with the suggestions of foreign merchants who offer to help you secure a bargain by deceiving customs officials in any way. Such transactions are frequently a setup, using the foreign merchant as an agent of US customs. (Another agent of US customs is TECS, the Treasury Enforcement Communications System, a computer that stores all kinds of pertinent information on returning citizens.) There is a basic rule to buying goods abroad, and it should never be broken: *If you can't afford the duty on something, don't buy it.* Your list or verbal declaration should include all items purchased abroad as well as gifts received abroad, purchases made at the behest of others, the value of repairs, and anything brought in for resale in the US.

Do not include in the list items that do not accompany you, i.e., purchases that you have mailed or had shipped home. These are dutiable in any case, even if for your own use and even if the items that accompany your return from the same trip do not exhaust your $400 duty-free exemption. In fact, it is a good idea, if you have accumulated too much while abroad, to mail home any personal effects (made and bought in the US) that you no longer need rather than your foreign purchases. These personal effects pass through customs as "American goods returned" and are not subject to duty.

If you cannot avoid shipping home your foreign purchases, however, the US Customs Service suggests that the package be clearly marked "Not for Sale" and that a copy of the bill of sale be included. The customs examiner usually will accept this as indicative of the article's fair retail value, but if he or she believes it to be falsified or feels the goods have been seriously undervalued, a higher retail value may be assigned. When sending packages worth less than $50 home, mark the package "Unsolicited Gift — Value Under $50" (again, it's a good idea to include a sales receipt). You can send one such parcel per address per 24-hour period, and it must be sent to a friend or relative, not to yourself.

Remember, the examiner is empowered to impose a duty based on his or her assessment of the value of the goods. The duty owed is collected by the US Postal Service when the package is delivered. More information on mailing packages home from abroad is contained in the US Customs Service pamphlet *Buyer Beware, International Mail Imports* (see below for where to write for this and other useful brochures).

A $5 to $10 per-person service charge (called a user fee) is now collected by airlines, and an $80 to $120 service charge is collected by cruise lines, to help cover the cost of customs checks. These charges are included in the quoted price when you purchase the ticket from the airline or cruise line.

FORBIDDEN IMPORTS: Narcotics, plants (unless specifically exempt and free of soil), and many types of food are not allowed into the United States. Drugs are totally illegal, with the exception of medication prescribed by a physician. It's a good idea to travel with no more than you actually need of any medication and to have the prescription on hand in case any question arises either abroad or when re-entering the US.

Any authentic archaeological find, colonial art, or other original artifacts cannot be exported from the Bahamas. They will be confiscated upon departure, and the violator runs the risk of being fined or imprisoned.

Tourists have long been forbidden to bring into the US any foreign-made, US-trademarked articles purchased abroad (if the trademark is recorded with US Customs) without written permission. It's now permissible to enter with one such item in your possession as long as it's for personal use.

The US Customs Service implements the rigorous Department of Agriculture regulations concerning the importation of vegetable matter, seeds, bulbs, and the like. Living vegetable matter may not be imported without a permit, and everything must be inspected, permit or not. Approved items (which do not require a permit) include dried bamboo and woven items made of straw; beads made of most seeds (but not jequirity beans — the poisonous scarlet and black seed of the rosary pea); cones of pine and other trees; roasted coffee beans; most flower bulbs; flowers (without roots); canned or dried fruits, polished rice, dried beans and teas; herb plants (not witchweed); nuts (but not chestnuts, acorns, or other nuts with outer husks); dried lichens, mushrooms, truffles, shamrocks, and seaweed; and most dried spices.

Other processed foods and baked goods are usually okay. Regulations on meat products generally depend on the country of origin and manner of processing. As a rule, commercially canned meat, hermetically sealed and cooked in the can so that it can be stored without refrigeration, is permitted, but not all canned meat fulfills this requirement. (The imported brands you see in US stores have been prepared and packaged according to US regulations.) So before stocking up on a newfound favorite, it pays to check in advance — otherwise you might have to leave it behind.

84 GETTING READY / Customs

The US Customs Service also enforces federal laws that prohibit the entry of black coral, and articles made from the furs or hides of animals on the endangered species list. Beware of shoes, bags, and belts made of crocodile and certain kinds of lizard, and anything made of tortoiseshell; this also applies to preserved crocodiles, lizards, and turtles sometimes sold in gift shops. Some protected species of coral — particularly large chunks of fresh coral and black coral in any form — are restricted (although most jewelry and other items made of coral usually are permitted). And if you're shopping for big-ticket items, beware of fur coats made from the skins of spotted cats. They are sold in many foreign countries, but they will be confiscated upon your return to the US, and there will be no refund. For information about animals on the endangered species list, contact the Department of the Interior, US Fish and Wildlife Service (Publications Office, Rm. 130, 4401 N. Fairfax Dr., Arlington, VA 22203; phone: 703-358-1711) and ask for the free publication *Facts About Federal Wildlife Laws.*

FOR FURTHER INFORMATION: The US Customs Service publishes a series of free pamphlets with customs information. It includes *Know Before You Go,* a basic discussion of US Customs requirements pertaining to all travelers; *Buyer Beware, International Mail Imports; Travelers' Tips on Bringing Food, Plant, and Animal Products into the United States; Importing a Car; GSP and the Traveler; Pocket Hints; Currency Reporting; Pets, Wildlife, US Customs; Customs Hints for Visitors (Nonresidents);* and *Trademark Information for Travelers.* For the entire series or individual pamphlets, write to the US Customs Service (PO Box 7407, Washington, DC 20044), or contact any of the seven regional offices — in Boston, Chicago, Houston, Long Beach, CA, Miami, New Orleans, and New York. The US Customs Service has a taped message whereby callers using touch-tone phones can get more information on various topics; the number is 202-566-8195. These pamphlets provide great briefing material, but if you still have questions when you're in the Bahamas, you can contact the US Customs representative at the US Embassy.

Sources and Resources

Island Tourist Offices

Below is a complete list of Bahamas and Turks & Caicos tourist offices in the US and Canada. These offices provide a wide variety of useful travel information and literature, most of it free for the asking. When requesting information, state your particular interests: accommodations, restaurants, special events, facilities for specific sports, activities, and so on. Because most of the material you receive will be oversize brochures, there is little point in sending self-addressed and stamped envelopes with your request.

Bahamas Tourist Offices
Atlanta (2957 Clairmont Rd., Suite 105, Atlanta, GA 30329; phone: 404-633-1793)

Boston (1027 Statler Office Bldg., Boston, MA 02116; phone: 617-426-3144)

Charlotte (4801 E. Independence Blvd., Suite 1000, Charlotte, NC 28212; phone: 704-532-1290)

Chicago (875 N. Michigan Ave., Suite 1816, Chicago, IL 60611; phone: 312-787-8203)

Dallas (World Trade Center, Suite 186, Stemmons Freeway, Dallas, TX 75258-1408; phone: 214-742-1886)

Detroit (26400 Lahser Rd., Suite 309, Southfield, MI 48034; phone: 313-357-2940)

Houston (5177 Richmond Ave., Suite 755, Houston, TX 77056; phone: 713-626-1566)

Los Angeles (3450 Wilshire Blvd., Suite 208, Los Angeles, CA 90010; phone: 213-385-0033)

Miami (255 Alhambra Circle, Suite 425, Coral Gables, FL 33134; phone: 305-442-4860)

Montreal (1255 Phillips Sq., Montreal, Quebec H3B 3G1 Canada; phone: 514-861-6797)

New York (150 E. 52nd St., New York, NY 10022; phone: 212-758-2777)

Philadelphia (Lafayette Bldg., 437 Chestnut St., Room 201, Philadelphia, PA 19106; phone: 215-925-0871)

San Francisco (44 Montgomery Center, Suite 503, San Francisco, CA 94104; phone: 415-398-5502)

St. Louis (555 N. New Ballas Rd., Suite 310, St. Louis, MO 63141; phone: 314-569-7777)

Toronto (120 Bloor St. E., Suite 1101, Toronto, Ontario M4W 3M5 Canada; phone: 416-968-2999)

Washington, DC (1730 Rhode Island Ave. NW, Washington, DC 20036; phone: 202-659-9135)

Turks & Caicos Tourist Offices
Miami (Turks and Caicos Reservation Center, 255 Alhambra Circle, Suite 312, Coral Gables, FL 33134; phone: 800-548-8462 or 305-667-0966)

New York (Caribbean Tourism Authority, 20 E. 46th St., New York, NY 10017; phone: 212-682-0435)

In addition, the Turks & Caicos tourist office offers the following toll-free information numbers: 800-441-4419 (for general information) and 800-282-4753 (for hotel reservations).

Books and Newsletters

BOOKS: Throughout GETTING READY TO GO, numerous books and brochures have been recommended as good sources of further information on a variety of topics.

The following is a list of books recommended for travelers headed for the Bahamas. It includes books intended to provide background information about the islands' history, a foundation for understanding what is found on the islands today, some ideas about what is happening around you that you may not personally witness, some solid fictional tales set in the islands, and a few books that call your attention to things you might otherwise not notice — such as exotic flora, local birdlife, and good buys. A few of the titles listed are out of print, but still warrant a trip to the library.

Caribbean Hideaways: The 100 Most Romantic Places to Stay by Ian Keown, 1991 (Prentice Hall, $16.)

Caribbean Ports of Call: A Guide for Today's Cruise Passenger by Kay Showker, 1987 (Globe Pequot Press, $14.95)

Dining and Snorkeling Guide to the Bahamas, 1988 (Pisces Books, $12.95)

The Outdoor Traveler's Guide: Caribbean by Kay Showker, photographs by Gerry Ellis, 1989 (Stewart, Tabori & Chang, $19.95)

Pelican Guide to the Bahamas, 1988 (Pelican, $11.95)

Romantic Island Getaways: The Caribbean, Bermuda and the Bahamas, by Radin & Fox, 1991 (John Wiley & Sons, $12.95)

The books described above may be ordered directly from the publishers or found in the travel section of any good general bookstore or sizable public library. If you still can't find a particular title, the following stores and/or mail-order sources also specialize in travel literature. They offer books on the Bahamas, along with guides to the rest of the world, and in some cases, even an old Baedeker or two.

Book Passage (51 Tamal Vista Blvd., Corte Madera, CA 94925; phone: 415-927-0960 in California; 800-321-9785 elsewhere in the US). Travel guides and maps to all areas of the world. A free catalogue is available.

The Complete Traveller (199 Madison Ave., New York, NY 10016; phone: 212-685-9007). Travel guides and maps. A catalogue is available for $2.

Forsyth Travel Library (PO Box 2975, Shawnee Mission, KS 66201-1375; phone: 800-367-7984 or 913-384-3440). Travel guides and maps, old and new, to all parts of the world. Ask for the "Worldwide Travel Books and Maps" catalogue.

Gourmet Guides (2801 Leavenworth St., San Francisco, CA 94133; phone: 415-771-3671). Travel guides and maps, along with cookbooks. Mail-order lists available on request.

Phileas Fogg's Books and Maps (87 Stanford Shopping Center, Palo Alto, CA 94304; phone: 800-533-FOGG or 415-327-1754). Travel guides and maps.

Tattered Cover (2955 E. First Ave., Denver, CO 80206; phone: 800-833-9327 or 303-322-7727). The travel department alone of this enormous bookstore carries over 7,000 books, as well as maps and atlases. No catalogue is offered (the list is too extensive), but a newsletter, issued three times a year, is available on request.

Thomas Brothers Maps & Travel Books (603 W. Seventh St., Los Angeles, CA 90017; phone: 213-627-4018). Maps (including road atlases, street guides, and wall maps), guidebooks, and travel accessories.

Traveller's Bookstore (22 W. 52nd St., New York, NY 10019; phone: 212-664-0995). Travel guides, maps, literature, and accessories. A catalogue is available for $2.

NEWSLETTERS: Throughout GETTING READY TO GO we have mentioned specific newsletters which our readers may be interested in consulting for further information. One of the very best sources of detailed travel information is *Consumer Reports Travel Letter.* Published monthly by Consumers Union (PO Box 53629, Boulder, CO 80322-3629; phone: 800-999-7959), it offers comprehensive coverage of the travel scene on a wide variety of fronts. A year's subscription costs $37; 2 years, $57.

The following travel newsletters also provide useful up-to-date information on travel services and bargains, as well as what's happening and where to go in the Bahamas:

Caribbean Travel Roundup (9 Stirling St., Andover, MA 01810; phone: 508-470-1971). This detailed fact sheet also provides information on Bahamas-related travel issues. At the time of this writing, this free information was available as a computer bulletin board service only, but the company was considering offering regular mail service.

Caribbean Treasures (160B Emerald St., Box 1290, Keene, NH 03431; phone: 603-352-3691). Issues highlight different areas of the Bahamas and provide recommendations on specific facilities and travel services. A year's subscription (9 issues) costs $54.

Caribbean Update (52 Maple Ave., Maplewood, NJ 07040; phone: 201-762-1565). Provides comprehensive monthly travel updates on various areas of the Caribbean and the Bahamas, as well information on economic and political status and recommended reading for further information. A year's subscription costs $120.

Hideaway Report (Harper Associates, Subscription Office, PO Box 300, Whitefish, MO 59937; phone: 406-862-3480). This monthly source highlights retreats — including island idylls — for sophisticated travelers. A year's subscription costs $90.

Travel Smart (Communications House, 40 Beechdale Rd., Dobbs Ferry, NY 10522; phone: 914-693-8300 in New York; 800-327-3633 elsewhere in the US). This monthly newsletter covers a wide variety of trips and travel discounts. A year's subscription costs $44.

Cameras and Equipment

Vacations are everybody's favorite time for taking still pictures and home movies. After all, most of us want to remember the places we visit — and show them off to others. Here are a few suggestions to help you get the best results from your travel photography or videography.

88 GETTING READY / Cameras and Equipment

BEFORE THE TRIP

If you're taking your camera or camcorder out after a long period in mothballs, or have just bought a new one, check it thoroughly before you leave to prevent unexpected breakdowns or disappointing pictures.

1. Still cameras should be cleaned carefully and thoroughly, inside and out. If using a camcorder, run a head cleaner through it. Always use filters to protect your lenses while traveling.
2. Check the batteries for your camera's light meter and flash, and take along extras just in case yours wear out during the trip. For camcorders, bring along extra Nickel-Cadmium (Ni-Cad) batteries; if you use rechargeable batteries, a recharger will cut down on the extras.
3. Trying out all the settings and features, shoot at least one test roll of film or one videocassette, using the type you plan to take along with you.

EQUIPMENT TO TAKE ALONG

Keep your gear light and compact. Items that are too heavy or bulky to be carried comfortably on a full-day excursion will likely remain in your hotel room, so leave them at home.

1. Invest in a broad camera or camcorder strap if you now have a thin one. It will make carrying the camera much more comfortable.
2. A sturdy canvas, vinyl, or leather camera or camcorder bag, preferably with padded pockets (not an airline bag), will keep your equipment organized and easy to find. If you will be doing much shooting around the water, a waterproof case is best.
3. For cleaning, bring along a camel's hair brush that retracts into a rubber squeeze bulb. Also take plenty of lens tissue, soft cloths, and plastic bags to protect equipment from dust and moisture.

FILM AND TAPES: If you are concerned about airport security X-rays damaging undeveloped film (X-rays do not affect processed film) or tapes, store them in one of the lead-lined bags sold in camera shops. This possibility is not as much of a threat as it used to be, however. In the US, incidents of X-ray damage to unprocessed film (exposed or unexposed) are few because low-dosage X-ray equipment is used virtually everywhere. However, when crossing international borders, travelers should know that foreign X-ray equipment used for carry-on baggage may deliver higher levels of radiation and that even more powerful X-ray equipment may be used for checked luggage, so it's best to carry your film on board. If you're traveling without a protective bag, you may want to ask to have your photo equipment inspected by hand. One type of film that should never be subjected to X-rays is the very high speed ASA 1000 film. The walk-through metal detector devices at airports do not affect film, though the metal film cartridges may set off the detector.

PERSPECTIVES

History

The Bahamas have always been closely linked to the United States. Not only are they geographically close — South Bimini lies just 50 miles off the coast of Florida — but they're also connected by common threads of history.

It was in the Bahamas, after all, that Christopher Columbus first stumbled upon the New World. On the moonlit night of October 12, 1492 — a date known to every American and Bahamian schoolchild — the lookout in the crow's nest on the caravel *Pinta,* the smallest of three ships in Columbus's fleet, sighted land. He had spotted Guanahani, the northeasternmost island in the Bahamas. (Some scholars say he actually saw Grand Turk Island or a smaller isle called Samana Cay, but never mind, they all are part of the Bahamian archipelago.) Columbus renamed the island San Salvador and claimed it for God and Spain.

Columbus didn't found the Bahamas, any more than Cortés inaugurated Mexico or Pizarro developed Peru, he was simply the first recorded European to set foot on these isles. The islands had been settled more than 5 centuries earlier by Arawak Indians who migrated to the Caribbean from South America. Columbus found the Arawak who lived in the Bahamas — they called themselves Lucaya — courteous and comely. ". . . their forms are well proportioned, their bodies graceful and their features handsome," he wrote in his diary. "Their hair is as coarse as the hair of a horse's tail and short. They wear their hair over their eyebrows, except a little hank behind, which they wear long and never cut." The Indians smoked pipes, drank maize beer, fished in stout dugout canoes, cultivated cassava and maize, and wove cotton cloth. Columbus's sailors were especially taken by their cotton hammocks, which soon became popular with European navies.

Columbus was also quick to notice the gold trinkets the Indians wore. But he and other Spanish explorers found no gold deposits in the Bahamas, and they soon set sail in search of more lucrative shores. When they found gold on Hispaniola (later to become Haiti and the Dominican Republic), they forcibly deported thousands of Lucaya from the Bahamas to work in the mines. Others were shipped off to Trinidad to dive for pearls. Less than 25 years after Columbus's first voyage to the Caribbean, the Indian population of the Bahamas had diminished drastically, depleted by war, deportation, and disease.

The next explorer to visit the Bahamas was Spaniard Juan Ponce de León, who, not content with the fortune he had earned trading in gold and slaves on Puerto Rico, sailed north in 1513 in search of Bimini, an island fabled to possess fabulous riches. He landed on several Bahamian isles — including Bimini, which proved cruelly disappointing — before bumping up against the east coast of Florida, which he mistook for another island. He found no gold in Florida, and no fountain of youth, and he died from a wound inflicted by an Indian arrow in 1521. He did leave a mark of sorts on the region, however, for he is credited with naming both Florida and the Bahamas. A fellow traveler, a historian named De Herrera, is said to have described the waters surrounding the Bahamas as *bajamar,* which in Spanish means "low tide."

COLONISTS AND PRIVATEERS

After the Spanish forsook the Bahamas in pursuit of gold and slaves, the islands languished for nearly a century. British sailors and colonists stopped by from time to time on their way to Bermuda and North America, but few stayed on. In 1625, French settlers established a short-lived outpost on Abaco Island, and 4 years later England staked out a formal claim to the Bahamas. The first permanent settlers, a group of dissident Puritans from Bermuda, arrived in 1648. Led by William Sayle, a former Governor of Bermuda, they called themselves the Company of Eleutherian Adventurers. Their ship was wrecked on the reefs, and they managed to scramble ashore on the island of Cigateo, which they renamed Eleutheria (now spelled Eleuthera), after the Greek word for "freedom." It was not an easy life. The colonists managed to survive by gathering ambergris and brasiletto wood — used to make a purple dye — hunting whales, and scavenging from the wrecks of Spanish galleons.

In 1656, another group of Puritans from Bermuda established a colony on an island they called "New Providence." (The "old" Providence, in Rhode Island, had been founded 20 years earlier.) In 1670, the island colonies were formally linked when King Charles II gave the Lord Proprietors of the Carolinas dominion over their Bahamian neighbors.

For more than a century, this connection made little difference to either side, for each was absorbed with its own problems. The Carolinians were embroiled in disputes with England, while the Bahamians simply struggled to eke out a living. The islands' thin, rocky topsoil yielded poor crops, and few large farms survived. Settlers on Exuma, Inagua, and Grand Turk managed to get by on the salt trade, and inhabitants of other isles survived by selling timber and ambergris.

The wars raging in Europe eventually provided the Bahamians with a more lucrative trade. To thwart its enemies in the Atlantic, England began to encourage "privateering" — attacks on vessels by private ships. The practice favored Crown and privateer alike: European shipping was disrupted at no cost to the British Treasury, and the pirates got to keep the loot. By the late 17th century, the Bahamas — with its secluded coves and uninhabited isles — had become the favored hideout for privateers. Nassau, the free-wheeling town on New Providence, was home to more than 1,000 buccaneers. Sir Henry Morgan and Edward Teach, better known as Blackbeard, held out there; so did Anne Bonney and Mary Read, two notorious female buccaneers. The Bahamian government did little to hinder them, for many local officials also profited directly from the trade.

Soon few ships were safe from their depredations. As the wars raged in Europe, the shifting alliances made it harder for privateers to tell friend from foe, and even British ships were pillaged by pirates. Spain and France, outraged by attacks on their vessels, sent ships to sack Bahamian towns. In 1718, King George I finally decided to bring the buccaneers to heel. He dispatched to Nassau a man named Captain Woodes Rogers, once a notorious buccaneer himself. Rogers hanged several pirates, shipped others off to English courts, and repelled another attack on the islands by the Spanish. With order more or less restored, the king declared the Bahamas a Crown colony and made Rogers its first royal governor. (The motto on the Bahamian crest — *Expulsis Piratis, Restituta Commercia,* or "Piracy Expelled, Commerce Restored" — survived until 1973, when the colony won its independence. The motto was changed to "Forward, Upward, Onward Together" by the country's prime minister, Lynden Pindling.)

In the end, though, Rogers's reforms accomplished little. The Bahamas remained poor, and settlers continued to find illegal activities more attractive than cotton farming and salt raking. In the late 18th century, residents of the Turks Islands shipped contraband to the American colonies. After war broke out in 1775, Bahamians ran guns and supplies to the colonists. When France entered the war, however, Bahamian allegiances quickly shifted to the side of the Crown. After Cornwallis surrendered at Yorktown, thousands of Tories — many of them wealthy planters from the South — set sail for Nassau, bringing their slaves with them. The Bahamians, never ones to slight guests, let them stay. In just 6 years, the population of the islands tripled.

One Loyalist, Andrew Deveaux, played a legendary role in the next episode of the islands' history. In 1781, Spain took advantage of the chaos in North America to capture the Bahamas once again. Deveaux, a lieutenant colonel from South Carolina, mustered 200 colonists and militiamen and retook Nassau. The Bahamas were formally ceded back to Britain 2 years later, under the terms of the Treaty of Versailles.

Many Tories found island life more difficult than they expected. Some settled in prosperous New Providence, but many moved to the Out, or Family, Islands, some of which had never been inhabited by Europeans. Chenille bugs and poor soil ruined their cotton crops, and in the 1830s the British abolished slavery, which soon brought an end to a free supply of labor. Many colonists lived hand to mouth, growing yams and beans, eating bonefish and conch, and "wrecking" — salvaging goods from ships destroyed on Bahamian reefs. During several years of the mid-19th century, half of the export earnings of the Bahamas came from the sale of scavenged goods.

CONTRABANDISTS

Prosperity returned with the American Civil War, when smuggling became profitable once again. Fast shallow-draft boats slipped past the Union blockade, running European manufactured goods from Nassau to Charleston and returning with bales of cotton. Profits were enormous: cotton worth 10 cents a pound in the South sold for $1 a pound in the Bahamas. More than 1,500

Bahamian ships carried goods to the South, many crossing several times: The *Robert E. Lee* made 21 runs. Captains could make several thousand dollars each trip. Flush with cash, they celebrated in bars and brothels in Nassau, which did a booming business.

With peace came the doldrums. Islanders returned to their vegetable plots and their scavenging. (To their disappointment, the British Admiralty sharply reduced the number of wrecks washing up on Bahamian shores in the late 1860s, when several lighthouses were built and navigational charts improved.) In 1866, the population — which numbered 47,000, 80 percent of whom were black — was hit by double disasters: a typhus epidemic and a hurricane. The survivors made a living trading various goods, all of them only marginally profitable. Conch shells were shipped from the Bahamas to Italy and France, where they were made into brooches until fashions changed and no one wanted them. Pineapples were exported from Eleuthera to the United States until restrictive tariffs and competition from Hawaii choked off trade. Sisal was grown and exported, but demand was slack except for a brief spell during the Spanish-American War, when sisal from the Philippines was in short supply. Other Bahamians earned a living diving for sponges, but in the late 1930s a fungus wiped out most of the crop.

By that time, however, a new trade had sprung up. From 1919 to 1933 — Prohibition years in the United States — the Bahamian economy revived. Rum running became as profitable as blockade running had been 70 years earlier. Ships based on New Providence, Grand Bahama Island, and Bimini slipped past the US Coast Guard to deliver cases of gin, whiskey, and rum to bootleggers up and down Biscayne Bay. When the Volstead Act was repealed in 1933, the trade dried up, and the islands once again sank into depression.

TOURISM AND TRADE

The 1930s saw the beginnings of what was to become a far more profitable Bahamian industry in the long run. Tourists, the Bahamians discovered, were a more reliable source of cash than contraband. Wealthy expatriates, attracted by the climate and low taxes, packed up and moved to the islands. Among the first was entrepreneur Sir Harry Oakes, who had made his fortune in Canadian gold mines. Oakes bought a Nassau hotel, renamed it the *British Colonial,* and turned it into one of the finest in the islands. Other hotels opened, and by the late 1930s up to 15,000 visitors were flocking to New Providence each year.

Though tourism fell off during World War II, the conflict indirectly promoted the tourist trade. The Duke of Windsor was Governor of the Bahamas from 1940 to 1945; he and his wife, American socialite Wallis Simpson, attracted a glittering set. (Their romance was immortalized in the still-popular *goombay* tune "Love Alone.") DC-3s flew well-heeled visitors in from the Eastern seaboard — it took 6 hours to fly from New York to Nassau, and 2 hours to fly from Miami, but no one seemed to mind — and wealthy European refugees bided their time in Nassau's fine hotels: the *British Colonial,* the *Fort Montagu,* and the *Royal Victoria.* Over the next 2 decades, tourism grew prodigiously, and by 1973, when the colony won its independence, the economy was thriving. Offshore banks, retired expatriates, divers and anglers, and day-tripping beachgoers and gamblers from New York and Miami all pumped money into the islands.

Since then, the government has made several attempts to diversify the economy. Citrus crops are cultivated on Eleuthera and Cat Island, crude oil is imported and refined, and rum, spiny lobster, fish, and pharmaceuticals are shipped overseas. But it hasn't all been mangoes and cream. Banks and insurance companies have been bruised by competing firms on Barbados and the Cayman Islands and by US regulations limiting banking secrecy. Per capita income is still under $10,000, and imports still outnumber exports, often by a wide margin. The government, once manipulated by the notorious Bay Street Boys, has been racked by new scandals, although the picture has brightened somewhat in recent years. The government also has made an effort to curb the drug trade, and tourism and real estate development have begun to show some signs of reviving.

TURKS & CAICOS ISLANDS

If you look at a map of the Bahamas, it's pretty clear why the residents of the Turks & Caicos Islands decided long ago to go their separate ways. This twin chain of tiny isles lies roughly 450 miles southeast of Nassau. In the mid-19th century, boats ferried mail from Nassau to Grand Turk only 4 times a year, and the only visitors to the islands were Nassau bureaucrats who came to collect the salt tax.

It was salt that had attracted settlers from Bermuda, who arrived in the Turks & Caicos in 1678. For more than a century, ships plied a lucrative trade between the salt flats on Grand Turk, Salt Cay, and South Caicos and Bermudian ports. After the American Revolution, scores of Loyalists fled to the western Caicos. Most of their cotton and sisal plantations eventually failed, but the slaves they brought with them stayed on, and many of the people who inhabit the islands today can trace their ancestry back to them.

Britain annexed the islands in 1799, largely for strategic reasons. The Turks & Caicos straddle the Windward Passage, which was plied by ships sailing from the Americas and the Caribbean to Europe. Nassau showed little interest in the islands, however, and in 1848, after years of squabbling, the Turks & Caicos were kicked out of the Bahamian General Assembly. In 1873, the islands fell under the formal control of the Governor of Jamaica. For the next 75 years, they were practically forgotten. Their residents, who numbered fewer and fewer each year, scraped by trading salt and fishing.

When Jamaica won its independence in 1962, the Turks & Caicos became an independent Crown colony. The salt trade came to an end shortly thereafter, and most "Belongers," as natives are called, made a living exporting conch and spiny lobster and cultivating small plots of corn and beans. Then tourists discovered the place. An airstrip and hotel were built on the island of Providenciales (known as Provo) in the late 1960s, and direct flights from

American cities began soon thereafter. (Today, nearly three-quarters of the visitors to the islands come from the US.) After *Club Med* built its *Turkoise* outpost on Provo's Grace Bay in 1984, the number of tourists visiting the islands doubled over 2 years. Though the government's reputation has been marred by recent drug and corruption scandals — several ministers have resigned since 1985 — the Turks & Caicos continue to draw tourists and investors. Lured by liberal tax laws, more than 6,000 offshore firms have relocated on the islands, and the tourist wave, though still small by Bahamian standards, shows no sign of abating.

Music and Dance

Singing and dancing come as naturally to Bahamians as breathing. Ride a bus, go to a party, watch kids at recess, step into a church on a Sunday morning, and you're bound to hear somebody singing. On the Family Islands and the Turks & Caicos, where links to the past are particularly strong, some villagers still dance English waltzes and quadrilles. Other Bahamian traditions, like *goombay* and the *junkanoo,* are shaped by African rhythms.

If there is one dance for which the islands are famous, it's the *junkanoo.* Traditionally performed by men to the syncopated beat of a goatskin drum, the dance has its roots in early colonial days, when slaves celebrated the few days of freedom granted them each year around the *Christmas* holidays. Always somewhat satirical, the dance eventually took on an overtly political cast — so much so that it was banned from time to time by the government. In the years since the Bahamas won independence, the *junkanoo* has become a symbol of national pride. A generation ago the dance was associated with poor kids and hooligans who wore masks to conceal their identities. Now it's popular even among the country's white-collar professionals. Teachers, architects, and lawyers don their *junkanoo* costumes each year, and Minister of Agriculture Perry Christie is one of the leaders of Nassau's most famous *junkanoo* groups, the *Valley Boys.*

The big dance of the year takes place on *Boxing Day* (December 26). Around 3 o'clock in the morning, *junkanoo* musicians invade the streets, beating drums and blowing bugles, tin whistles, and conch shells. Cowbells are struck with wooden sticks, creating a distinctive "kuh-lick." (The sound is said to have inspired the name of a popular Bahamian beer, Kalik.) Teams of elaborately costumed dancers — as many as 500 to a group, each representing a neighborhood or town — shuffle and jive down the street. In Nassau, the *Valley Boys* from Centerville compete against the *Saxon Superstars* from Fort Fincastle (their archrivals), the *Music Makers* from Grant's Town, the *Vikings* from Chippingham, the *Fancy Dancers* from Kemp Road, and the *Congos* from Fox Hill.

The rivalry is intense. (It's a little like the sparring among Rio's samba schools during *Carnaval.*) Drummers bang out competing rhythms, some slow, some fast, all heavily syncopated. Each team vies for the best theme: Some groups are Vikings, others Roman centurions, Lucaya Indians, or Spanish conquistadores. In recent years, the costumes, like the floats in the *Macy's Thanksgiving Day* parade, have gotten increasingly wild (and in the eyes of some, increasingly commercial as well). A few years ago, the *Saxon Superstars* chose the theme "Invasion of the Arthropods." Some *Saxons* came as flies with red-and-white compound eyes and 9-foot wings; others were cocoons, giant spiders or butterflies, or praying mantises.

Over the years, the costumes have become fabulously elaborate. In colonial times, dancers simply adorned their clothes with rags or sea sponges. The headpieces for the costumes worn today can tower 10 or 12 feet high, and many costumes weigh more than 100 pounds. Most dancers wear a headdress, a caparison vest that can extend several feet above the shoulders, and a giant hoopskirt — all made from cardboard decorated with thin strips of crêpe paper glued on meticulously by hand. The crêpe paper is cut to different widths, depending on the effect the dancer wants to create: There is "fluff fringe," "carpet fringe," and extra-fine "painting fringe" for areas that require a lot of detail. Dancers spend 2 or 3 months making their costumes, following the instructions of their team's master designer, and great pains are taken to conceal their team's theme from the competition.

The costumes worn on *Boxing Day* are particularly large and elaborate; they're so cumbersome that it's hard to put them on, let alone dance in them from 3 in the morning until well after dawn. It's a point of pride, though, to endure the weight uncomplainingly; the heavier the costume, the more macho the dancer. The costumes worn for the *New Year's Day junkanoo* are lighter and less cumbersome, and the dances performed then are sprightlier and more athletic than those performed for the *Boxing Day* parade.

The origins of the dance are obscure. Some say *junkanoo* is a corruption of "John Canoe," a slave purportedly brought to the islands from America, but the story is probably apocryphal. Nor does the dance have its roots in Christian tradition, as the pre-*Lenten* festivals of *Carnival* and *Mardi Gras* do. The rhythms of the dance are indisputably African, imported by the slaves brought to the islands from the American South and the Caribbean. The dances sometimes have a satiric edge. In colonial times, some *junkanoo* dancers dusted their faces with flour and parodied the cruelties of their masters. After slavery was abolished, the dance sometimes became a subtle form of social protest. The elite identified it — wrongly or not — with hooliganism and violence. The government banned it in 1899 and again in 1942, following a riot over discriminatory wages.

The *junkanoo* dances have always been warlike, in a playful sort of way. Teams of dancers "rush" at each other in mock battles, like the jousts between the Sharks and the Jets in *West Side Story*. Today, some of the dances still have a vaguely bellicose air, but many are free-form: part jive, part shuffle, part dazzling acrobatics. Old taboos are gradually being broken. Women were barred from the *junkanoo* for many years — ostensibly because the dances were too violent — and though some teams still claim that women bring bad luck, a few are accepting them as dancers. (Drumming, though, is still an exclusively male purview.)

Like the *junkanoo,* a few other dances performed in the Bahamas have been around since colonial times. On Cat Island, one of the most tradition-bound isles in the Bahamas, no wedding feast is complete without a waltz, a two-step, or a quadrille. Introduced to the islands by English settlers, the dances have acquired a Bahamian flavor over the years. Dancers of the quadrille stand in two long lines, clapping and swapping partners and twirling around to music in stately 4/4 time. The music is provided by a "rake-and-scrape" band: a trio playing a concertina, a saw scraped with a knife, and a washtub bass, with a guitar player sometimes joining in. As the dancers shuffle and bow, the old men cut a fancy caper or two, and the musicians sing songs such as this one:

> *Good morning, Mister Fisher!*
> *Good morning, Father Brown!*
> *Have you any black crabs?*
> *Please sell me one or two.*
> *Bonefish bite him,*
> *I have no bait to catch 'em,*
> *Every married man*
> *Catch he own bonefish!*

Other traditional dances are not quite so genteel. Parties in Nassau and Lucaya may end with a "jump-in dance" performed by dancers to the sound of a goatskin drum that beats out the rhythm: Ba-ba-ba-ba-*boom!* Ba-ba-ba-ba-*boom!* The dancers form a circle; on the heavy downbeat, one of the participants jumps into the ring and goes through some gyrations, which can range from mildly provocative to salacious — depending on the hour and the crowd. The dancer then picks another to jump into the ring. The dance is possibly a grown-up version of the ring games played by Bahamian children since colonial times, such as the one performed to this ditty:

> *Blue Hill, water dry*
> *Nowhere to wash my clothes*
> *I remember the Saturday night*
> *We had boilfish and johnnycake*
> *Santippy* [a centipede] *knocked on my door last night*
> *I thought it was Johnny, and I say:*
> *Slam, Bam!*

. . . and when the kids shout *Bam!,* the child in the center of the ring does a cut-up dance.

Singing comes naturally to Bahamians. Schoolkids chant and sing their clapping games ("Ask my mother for fifty cents/ To see the wild elephants jump the fence/ They jump so high they touch the sky/ And never come back 'til the fourth of July"), old women on Crooked Island march around the church singing hymns that date back to colonial days, and voices are raised for every family event — from christenings to weddings to wakes.

It's not surprising that many folk songs are religious, given the fact that many islanders' social lives revolve around their church. On some islands, particularly Andros, men still sing "rhyming spirituals," which recount a biblical story. The lead singer takes the melody, and the rest harmonize; the songs are sung a cappella, and the singers improvise as they go along. The words of some of the anthems sung by Bahamian church choirs resemble some of the old hymns written in the South before the Civil War. In Baptist and Pentecostal churches throughout the Bahamas, communicants celebrate by "rushing" — a foot-stamping, hand-clapping, singing-and-wailing promenade up and down the aisles. The dance reaches an especially fevered pitch on *New Year's Eve,* when the minister calls out in a stentorian voice: "Watchman, watchman, what is the hour?" and a man in the congregation shouts back the time. As midnight approaches, the congregation's frenzy grows, as if doomsday were at hand.

Wakes are also celebrated with singing, even on relatively Americanized New Providence and Grand Bahama islands. Friends and relatives gather at the home of the bereaved; if the house is small, the crowd spills out into the garden and the street. The women may sing a few anthems or "settin' up songs," and then the men take over, singing tune after tune, in harmony and without accompaniment. Some of the songs, like "Lay Down My Dear Brother," have a strong thumping downbeat every four counts — rather like the beat of the big bass drum played at Bahamian funeral processions.

Ballads are nearly as popular as hymns. Some recount historical events, such as the landing of the Eleutherian Adventurers in the 17th century, or the sinking of three boats in Nassau Harbour. Others recount the legends from buccaneering days. The popular "Ballad of Captain Morgan" tells the story of the pirate's treasure trove on the island of Andros, which is said to be guarded by Morgan's ghost. Fishermen still sing sea chanteys, some of which may have been brought here a century or two ago by English sailors.

While many of the island's folk tunes have gone unrecorded, a few Bahamian folk singers have won wider recognition. Two of the best died several years ago. Raspy-voiced Joseph Spence popularized many religious tunes and ballads, including "The Wreck of the Ethyl, Myrtle, and the Victoria" and "Out on the Rolling Sea Jesus Speak to Me." Alphonso Higgs, better known as Blind Blake, made several recordings, including renditions of spirituals such as "Run, Come See Jerusalem." Bahamian composer and director Clement Bethel, who died in 1987, carried on the tradition in his folk opera *The Legend of Sammy Swain,* which is set on Cat Island. One of his pupils, Nassau lawyer and musician Cleophas Adderley, Jr., has written a popular folk opera called *Our Boys* that tells the story of the day in 1980 when Cuban MIGs attacked a Bahamian naval vessel, killing four members of the Royal Bahamian Defence Forces.

Tourists who visit a Bahamian bar will probably find that the music playing on the radio or the jukebox is the kind known here as *goombay.* The name — spelled "gombey" on neighboring Bermuda, which has a similar musical tradition — is derived from a Bantu word meaning "drum" or "rhythm." The soul of the music is the goatskin drum — the same drum played for the *junkanoo.* Traditionally, the drums are made from goatskins soaked in lye and tanned and stretched over both ends of a wooden barrel. Like many African drums, they are tuned to specific pitches. To adjust the pitch, the drum is held over a fire to soften the skin, which can then be stretched or loosened. (*Junkanoo* drummers, who must tune their drums as they march, carry along a tin of Sterno to heat their drums.)

Unlike *junkanoo* music, which is dominated by the heavy beat of the *goombay* drums, *goombay* music is softer and more melodic. A saxophone takes the lead in some *goombay* songs, or a concertina may put on a gentle harmony. Like calypso, the native music of the southern Caribbean, *goombay* has left its mark on Bahamian popular music. The 1940s *goombay* tune "Love

Alone," which celebrated the romance of the Duke and Duchess of Windsor — the Duke of Windsor was Governor of the Bahamas during World War II — was a smash hit. If you spend a few nights at the clubs in Nassau — try *Drumbeat* on West Bay Street, owned by singer Peanuts Taylor — you're bound to find somebody who still plays it.

Modern Bahamian musicians are an eclectic bunch. Listen carefully to the lyrics in singer Eddie Minnis's calypso-and-*goombay* tunes: They bristle with gibes at local social conventions. The homespun tunes of Toby MacKay, better known as "Exuma, the Obeah Man," draw on Family Island folk traditions. Composer Kendal Stubbs has crossbred *junkanoo* rhythms with what he calls "marketable popular sounds" to create "junkafunk." Ah, yes. Given a good bottle of rum and a couple of hours to improvise, Bahamian musicians can come up with just about anything.

Religion and Religious Heritages

The Bahamians, if a sweeping generalization can be made, are a very religious people. This may escape the notice of tourists who spend their time in the nightclubs and casinos in Freeport and Nassau, but those who spend time off the beaten track will discover that it's true. In many Bahamian families — rich and poor — the church is the center of social life; the chef of one of the finest restaurants in the Bahamas takes time off on Wednesdays to rehearse his trumpet solos with the church band. Religion and folklore are intertwined. On Crooked Island, women sing "I'm Goin' Home on the Mornin' Train" — a hymn reminiscent of the spirituals brought by the slaves of Southern pro-British Loyalists 200 years ago. In Baptist and Pentecostal churches, communicants celebrate by "rushing" — a joyous procession that recalls the *junkanoo*.

It's a little ironic that the Bahamas never became a Catholic country, given that the first mass heard in the New World was said here in 1492 by a priest traveling with Christopher Columbus. It's ironic, too, that the Bahamas didn't remain devoutly Puritan, given the fervor of the Bermudian settlers who colonized Eleuthera during the mid-17th century. Historians can probably come up with a half-dozen reasons why the Bahamas didn't turn out like Anglican Bermuda or Catholic Hispaniola. Suffice it to say that no single religion has ever held sway here. Baptists predominate today. Twenty-nine percent of the population are Baptist, 23 percent are Episcopalian, and Catholics are a close third, with 22 percent.

Aside from the band of Puritans who founded a utopian community on Eleuthera in 1648, the Protestant church exerted little influence over public affairs in the Bahamas until the late 18th century. A few brave souls came over from England to proselytize, but they found many of the natives indifferent. The Reverend William Guy, who sailed from London to New Providence in 1731, claimed to have baptized 128 Bahamians, though only a few dozen faithfully listened to his sermons. And fiery sermons they must have been, for preachers found plenty to rail against in the days when buccaneering was the most lucrative occupation on the islands and when many poor Bahamians — baptized or not — made a living by "wrecking" — scavenging ships that ran aground on reefs and shoals offshore.

It was only after the end of the American Revolution that the Anglican church acquired any sort of official status. Many of the Loyalists who fled to the Bahamas were solid Anglicans, and their faith took root more successfully than their crops of cotton and tobacco. By the close of the 18th century, most of prosperous New Providence's leading citizens were members of the Church of England. They wielded such influence that in 1795 the Bahamian parliament passed a law requiring the state to turn over all revenues from the sale of liquor licenses to the Church of England — a sort of "Rum for Jesus" trade. The legislature also gave the Anglican Vestry the power to manage the public market, crack down on illegal use of weights and measures, and fine unscrupulous merchants (money collected from fines went directly into the church's coffers).

As the Anglicans' influence grew, so did their intolerence. Catholics were anathema, and Methodists and Baptists — who came to the Bahamas from America — were dismissed as "dissenters." (Presbyterians, who founded St. Andrew's Kirk on New Providence in 1810, were grudgingly accepted.) The intolerence of the Anglicans had a racial cast. Unlike the Anglican hierarchy in Bermuda, which forced slaves to attend church services, the Anglicans of the Bahamas did their best to ignore blacks. Some Bahamian plantation owners maintained that Christ's preachings about equality would demoralize their slaves — or, worse yet, cause them to rebel.

As a result, few blacks — free or slave — joined the Anglican fold. Most blacks continued to practice their own religion, a blend of animism, West African tribal ritual, Islam, Christian symbolism, and shamanistic rites called obeah. From the mid-19th century onward, however, many blacks gradually abandoned their traditional faith. Baptist, Methodist, and Moravian ministers wooed black converts — though the Anglican elite didn't make their task easy. A Methodist missionary, the Reverend William Turton, who came to the Bahamas from Barbados in 1800, complained he was undermined by "slander, petty persecutions, and impertinent officialdom."

Despite the harassment, the dissenting congregations continued to grow. They were aided by a national scandal. In 1866, a hurricane swept through the islands, destroying several churches. In the aftermath of the storm, the National Treasury managed to scrape together funds to repair some of the churches — the Anglican ones. Non-Anglican churches, such as Trinity Methodist in Nassau, were left in ruins. Infuriated "dissenters" raised such a fuss that, in 1869, the legislature revoked the Anglican church's official status.

The move was a severe blow to many Anglican churches, whose well-heeled members were unaccustomed to digging into their own pockets to support their congregations. Their loss was their competition's gain. Some blacks joined Methodist churches. (Hardly paragons of equality, the Methodist congregations also were generally split along racial or class lines.) The more egalitarian Baptists gained even more members. (Legend had it that a runaway slave from America named Sambo Scriven brought the Baptist faith to the islands — a story that may have boosted the denomination's popularity.) The black man in the Bahamas, observed British diplomat C. S. Salmon, who served in the British West Indies for several years during the mid-19th century, "prefers being a dissenter to being a state churchman, notwithstanding the social dignity supposed to be attached to the latter. He sees and feels that he is regarded [by white Anglicans] more as a pariah than anything else."

Meanwhile, the Anglicans were split by another controversy. The schism pitted Ritualists — who wanted to revive old rites that predated the church's split with Rome in Henry VIII's time — against the Prayer Book faction, which wanted to keep the modern church's rituals as they were. By the turn of the century, the Ritualists had gained the upper hand in the Bahamas, and many of their foes had abandoned the faith and joined the Methodists. To bolster their shrinking congregations, Anglican ministers began for the first time to seek followers among the black community.

Catholics were late in coming to the island, with the exception of two early visitors: Christopher Columbus and Juan Ponce de León. One of the first priests to visit came by accident. Father Gibbons, a native of Baltimore, was shipwrecked in 1853 while traveling from Dublin to New Orleans, and he was stranded for a time on Grand Bahama. During the years that followed, a handful of other priests arrived, and the churches they founded were supervised by the Diocese of New York. In 1891, an ailing Benedictine monk from a Minnesota abbey landed in Nassau. Father Chrysostom Schreiner came to the islands for his health — he suffered from tuberculosis — and had no interest in staying, for he found the islanders too steadfastly Protestant to be susceptible to persuasion. During his stay, he chartered a boat and sailed to the islands that Columbus had visited in 1492. (The Bahamian government was laying plans at the time for the celebration of the 400th anniversary of the discovery of the New World.) A storm arose while he was en route, and his ship was dashed against a reef. In gratitude for his rescue, he decided to stay in the islands. And stay he did — for 37 years, until his death in the rectory of Holy Saviour Church in Cockburn Town, on the island of San Salvador.

Today, one in ten Bahamians is Catholic. Although most islanders are Protestant, a number of other sects — Seventh-Day Adventists, Jehovah's Witnesses, Christian Scientists — have taken root. A Greek Orthodox church, a Baha'i temple, and a mosque stand among the tall gray spires of the Anglican churches in Nassau, and there is a Jewish synagogue in Freeport.

While there are fewer historic churches in the Bahamas than in, say, Bermuda or the Dominican Republic, some merit a visit. The Hermitage on Cat Island has the finest setting: atop Mt. Alvernia, the highest point in the Bahamas (the mountain is only 206 feet above sea level, but the view from the top is nonetheless impressive). The Hermitage's hand-hewn limestone chapel, bell tower, and house were built in the 1940s by John Hawkes, a former Anglican missionary known as Father Jerome after his conversion to Catholicism. Two of the oldest churches in the Turks & Caicos Islands are in Cockburn Town on Grand Turk: One is Methodist; the other, St. Thomas, is Anglican.

Island Food and Drink

Bahamians are fiercely nationalistic, and they're just as proud of their native dishes. Bahamian food is soul food, pure and simple, and visitors who are fond of red beans and rice or corn pone will feel right at home here. Over the years, many culinary traditions have left their mark on the local fare. Some Bahamian dishes are based on old English recipes; others were introduced by the Tories who settled here after the American Revolution. Hot red peppers from the West Indies spice up native stews, and the sesame-seed *benne* cakes beloved by Bahamian children are akin to some West African sweets. The farther east you go in the islands, the more traditional the food becomes. In parts of the remote Family Islands and the Turks & Caicos Islands, women still grind the corn for their grits by hand, and bake their johnnycakes over a wood fire.

If there's one food that's quintessentially Bahamian, it's the queen conch. The mollusk (pronounced *conk*) is virtually a national symbol — the Bahamian equivalent of American apple pie. It's prepared in dozens of ways; of them, conch salad is perhaps the tastiest. On Saturday or Sunday mornings, many Nassau families make their weekly conch-salad pilgrimage to Potter's Cay. They order the salads from a "conch man," who hammers a hole in the conch's cone-shaped shell, extricates the tough muscle, dices and salts it, and sprinkles it with lime or the juice of a sour orange. (Conch is tough and must be marinated, or "scorched," to make it palatable.) Diced onions, tomatoes, and hot peppers are mixed in, and the salad is spooned into a plastic bag and left to marinate for a while. Conch is also pounded, or "cracked," coated with batter and deep-fried, and simmered in bisques and chowders. (Be prepared for the teasing that conch is an aphrodisiac.) For a sampling of all these preparations, go to *Mandi's Conch* restaurant in the town of Palmdale in eastern New Providence, where conch is the only food on the menu. On *Discovery Day* (October 12), MacLean's Town on Grand Bahama holds a conch cracking competition: the first to crack and clean 25 conchs gets the prize. (Tourists can enter, but shouldn't expect to win.) Frugal Bahamians put leftover conch shells to good use. Musicians use them as horns; artisans turn them into jewelry; and the shells line sidewalks and graves.

If conch is the national food, spiny lobster is a close second. A type of crayfish (or crawfish, as Bahamians say), it thrives in many parts of the Bahamas, and it has made many of the fishermen of Eleuthera and South Caicos rich. The lobsters, which are most plentiful between October and July, can weigh up to 7 pounds; most of those sold at Potter's Cay weigh 2 or 3 pounds. Considered poor man's food a generation or two ago, it's now a delicacy, and export demand has driven up prices enough to put it beyond the reach of many Bahamian families. Like all shellfish, the fresher it is, the more simply it can be prepared. A fresh, tender spiny lobster needs little more than lemon and drawn butter to make a perfect dish. Older, tougher lobsters require more elaborate preparations: The meat can be minced, cooked until it's dry and flaky, and sautéed with onions, tomatoes, and hot peppers.

Of the many game fish that swim in these waters, grouper is perhaps the most popular. Bahamians eat two kinds: striped Nassau grouper, which is plentiful from November to January; and yellowfin grouper, or rockfish, in season from February to April. Grouper is grilled, sautéed, and served with a dash of lime, or sliced into thin fingers and deep-fried. (Other large fish, such as wahoo and snapper, are prepared in the same ways.) Some of the tastiest preparations, though, aren't likely to turn up on tourist menus. Bahamian fishermen, for instance, sauté grouper livers and roe with onions, hot peppers, and a pinch of bay leaf or thyme. Smaller fish — grunts, porgies, jacks, and margate, or "margaret," as the natives say — are steamed, made into chowder, or simmered in a simple stew called "boilfish," a popular breakfast dish. On the Family Islands, where electric refrigerators arrived not too long ago, dried fish are still a staple. Dried turbot, grunt, or conch are tossed into a pot of boiling water, mixed with onions, cassava, and a bit of salt pork, and simmered for hours over a wood fire.

Many of these dishes would be bland if it weren't for a dash or two of hot peppers. Some of the peppers found here were probably introduced from the West Indies; others are similar to Mexican varieties. Most common are the flame-red peppers about the size of a jalapeño; they're steeped in dark rum and served as a condiment with meat and fish. Of all the varieties eaten in the Bahamas, the goat pepper is the most scorching. Pale yellow and nearly round, it's known as the Scotch Bonnet in parts of the West Indies (*habanero* in the Yucatán). The pepper is so hot that a drop of juice on the skin will raise a welt. (Never, never eat the seeds — they're the hottest of all!) Bahamian cooks mince them finely and toss them into a bowl of conch salad or a kettle of boilfish.

Most Bahamians seem inured to the effects of hot peppers, but tourists who have suffered an overdose can do what the Mexicans do: Don't drink water, eat starch. There are plenty of Bahamian breads that will do the trick. Perhaps the most popular is johnnycake, an eggless, yeastless bread that's similar to a heavy biscuit. (It's an essential accompaniment to boilfish.) Introduced generations ago from the West Indies — probably from Jamaica — the bread was popular because it could be stored for weeks or months, like Swedish hardtack. During colonial times, ships stocked up on it to sustain crews during long voyages. (Johnnycake is probably a corruption of "journeycake.") In the Bahamas, the bread is made from unbleached wheat flour, vegetable oil, salt, and unsweetened condensed milk; fresh grated coconut is often added. Unlike the johnnycakes served in some parts of the Caribbean, the Bahamian version is baked, not deep-fried. Family Island women pat the dough out into rounds and place them in an iron pot. The pot is covered and set over a wood fire, which imparts a smoky taste to the cakes.

The classic Bahamian comfort food is peas 'n' rice. Like red beans and rice in New Orleans, it has become a cultural emblem. There is no fixed recipe: Cat Island cooks may prepare it differently from cooks in the Caicos Islands or on New Providence. Two ingredients never vary: white rice and pigeon peas, a dusky little legume that turns nut-brown when cooked. (In a pinch, black-eyed peas can be used as a substitute.) Traditionally, dried pigeon peas are soaked overnight and boiled; some Family Islanders cook them in coconut milk, which imparts a rich flavor. Cooks season the peas and rice with whatever strikes their fancy: diced bits of sautéed salt pork, onion, green pepper, and celery are commonly added, with a sprig of thyme or a dash of black pepper.

Cassava, brought to the islands by the Lucaya Indians, is another popular down-home food. Once squeezed of its poisonous juices, it is cubed and boiled like a potato, dried and stirred into soup as a thickener, or baked into heavy yeastless bread. Hominy grits, which may have been introduced to the islands by Southern Loyalists, are a breakfast favorite. While many cooks on the western islands buy instant grits exported from the US, some Family Islanders still grind their own with a hand mill. Often several varieties of corn — red, white, yellow — are ground together. Travelers to some remote cays may see an even rarer sight: a farmer or his wife pounding dried corn in a large wooden trough. Rice, which in the Bahamas is cheaper than potatoes, is another common staple. In poor households, leftover rice is used as a "pullover" to stretch a dish of sautéed pumpkin or squash.

Plantains, a banana-like fruit and a staple in the tropics, are cooked here in many ways. Bahamian cooks boil them, deep-fry them, sauté them, or bake them whole in their skins. One Nassau restaurant makes a delicate plantain mousse seasoned with scallions. And breadfruit and arrowroot are used to fill out or thicken some dishes.

Many Bahamian meat stews have been influenced by West Indian cooking. *Souse,* a pork stew, is popular here and throughout the Caribbean region, from Jamaica to Belize to Guyana. The fundamental ingredient in Bahamian *souse* is pig's feet, or "trotters"; a couple of pig's ears and tails may be thrown in for good measure. The meat is boiled with onions, bay leaves, and allspice, and the gelatin from the bones makes a delicious aspic. Many Bahamian families once ate this economical dish every Saturday night. Chicken and sheep's tongue *souse* are popular, too, though they're less common. Stews and curries made with mutton — which in the Bahamas can mean mutton, lamb, or goat — are popular as well. (Most of the beef eaten in the islands is imported frozen.) Many meats are steamed, a slightly misleading culinary term. Bahamian steamed chicken, for instance, is actually similar to a French *daube,* in which sautéed meat is simmered in a reduced stock seasoned with onions and vegetables.

Bahamian vegetables are a treat. They're generally fresher and less doctored up than their American supermarket counterparts: The tomatoes aren't gassed, and cucumbers aren't smothered with wax to make them shiny. Much of the produce is grown on the Family Islands and shipped by mail boat to New Providence and Grand Bahama. Sweet white Exuma onions are said to rival Vidalias from Georgia, and the tomatoes from Long and Cat islands are said to be the best. Avocados — called "pears" — are another local favorite: Natives eat them out of their hand, sprinkled with salt and lime juice.

Traditional Bahamian desserts tend to be cloyingly sweet. The national favorite, guava *duff,* is a variant of a classic English dessert. Blanched and peeled, white guavas are spread on a rich biscuit-like dough, which is rolled up and wrapped in cheesecloth. The *duff* is boiled for an hour or two, cooled and sliced, and served with a frothy butter sauce flavored with dark rum. Coconut is the essential ingredient in many desserts: coconut *duff,* coconut cream pie, coconut *jimmy* (a sort of turnover), and pink-and-white striped coconut bars made with enough sugar to ruin several molars. Bread pudding is another English favorite, as is the rich *Christmas* fruitcake, which is soaked for up to a year in brandy or dark rum.

Those who aren't fond of sweets will find plenty of fruit to eat. There are red-and-green Hayden mangoes imported from Haiti, sweet pineapples from Eleuthera, peanut-shape watermelons with delicious crimson flesh, tiny "sugar bananas," sapodillas, luscious pink grapefruit from Abaco, tamarinds, and yellow hog plums that taste a little like mangoes. Astringent sea grapes and green mangoes are boiled up into preserves and chutneys, and unripe "jelly coconuts" are cracked open and eaten with a spoon.

Fruits are the base of many Bahamian drinks. Grapefruit and a dash of Campari are the essential components of a Bahama Delight. Three juices go into a Bahama Mama: apple, orange, and coconut; there's a little rum, Triple Sec, and grenadine in it, too. Orange juice and lemon juice, dark and light rum, and Tia Maria make a Yellow Bird; and the local version of a mint julep is made with lime, light rum, and champagne.

Those seeking a great traditional dish needn't sail to a remote Family Island cay. Native cooking has come into vogue in recent years, just as native American fare did not too long ago in the US, and many fine restaurants on New Providence, Bimini, and Grand Bahama are adding native dishes to their menus. A few chefs, such as *Graycliff*'s Philip Bethel, have revived many traditional favorites, lightening them a bit, brightening them with new herbs and spices, and spiffing up their presentations. Bethel, for instance, has concocted a light, trifle-like version of guava *duff,* a reduced and enriched version of grouper stew topped with vol-au-vent, roast pheasant with Eleuthera pineapples, and a pigeon-pea soup similar to a Tuscan minestrone. Island dining has come into its own.

Flora, Fauna, and Fertile Lands

It's hard to say exactly how many islands belong to the Bahamas — it depends on how you define an island. Most Bahamians live on fewer than a dozen isles, among them Andros, Grand Bahama, Great Abaco, Great Inagua, and hairpin-thin Eleuthera. The largest Bahamian island, Andros, is 111 miles wide; the smallest is little more than a large rock. If you count every one, the Bahamian archipelago comprises more than 700 isles and 2,000 tiny cays scattered over 90,000 square miles of the West Atlantic. They stretch from Bimini, just 50 miles off the coast of Florida, to Mayaguana and the Inaguas, nearly 700 miles to the southeast. (The Turks & Caicos chain, located even farther east, belongs — geographically speaking — to the Bahamian archipelago, but it has been governed separately for more than 100 years.)

Sometime when you're out lazing in a boat somewhere among the Bahamas, look around at the tiny green isles that surround you. In a couple of centuries, many of the islands you see will have grown a bit larger. Some may have split in two; others may have disappeared altogether. The geography of the archipelago is always changing: if you were to compare a seaman's chart drawn in 1940 with one used today, you would probably notice some subtle differences.

The reason for this lies in the way the islands are made. The Bahamas rise from the bumpy floor of a great submarine plateau. Over many millennia, colonies of coral anchored themselves to seamounts, forming reefs that eventually broke above the surface of the water. Bahamians call these islets cays (pronounced *keys*), after the Arawak word *cairi*. The process of island building isn't always slow and delicate. Hurricanes can sweep through in a few days, splitting islands in two or creating new ones. One powerful storm can cut a channel through a reef, dividing it in half, or expose a sandbar to unite two islands.

Shifts in global climate have also changed the shape of the islands, sometimes in dramatic ways. The Bahamas are so low — elevations seldom exceed 150 feet, and the highest point in the entire archipelago, Mt. Alvernia on Cat Island, towers a mere 206 feet — that they have been swallowed up by the sea more than once during their long history. When the global climate warms, the polar ice caps melt, sea levels rise, and the Bahamas take a dive until the mercury falls again. Sea levels have been rising since the last Ice Age began to wane 20,000 years ago, and if the trend continues, the islands may be due for another bath. Not to worry, though. It won't happen anytime soon, and when it does, it will be too gradual for tourists to notice — unless they're planning to spend several decades (or even centuries) on the beach.

All that aside, the climate of the Bahamas is just about as close to perfect as it can get. The Gulf Stream protects the archipelago from temperature extremes, and frosts are unheard of, at least in recent times. In winter, temperatures hover around 72F, while in summer the trade winds keep the mercury from climbing above the mid-80s. About 50 inches of rain fall each year (the northwestern isles are wetter, and the southeastern ones are drier). There are twin rainy seasons: in June and July, and in September and October. Hurricanes occasionally blow through during the fall. Storms are in fact essential to the local ecology, for there are few rivers and freshwater lakes in the Bahamas; many houses have a cistern for collecting precious rainwater. (The coralline limestone from which the islands are made is so porous that rain percolates through the rocks like water in a coffeepot. Wells can tap this rainwater, which floats on top of the denser saltwater, but if the water is disturbed, it quickly turns brackish.)

FLORA

To many people, the Bahamas conjure up images of palm-fringed beaches and little else. In fact, the islands are home to a wide variety of plant life. The larger islands — particularly Andros, Grand Bahama, and Great Abaco — are still heavily forested, and visitors can still see stands of virgin timber, though logging companies cut down many of them in the early 20th century. Wild tamarinds and acacias grow here; so does the tulip tree, whose scarlet blossoms are large enough to serve as birdbaths; the flamboyant, which has slightly smaller fire-red flowers; the frangipani, which bears deliciously fragrant star-shaped blossoms; and the tall and stately breadfruit tree, which is said to have been introduced to the Caribbean by Captain Bligh, who brought a shipload of seedlings to Jamaica from Tahiti in 1794. The mahogany, whose close-grained wood was much favored by Bahamian shipbuilders, still flourishes here; you can identify it by its oak-like leaves and bright orange blossoms. Wispy casuarinas, an evergreen native to Australia, cast delicate shadows on the sand near the shore.

Among the most useful trees is the lignum vitae, a short tree with tiny indigo-colored flowers. Its wood, which is so dense it doesn't float, makes fine bowling balls, and the Arawak made a potion from its bark to treat syphilis. (Spanish explorers took seedlings of the lignum vitae to Europe, where medicines derived from the bark were used to treat the "sailor's disease" for 400 years.) Cascarilla, a West Indian shrub belonging to the spurge family, grows wild on some of the Family Islands. Its aromatic bark is used to flavor Campari, the Italian liqueur, and to make incense. One tree should be avoided. The manchineel — the name is a corruption of the Spanish diminutive for apple — secretes a venomous milky white juice and bears a poisonous fruit called the death apple. Warning: Don't stand under a manchineel during a storm, for the rain running off the leaves can burn your skin.

Some plants have adapted cleverly to their environment. The mangroves

PERSPECTIVES / Flora and Fauna

that thrive in brackish waters near the coast survive their hostile habitat by secreting salt through their leaves. Their tangled prop roots trap silt and organic debris, actually helping the islands to grow. Cacti thrive in the dry, sandy soil on some of the Family Islands and the Turks & Caicos. If you walk through the dunes — mind the needles! — you can find prickly pears, which bear a delicious fruit; old man cacti, named for their beard-like tufts; and spindly candle cactus. Grand Turk Island gets its name from a bulbous green cactus topped with a little red cap that reminded some early settlers of a Turkish fez.

In all, more than 950 varieties of plants have been collected here, including 56 species found only in the Bahamas. The yellow elder — the national flower — brings forth its trumpet-shape blossoms from October to December. Stately poinsettias bloom around *Christmas* (they're far lovelier than the anemic little plants sold at every American grocery store in December). Purple-flowered railroad vines and low-lying sea grapes flourish along the beach. Heart-shape flamingo flowers, angel's trumpets, birds of paradise, torch ginger, and myriad shades of oleander and bougainvillea grow here as well.

Mangoes, passion fruit, pomegranates, and custard apples are here for the picking. So are guavas, which the Arawak brought to the islands from South America. They also brought cassava, a squat shrub about 6 feet high whose roots are boiled, grated, and made into a coarse bread. The mammee, or marmalade tree, bears an apricot-colored fruit that's delicious stewed or cooked into jelly. If you peel off the spiny green skin of the soursop (called a *guanabana* in the Spanish-speaking islands of the Caribbean), you'll find a luscious pinkish white fruit underneath. The tropical evergreen tree known as the sapodilla (the name is a corruption of the Aztec word *tzapotl*) oozes a milky fluid that Mesoamerican Indians made into chewing gum; its fruit, which is covered with a rough reddish skin, tastes a little like a kiwi.

ALL AT SEA

If there is a national animal in the Bahamas, it should by rights be coral. Every island in the archipelago is made of the skeletons of these humble little polyps. Sensitive and slow-growing — most perish in waters cooler than 70F, and many grow less than an inch a year — they can form massive structures if left undisturbed. The 100-mile-long barrier reef off Andros, for instance, is the third-largest in the world.

Several kinds of coral grow here. Tough elkhorn and brain coral live on the fringes of reefs where the sea pounds the hardest. Delicate, fast-growing staghorn coral, which grows up to 4 inches a year, flourishes in calmer waters. Black coral and fire coral — which, if you want to split hairs, are not really corals at all — live here, too. The pink and purple tints of some corals are borrowed finery — they come from symbiotic algaes. Resist the temptation to pluck a piece of coral or two — it's against the law, and in any case it smells to high heaven when it's plucked from the water and the organic matter inside starts to decay.

The seas that surround the Bahamas are lively indeed. Humpback whales congregate near the Turks Islands from mid-January to March. (The sperm and pilot whales hunted by 19th-century fishermen have largely disappeared from these waters.) Sea bass the size of small dinghies lurk in deep waters. Schools of angelfish — some blue and green, some silvery, some black with yellow speckles — glide by. (They all seem to be pouting.) Slender trumpet fish, jewfish and parrot fish, and scarlet cardinals dart between the sea fans and anemones. Schoolmasters, tropical snapper, survey the waters with a dour look. Sergeant majors, named for their sporty black and yellow chevrons, are more cheerful. Puffer fish blow themselves up like balloons to scare off predators; red long-spine squirrelfish intimidate their enemies by widening their eyes. The trunkfish's bony carapace protects him from marauders, while the surgeonfish wards off foes with his lancet-like tail.

The marine life here is for the most part benign, but divers and snorkelers should be on the lookout for the occasional shark or barracuda. (Sharks aren't likely to attack unless the water's murky, which is rare in the Bahamas, or unless they mistake you for a tuna.) Visitors should also be on guard against sea urchins, whose spikes can sting badly (local divers will tease you that a drop of urine quickly numbs the pain). Fire coral — which isn't coral at all, but a relative of the jellyfish and Portuguese man-of-war — also delivers a venomous sting.

ON THE HOOK

It's true, if clichéd: The islands are an angler's paradise (see *Quintessential Bahamas,* in DIVERSIONS). Of all the game fish here, the blue marlin gets the most press. Fast, strong, and cunning, they're as macho as fish get. The largest ever caught here on a 130-pound line weighed more than 700 pounds. Look for them off Bimini, Cat Island, Walker's Cay, and Grand Bahama. Whether marlin are as great to eat as they are to catch is a matter of debate. Most fishermen say fresh marlin tastes so-so, but properly smoked, it can be delicious.

Any time but summer is the right time to fish for wahoo, a tasty type of mackerel that can weigh up to 150 pounds. These fast and cunning fish can be found in deep waters off New Providence and Eleuthera. Bluefin tuna, the giant of the mackerel family, appear in the western Bahamas in the late spring and early summer. Yellowfin and bonito are most plentiful in summer; amberjack, sailfin, and dolphin appear in winter. The "passing jack" shows up in the Gulf Stream west of Bimini for a few weeks in midsummer. Grouper and snapper stick around all year; they lie near the bottom and can be caught with weighted lures. The feisty bonefish, the favorite of light-tackle fishermen, feeds on crabs just offshore. Delicious small fry — grunts, porgies, and margate — also feed in the flats near the shore.

The most popular catches are shellfish. Most prized is the spiny lobster, a type of crayfish (or crawfish, as the natives say), which was considered poor man's fare 40 or 50 years ago. Whether they're encased in puff pastry and served with saffron cream sauce in a posh Nassau restaurant, or grilled over a fire on a beach on a remote Family Island cay, they're excellent. Conch (pronounced *conk*) is another local favorite. Bahamian shellfish are also exported to Europe and North America. It's a lucrative trade: Exports of conch and spiny lobster bring in millions of dollars, accounting for more than three-fourths of the country's total foreign exchange earnings during some years.

FAUNA

More than 200 species of birds have been spotted on the islands. Roughly half are migrating species from North America that — like most tourists — flock to the Bahamas during the winter. Flamingos nest on many of the islands, and more than 20,000 live on the 290-square-mile reserve on Inagua. Egrets, herons, pelicans, and strawberry-pink spoonbills stalk the brackish marshes on Inagua and other islands. Pintails, wood star hummingbirds, and brilliant green parrots are common; rare Cuban crows and grassquits are harder to spot. (The black-and-yellow banana quit, which pecks holes in flowers to suck their nectar, is so fond of sweets that it will snatch the sugar lumps from your seaside table.) Several species of native and migratory game birds can be hunted from April through September, including guinea and marsh hens, mourning doves and Key West quail doves, ring-necked pheasants, and many kinds of wild ducks and geese.

Few mammals are indigenous to the islands. Arawak Indians introduced a small, yellow, non-barking dog from South America, but the last of these died centuries ago. The Arawak may have also imported the hutia, a South American rodent prized for its succulent meat. Now nearly extinct, the hutia lives on Atwood Cay and a few other remote Family Islands. Wild horses and pigs — the descendants of those brought by the European settlers — roam the forests of Abaco, and feral donkeys graze on the scrubby plains of Inagua. Rats and raccoons hitched a ride to the islands sometime around the 17th century.

The animals native to the islands are hardly threatening. Iguanas look ferocious, but in fact they're mild-mannered vegetarians. Their numbers have fallen drastically, for locals covet their meat, and they are now protected by law. Snakes, lizards, and frogs are common, but all are harmless. Bats roost in limestone caves throughout the Bahamas, and their guano is collected for fertilizer.

FRUITS OF THE SOIL

Soil, like water, is a precious commodity. As the early colonists found, the rich black topsoil found on many of the islands is fertile but very thin, and its nutrients are quickly exhausted. Large-scale farming is also hindered by the hard and bumpy limestone surface of the islands, which is pocked with depressions called "banana holes." All told, only 2 percent of the land in the Bahamas is arable.

Many early attempts at large-scale farming failed. Loyalists who fled the

American colonies after the Revolution planted nearly 5,000 acres of cotton in the Family Islands in the years following the war, but chenille bugs soon spoiled their crops. Family Islanders tried to raise tobacco, too, but the land gave out within a generation. Sugar Loaf pineapples — said to be the finest in the world — were canned on Eleuthera and New Providence from the 1850s to the 1890s, but US tariffs and competition from Hawaii destroyed the market for the fruit, and little is exported today. Sisal was raised for a time on some of the Family Islands, but Bahamian producers couldn't compete with growers in the Philippines and Mexico, and only a little is raised today. Cotton and sisal still grow wild on some of the islands where they were once cultivated.

Many colonial planters eventually abandoned their farms, and their slaves were left to fend for themselves. Over the years, the descendants of those slaves learned to eke out a living from the land and sea. Many of the farming techniques they developed still survive in isolated communities on the Family Islands. On Eleuthera and a handful of other isles, farmland, or "commonage,"' is handed down from father to son. Crops are rotated so that the fragile soils aren't depleted of nutrients. On Cat Island, farmers still practice slash-and-burn agriculture, as the Arawak Indians did many centuries ago.

Potatoes are cultivated on the sandy stretches near the coast known to natives as "white land." Tomatoes and watermelons flourish in the "red land" soils in the interior. (Try the extra-juicy tomatoes from Long and Cat islands that are sold on Potter's Cay in the Nassau market.) The sweet onions from Exuma are said to taste like Vidalias and the onions grown on Maui in Hawaii. Oranges and limes grown on the Family Islands are shipped to restaurants and hotels on New Providence and Grand Bahama. Bananas, cucumbers, pigeon peas, Guinea corn, cassava, yams, prickly pears, okra, sweet and hot peppers, onions, melons, and many other crops are carefully tended on small farms and family plots.

A few crops are exported. Pineapples are still harvested on Eleuthera (go to the *Pineapple Festival* in Gregory Town if you're visiting in July). Mangoes are raised on Eleuthera and other isles and canned at seven plants in the Family Islands. Coconut palms, which flourish throughout the islands, are cultivated commercially in some areas. Most coconut meat is consumed locally, but the oil is extracted and made into cosmetics and suntan products. Sea Island cotton is harvested on some of the Family Islands, and some natives still tend small plots of indigo, an herb that yields a deep blue dye.

Folk Legends and Lore, and Crafts

Storytelling is still a fine art in the Bahamas. The tales that are spun here on wharfs and shady front porches are part of a rich and varied tradition. An African proverb or an English sailor's ditty may pop up in a story, or the plot may echo a Grimm fairy tale — only hereabouts the good children are rewarded with a bowl of stewed conch, not gingerbread.

The oral tradition is strongest on the Family Islands, where electricity and television arrived just a few years ago (some of the remote villages still aren't electrified). Some of the old women on Crooked Island still sit by the sea and tell old tales to their grandchildren, and there was — or perhaps still is — a very old lady in the town of Pirate's Well on Mayaguana who was famous for her stories. Don't expect shy Family Islanders to divulge their tales willingly, no matter how polite and helpful they are. "What, those old lies?" they're likely to say — or, perhaps, "Let me tell you something from the Bible — that's better for you."

Years ago, people on the Family Islands would tell stories around the kitchen hearth at night. Many of the kitchens in the villages on remote cays were housed in separate buildings, to keep the heat away from the main house. The kitchens were usually divided into two rooms: a storage room in front, with hooks for horse tack and bins for corn and pigeon peas, and a large hearth in the back. At night, slaves and free blacks would sit by the fire plaiting straw and shelling peas, taking turns telling stories to keep awake. Many began with a riddle or a proverb, as many of the stories do today.

Today, some of those proverbs and riddles still crop up in everyday speech. When little Bahamian girls make mud pies, they chant, "Nyam, nyam, dirty dog" — *nyam* is a West African word meaning "eat" that was probably introduced to the Bahamas by slaves more than 200 years ago. "If you can't cut bait, get out of the boat," Bahamian executives say to lazy employees. (The proverb is said to be a favorite of Prime Minister Lynden Pindling.) "The higher a monkey climbs, the more his tail shows," a Bahamian mother warns her overambitious children. Picky eaters are told, "A hungry dog will eat raw corn" — a variant of a West African saying meaning "Be thankful you've got something to eat." Mothers tell their daughters, "Girl, your hair looks like a *hurra* nest today" — a *hurra,* on some islands, is a mythical bird that makes an enormous, untidy nest. Some proverbs warn about the mischievous *chickarnie,* a red-eyed, three-fingered, and three-toed creature who lives in the woods on the island of Andros. When a Nassau boy asks his father,

"When can I drive the car?" the answer is invariably, "When chicken grow teeth."

Just as slaves brought their proverbs to the islands, European settlers brought their fairy tales, and over the years they acquired a local patina. The tale known to Bahamian children as "B'er Jack" — short for Brother Jack — "and de Snake" is "Jack the Giant Killer" dressed up in tropical clothing. Another popular Bahamian story, "The Woman and the Bell-Boy" (it's not, by the way, set in a Nassau hotel), borrows from the Grimm tale "The Golden Billy Goat." In the Bahamian version, a boy ventures into the woods and meets an old woman, whose company he spurns. Furious, the woman (who's a witch) turns him into a stick of wood, a rock, a piece of iron, and a bell before she tires of the game and sets him free.

Some tales are a hodgepodge of English, French, African, and Caribbean folklore. A popular tale about B'er Rabby — the Bahamian incarnation of Brer Rabbit, the invention of American writer Joel Chandler Harris — features a goat named B'er Bouki (from the French word *bouc,* meaning "he-goat"), a rooster that crows a very English "cock-a-doodle-doo," a door that swings open after the words "open *kafeysha*" are intoned, and a character who is rewarded with a meal of peas and rice, stewed conch, and *benne* cake. (The latter, which derives its name from a West African word for sesame, is a sweet snack made from sesame seeds.) In another Bahamian tale, the rabbit saves B'er Bouki from the jaws of a hungry lion. (Neither rabbits nor lions inhabit the Bahamas, where the closest thing to a ferocious beast is the mild-mannered iguana.) Such tales may be variants of African trickster tales, some of which describe the adventures of a wise hare and a silly goat.

Some Bahamian tales are extended jokes, like the tale about the man who told his wife to save money for a rainy day. A vagrant who overheard the conversation between the pair waits until the husband leaves and then introduces himself to the wife as "Mr. Rainy Day." (You can guess the outcome.) There are joke stories about preachers who misread their sermons and make mortifying mistakes. There are ghost stories, such as the tales of the beautiful woman who sheds her skin at night and sucks human blood so that she can assume her lovely shape in the morning.

Other tales describe quests for buried treasure, such as the story about Morgan's Bluff on the island of Andros, where buccaneer Henry Morgan was said to have hidden his fortune. Sometimes a spirit comes to a person in a dream and tells where to find a buried treasure. In some stories, a ghost appears to a treasure seeker in midday; to keep the ghost from melting away before it can divulge the location of the loot, the treasure seeker must cut a finger and let the blood drip on the ghost, or must surround it with a circle of corn. These rituals may be linked to obeah, the voodoo-like rites practiced by Bahamian slaves.

Many Bahamian stories close with a bit of nonsense, such as "When I die, bury me in a pot of candle grease" or "The monkey chewed tobacco and spit white lime." Others conclude with a silly ditty: "E-bo-ban, my story's end/if you don't believe my story's true/ask my captain and my crew." These flourishes may be rooted in African oral tradition or possibly in English tales such as this one, which ends: "Be bow bended, my story's ended/If you don't like it, you may mend it/a piece of puddin' for telling a good 'un/a piece of pie for telling a lie."

Folk medicine, like folktales, still survives in the Bahamas, particularly on the far-flung Family Islands. Few doctors live on the remote cays in the eastern Bahamas, and well-stocked pharmacies are few and far between. When islanders catch a cold or the flu, they resort to bush medicine. A few remedies that keep the sniffles away: an infusion of the leaves of the gale-of-the-wind plant, with a dash of lime and salt (drink it steaming hot); or tea made from the leaves of horsebush or salvebush or the bark of a sweetwood tree. (The bark of a relative of the sweetwood tree is used to flavor Campari, the Italian liqueur.)

Aloe (or aloes, as it's often called here) is a universal cure-all, the Bahamian equivalent of ginseng. Sunburn, acne, and insect bites are treated by splitting one of the plant's fleshy leaves and rubbing the sticky green juice on the skin. Peeled slices of the leaves are said to alleviate constipation, and diabetics drink a liquid made by soaking aloe in water overnight.

Visitors who spend an hour or so with a Bahamian herbalist — there are even a few in Nassau — will learn all sorts of things. Rheumatism is treated with an infusion of mango leaves; gout is soothed by tea made from the bark of the lignum vitae. (The bark of this tree, whose name means "wood of life" in Latin, was used for centuries in a potion for treating syphilis.) Children who come down with chicken pox are told to soak in a bath sprinkled with twigs from a pigeon pea bush; those who have measles bathe in water steeped with leaves from the tamarind tree. The juice of the prickly pear is said to cure dandruff, and hypertension is soothed with infusions made from the leaves of soursop or breadfruit trees.

BAHAMA CRAFTS

In colonial days, when resources were scarce, women wove baskets and mats out of straw or palmetto fronds. The craft has become a national cottage industry, and women can learn the art in government-sponsored classes. Their wares are displayed at markets in Freeport and Nassau. (Most are unbearably touristy.) Take care if you buy: Some baskets are woven outside the Bahamas and are hand-finished on the islands. If you look hard, though, you can find authentic pieces. Some have lacy openwork, some are tightly whorled, and many are brightly colored. They're woven in traditional designs with lovely names like shark's teeth, Jacob's ladder, Bahama mama, fish gill, lace-edge, and peas 'n' grits.

THE ISLANDS

BAHAMAS

The Bahamas are in a class of their own. They're not Caribbean, for the archipelago is just a bit too far north. They're not Bermuda, though many Bermudians settled there early on. And they're definitely not America, though Bimini is closer to Florida than Miami is to Palm Beach.

It's too easy to classify the Bahamas as a generic tropical resort: the sort of place where you sit, rum cocktail in hand, looking out over a perfect stretch of white sand, and an endless expanse of turquoise blue ocean beyond that. Not that there aren't great beaches, and not that the Bahamas don't have their share of tropical clichés. But though the casinos may seem a bit dated — is that Eydie Gormé singing in the bar? — and the straw markets and Bay Street souvenir shops are just a mite too commercial, that's not all there is to see there. If you're willing to explore, if you don't mind an occasional bumpy road or desultory ferry schedule or islands where people communicate by CB radio and where goats outnumber TV sets, the Bahamas can be very much worth the trip. And the culture here — junkanoo dances, rake-and-scrape bands, goombay music, rollicking island ballads and sea chanteys, sizzling-hot cooking — is lively and unique.

Tourists discovered the Bahamas during the Gatsby era, sometime after World War I. But the crowds didn't start arriving for another 20 or 30 years. The cream of British society had been coming here for ages — Neville Chamberlain ran a sisal plantation on Andros, Lord Mountbatten and Sir Winston Churchill came here for a bit of sun, and the Duke of Windsor came here to dabble in politics after he gave up the throne to marry Wallis Warfield Simpson. But then the brash North Americans took over, and the tourist industry really took off. Sir Harry Oakes, who had made a fortune in Canadian gold mines, set about building Nassau hotels. Railroad baron and Florida real-estate developer Henry Flagler launched several projects here. So did American entrepreneur Wallace Groves, who built Freeport from the ground up during the early 1950s.

Early on, tourists generally came to the Bahamas in the winter, and the hotels in Nassau were shuttered for the rest of the year. When the big resorts were built here in the 1950s, the pattern started to change. The Bahamas, like Florida, finally discovered summer. Of the 3.5 million tourists who visited the islands in 1990, a good number came during the off-season — even in the hottest days in June and July. Over the years, the islands have begun to attract a different crowd. Though Prince Charles and Princess Di may hop over for a brief stay on Windermere Island, most of the tourists who vacation here are more average types. And unlike the majority of the crowd that came here not so long ago, many visitors don't just come to gamble at the casinos in Nassau and to shop on Bay Street and in the malls in Lucaya. Cable Beach, just west of the capital, Nassau, on New Providence, attracts some 400,000 visitors a year, as does tiny Paradise Island, just across the bridge from downtown Nassau. And the Family Islands — once known to Juan Trippe, Henry Luce, and God alone — are finally being discovered by adventuresome tourists.

The question is whether you will like what you find here. And the answer is, "That depends." For dedicated divers, yachtsmen, and fishermen, the response is 99% yes. Most gamblers and many golfers will be happy in Freeport/Lucaya and Nassau/Paradise Island, where the casinos and championship golf courses make up for the lack of authentic island atmosphere. And cruise ship crowds and diminishing chic notwithstanding, parts of New Providence — pretty old buildings, fringe-topped surreys, straw-market hustle — and Paradise Island still have viable charms. If you haven't returned recently, you're in for a pleasant surprise: Most of the dowager hotels have been spiffed up, and work continues on a long-range, multimillion-dollar harbor expansion of the Port of Nassau.

But the quest to build a tourist's paradise here hasn't always been easy. In the early days of self-government — ages ago, in the mid-1960s — many visitors to Nassau and Freeport were met with a distinctly chilly reception. (Blessedly, most of the Family Islanders remained as gracious as ever.) But time and the persistent efforts by both the government and local hoteliers have had some effect. Despite a government that seems mired in self-interest, scandal, and indifference, the island economy seems to be on the upswing. And many Bahamians have come to the realization — cynical or not — that tourism is vital to their own prosperity and interests. That doesn't mean there still aren't difficulties and discourtesies between islanders and visitors, but relationships seem to be getting better and a bit more pleasant.

BAHAMAS AT-A-GLANCE

FROM THE AIR: Counting every reef, rock, and bump, there are some 700 islands and 2,000 cays in the Bahamas, scattered over 90,000 square miles of the Atlantic Ocean. The archipelago stretches for 760 miles, from Bimini, just 50 miles off the coast of Florida, to a point just above the Windward Passage separating Cuba and Haiti.

The city of Nassau, the Bahamas' capital and chief port of entry, is at 25°05' N latitude, 77°25' W longitude on the island of New Providence, near the middle of the group. The Bahamas' other major resort center — also with an international jetport — is Freeport/Lucaya on Grand Bahama Island, less than 60 miles east of Florida. The flight from Miami to Nassau or Freeport takes less than 45 minutes; New York is 1,100 miles and 2½ hours by air; Toronto, 1,500 miles and 3 hours.

SPECIAL PLACES: The favored destination for tourists since rumrunners came here to squander their fortunes in Prohibition days, New Providence is still worth a visit. Though the scene on Paradise Island has gotten a bit threadbare, and the casinos in Nassau and Cable Beach are as packed as a stadium on *Super Bowl Sunday,* there is still plenty of genuine excitement and charm to be found here. Nassau has more historic buildings and museums than any other town in the Bahamas. Lyford Cay, the super-exclusive residential neighborhood on the west end of New Providence Island, with its grand mansions tucked behind the palmettos and casuarinas, is really the only remaining echo of days as a chic retreat for the rich and famous. (Hire a guide to find the hideaways of various luminaries, from Prime Minister Lynden Pindling to pop singer Julio Iglesias.) Freeport and Lucaya, on the other hand, are of hardly any historical interest, unless you're 16 and the Cuban missile crisis and the *Beatles* seem antediluvian, for they date from the 1950s and early 1960s. But if baccarat is your game and pristine white beaches your passion, you won't find Freeport/Lucaya disappointing. Tourists who crave tradition should jump in a car — preferably one with sturdy shocks — and tool down to the village of West End at the western (where else) tip of Grand Bahama. The road winds by a handful of fishing villages, some secluded coves — great for diving and bonefishing — and tropical gardens before it runs smack into the center of West End, where smugglers plied a brisk trade in Al Capone's heyday.

All the Bahamian isles, with the exception of New Providence and Grand Bahama and their neighboring cays (pronounced *keys*), come under the rubric of the Family Islands (which include the Abacos, Andros, the Berry Islands, Bimini, Cat Island, Eleuthera, San Salvador, and the Exumas). Colonial traditions are stronger here than they are on New Providence and Grand Bahama, and some towns — Harbour Island just off Eleuthera, Hope Town just off Great Abaco — look like Cape Cod with palm trees. A few of the islands were discovered by adventuresome tourists some time ago, and have well-developed resorts, marinas, and dive facilities. Walker's Cay in the Abacos, George Town in the Exumas, and Windermere Island off Eleuthera — to name just a few — have world class resorts and/or water sports facilities. Game fishermen set their compasses straight for Alice Town on North Bimini, which is an angler's paradise. Accommodations and amenities on some islands range from good to rustic to primitive, but that doesn't mean they should be passed by. The amenities on Cat Island and historic San Salvador (supposedly Columbus's first landing in the New World) are hardly luxurious, but they both have terrific beaches and diving spots. And if you're looking for tradition, Cat Island has plenty of it: If you're lucky, you might hear a rake-and-scrape band, or see a wedding couple dancing an old English quadrille. The giant reef off the east coast of Andros is a must for serious divers, and blue-water sailors head for the secluded anchorages in the Abacos and the Exumas. But the islands aren't just for sports fanatics. You can stroll on a rose-tinted beach and search for sand dollars, watch a regatta, visit a historic hermitage or a tropical garden, or dine on barbecued spiny lobster at a deserted cove.

- **EXTRA SPECIAL:** The 25-year-old *Underwater Explorers Society* (*UNEXSO*) is one of the most successful dive operations in the world. Located across from the *Lucayan Beach* hotel, the complex includes such marine attractions as the *Museum of Underwater Exploration,* featuring displays, movies, and multimedia presentations depicting Bahamian dives and deep-sea discoveries. Another attraction, the "Dolphin Experience," lets visitors swim with six dolphins ($59 per person), while a new program, the only one of its kind, permits scuba divers to see and swim with wild dolphins in the open ocean. "Shark Shot Reef" allows divers to hold and be photographed with sharks (fiberglass, that is). Non-divers can take resort or full-certification courses here, taught by highly qualified staff. Videotapes of your experiences are also available (phone: 373-1250; dive shop, 373-1244; in the US, 800-992-DIVE).

- **ANOTHER EXTRA SPECIAL:** The Bahamaian government's People-to-People Programme has a roster of more than 500 islanders lined up to entertain interested visitors with a "truly Bahamian experience." Hosts and guests are matched ac-

124 BAHAMAS / Local Sources and Resources

cording to mutual interests and hobbies. To participate, contact the People-to-People coordinator (phone: 326-5371), your hotel's social desk, or a tourist office information bureau. It's free.

■ **THE OUTLYING ISLANDS:** The seven primary Family, or Out, Islands — including the picturesque Abacos (Great Abaco, Little Abaco, and its neighboring cays); Andros, the largest of the Bahamas; Bimini, famous for its game fishing; Cat Island, once home to Sidney Poitier; history-rich Eleuthera and San Salvador; and the incredible diving sites off the Exumas — are covered in detail in DIRECTIONS.

LOCAL SOURCES AND RESOURCES

LOCAL TOURIST INFORMATION: In Nassau, the tourist offices offer information on special events, sightseeing advice, arrangements for the abovementioned People-to-People Programme, and answers to any questions. They are open daily at four locations: two at the airport, one in the arrivals area (8:15 AM to 10:30 PM; phone: 327-6833) and the other in the departure area (9 AM to 5 PM; phone: 327-6782); and two downtown, in Rawson Square (8:30 AM to 5:30 PM; phone: 328-7810) and at Prince George Dock (8:30 AM to 4:30 PM; phone: 325-9155). On Grand Bahama, there's a Visitors' Information Centre at Port Lucaya (phone: 373-8988), at the airport (phone: 352-2052), and at the *International Bazaar* (9 AM to 5 PM weekdays; 10 AM to 2 PM Saturdays; closed Sundays and holidays; phone: 352-6909). At present, there are two tourist offices on the Family Islands: On Andros, the North Andros Tourist Office is in Nicholl's Town (phone: 329-2167); on Eleuthera, the tourist office is at Governor's Harbour (phone: 332-2142 or 332-2143).

The Bahamas Ministry of Tourism's Treasure Card, available at no charge to US citizens visiting the Bahamas, entitles travelers to discounts of up to 50% at participating restaurants, shops, and attractions throughout the islands. For more infomation, contact the tourism office or your hotel desk.

Local Coverage – Several digest-size guides, free to visitors and available locally, provide current information on shopping, sightseeing, restaurants, nightspots, island food, and lore. These include *What-to-Do: Nassau, Cable Beach & Paradise Island; Pocket Guide to the Bahamas; Dining and Entertainment Guide: Nassau, Cable Beach, Paradise Island;* and *Best Buys in the Bahamas.* The *Bahamas Handbook* ($13.95) goes into Bahamian life in depth for the benefit of potential (business) investors and those considering buying property or moving to the islands. The quarterly *Bahamas* magazine carries full-color features on island destinations and tourism industry news.

On the Family Islands, *Abaco Life*, available at the Abaco Chamber of Commerce, provides current information about the island; the *Family Islands Travel and Map Guide* is available at no charge at some Bahamas hotels and through the Bahamas Family Islands Promotion Board, 1100 Lee Wagener Blvd., Suite 206, Ft. Lauderdale, FL 33315 (phone: 305-359-8099).

Two daily newspapers are published in Nassau: the *Tribune* and the *Nassau Guardian*. The *Freeport News* is published in Freeport. *The New York Times, Wall Street Journal, USA Today,* and *Miami Herald* are available on newsstands on the day of publication; other major North American newspapers are also flown in daily.

TELEPHONE: The area code for the Bahamas is 809.

GETTING AROUND: Taxi – Readily available at airports and hotels in Nassau and Freeport. Cabs are metered at rates fixed by law: $2 for the first quarter mile and 30¢ for each additional quarter mile for one or two passengers; $3 for each additional passenger, 50¢ for each bag in excess of two; children under 3, no charge. Approximate fares for one or two passengers from Nassau International Airport: to downtown Nassau, $16; to Cable Beach hotels, $12; to *Divi Bahamas Beach,* $10; to East Bay Street hotels, $18; to Paradise Island (including $2 toll), $23. From Freeport International Airport to hotels in the Freeport or Lucaya area, about $8. On the outlying islands, the unmetered taxi rates may run slightly higher but are negotiable. The usual tip is 15% of the fare. Many taxi drivers are good, knowledgeable, and/or amusing guides to their particular islands. Ask your hotel to recommend one; rates in Nassau and Freeport are about $15 to $20 per hour for a five-passenger cab.

On the Family Islands, taxis are available at the individual island airports. Approximate fares for two passengers are as follows: on the Abacos, $10; Andros, $20; Bimini, $3; Cat Island, $45; Eleuthera, $20 to $40; Harbour Island (off Eleuthera), $11 for taxi to ferry and taxi to hotel from ferry; San Salvador, $10; the Exumas, $25.

Jitney – Minibuses run from outlying sections of New Providence to downtown Nassau at rates starting from 50¢, and in Freeport bus rides between Freeport and Lucaya cost 75¢. They're fast, inexpensive, and comfortable. Many Cable Beach and Paradise Island hotels provide free shopping bus service to Rawson Square for their guests several times a day.

Car Rental – Daily rates with unlimited mileage range from about $70 to $110, depending on make of car and season; weekly rates range from $300 to $550. Gas, which runs about 20 to 30¢ more per gallon than in the US, is extra. There are a number of local rental agencies operating in the Nassau–Cable Beach–Paradise Island area, including *Hilton* (phone: 322-4080); *McCartney* (phone: 328-0486); *Poinciana* (phone: 393-1720); *Teglo* (phone: 362-4361); and *Wallace* (phone: 393-0650). In addition, international agencies in Nassau include *Avis* (phone: 363-6380; airport, 327-7121; Paradise Island, 363-2061); *Budget* (phone: airport, 327-9000; Paradise Island, 363-3095); and *National* (phone: airport, 327-7301; downtown, 325-3716). In Freeport, rental agencies include *Avis* (phone: airport, 352-7666; Lucaya, 353-1102); *Hertz* (phone: airport, 352-9250; Lucaya, 373-1444); and *National* (phone: airport, 352-9308; *Xanadu Beach* hotel, 352-6782, ext. 1000).

You can also rent a car on some outlying islands, but it won't be a late model, and chances are it will have traveled some pretty rough roads before it gets to you. So be sure to check its tires (including the spare) and general condition, and listen to the motor before accepting delivery. There isn't always a phone handy in case of a breakdown. On Great Abaco, try *H & L Car Rentals* (in Marsh Harbour; phone: 367-2840 or 367-2854); on Eleuthera, *El-Nik's Rent-A-Car* (in Palmetto Point; phone: 332-2523 or 332-2538), *Munroe's Rental Cars* (in Tarpum Bay; phone: 334-4245), or *Dingle Motors Service* (in Rock Sound; phone: 334-2031); on Great Exuma, *Exuma Transport* (in George Town; phone: 336-2101).

US and Canadian driver's licenses are valid, but remember: *Drive on the left.*

Motor scooter rentals are increasingly popular in Nassau, at Cable Beach, and on Paradise Island, as well as in Freeport/Lucaya; they're also available on Eleuthera and in George Town, Great Exuma. Hotels have their own stands or will direct you to the nearest outlet. Rates run about $23 to $28 (plus a $20 deposit) per bike for an 8 or 9 AM to 5 PM day; most have an extra seat behind the driver. Standard two-wheel bikes rent for about $10 a day.

Sightseeing Bus Tours – Local operators offer a wide variety of sightseeing tours on both New Providence and Grand Bahama islands — though it's more fun to explore Nassau on your own (walking, in a buggy, on a motor scooter, or with a taxi driver; for further information, see walking/driving tours in DIRECTIONS). And there isn't that much to a Freeport tour. The *Great Bahama Taxi Union* offers 3-hour taxi tours to groups for $15 per person, or limo tours for 2 people for $35 per hour (phone: 352-7858; airport taxi stand, 352-7101). Your hotel travel desk is the best place to find out what's offered and for how much. *Majestic Tours* (phone: 322-2606) runs, among other things, a nightclub tour of Nassau and Paradise Island that has garnered rave reviews. If you're hesitant about roaming on your own, ask your hotel travel desk to book a table for the dinner show at Peanuts Taylor's *Drumbeat Club* (Bahamian sounds) in Nassau, at *Le Cabaret Theatre* (Vegas-style glitter) on Paradise Island, the *Crystal Palace Theater* at Cable Beach (see *Nightlife* for further suggestions) — and get a good driver to take you and bring you home.

At least once — maybe for part of a Nassau tour — take your pick of the fringe-topped surreys lined up at Rawson Square or on Frederick Street, just off Bay Street, and clip-clop around town for a while. Often a horse with a hat you admire has a driver you'll like, too. His commentary will be worth the $10 per hour for up to three people. The Freeport alternative: sociable buses that make a 2-hour all-around tour for about $12.50 to $15 per person.

Sea Excursions – Small glass-bottom boats at the Prince George Wharf charge about $10 per person for an hour's Sea Gardens tour, but the ultimate glass-bottom trip is aboard the 97-foot *Nautilus,* departing from Deveaux Street Dock (off Bay St.; phone: 325-2871 or 325-2876). This "surface submarine" charges $15 per person for a 2-hour daytime harbor/Sea Gardens cruise, or $25 for the night ride (which includes dinner at *Capt. Nemo's*). Also Nassau-based is the catamaran *Tropic Bird,* which sails from Prince George Wharf for a 3-hour sea tour with music by a goombay band and a swim on a remote beach; departures are at 10:15 AM Mondays through Saturdays ($15 per person; phone: 322-4941 or 322-1340). The sailing schooner *Wild Harp* leaves the *Yacht Haven*'s dock for a lunch cruise with calypso music and a swim on a secluded Rose Island beach; about $35 per person includes wine and an island picnic (10 AM daily, returning 2 PM; sunset supper cruises too; phone: 322-1149). The *Calypso* has a similar excursion to isolated Blue Lagoon Island for about $35 per person (phone: 363-3577 or 363-3578). In Freeport/Lucaya many boat trips are available, including the "World's Biggest Glass-Bottom Boat," which leaves the *Lucayan Beach* resort dock at 10:30 AM, 12:30 PM, and 2:30 PM daily for tours of the reefs off the coast (12$ per person; phone: 373-1269). In both Nassau and Freeport/Lucaya, hotel tour desks can provide information on other picnic and cocktail sails.

Mail-boat trips that connect the outlying islands with Nassau and Freeport and with each other can provide offbeat travel inexpensively. For example, from Potter's Cay Dock, Nassau, to South Andros, a 4- to 6-hour trip, usually on Tuesdays (schedules are haphazard), costs about $20 per person one way; but book an island bed before you leave.

Local Air Services – There are no prepackaged local air tours, but *Bahamasair* (phone: 327-8451), Nassau's *Trans Island Airways* (phone: 327-8329), Ft. Lauderdale's *Red Aircraft* (phone: 305-523-9624), and Freeport's *Taino Air Service* (phone: 352-8885 or 352-8886) are available for charter island-hopping trips; rates are based on mileage and size of aircraft. More than 45,000 private planes fly into the Bahamas each year. They're required to land first at an official port of entry (West End on Grand Bahama and South Bimini are the two closest to the US), and to file a Declaration of Private Aircraft (forms available at most US airports) and the usual immigration cards distributed on arrival. An air navigation chart is free from any tourist office branch. There are small-plane landing strips in the Abacos, on Andros, the Berry Islands, Bimini, Cat Island, Eleuthera, the Exumas, Long Island, and San Salvador — among others. Most of the Bahamas' 52 airports and strips have 100-octane fuel. Pilots can get up-to-date information by calling the Bahamas Pilot Briefing Center (phone: in the US, 800-327-7678).

SPECIAL EVENTS: Holidays when shops and businesses are closed are *New Year's Day, Good Friday, Easter Monday, Whitmonday* (seventh Monday after *Easter*), *Labour Day* (first Friday in June), *Independence Day* (July 10), *Emancipation Day* (first Monday in August), *Discovery* — or *Columbus* — *Day* (October 12), *Christmas,* and *Boxing Day* (December 26). Both *Boxing Day* (December 26) and *New Year's Day* are occasions for junkanoo parades, with celebrants in fantastic crêpe-paper costumes and masks bounding along to the rhythm of cowbells, goatskin drums, and whistles. Goombay, the ongoing summer celebration, offers visitors a variety of folklore and cultural events.

Special events on the sporting calendar are too numerous to list, but among the most famous are more than 20 annual sport fishing tournaments, including the prestigious 6-tournament *Bahamas Billfish Championship* competition, which begins in March and ends in June. Popular regattas include the *Family Island Regatta,* held each April at George Town, Great Exuma; *Regatta Time,* held in June at Marsh Harbour, Great Abaco; and the *Green Turtle Yacht Club Regatta Week,* a July event at Green Turtle Cay, off Great Abaco. Information on these and other sporting events — golf and tennis tournaments, windsurfing competitions, powerboat races, and all the rest — is available through the Bahamas Sports Line (phone: in the US, 800-32-SPORT).

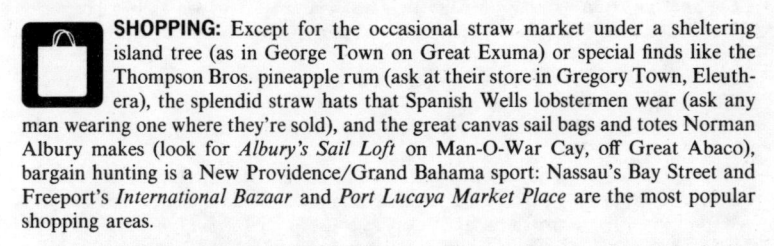

SHOPPING: Except for the occasional straw market under a sheltering island tree (as in George Town on Great Exuma) or special finds like the Thompson Bros. pineapple rum (ask at their store in Gregory Town, Eleuthera), the splendid straw hats that Spanish Wells lobstermen wear (ask any man wearing one where they're sold), and the great canvas sail bags and totes Norman Albury makes (look for *Albury's Sail Loft* on Man-O-War Cay, off Great Abaco), bargain hunting is a New Providence/Grand Bahama sport: Nassau's Bay Street and Freeport's *International Bazaar* and *Port Lucaya Market Place* are the most popular shopping areas.

■ **Good News:** The Bahamian government has abolished customs duty on a wide variety of goods, including china, crystal, and glass; perfume; jewelry; clocks and watches; leather goods; cameras and photographic accessories; linen; sweaters; and liquor, making the Bahamas competitive with many of the islands in the Caribbean in the duty-free category.

There are particularly good bargains on Japanese and European merchandise, though not all imported goods cost less in the Bahamas than in the US. A department store catalogue brought along for on-the-spot price comparisons will be a big help; otherwise, do some pre-trip browsing at home and take notes. Be sure to check prices in stateside discount outlets, particularly if you intend to shop for cameras or electronic equipment, because Bahamian savings on these items are usually quoted as X percent below a "manufacturer's suggested list price" — which is normally higher than you'd have to pay at home. And don't buy an unfamiliar brand of watch, camera, radio, tape recorder, or anything else that might need repairs without making sure there's a stateside service shop that will honor its warranty. Some final advice: Save steps by checking a local source like *Best Buys in the Bahamas, What-to-Do,* or the *Pocket Guide* to find out which stores specialize in the things for which you're looking, and start out early to find the stores least crowded and the salespeople most cheerful.

Local crafts — mostly straw items from hats to handbags, totes, baskets, and the like — are the raison d'être for the *Straw Market,* in its own big building (at the foot of Market St., on Bay), where bargaining before you buy is accepted and expected.

Most shops are open Mondays through Saturdays from 9 AM to 5 PM, and, in Freeport, sometimes until 6 PM. A few close one afternoon a week (usually on Thursdays, Fridays, or Saturdays).

NASSAU

Ambrosine – The toniest boutique in town, it features designer-name fashions. Marlborough St. between West and Nassau Sts. (phone: 322-4205).

Barry's – Big on everything British — woolen sweaters, suits, men's furnishings; also *guayabera* shirts, dashikis, and gold, silver, and jade jewelry. Bay and George Sts. (phone: 322-3118).

Bernard's – Substantial savings on Wedgwood and Royal Copenhagen china, Baccarat and Lalique crystal, Ernest Borel Swiss watches, gold jewelry. Bay St. between Charlotte and Parliament Sts. (phone: 322-2841).

Brass and Leather Shop – Imported English and European horse brasses, teapots, bookends, lots of gift ideas; plus good-looking belts, wallets, luggage from *Gucci* and *Bottega Veneta.* Charlotte St. just off Bay St. (phone: 322-3806).

Cartier – Jewelry, watches, scarves, pens, sunglasses, and other items from this exclusive French house. Bay St., opposite *Nassau Shop* (phone: 322-4391).

Cellar Wine Shop – Just as the name suggests: a large stock of wines. Two locations: Bay and Charlotte Sts. (phone: 322-4164) and *British Colonial Beach Resort Arcade* (phone: 322-8911).

Coin of the Realm – Maps, stamps, coins, and numismatic souvenirs. Charlotte St. off Bay St. (phone: 322-4862 or 322-4497).

Cole's of Nassau – Designer swimwear and sports clothes. Bay St. (phone: 322-8393).

Fendi – Clothes from the famous designer. Charlotte and Bay Sts. (phone: 322-6300).

Gold & Diamonds – Gold Bahamian charms; jewelry made from gold coins recovered from Spanish treasure ships. Bay St. opposite the *Straw Market* (phone: 322-1851).

Greenfire – For Colombian emeralds "direct to you, at substantial savings." At the *Paradise Towers* hotel (phone: 363-2748).

Gucci – Designer fashions for men and women from this famous label. Bay St. and Bank La. (phone: 325-0561).

Island Shop – Scores and scores of books: novels, mysteries, best sellers, and all kinds of information on the Bahamas; film and camera supplies. Frederick and Bay Sts. (phone: 322-4183).

John Bull – The town's best selection of cameras and accessories, plus Rolex and Seiko watches; also an extensive jewelry collection, Limoges porcelain, English bone china, crystal, and calypso records. Bay St. between East St. and Elizabeth Ave. (phone: 322-3328/9).

K. F. Butler – Large stock of whiskey, rum, and liqueurs at good prices. Marlborough and West Sts. (phone: 322-2092).

Leather Shop – Handbags, belts, and accessories by Ted Lapidus, Lanvin, and others. Two locations: Saffey Sq. on Bank La. (phone: 325-1454) and Parliament St. off Bay St. (phone: 322-7597).

BAHAMAS / Local Sources and Resources 129

Lightbourn's – Biggest perfume selection in town, at even bigger savings. Bay and George Sts. (phone 322-2095).

Linen and Lace – All sorts of lavish table and bed linen up to and including hibiscus-embroidered tea cozies, printed linen tea towels attractive enough for wall hangings. Bay St. (phone: 322-4266).

Little Switzerland – China, crystal, figurines, silver, jewelry, watches, coins, antiques, and perfume. Three locations: Bay Street, opposite the Royal Bank of Canada (phone: 322-2201); Bay and Charlotte Streets (phone: 325-7554); and Bay Street, opposite the *Straw Market* (phone: 322-1239).

Marlborough Antiques – Maps and prints; limited-edition artwork; Georgian, Victorian, and Edwardian furniture, bric-a-brac, and collectibles from the UK. Corner of Marlborough and Queen Sts. (phone: 328-0502).

Nassau Shop – The town's largest department store, it has good buys on French perfume, watches, jewelry, British knitwear for men and women. Bay St., between Frederick and Charlotte Sts. (phone: 322-8405/6).

Perfume Shop – Fragrances for women and men at 20% to 40% off US prices. Bay and Frederick Sts. (phone: 322-2375).

Pipes of Peace – Pipes, cigars, cigarettes, lighters, plus cameras and English candies. Bay St. between Charlotte and Parliament Sts. (phone: 325-2022).

Pyfrom's – The town's biggest stock of out-and-out souvenirs — dolls, steel drums, Nassau T-shirts and sweatshirts, you name it. Bay St. between Frederick and Charlotte Sts. (phone: 322-2603).

Scottish Shop – Tams, clan jewelry, tartan ties, scarves, and kilts. Charlotte St. off Bay St. (phone: 322-4720).

Solomon's Mines – Suitably dazzling collection of bone china, Waterford and Swedish crystal, figurines, jewelry. In the Bernard Sunley Building, Bay St. (phone: 322-8502).

Treasure Box – Nicely done conch and coral jewelry. Bay St. near Market St. (phone: 322-1662).

Treasure Traders – Imported china, crystal, and cutlery. Bay and George Sts. (phone: 322-8521/2).

FREEPORT/LUCAYA

The big *International Bazaar* is so full of so many things that it can get quite confusing. Started some 20 years ago, in the past few years it had become slightly run-down. A refurbishment, however, has given it a new look, and junkanoo parades are now held every afternoon. Don't try to sort it out without a map (pick one up at the Tourist Information Centre near the Scandinavian Section) and your list of comparative prices.

Basically there are two sorts of merchandise for sale: imports that are bargains because there is no customs duty on them, and imports that may be good buys because you like them, but for which you'd pay about the same price back home. One Nassau shop — *Pipes of Peace* (see listing above) — has bazaar branches selling similar merchandise. The big *Ginza* import store is the Freeport version of Nassau's *John Bull*, with similar buys on cameras, watches, jewelry, and more. *Solomon's Mines* is good for china, crystal, and pottery. *Midnight Sun* stocks all the best Scandinavian names — crystal by Iittala, Kosta, Orrefors, Holmegard; Bing & Grøndahl, Royal Copenhagen porcelain — plus Daum, Lalique, and Baccarat, most at 25% or more below US prices. *Thai Crystallery* and the *Discount Bazaar* are also centers for import bargain shopping. And don't overlook *Port Lucaya,* Freeport's multimillion-dollar marketplace with 85 boutiques, 23 restaurants, bars, and specialty food shops, 40 straw vendors, 11 arts and crafts shops, and daily Bahamian entertainment, near the *Lucayan Beach* resort.

Azteca de Oro – Bright Mexican shirts, caftans, jewelry. In the Spanish section of the *International Bazaar* (phone: 352-5545).

Bahamian Tings – Featured here are gift items and souvenirs. Poplar Crescent, west of the center of Freeport (phone: 352-9550).

Bata – Lots of shoes for men and women. Downtown, in the *Churchill Square Shopping Centre* (phone: 352-7545).

CariBah – Great island batik cloth and clothes made from it. At the *International Bazaar* (phone: 352-5946).

Far East Traders – For lace tablecloths and linen (don't miss the shell shop upstairs). In the Hong Kong section of the *International Bazaar* (phone: 352-5369).

Fragrance of the Bahamas – Mix your own special scent at this perfumery. In the *International Bazaar* (phone: 352-9391).

Freeport Jewelers – The main lures are 18-karat gold chains and other fine jewelry. In the *International Bazaar* (phone: 352-2004).

Gucci – Watches, handbags, scarves, shoes, and wallets from the famous designer. In the *International Bazaar* (phone: 352-4580).

Island Galleria – Handsome jewelry (especially coral, crystal, china, and artworks). In the *International Bazaar* (phone: 352-8194).

London Pacesetter – British imports and sports clothes. In the *International Bazaar* (phone: 352-2929).

Mademoiselle – European fashions for young and old. In the Hong Kong section of the *International Bazaar* (phone: 352-9182).

Parfum de Paris – Everything scentsible from France. In the French section of the *International Bazaar* (phone: 352-8164).

Penny Lane – Pretty, exotic things from the Orient. In the *Port Lucaya Marketplace* (phone: 373-2263).

UNEXSO – Gift items, Oriental designs. Port Lucaya, opposite the *Lucayan Beach* hotel (phone: 373-1244).

SPORTS: To first-rate golf, tennis, and every kind of water sport, the Bahamas adds a toll-free hotline to handle queries on sporting events and facilities throughout the islands: Dial 800-32-SPORT (more prosaically, 800-327-7678.) Meanwhile, you'll find:

Boating – Lots of possibilities on both a large and small scale. Most island hotels have Sailfish, Sunfish, and sometimes Hobie Cats to rent (about $15 to $30 for the first hour, $10 per hour after that) for small-craft sailing. Island resorts often have Boston Whalers or other outboards available, at widely varying rental rates (they're sometimes free to guests).

For yachting enthusiasts, the Bahamas' calm open waters, safe bays, and vast number of anchorages (not to mention the swimming and diving waters found in and near them) make this an exceptionally fine cruising area. All sizes and types of boats are available for charter to experienced skippers. Arrangements can be made through a travel agent, your hotel, and specialists like *Nassau Yacht Haven* (phone: 393-8173).

On the outlying islands, *Abaco Bahamas Charters* (Hope Town on Elbow Cay; phone: in the US, 800-626-5690 or 800-327-2276) and *Marsh Harbour Marina* (Marsh Harbour on Great Abaco; phone: 367-2700) also offer boats for charter. Bareboat charters are a specialty of *Bahamas Yachting Services* (at Marsh Harbour on Great Abaco; phone: 367-2080; in the US, 800-327-2276).

Well-equipped marinas on a number of islands provide water, fuel, food, ice, showers, and sometimes a bed for the night. In the Nassau/Paradise Island and Cable Beach areas, they include *Hurricane Hole Marina* (phone: 363-3600); *Nassau Yacht Haven* (phone: 393-8173); and *Nassau Harbour Club* (phone: 393-0771). On Grand Bahama: *Lucayan Harbour Inn Marina* (phone: 373-8888); *Running Mon Marina* (phone: 352-6834); and *Xanadu Marina* (phone: 352-6782, ext. 1421).

Marinas on the outlying islands include the following: In the Abacos: *Green Turtle Marina* (phone: 367-2572); *Marsh Harbour Marina* (phone: 367-2700); and *Conch Inn Marina* (phone: 367-2800). On Andros: *Andros Beach Hotel Marina* (phone: 329-2582). In the Berry Islands: *Great Harbour Cay Marina* (367-8123) and *Chub Cay Marina* (phone: 325-1490). On Bimini: *Bimini Blue Water* (phone: 347-2166); *Brown's Marina* (phone: 347-2227); and *Weech's Docks* (phone: 347-2028) — all on North Bimini. On Harbour Island, off Eleuthera: *Romora Bay Club* (phone: 333-2325) and *Valentine's Yacht Club* (phone: 333-2142). On Spanish Wells, off Eleuthera: *Spanish Wells Beach* resort (phone: 333-4371). In the Exumas, on Staniel Cay: *Happy People Marina* (phone: 355-2008). On Long Island: *Stella Maris Marina & Yacht Club* (phone: 336-2106).

For complete detailed cruising information — including small charts, landfall sketches, anchorages, and approach descriptions — *The Yachtsman's Guide to the Bahamas* is invaluable; it's $22.95, plus postage, from Tropic Isle Publishers, PO Box 610935, N. Miami, FL 33261-0935 (phone: 305-893-4277).

Cricket – This cousin of US baseball is played on pitches (fields) ranging from exquisitely manicured greens to vacant lots. Cricket is a spectator sport that is also a social event, much like *Carnival*. For upcoming matches, check with the tourist board of the island you plan to visit or consult the sports section of the island newspaper.

Golf – In a very, very flat country, the design experts have managed to craft an amazing number of challenging courses — 14 full-scale 18-holers and several 9-holers. Grand Bahama is the champ with five: in Freeport/Lucaya, the two 18-hole courses at the *Princess Tower* (phone: 352-6721), the *Ocean Reef Golf and Country Club* (phone: 373-4662), the *Atlantik Beach* resort's *Lucaya Golf and Country Club* (phone: 373-1066), and the *Fortune Hills Golf and Country Club* (phone: 373-4500). Nassau and Paradise Island have four 18-hole championship golf courses between them: the *Cable Beach Golf Club* (phone: 327-6000), *Divi Bahamas Beach Resort and Country Club* (phone: 362-4391), *Paradise Island Golf Club* (phone: 363-3925), and *Lyford Cay Club* (private membership only).

There are also golf courses on the outlying islands at *Great Harbour Cay* in the Berry Islands (9 holes; phone: 367-8838; in the US, 800-343-7256), and at the *Cotton Bay Club* (18 holes; phone: 334-6156) on Eleuthera. All 18-hole courses have complete facilities: rental carts and clubs and resident pros. Greens fees average $15 to $20 a round in winter, somewhat less in summer.

Horseback Riding – Along lanes of casuarinas and sea grape–lined beaches, it's a beautiful way to go — especially in the early morning. There are stables at Coral Harbour on New Providence (*Happy Trails;* phone: 323-5613) and in Freeport (*Pinetree Stables;* phone: 373-3600). A 1½-hour ride costs about $20.

Kayaking – An ideal way to explore hard-to-get-to areas, kayaking is fast becoming a popular activity in the Bahamas. Kayaks are almost impossible to capsize, move faster than canoes, are relatively easy to maneuver, and can even be equipped with sail rigs. *Ibis Tours* offers 8-day kayaking expeditions through the Exuma cays; the outfit provides kayaks, life jackets, tents, sleeping bags, mattress pads, food, and even pillows. The trip costs about $1,000, and novices are welcome. For more information, write to *Ibis Tours,* 5798 Sunpoint Circle, Boynton Beach, FL 33437, or call 800-525-9411.

Regattas – All year long, for both sail and power boats. Among the major annual events: the *Miami-Nassau Race* and *Nassau Cup Yacht Race* in February (sometimes March); *Bahamas "500" Powerboat Race* in June; *Regatta Time in Abaco* in late June and early July; *Green Turtle Yacht Club Regatta Week* in July; *Cat Island Regatta* in August; *Discovery Day Regatta* in October; and the *Miami-Nassau Powerboat Race* in December. Most fun: the *Family Island Regatta* (sometimes pronounced *regretta*), a fierce competition for island workboats held every April in George Town in the Exumas. There are only two rules: Don't bump, and throw no man overboard. Every

132 BAHAMAS / Local Sources and Resources

vessel that can goes to George Town to race or watch, making this one of the all-time great parties afloat and ashore.

Shelling – Escorted tours for shell collectors — either wading or snorkeling — on Eleuthera include round-trip air transfers, hotel, and daily guided trips to the shelling area. Contact *Shells of the Seas,* PO Box 1418, Ft. Lauderdale, FL 33302 (phone: 305-763-7516).

Snorkeling and Scuba – Incredible visibility, scores of reefs and drop-offs close to shore, and the rich variety of Bahamian marine life make a number of these islands great sites for underwater exploration. Masks and flippers can be borrowed or rented for a small fee (usually less than $5 a day) at almost every hotel beach, and snorkeling is casual fun at all of them. First-rate guides and instruction are available at many island sites. These are some of the best:

In Nassau/Cable Beach/Paradise: All hotels can arrange for certified instruction, many at their own pools and off their own beaches through qualified concessionaires. *Peter Hughes's Dive South Ocean* (at the *Divi Bahamas Beach Resort and Country Club;* phone: 362-4391), *Bahama Divers* (at the *Pilot House;* phone: 393-5644 or 393-1466), and *Nassau Undersea Adventures* (phone: 327-7862) rent scuba and snorkeling equipment and arrange diving trips. Among the best sites are Rose Island Reefs close to Nassau harbor (a good place for novices to try their fins); the wreck of the *Mahoney* (a steel-hulled ship sunk in 30 feet of water just outside the harbor); Goulding Cay Reefs at the far western end of the island (favorite "set" for underwater movies); Gambier Deep Reef off Gambier Village (80 to 90 feet down); Green Cay heads and elkhorn coral stands (off Green Cay, 40-foot depth); Booby Rock Channel (large fish population, strong current; boat needed); South Side reefs (tiny, isolated reefs; good snorkeling, bad boating due to shallowness); and Clifton Pier Drop-off, off the south shore of New Providence (sheer drop starting at 110 feet; for experienced divers only).

In Freeport/Lucaya: The *Underwater Explorers Society (UNEXSO;* phone: 373-1250; in the US, 800-992-DIVE; the "Dolphin Experience" and dive shop, phone: 373-1244) has what is certainly the most complete setup for instruction and dive trips in the islands, and probably one of the best anywhere in the world — including an instruction tank 18 feet deep where beginners can really master fundamentals to a degree impossible in shallow hotel pools. They're tops in all departments. Interesting dive sites around Grand Bahama include Treasure Reef, where the $1.2-million Lucaya Treasure was discovered in 1964; the Wall and Black Forest Ledge (a 1-mile drop-off starting 125 feet down off the south shore); Zoo Hole, 5 miles west of Lucaya (fantastic fish variety); the Caves (heavy reef coral formations, very tame fish); and *Theo's Wreck* (a 230-foot steel freighter on its side in 100 feet of water, perched on a ledge), the object of a scheduled dive every Wednesday. *UNEXSO* also offers the "Dolphin Experience," the only program in the world that allows scuba divers to mingle with free swimming wild dolphins in the open ocean.

On the outlying islands: In the Abacos, rentals and dive trips can be arranged at *Dive Abaco* (Marsh Harbour; phone: 367-2014 or 367-2787) and *Walker's Cay Dive Shop* (Walker's Cay; phone: 352-4671 or 352-5252; in the US, 800-432-2092). The best diving spots are coral-lined Devil's Hole, 2,000-acre Pelican Cay National Park (between Lynyard and Tilloo cays south of Marsh Harbour); also Scotland, Spanish, and Deep Water cays, and the wreck of the Union warship USS *Adirondack,* 20 feet down. On Andros, *Small Hope Bay Lodge* (near Fresh Creek; phone: 368-2014; in the US, 800-223-6961) has complete dive facilities and offers resort course, rentals, trips, and underwater photography courses; so does *Andros Undersea Adventures* (at the *Andros Beach* hotel at Nicholl's Town; phone: 329-2582; in Florida, 305-359-0065; elsewhere in the US, 800-327-8150). The Andros Barrier Reef, 12 to 20 feet down, with its deep outside drop-off and plunging blue holes, is a truly spectacular site. On Bimini, *Bimini*

Undersea Adventures (on North Bimini; phone: 347-2089; in Florida, 305-763-2188; in the rest of the US, 800-327-8150) provides boat and equipment rentals and guided dive trips; the most intriguing sites are the submarine stone formations off North Bimini, believed by some to be the remains of the Lost Continent of Atlantis, and more than a dozen sunken ships off North Rock Light and South Bimini. In the Exumas, *Exuma Divers* (in George Town; phone: 336-2710) and *Exuma Aquatics* (at the *Pieces of Eight* hotel outside George Town; phone: 336-2600) have dive boats and equipment; the Exuma National Land and Sea Park sea gardens 3 to 10 feet below the water's surface are beautiful for snorkeling; Thunderball Grotto (at Staniel Cay), Mystery Cave (off Stocking Island near George Town), and the wreck of a 1560 privateer (off Highborne Cay) are the best dive sites. On the main island of Eleuthera, equipment and information are available at the *Cotton Bay Club* (near Rock Sound; phone: 334-2101); dive sites include the maze of coral reefs in Six Shilling Channel between Eleuthera and Nassau, a steamship wreck off the northern coast, Egg Island reef northwest of Current, and — are you ready? — a wrecked *train* that went down with a Cuba-bound barge off North Eleuthera. On Harbour Island, the *Romora Bay Club* (south of Dunmore Town; phone: 333-2325) is fully equipped for instruction and trips; *Valentine's Yacht Club* (phone: 333-2142) also boasts a first-rate scuba/snorkeling/fishing setup. On Spanish Wells, off Eleuthera, *Spanish Wells Beach* resort club (phone: 333-4371) provides facilities for its own guests and others. In the Berry Islands, the *Chub Cay Club* (phone: 325-1490) has diving equipment, boats; sites include Mamma Rhoda Rock, Whale Cay reefs, Hoffman Cay, and a mystery wreck with cannon between Little Stirrup and Great Stirrup cays. On Long Island, *Stella Maris Inn* (phone: 336-2106) features snorkel trips and has a diving center.

Spectator Sports – Cricket, soccer, and rugby are played in season on *Haynes Oval* near Fort Charlotte in Nassau and on fields in Freeport and throughout the islands. Weekends are the big game times; consult local newspapers for specific schedules and details. At this writing there is no horse racing in the Bahamas.

Sport Fishing – Bahamian waters are great grounds for tuna (Allison, bluefin), barracuda, amberjack, bonefish, marlin (blue and white), dolphin, grouper, kingfish, sailfish, tarpon, and wahoo. More than 20 tournaments open to residents and visitors are scheduled every year, including the annual 6-tournament *Bahamas Billfish Championship,* beginning in March and ending in June. Fishermen out of Bimini alone hold 50 world's records. Hotels and marinas can arrange fishing trips. Rates for parties of two to six — including boat, crew, fuel, bait, and tackle — run from about $300 for a half day up to about $500 for a full day's sport.

Swimming and Sunning – There are hundreds of miles of sandy beach on these 700 islands: from dusty pink to gleaming white; long, shining expanses and small crescent coves — all washed by a sea that is truly, incredibly clear. If you're staying in Nassau, on Cable Beach, on Paradise Island, or in Freeport/Lucaya, chances are your hotel will be built on its own stretch of sand; if not, it will have made arrangements for its guests to use a beach close at hand. On the islands, the beach is either right there or a short stroll away. And many hotels have pools. But that's only the beginning. Whatever your hotel's facilities, there's lots more shore out there waiting when you feel the need for a change of beach scene. Among the most beautiful: Saunders Beach and Love Beach on the north shore of New Providence (Nassau's island) and Adelaide and South Beach on its south shore; Paradise Beach and the *Pirate's Cove Holiday Inn*'s perfect semicircular cove on Paradise Island; Taino Beach on Grand Bahama. Great Harbour Cay, on the Berry Islands — one of the handsomest beaches in the Bahamas — offers good shelling.

The outlying islands also boast some excellent beaches. There are 2 miles of fine white sand lining the shore at Staniard Creek on Andros; Stocking Island off George Town

134 BAHAMAS / Local Sources and Resources

on Great Exuma (an ideal destination for day sailing trips, private picnics); the fantastic length of pink beach on Harbour Island, off Eleuthera; the miles-long coral sand shore east of Governor's Harbour, Eleuthera; and the whole sandy rim of unspoiled Mayaguana, a virtually undiscovered island east of Acklins Island, with no accommodations but the best shelling in the Bahamas.

Tennis – The largest court complex is at the *Club Med* on Paradise Island, with 20 clay-composition courts (8 lighted), plus a full staff of instructors, instant replay TV, ball machines, and all the latest teaching paraphernalia; *Club Med* on San Salvador features 12 courts. On Paradise Island are 12 so-so courts for day or night play at the *Paradise Island* resort, another 9 Har-Tru at the *Ocean Club* (4 lighted), and courts at the *Harbour Cove Inn, Marriott Beach Club, Pirate's Cove Holiday Inn,* and *Sheraton Grand.* On Cable Beach, the *Nassau Beach* hotel has 6 courts, the *Ambassador Beach* has 8, and the *Crystal Palace* has 12; the *Divi Bahamas Beach* hotel has 4 courts at the southwestern corner of New Providence. Hotels with tennis facilities in the Freeport/Lucaya area include the *Atlantik Beach* (8 courts), *Bahamas Princess* (12 courts), *Radisson Resort on Lucaya Beach* (2), and *Xanadu Beach* (3); on the outlying islands, the *Cotton Bay Club* on Eleuthera also has a top layout (4). Court time usually is free to guests and available to non-guests at a fee of about $5 to $7 an hour, more for night play.

Water Skiing – The best sea sites are off Nassau's Cable Beach, around Paradise Island, and on the protected waters around Freeport/Lucaya; some of the larger outlying island resorts (Eleuthera's *Club Med,* for example) also have boats and equipment, though most prefer to concentrate on diving; rates run from about $15 and up for a 20-minute tow. Nassau/Paradise and Freeport/Lucaya also offer parasailing on a parachute towed behind a speedboat (about $25 a ride) and spinnaker flying (riding a trapeze suspended from a wind-filled sail).

Windsurfing – Increasingly popular, especially on Nassau's Cable Beach (site of the *Annual Bahamas International Windsurfing Regatta*) and on Paradise Island; at Grand Bahama's *Atlantik Beach* resort.

Windsurfing on the outlying islands is available in the Abacos at Hope Town, Walker's Cay, and Green Turtle Cay; on Harbour Island, just off Eleuthera; on Andros; at Pittstown Point on Crooked Island; and at *Stella Maris* on Long Island. More and more water sports centers offer sailboard rentals, too.

NIGHTLIFE: Though some islands tend to be quiet after dinner — with maybe a little bar talk or terrace sitting — there's plenty happening on the Nassau/Paradise Island scene and in Freeport/Lucaya. Nassau/Paradise offers the greatest variety, starting with two casinos — the enormous *Paradise Island Casino* and the similarly enormous *Crystal Palace Casino,* a purple extravaganza on Cable Beach (a reincarnation of the casino at the former *Cable Beach* hotel). Accessible from the latter are the *Crystal Palace's* 800-seat *Palace Theater,* where the Las Vegas–style show, *Jubilation,* takes the stage nightly (admission: $30 per person, or $40 for dinner and the show; phone: 327-6200), and the 2-story *Fanta-Z Disco.* At the *Paradise Island* resort, next door to its casino, the 550-seat *Le Cabaret Theatre* stages big, girly, Vegas-gone-island-type shows nightly except Sundays (admission: $27 per person, show only, or $42 for dinner and the show; phone: 363-3000); the resort's *Tradewinds Calypso Show Lounge* features Bahamian entertainment. Also on Paradise Island, the *Paradise Island Casino's Club Pastiche* and the *Holiday Inn's Pirate's Cove* are the discos to know. Out Cable Beach way, besides the *Crystal Palace* spots, one of the liveliest hotel scenes is apt to be the *Nassau Beach's Rum Keg* — loud and crowded with dancers. There are jumping "island" shows (flaming limbos, drums, frenetic dancers) at the *Nassau Beach* hotel on Thursday "Junkanoo" nights. But wonder-drummer Peanuts Taylor's *Drumbeat Club* (on West Bay St.; phone: 322-4233) is more fun and lots more genuinely Bahamian; and run, don't walk, to hear a singer named Eloise wherever she's playing — she's a one-woman special event. Also on West Bay Street, at Saunders Beach, is the *Colosseum,* which features a band that plays Bahamian music, reggae, and disco. Open until 3 AM (phone: 322-7195). Another late-night venue with live music is the *Waterloo* (on East Bay St.; phone: 393-1108).

In Freeport/Lucaya, most nightly events take place near the *Princess Casino,* where you can play for keeps until 4 AM; the *Casino Royale Theatre* is the big showplace. A second casino is at the *Lucayan Beach* resort, which also has a revue, at the *Flamingo Showcase Theatre.* The *Sultan's Tent* disco at the *Princess Tower* is worth checking out, as is the *John B. Club,* also at the *Princess,* which also offers live Bahamian music. Lucaya's hot spot, *Club Estee,* is also a big sound scene. Island shows play the *Castaways* and *Yellow Bird.*

BEST ON THE ISLANDS

CHECKING IN: After a shakedown and realignment period that yielded substantial improvements in the government properties, the hotel situation in Nassau/Paradise Island and Freeport/Lucaya has improved significantly, with many major resorts spending millions of dollars on much-needed renovations and room refurbishment. Meanwhile, established inns on the outlying islands — with their stunning beaches, relaxed sports, and genuinely personal service — continue to delight repeat guests.

Most Nassau/Paradise and Freeport/Lucaya hotels quote European Plan (EP) rates (without meals); more resorts on the islands beyond — where there aren't that many places to eat out — include breakfasts and dinners (Modified American Plan, MAP), sometimes all meals (American Plan, AP), in their rates. A 4% government room tax plus a 4% resort levy are added to all hotel bills, and many hotels now add a 10% or 15% service charge to the bills. Expect to pay $150 and up in winter for a double room without meals in a hotel listed here as expensive; between $100 and $145 in one designated moderate; and less than $100 in inexpensive digs. Some hotels offer MAP add-ons (covering breakfast and dinner) for about $20 to $45 per person a day. Between late April and mid-December, prices in all categories drop by about 30% to 50%. All telephone numbers are in the 809 area code unless otherwise indicated.

NASSAU–CABLE BEACH, NEW PROVIDENCE

Ambassador Beach – A Wyndham property, this U-shape 400-room structure has 1,800 feet of white sand beach, a pool, 8 tennis courts, and several bars and restaurants. Water sports, including scuba diving and fishing, are available. It's across the road from the *Cable Beach* golf course. On Cable Beach (phone: 327-8231; in the US, 800-822-4200; fax: 327-6727). Expensive.

Coral World Villas – Here, on the private island of Silver Cay, close to Nassau's harbor entrance, are 22 individually decorated villas, each with a kitchenette and private swimming pool. Guests enjoy complimentary ferryboat service to the mainland and free admission to the *Coral World* aquatic attractions. Silver Cay (phone: 328-1036; in the US, 800-328-8814; fax: 323-3202). Expensive.

Crystal Palace – *Carnival Cruise Lines'* $240-million, 1,539-room resort — the largest in the Bahamas — is a popular place to stay in the Nassau–Cable Beach area. Rooms are dispersed among the Casino Tower, also called the Crystal Tower, built on the site of the former *Emerald Beach* hotel, the recently renovated Riviera Tower, formerly the *Cable Beach* hotel, and the four Palace Towers. The candy-colored Crystal Tower has 255 luxury rooms with lovely sea views; the Riviera Tower nearby adds another 672 rooms and suites to the count; and the Palace Towers have 612 rooms. The property boasts a bewildering array of bars, restaurants, and recreation areas, a casino that vies with the one on Paradise Island as the largest in the Bahamas, a spectacular cabaret and 2-story disco, extensive sands, a landscaped pool deck with 100-foot water slide, two lagoons, facilities for sail sports, snorkeling, and scuba, 18 holes of golf, 12 tennis courts (5 lighted), and 3 racquetball and 3 squash courts. On Cable Beach (phone: 327-6000 or 327-7070; in the US, 800-222-7466; fax: 327-6801). Expensive.

Graycliff – The very small (12 rooms, 2 suites) and quietly elegant former home of Lord and Lady Dudley, across from Government House. No sports, but grassy gardens, a small pool, and the atmosphere of a genteel private house. Perfect for the discriminating clientele it attracts; far from the casino and glitter mobs. A member of the prestigious Relais & Châteaux group, it boasts the island's best restaurant (see *Eating Out*). West Hill St. (phone: 322-2796; fax: 326-6110). Expensive.

Le Meridien Royal Bahamian – Retains its quiet elegance and the feel of a private club, which it once was. There are 145 good-size rooms in its 6-story Manor House tower, and 25 more in 10 garden-surrounded villas (2 with private pools, sunrooms, wet bars, whirlpool baths in master suites) that offer special concierge service. Health spa, big pool terrace, beach with extensive water sports, outdoor café and handsome dining room, cocktail and evening entertainment in season. On Cable Beach (phone: 327-6400; in the US, 800-543-4300; fax: 327-6961). Expensive.

Nassau Beach – A 410-room fixture in the heart of Cable Beach, the liveliest, most jovial on this shore. Lots of land and water sports; planned activities; happenings day and night; the *Beef Cellar* (see *Eating Out*) and other restaurants, including, next door, the *Frilsham House,* are under the same management. Tennis and non-motorized water sports at no extra charge. Good choice if you're up for convivial but not overpowering action. A Forte hotel. On Cable Beach (phone: 327-7711; in the US, 800-225-5843; fax: 327-7615). Expensive.

British Colonial – Once the social queen of them all (along with the late, lamented *Royal Victoria*), the pink palace, affiliated with Best Western, these days has 325 guestrooms, fresh-faced public rooms, the highly recommended *Bayside Buffet* (see *Eating Out*), as well as another restaurant, *Blackbeard's,* and ... *McDonald's.* The grande dame has lost much of her elegant charm, but the location — in the heart of Nassau at No. 1 Bay Street — is still prime. Bay St. (phone: 322-3301; in the US, 800-327-0787; fax: 322-2286). Moderate.

Casuarinas of Cable Beach – This attractive, homey, 76-apartment complex offers a choice of 1- or 2-bedroom, efficiency, and studio setups. Rec room, pools on site; other sports and activities arranged by staff. Pool bar; the *Round House* restaurant specializes in Bahamian food, for about 60% of what you'd pay in casino hotels (see *Eating Out*). Owner Nettie Symonette, a well-known local businesswoman, has trained her staff in the art of personalized service — one of this resort's attractions. West Bay St. on Cable Beach (phone: 327-7921 or 327-8153; in the US, 800-327-3012; fax: 327-8152). Moderate.

Ocean Spray – Directly across the street from Lighthouse Beach and a short stroll to West Bay Street, with 30 rooms, an open sun roof overlooking the ocean, and a European-style restaurant (phone: 322-8032; in the US, 800-327-0787; fax: 325-5731). Moderate.

Pilot House – Across from the marina, a great favorite with sailors and people who like informal, but pleasant, personal service. The quality level of the accommodations in this 125-room hotel has fallen lately, however, with considerable wear and tear now visible. Ask to see the room first. Small pool, 2 restaurants; there's also alfresco dining in the garden. Off East Bay St. (phone: 393-3930; fax: 393-7887). Moderate.

Towne – Simple, in town, personably managed, with 46 rooms. Friendly, but no frills; favorite for short stays, business travelers. There is a small swimming pool, and the restaurant serves island specialties. George St. (phone: 322-8450; in the US, 800-327-0787; fax: 328-1512). Moderate to inexpensive.

Olympia – Near Lighthouse Beach just west of downtown, with 50 refurbished and air conditioned rooms, some with balconies and sea views. There's also a lively pub and a restaurant on the premises. West Bay St. (phone: 322-4971; in the US, 800-327-0787; fax: 325-2938). Inexpensive.

Parthenon – On the edge of downtown Nassau, with 18 air conditioned rooms, each with a porch or patio. Arrangements can be made for golf, tennis, fishing, sailing, water skiing, and island tours. West St. (phone: 322-2643; in the US, 800-327-0787). Inexpensive.

PARADISE ISLAND

Merv Griffin's Paradise Island – The resort's two main buildings were once separate hotels in their own right. With the *Paradise Island* resort and casino, they make up what was, until the advent of *Carnival's Crystal Palace,* the most extensive resort complex in the Bahamas, offering a total of more than 1,200 guestrooms and suites, an 18-hole championship golf course, 2 health clubs, a shopping arcade, 2 pools, 12 tennis courts, and 3 miles on Cabbage Beach. Guests have their choice of a dozen restaurants (see *Eating Out* for a few of them) and another dozen bars and nightclubs, not to mention the dinner theater (*Le Cabaret Theatre*) at the casino, which, at 30,000 square feet, is one of the largest gaming facilities in the world. The Paradise Concierge program offers VIP floors with separate check-in, concierge services, separate elevators with passkeys, and a hospitality lounge. Included in the room count is the luxury wing on the beach devoted exclusively to guests of Club Paradise, an all-inclusive — everything from sports to meals — package program (phone: in the US, 800-321-3000; in Miami, 305-895-2922; in Ft. Lauderdale, 305-462-1370; fax: 363-3703). Expensive.

Ocean Club – Built in the 1930s as a private home (2 colonnaded stories around a pink patio), bought by millionaire Huntington Hartford in the 1950s, who converted it to an exclusive club, and owned since the 1960s by Resorts International, this is certainly the handsomest place on Paradise Island — or Nassau, for that matter. Secluded, with a backdrop of the Versailles Gardens that Hartford completed, it has 71 balconied rooms, all (except for the 12 simple tennis cabañas) with fans, air conditioning, satellite television, and mini-bars; the 5 private villas have Jacuzzis and enclosed patios. Beautiful big pool, 9 clay tennis courts (4 lighted), beach, golf nearby. Total, quiet luxury with a lovely galleried dining courtyard, the *Courtyard Terrace* (see *Eating Out*), graced with pond and fountain (phone: 363-3000; in the US, 800-321-3000; fax: 363-2501). Expensive.

Sheraton Grand – There are 360 rooms in this recently renovated beachfront high-rise, each with a refrigerator, cable TV, mini-bar, private balcony, and direct-dial phone; the two upper floors, called the Sheraton Towers, are VIP territory — offering use of a special lounge serving complimentary continental breakfast, wine and cheese in the afternoon, and evening cocktails. In addition, there are 12 oceanfront suites; a spectacular array of beach and water sports activities; and the elegant *Rotisserie* restaurant (see *Eating Out*) and the *Verandah and Terrace* restaurant, serving a Wednesday-night Chinese buffet and a Saturday-night Italian buffet. Other features include tennis, a pool with a waterfall, and a shopping arcade (phone: 363-2011; in the US, 800-325-3535; fax: 363-3193). Expensive.

Club Land'Or – Set in a quiet cove on a lagoon opposite the *Paradise Island* resort's Britannia Towers building, this small and charming resort has 72 1-bedroom villas with fully equipped kitchens and private patios or balconies. Facilities include a swimming pool, lovely courtyard, excellent *Blue Lagoon* restaurant (some of the best seafood on the island), and the *Oasis Bar* with piano entertainment. The emphasis is on attentive and personalized service, with an extensive daily activities program (phone: 363-2400; in the US, 800-321-3000; fax: 363-3403). Expensive to moderate.

Harbour Cove Inn – A breezy 250-room high-rise overlooking Nassau Harbour (a water taxi takes guests across to town), with a recently enlarged manmade stretch of sand, a pool, and first-rate tennis courts. It's altogether pleasant and nicely decorated (phone: 363-2561; in the US, 800-223-0888; fax: 363-2561). Expensive to moderate.

Bay View Village – This beautiful, lushly landscaped resort, with privacy its primary attraction, offers 54 1-, 2-, or 3-bedroom units in either villa, townhouse, apartment, or penthouse configurations, all with complete kitchens, private balconies, and patios or garden terraces. Other features include 3 swimming pools, a tennis court, daily maid service, and an extremely charming staff. Five minutes' walk to beaches, casino, and other attractions (phone: 363-2555; in the US, 800-321-3000; fax: 363-2370). Moderate.

Club Med – It has the familiar theme and camaraderie, but with a definite emphasis on tennis (20 courts, teaching staff, TV playback). Plus all the usual *Club Med* pursuits — from morning yoga to late-night disco. Families are welcome; a Mini-Club for children, with supervised activities, gives parents a rest. All double accommodations (300 rooms), with an unusual number of double beds available. Some singles at extra charge. Weekly rates cover all activities (including tennis instruction) and all meals, including house wines (phone: 363-2640; in the US, 800-258-2633). Moderate.

Comfort Suites – Opened in 1991, it has 150 junior suites with satellite TV, serving bars, and coffeemakers. Complimentary continental breakfast; coin-operated laundry on the premises. Near the *Paradise Island* resort and casino, its guests have full access to facilities at the resort (phone: 363-3680; in the US, 800-228-5150; fax: 363-2588). Moderate.

Marriott Beach Club – A time-share ownership division of this hotel chain, it has 44 2-bedroom villas, each with satellite TV, fully equipped kitchen, sunken tubs, and large balcony. Discounts for *Paradise Island* golf course. On the beach, it has 2 pools and 2 tennis courts. PO Box 890, Lakeland, FL (phone: 363-2523; in Florida, 813-688-7700; elsewhere in the US, 800-228-9290). Moderate.

Paradise Paradise – This informal, low-rise hotel is on the beach for which the island was named. It has 100 balconied rooms, a pavilion restaurant, and cocktail lounge; the "sports inclusive" rates (covering sailing, snorkeling, windsurfing, water skiing, hydroslides, day and night tennis, aerobics, volleyball, bicycling, and so on) make it a noteworthy Paradise buy (phone: 363-3000; in the US, 800-321-3000; fax: 363-2540). Moderate.

Pirate's Cove Holiday Inn – Don't even think of associating this resort with most of its roadside American counterparts. Its 535 high-rise rooms rate a luxury label. Features include a setting on Pirate's Cove, a beautiful lagoon with a fine beach, a huge free-form swiming pool, theme poolside buffets, tennis courts, a shopping arcade, a pleasant café (see *Eating Out*), and a host of water sports and guest activities (phone: 363-2100; in the US, 800-HOLIDAY; fax: 363-2206). Moderate.

Sunrise Beach – On the beach with 35 1- and 2-bedroom villas (rental and timeshare), with full kitchens. The setting is lovely, with a pool, grotto, and elegant European-style decor (phone: 363-2308; in the US, 800-451-6078; fax: 363-2308). Moderate.

Villas in Paradise – Comfortable resort accommodations in 25 1- and 2-bedroom apartments and 1- to 4-bedroom villas, 15 of which feature private swimming pools in enclosed patios. All units have fully equipped kitchens and 2 full baths. Complimentary rental car for 1 day is included with a 7-night stay (phone: 363-2998; in the US, 800-321-3000; fax: 363-2703). Moderate.

WESTERN NEW PROVIDENCE ISLAND

Divi Bahamas Beach – In the southwestern corner of the island, it has the Peter Hughes *Dive South Ocean* dive shop and water sports center and an 18-hole Joe Lee–designed golf course with resident pro and complete pro shop to lure guests away from the bright lights and big city. There are 130 beachfront rooms and 120 others with their own patio or terrace, in buildings stretched along a mile and a half of oceanfront property. Two dining rooms, including the elegant *Papagayo* restaurant (phone: 362-4391; in the US, 800-367-3484; fax: 362-4728). Moderate.

GRAND BAHAMA

Deep Water Cay – Small and exclusive, this newly refurbished lodge attracts celebrities and keen sport fishermen. It offers 1 luxury cottage and 7 smaller cottages, a private airstrip, and superb bonefishing. Closed August and September. East End (phone: 359-4831; in Florida, 407-684-3958; fax: 359-4831). Expensive.

Xanadu Beach – This place, which once served as home for the late billionaire Howard Hughes, has been bought by Mexican developers who plan further facelifts for its Cabana Marina wing and multistory Coral Tower, plus improvements to the marina and beachfront. Facilities at this 186-room hotel include a pool, 3 lighted tennis courts, a 70-slip marina for large yachts, 3 restaurants, a disco, and good service. Freeport (phone: 352-6782; fax: 352-5799). Expensive.

Atlantik Beach – A Swiss-owned property, next door to the *Lucayan Beach,* this beachfront resort has 175 guestrooms, including 42 suites with a fresh look, kitchens, TV sets, phones, and mini-bars. Facilities include a good 18-hole golf course at the *Lucaya Golf and Country Club,* which is not far away and owned by the hotel, 8 tennis courts, a beach club on a fine beach, most water sports (including a boardsailing school), a shopping arcade, and 3 restaurants. Lucaya (phone: 373-1444; in the US, 800-622-6770; fax: 373-7481). Expensive to moderate.

Bahamas Princess – Another case where two formerly separate hotels and a casino have been combined into one big resort — 2,500 acres, with extensive public spaces and an essentially group-oriented approach to resort life (intimate island atmosphere is not the strong suit here). Accommodations are in the tower (394 rooms) and the country club (469 rooms). The former, within strolling distance of the *International Bazaar,* adjoins the *Princess Casino* and is more gambling-oriented; the latter, across the road, is more informal. Guests in either wing have access to the property's 2 championship 18-hole golf courses, 12 tennis courts, 2 pools, 9 restaurants (see *Eating Out*), 6 bars, 2 nightclubs, and the casino showroom. No beachfront — guests use the free shuttle bus to the *Xanadu Beach Club,* exclusively for *Xanadu Beach* and *Princess* guests. Inexpensive packages — especially off-season — are available. Freeport (phone: 352-6721 or 352-9661; in the US, 800-223-1818; fax: 352-6842). Expensive to moderate.

Lucayan Beach – This 247-room resort rests on 1½ miles of white sand beach, with a huge casino right on the beach, 4 restaurants, and the *Flamingo Showcase Theatre*, a Las Vegas–style cabaret. The *Underwater Explorers Society* dive shop and water sports center offers guests a full range of aquatic activities. Besides regular hotel rooms, there are more elegant (and pricier) rooms in a beachfront wing, each with private access to the sand from a waterfront balcony (phone: 373-7777; in the US, 800-772-1227). Expensive to moderate.

Radisson Resort on Lucaya Beach – Formerly the *Holiday Inn Lucaya Beach*, this 505-room hotel has been extensively refurbished in a tropical-floral motif and continues to offer a gallery of shops, bars, restaurants, discos, a cabaret, health facilities, and a pool. A popular family resort with a full complement of land, beach, and water sports activities. Lucaya (phone: 373-1333; in the US, 800-835-3597; fax: 373-8662). Expensive to moderate.

Silver Reef – This health spa offers 2- or 7-day packages at its water-view villas. Exercise, "body pampering," hair styling, and collagen treatments available. Lucaya (phone: 373-8802; in the US, 800-458-9772; fax: 373-3332). Expensive to moderate.

Running Mon – Freeport's newest, this pastel-pink marina resort offers 32 cool, comfortable rooms with tile floors and bathrooms. The glass-sided hexagonal restaurant, which serves fresh seafood and Bahamian dishes, overlooks the 66-slip marina, which features a marine supply shop. Free bus service to the *Princess Casino* and the *International Bazaar*, as well as to *Xanadu Beach*. Kelly Court and Knotts Blvd. (phone: 352-6834; fax: 352-6835). Moderate.

Lucayan Marina – An official Bahamas port of entry, on Lucayan Bay, across the water from its sister hotel, the *Lucayan Beach*. It offers 148 rooms, all recently redecorated in soft earth tones; a 150-slip, full-service marina; commissary and restaurant; pool; and free ferry service to the *Lucayan Beach*. Lucaya (phone: 373-8888; in the US, 800-772-1227; fax: 373-2826). Inexpensive.

THE ABACOS

Great Abaco Beach – One of Great Abaco's most charming spots, it has 20 deluxe rooms and 6 luxury villas, all overlooking the water. The hotel adjoins *Boat Harbour Marina*, which boasts 180 slips and complete marina services. An excellent scuba program is offered through the legendary Captain Skeet LaChance's *Dive Abaco*. There also are good restaurants, 2 tennis courts, and lots of camaraderie — the pleasant staff has won many enthusiastic returnees. Marsh Harbour, Great Abaco (phone: 367-2158; in the US, 800-468-4799; fax: 367-2819). Expensive.

Walker's Cay Club – All the comforts (smartly done rooms, restaurant, bar) in a palm-fringed setting with 2 pools, a fine shelling and swimming beach, and a 75-slip marina. All kinds of fishing possibilities — deep-sea, reef, bone, with native guides — plus scuba (certified instruction, choice dive sites). Populated year-round by an eclectic cast of serious sport fishing pros and those chasing world-record billfish. The hotel offers 62 double rooms, 4 villas, and 4 private suites, all with sea views. Packages include airfare from Ft. Lauderdale. Walker's Cay (phone: 352-5252; in Florida, 305-522-1469; in the rest of the US, 800-432-2092; fax: 359-1414). Expensive to moderate.

Abaco Inn – A small gem, ensconced between the Atlantic on one side and the calm blue of White Sound on the other — which means lazy swimming and alfresco dining oceanside, or in the new indoor restaurant. With 12 rooms, a unique swimming pool shaped into the shore by the ocean, first-rate diving, fishing, surfing, and windsurfing. The restaurant is one of the best in the Bahamas, specializing in lobster, snapper, and grouper. This inn is special. Hope Town, Elbow Cay (phone: 366-0133; in the US, 800-468-8799; fax: 366-0113). Moderate.

Bluff House – Perched on a hilltop with a picture-postcard view of the tiny town of New Plymouth, it has 26 rooms and villas. There's a marina, beach, tennis, saltwater pool; sailing, snorkeling, fishing, exploring, and loafing are the favorite local sports. Green Turtle Cay (phone and fax: 365-4247). Moderate.

Conch Inn – A favorite with scuba divers and yachting enthusiasts, this newly renovated inn-marina enclave is full of cheerful charm and affable boating people. Rooms that don't look like much from the land side are fresh and pretty inside, each with a harbor-viewing balcony and air conditioning. The minuscule pool is the scene of large water polo action; fishing, boating, and just sitting on the beach are all easily arranged. The coffee shop serves breakfasts, fine chowder, fritters, fish, and burgers; and there is a small, handsome restaurant. Marsh Harbour, Great Abaco (phone: 367-2800; fax: 367-2890). Moderate.

Green Turtle Club – One of the Abacos' most charming island enclaves, with its own 32-slip marina. It is a center for all sorts of waterborne activity (power- and sailboating, fishing, skiing, and scuba diving). There's a choice of 3 beaches (or the pool); some of the 30 rooms (with French fabrics and hardwood floors) are in cottages with their own boat slips. Sociable evenings and dockside alfresco dining are arranged by the friendly management. Green Turtle Cay (phone: 365-4271; in the US, 800-825-5099; fax: 365-4272). Moderate.

Hope Town Harbour Lodge – A former island commissioner's home is the nucleus of this relaxed resort, with its own dock on one side and beach on the other, right in the heart of Hope Town. Sailing, scuba, snorkeling, water skiing, and deep-sea fishing are all daily possibilities. Next to the swimming pool is a friendly bar that does informal lunches, a traditional meeting spot for locals in this cozy little town. With 21 brightly painted rooms and 1 cottage. Elbow Cay (phone: 366-0095; in the US, 800-626-5690; fax: 366-0286). Moderate.

Lofty Fig Villas – In the heart of Marsh Harbour, each of the 6 cottages of this small, reasonably priced property is furnished in a sea-island motif with glass doors leading onto beautifully landscaped gardens. There also is a pool on the property. Marsh Harbour, Great Abaco (phone: 367-2681). Moderate.

New Plymouth Inn – This charming in-town choice is in New Plymouth's most elegant old residence, beautifully maintained, with high-ceilinged, cozy rooms out of another century. Friendly American management. Green Turtle Cay (phone: 365-4161; fax: 365-4138). Moderate.

Guana Beach – A suitably unpretentious island inn for those who *really* want to get away from it all; with a small marina at the front and a superb beach at the back of the property. The small island is completely ringed by gorgeous, deserted beaches. Friendly bar and extremely informal restaurant. Great Guana Cay (phone: 367-3590). Moderate to inexpensive.

Treasure Cay – Probably the Abacos' finest resort complex, it is clustered around a wide, crescent-shape expanse of exquisite white sand dotted with coconut palms. The property, which boasts a 150-slip marina, has snorkeling, scuba, fishing, sailing, windsurfing, water skiing, and other beach and water sports, as well as an 18-hole golf course and tennis courts. There are 97 spacious, comfortable rooms with sea views and 13 luxury beachfront villas, plus a variety of restaurants that range from haute cuisine to alfresco to buffet. Treasure Cay (phone: 367-2570; in the US, 800-327-1584; fax: 367-3362). Moderate to inexpensive.

ANDROS

Coakley House – This diving resort is just across the bay from *Small Hope Bay Lodge,* its parent establishment. Housed in a mansion that was once owned by the Crown, it sleeps four to six people. Diving is available through *Small Hope Bay Lodge* (phone: 368-2014; in the US, 800-223-6961: fax: 368-2015). Expensive.

Emerald Palms – An elegant seaside spot that has 18 richly decorated poolside rooms with sea views, 2 oceanfront suites, a bar, and a first-rate restaurant. Congo Town (phone: 329-4661; in the US, 800-835-1018; fax: 329-4667). Expensive.

Lighthouse Yacht Club and Marina – A splendid new air conditioned, 20-room (all with king-size beds and TV sets) property, it has a 15-slip marina and diving opportunities available through *Small Hope Bay Lodge.* Also on the premises are a pool and a large restaurant. Andros Town (phone: 368-2308; in the US, 800-825-5099). Expensive.

Andros Beach – This 10-room inn (plus 3 cottages) attracts divers with its *Andros Undersea Adventures Dive Shop.* There's also a lovely beach, a pool, beachside bar, and lush gardens for strolling. Nicholl's Town (phone: 329-2582). Moderate.

Cargill Creek Lodge – Popular with fishermen, this tastefully furnished, Mediterranean-style cottage colony has satellite TV, a gameroom, a dive center, a bar, and a seafood restaurant. Cargill Creek (phone: 329-5129; fax: 329-5046). Moderate.

Small Hope Bay Lodge – A resort for dedicated divers and discriminating travelers, with 20 rooms on a palm-lined beach. Daily diving trips to the reef a mile offshore; underwater photography seminars. Snorkeling, fishing, beach-based hot tub, too. Very informal; management has been known to scissor off neckties on sight. Great relaxed fun, nice people, extended-family atmosphere. The origins of that fabulous, colorful line of Androsia batik fashions are here; ask about the factory. Closed September through October. Fresh Creek (phone: 368-2014; in the US, 800-223-6961; fax: 368-2015). Moderate.

Nottages Cottages – Overlooking Behring Point, this hotel has 10 rooms, a bar, a dining room serving native seafood dishes, and one 2-bedroom cottage. Behring Point (phone: 329-5293). Inexpensive.

BERRY ISLANDS

Chub Cay Club – Condominiums clustered around a complete marina, where life focuses on deep-sea and bonefishing, diving, boating. Only 15 rooms are open for public rental; restaurant, tennis courts, and villas are limited to members. Small commissary on premises. Excellent diving facilities. Chub Cay (phone: 325-1490 or 324-7800; in the US, 800-662-8555). Expensive to moderate.

BIMINI

Bimini Big Game Fishing Club – Exactly what its name says. Simple and friendly, with a marina admirably set up to arrange deep-sea and bonefishing charters. There's a pool, tennis court, and a pair of bars that tend to liven up when the boats come in. With 50 newly refurbished rooms, owned and comfortably run by the Bacardi rum people. Alice Town, North Bimini (phone: 347-2391; fax: 347-2392). Moderate.

Blue Water Marina – A small, simple 12-room inn overlooking the sea, up the hill from the marina, it's home to several fishing tournaments each season, but open to non-anglers, too. Good restaurant and friendly bar. Anchorage, North Bimini (phone: 347-2166; fax: 347-2293). Moderate.

Compleat Angler – Ossie Brown's decades-old hotel is one of the funkiest places in all of the Bahamas. Hemingway used to hang out here, and it still attracts an extraordinary cast of characters. Great people watching at the bar and in the lobby. Bar walls are lined with hundreds of photos, forming a chronology of Bimini's fishing tournament history. Though not for everyone — there are only 12 plain, noisy rooms — this place is worth seeing. Alice Town, North Bimini (phone: 347-2122; in the US, 800-327-0787). Inexpensive.

CAT ISLAND

Fernandez Bay Village – A lovely, lazy group of 11 villas, sized to sleep two to eight people, each individually and appealingly decorated and endowed with all the housekeeping essentials, including maid and laundry service; grocery on property, also a restaurant. Situated on 50 acres of land fronting one of the most beautiful beaches in the Bahamas, it's ideal for swimming, sunning, beachcombing, snorkeling; fishing, small-boat sailing, windsurfing, too. Fernandez Bay (phone: 354-5043; in Florida, 305-792-1905; elsewhere in the US, 800-940-1905). Moderate.

ELEUTHERA

Cotton Bay Club – As one of this island's most luxurious resorts, it has served as the private playground for President George Bush, Richard Nixon, and Sidney Poitier, among lots of other notables. There's great golf (an 18-hole Robert Trent Jones, Sr. course), terrific tennis (4 courts), water sports, fine fishing from the nearby marina, 2 miles of gleaming white sand beach, and an air of deep-seated well-being. Good-looking clubhouse with a small pool and an inviting dining room. There are 77 rooms in clubhouse and beachside cottages, and the acquisition of the neighboring 50-acre estate of industrialist Edgar Kaiser adds a 6-bedroom villa with its own pool to the complex. Near Rock Sound (phone: 334-6156; in the US, 800-223-1588; fax: 334-6082). Expensive.

Windermere Island Club – A discreetly luxurious, tranquil, beautifully cared for islet reached by bridge, where the seclusion-seeking rich and famous (Prince Charles and Princess Di, for example) find the local lifestyle to their liking, spending their days playing tennis, boating, windsurfing, water skiing, bonefishing, snorkeling, or sunning on the private beach or beside the pool. Now owned by the Venice Simplon–Orient Express folks, there are 21 handsome rooms, 10 suites, 7 cottages, 10 apartments; clubhouse with lounge, bar, dining room (ties and jackets at night), occasional entertainment. It's 18 miles from Rock Sound Airport (phone: 332-6003; in the US, 800-237-1236; fax: 332-6002; or write to *Venice Simplon–Orient Express Hotels,* 1155 Ave. of the Americas, New York, NY 10036). Expensive.

Winding Bay – Lining a strip of pink sand beside what was once the beach house of an American millionaire (he was one of the island's original developers), with fishing, diving facilities, small sailboats, and snorkel gear for rent. Two lighted tennis courts, *Cotton Bay Club* golf privileges. There are 36 rooms in good-looking natural stone cottages, all with patios. Near Rock Sound (phone: 334-4055; in the US, 800-835-1017; fax: 334-4057). Expensive.

Club Med Eleuthera – Located 8 miles from Governor's Harbour Airport, this complex has 300 air conditioned, double rooms in beach- and garden-front settings. The village on the property houses a dining room, open-air cocktail lounge, disco and dance floor, theater, and boutique. There is also a pool and 8 tennis courts; a nearby marina offers water sports facilities. Perfect for families, it welcomes children ages 2 and up. Near Governor's Harbour (phone: 332-2270; in the US, 800-CLUB-MED; in New York City, 212-750-1687). Moderate.

Cambridge Villas – Located in the heart of the pineapple-growing area, with 25 air conditioned rooms, all equipped with mini-refrigerators and 4 of them with cooking facilities. A saltwater pool, restaurant, and disco are on premises. Free transportation to beaches, where surfing is good. Gregory Town (phone: 322-0080; in the US, 800-327-0787; fax: 332-0142). Inexpensive.

HARBOUR ISLAND, OFF ELEUTHERA

Dunmore Beach Club – Probably Harbour Island's most exclusive enclave for the shyly rich and famous (it was a private club for 25 years), a favorite with yacht captains. It's small, with only 12 rooms — try to book in the "Pink" or "White" cottages — and renowned as having the best restaurant on the island. There's a long beach, tennis, and a variety of water sports nearby. Near Dunmore Town on Colebrook La. (phone: 333-2200). Expensive.

Ocean View Club – With 9 smartly decorated rooms, this relaxing (some would say decadent) resort caters to Europeans, film crews, fashion models, and the like. Although it is right on the beach, the hotel offers no organized sports. The owner, who shuns publicity, has managed to preserve an aura of mystery about the place. The excellent restaurant, which features long, communal tables, serves continental fare (phone: 333-2276). Expensive.

Romora Bay Club – This lovely inn has a total of 35 rooms in the main house and cottages. Once a private home, it overlooks terraced flower gardens and a small cove. Main-house dinners are an occasion (book a table early, even if you're a hotel guest). Diving and other water sports are very popular. There are scuba (including instruction) and snorkel trips daily, a tennis court, a hot tub, a big beach a few minutes' stroll away, and a coveside pavilion for lunch buffets, sunset gatherings, and informal nighttime entertainment. On Colebrook La. (phone: 333-2325; in the US, 800-327-8286; fax: in Florida, 305-427-2726). Expensive.

Coral Sands – A congenial 33-room complex overlooking the beach, where most guests spend their days. Water sports, free snorkeling, sailing, tennis (charge only for lighting). Known for its delicious home-style food, good wine, inviting atmosphere, and informal and entertaining evenings, especially Fridays. Chapel St. (phone: 333-2350; in the US, 800-468-2799; fax: 333-2368). Expensive to moderate.

Pink Sands – Family resort at the edge of the island's incredibly beautiful pink (honest!) sand beach. Nice sense of privacy in 42 cottage rooms. Three tennis courts, boating; fishing arranged with local skippers. Snorkeling, windsurfing, and Sunfish all complimentary. Dining room, bar. Chapel St. (phone: 333-2030; in the US, 800-729-3524; fax: 333-2060). Expensive to moderate.

Runaway Hill Club – An intimate Bahamian-style inn overlooking a hillside pool and lovely wide beach. Only 8 rooms (the 5 in the main house are best), tastefully (if simply) decorated, with terra cotta floors, white wicker, and *Casablanca*-style ceiling fans. Good restaurant (reservations advised), and a calypso group on Tuesdays in the winter. Closed September through October. A half mile from Dunmore Town (phone: 333-2150; in the US, 800-327-0787). Expensive to moderate.

Valentine's Yacht Club – Right on the sound, this small 21-room inn also has its own pool, and a following of fishing, diving, and yachting folk. Sailing, snorkeling, diving; bone, bottom, or reef fishing arrangements. Informal, but a thoughtful management and staff are always ready to help. Dunmore Town (phone: 333-2142 or 333-2080; in the US, 800-327-0787; fax: 333-2135). Moderate.

EXUMAS

Flamingo Bay – A half mile south of George Town, it's a favorite rendezvous for international yachtsmen. Includes 30 rental villas set in 1,300 acres of hills and beaches. Queen's Highway East (phone: 336-2661). Expensive.

Peace and Plenty – A classic island hostelry with 32 air conditioned rooms and an informal guesthouse atmosphere, agreeable staff. Virtually in town, with a small swimming pool overlooking the harbor. Ferry service to the beach club (with bar and snack service) on beautiful Stocking Island, just across the water. Fishing, sailing, snorkeling arranged. Some evening entertainment. The bar is the local meeting and greeting place. Queen's Highway in George Town (phone: 336-2551; in the US, 800-525-2210; fax: 336-2093). Moderate.

Staniel Cay – This small, private yacht club has cottages with balconies overlooking the marina, a cozy bar, and a restaurant serving native and American seafood dishes. Boating and diving facilities available. Staniel Cay (phone: 355-2024). Moderate.

Two Turtles Inn – A tropical hardwood 2-story-cabin colony set around a stone courtyard overlooking Elizabeth Harbour, it has a good restaurant serving fresh seafood, and a popular bar. Friday night is barbecue night for most local residents. Cycling, boating, and tours of the island can be arranged. George Town (phone: 336-2545; fax: 336-2670). Inexpensive.

LONG ISLAND

Stella Maris Inn – Rambling cottage resort with 50 air conditioned rooms in apartments, cottages, or villas. Extensive diving facilities, including instruction, day and night dives, island day and overnight cruises. Compressors and training tank on premises. Also sailing, fishing, snorkeling, windsurfing, water skiing. Three swimming pools, 2 tennis courts. Informal outdoor patio with fireplace, where barbecues take place Wednesday nights, pool, beach, and cave parties. Stella Maris (phone: 336-2106; in the US, 800-426-0466). Moderate.

RUM CAY

Rum Cay Club – The island's only resort, designed for dedicated divers and snorkelers, it offers authorized *PADI* instruction and certification, deep-sea and sandy-flat fishing programs, hiking, underwater photography, and private charter service from Ft. Lauderdale (phone: in the US, 800-334-6869 or 800-327-8150). Expensive.

SAN SALVADOR

Club Med – Overlooking Bonefish Bay and the sparkling Caribbean waters, this "Columbus Isle" village is ideally situated on 3½ miles of beautiful pristine beach. Guests can engage in all the *Club Med* activities — from morning calisthenics and dancing the night away to supervised programs for adults and children alike. The 300 large rooms are equipped with TV sets and telephones. Weekly rates include all activities (including diving certification and tennis instruction), all meals (with wine at lunch and dinner), and entertainment (phone: in the US, 800-CLUB-MED). Moderate.

Riding Rock Inn – This longtime favorite haunt of scuba buffs has 24 rooms, a pool, tennis, and 4 apartments available for rent. Excellent dive facility, complete with photo lab and instruction. Easy walk to town. Good vacation packages, with airfare included from Ft. Lauderdale (phone: 332-2694, ext. 215; in Florida, 305-359-8353; in the rest of the US, 800-272-1492). Moderate.

EATING OUT: Meals in the larger Nassau/Paradise Island and Freeport/Lucaya hotels tend to be expensive and unimaginative, with too many "turf and surf" specials that do justice to neither the filet mignon nor the lobster tail involved. When it comes to good restaurants, the Freeport/Lucaya choice is limited, and the Family Islands are, with some notable exceptions, lacking in

146 BAHAMAS / Best on the Islands

restaurants that offer much beyond local fare. Nassau does somewhat better, with several places where first-rate chefs use their continental skills to make the most of fresh local fish and seafood (except for chicken, most meat is imported frozen). There are also some tasty Bahamian places where prices — while hardly inexpensive — tend to be somewhat gentler, and the food is home-cooked and good. Favorite island dishes include lots of conch (pronounced *conk*) served as "salad" (ceviche), fritters, chowder, and "cracked" (that is, pounded thin and deep-fried); spiny lobster; baked Bahamian crab; broiled or boiled grouper (the latter a favorite Bahamian breakfast, really a nicely spiced fish stew); and peas (really beans) and rice. On the outlying islands especially, most bread is locally baked — fresh, crusty, and delicious. Sweet, fresh Eleutheran pineapple turns up frequently as a breakfast starter or a dessert. And rum, in just about any form, is the favorite local drink. Expect to pay $60 or more for a meal for two at the restaurants we have listed in the expensive category; $30 to $60 in moderate restaurants; and under $30 in those restaurants considered inexpensive. Prices do not include wine, drinks, or tip. Dining plans appear from time to time, and they are generally a good choice for those who want to dine around, because you usually enjoy unrestricted choices from the menu. All telephone numbers are in the 809 area code unless otherwise indicated.

NASSAU

Beef Cellar – Small, cozy, with a limited menu: appetizer, soup, dessert, and filet mignon — which you broil just the way you like it on a brazier at your table. Reservations advised. Major credit cards accepted. In the *Nassau Beach* hotel, Cable Beach (phone: 327-7711). Expensive.

Buena Vista – In a rambling house built in the early 1800s, one of the pleasantest all-around eating experiences in Nassau. Soothing atmosphere, deft service, excellent food. A number of great grouper recipes (en coquille, au gratin, baked in white wine sauce, or Bahamian-style), delicate veal Buena Vista; incredible cold soufflé desserts. Prettiest in warm weather, when tables are set in the garden. Dinner only; closed Sundays; reservations essential. Jackets not required, but suggested. Major credit cards accepted. Delancey St. (phone: 322-2811). Expensive.

Frilsham House – The former colonial home of a British newspaper baron is now one of Nassau's most sophisticated restaurants, with mahogany furniture, fireplace, and two Bahamian chefs, fresh from France, specializing in continental cooking along with the ever-popular conch chowder. Reservations necessary. Major credit cards accepted. Next to the *Nassau Beach* hotel, Cable Beach (phone: 327-7639). Expensive.

Graycliff – Leisurely continental and Bahamian lunches and dinners served with true English elegance in the house that was once the home of Lord Dudley, the Earl of Staffordshire, and is now a small, Relais & Châteaux–affiliated property. The menu includes perfectly steamed fresh lobster, elegant grilled grouper with white truffles, tender *nodino di vitello* (a special cut of veal rarely found outside Italy), luscious chocolate mousse, and lots more. Cocktails are served in the antiques-filled drawing room; service is perfect, the wine list notable, and the ambience unforgettable. Reservations necessary. Major credit cards accepted. West Hill St. opposite Government House (phone: 322-2796). Expensive.

Ivory Coast – Despite the place's all-pervasive African theme — from carved masks, stuffed animals, and servers in khaki outfits and pith helmets to the cocktail lounge, called the *Casablanca Piano Bar* — the fare consists of mostly grilled, broiled, or smoked meat and seafoods. Reservations advised. Major credit cards accepted. East Bay St. (phone: 393-0478). Expensive.

Sun And . . . – Indoor-outdoor dining around a fountain-centered patio or in a wood-paneled main dining room, depending on the weather. The romantic atmosphere — glinting crystal, silver, candlelight — is a big draw; book well in advance. The conch chowder is memorable, and you might follow it with a poached grouper soufflé, veal piccata, or roast rack of lamb. Dinner only; closed Mondays and the months of August and September. Jackets preferred; reservations necessary. Major credit cards accepted. Lakeview Dr., off East Shirley St. — take a taxi so you won't miss the turn (phone: 393-1205). Expensive.

The Cellar – Choice of dining in an English-style pub or outdoor garden patio on local seafood such as grouper fingers, cracked conch, grouper in white wine sauce, or seafood coquille. Entertainment Monday, Friday, and Saturday evenings. Reservations advised. Major credit cards accepted. 11 Charlotte St. (phone: 322-8877). Moderate.

Mai Tai – For Chinese/Polynesian fare in pleasant surroundings overlooking gardens bordering a lake. Lunch to 3 PM, dinner till midnight. Reservations unnecessary. Major credit cards accepted. Waterloo Lodge, East Bay St. (phone: 393-5106 or 393-3088). Moderate to inexpensive.

Pick-A-Dilly – Continental and Bahamian specialties served in an indoor/outdoor garden (wear a jacket during the winter) complete with tropical birds, and a calypso singer most evenings. Conch chowder, turtle pie, and various curry dishes are specialties. Complimentary salad bar; exotic drinks. The bar is popular with local lawyers at cocktail time. Lunch from 11:30 AM to 4 PM; dinner from 6 to 10:30 PM. Reservations advised. Major credit cards accepted. 18 Parliament St. (phone: 322-2836). Moderate to inexpensive.

Roselawn Café – Italian specialties with live entertainment evenings from 6:30 till late. Open for lunch from 11:30 AM to 2:30 PM. Reservations unnecessary. Major credit cards accepted. Bank La., off Bay St. (phone: 325-1018). Moderate to inexpensive.

Round House – Part of the *Casuarinas* complex out Cable Beach way, where Nettie Symonette does delicious things with old Bahamian recipes — naturally, and especially, fresh fish and seafood. Closed Tuesdays. Reservations necessary. Major credit cards accepted. West Bay St., Cable Beach (phone: 327-7921/2). Moderate to inexpensive.

Tony Roma's – Tender, meaty baby back ribs, crispy loaves of onion rings, and barbecued chicken are the standard fare at the two island outposts of the familiar mainland chain. Reservations unnecessary. Major credit cards accepted. Two locations: East Bay St., at the foot of the Paradise Island Bridge (phone: 393-2077), and West Bay St., at Saunders Beach (phone: 325-6502). Moderate to inexpensive.

Traveller's Rest – Fine Bahamian dishes, great drinks, good Sunday "jump-up" with music. Closed Wednesdays; reservations advised. Major credit cards accepted. This place is 10 miles from Nassau. In Gambier, on West Bay St. (phone: 327-7633). Moderate to inexpensive.

Bayside Buffet – At the *British Colonial,* on the water, it's the best dining value in Nassau for lunch or dinner, if you crave buffet-style extravaganzas, and this one is high quality. Reservations advised. Major credit cards accepted. Bay St. (phone: 322-7479). Inexpensive.

Mandi's Conch – The Bahamas' national dish, prepared every way you can imagine: conch chowder, conch salad, cracked conch, conch fritters, conch burgers . . . Nothing, in fact, but conch, except for side dishes like salads, coleslaw, and French fries. Reservations unnecessary. No credit cards accepted. At the corner of Arundel St. and Mount Royal Ave. in Palmdale; a little out of the way, but well worth the trip (phone: 322-7260). Inexpensive.

Poop Deck – Bahamian favorites like cracked conch and grouper share the menu with steaks and spaghetti. Sandwiches served at lunch. Informal, with a fine marina view; a popular hangout for boating people. Reservations advised. Major credit cards accepted. Nassau Yacht Haven, East Bay St. (phone: 393-8175). Inexpensive.

Tamarind Hill – A delightful inland retreat in a converted Bahamian cottage. The menu is strong on local dishes, and the English beer on tap and the live music are big attractions. Reservations unnecessary. Major credit cards accepted. Village Rd. (phone: 323-1306). Inexpensive.

PARADISE ISLAND

Boathouse – Overlooking Paradise Lagoon, it features steaks sizzled to your taste on tableside grills; seafood, too. Reservations advised. Major credit cards accepted. At the *Merv Griffin Paradise Island* resort (phone: 363-3000). Expensive.

Café Martinique – Gilded dining in a former home surrounded by greenery and water views — an intimate setting rare on Paradise Island. The continental menu is usually skillfully done. Service can vary from excellent to exasperating. But if you're lucky, dinner here can be elegantly rewarding. Reservations necessary. Major credit cards accepted. At the *Merv Griffin Paradise Island* resort (phone: 363-3000). Expensive.

Courtyard Terrace – One of the prettiest dining spots in the Nassau area, it features alfresco dining framed by swaying palms in a galleried courtyard with a fountain. Chefs are Swiss and Irish; service is sometimes slow, but the setting is worth the often only average cuisine. Reservations essential. Major credit cards accepted. At the *Ocean Club* hotel (phone: 363-2501 or 363-3000). Expensive.

Rotisserie – Nothing exotic, but everything done with flair, from appointments and service to food preparation and wine selection. Notable starters include marinated seafood in a *sauce caribe* and cauliflower soup with shrimp. Surf and turf here becomes a superb *filet de boeuf grillé* and *langouste fraîche*. Jackets required. Reservations necessary in season and on weekends. Major credit cards accepted. In the *Sheraton Grand* (phone: 363-2011). Expensive.

Villa d'Este – Another of the deluxe dining places appended to the *Paradise Island* resort complex, in the Britannia Towers. The decor is unconvincing mock Mediterranean, but the menu is Italian with some tasty pasta dishes and plenty of veal — a good place to get away from grouper if you've been here a while. Reservations necessary. Major credit cards accepted. At the *Merv Griffin Paradise Island* resort (phone: 363-3000). Expensive.

Coyaba – A *Trader Vic's* look-alike setting, with excellent Polynesian and Chinese food. Reservations advised. Major credit cards accepted. *Merv Griffin Paradise Island* resort (phone: 363-3000). Expensive to moderate.

Paradise Pavilion – Best view on Paradise Island, right on the water overlooking Nassau Harbour and downtown. The steaks are good; barbecue and seafood satisfactory. Casual dress. Reservations unnecessary. Major credit cards accepted. On the beach between *Paradise Paradise* and *Pirate's Cove Holiday Inn* hotels (phone: 363-3000, ext. 29). Expensive to moderate.

Junkanoo Café – Buried in the *Pirate's Cove Holiday Inn,* it offers an attractive selection of sandwiches, salads, and lighter entrées for lunch and dinner. The grilled chicken breast teriyaki sandwich is filling and fairly priced. No reservations. Major credit cards accepted (phone: 363-2100). Moderate.

Island – The only thing still operating at the old *Chalk's* airline terminal just off Paradise Beach Drive, and the only genuinely Bahamian restaurant on the island. Open for breakfast, lunch, and dinner, with such dishes as boiled fish and grits, conch fritters, stewed conch, chicken, or fish, steamed pork chops, and spareribs, all served with hearty homemade bread. Open daily. No reservations. No credit cards accepted (phone: 363-3153). Inexpensive.

FREEPORT/LUCAYA

Crown Room – Best bet for preshow or pre-casino dining at the *Princess,* although the standard fare, while well prepared and efficiently served, offers no surprises or spices. Closed Mondays. Reservations advised. Major credit cards accepted. *Princess Casino* (phone: 352-6721). Expensive.

Lucayan Country Club – Away from the hotel bustle, popular with residents for its true country club ambience. The menu, in the international Freeport tradition, offers standard fare at top prices. Closed Sunday evenings; reservations advised. Major credit cards accepted. At the *Lucaya Golf and Country Club,* Albacore St. off Sgt. Major Dr. (phone: 373-1066). Expensive.

Rib Room – A snug but unsurprising hideaway that goes the escargots, prime ribs, surf 'n' turf, cherries jubilee route — all nicely done and nicely served. Closed Tuesdays and Wednesdays. Reservations necessary. Major credit cards accepted. In the *Princess Country Club, Princess Tower* (phone: 352-6721). Expensive.

Captain's Charthouse – All kinds of steaks (sirloin, teriyaki, New York strip), prime ribs, lobster and shrimp in season. Reservations advised. Major credit cards accepted. East Sunrise Hwy. at Beachway Dr. (phone: 373-3069). Expensive to moderate.

Guanahani's – Garden and waterfall view, soothing music for a welcome change, if not very exciting fare. Start with deep-fried grouper fingers; then try Bahamian lobster and fish pot or ribs and chicken; chocolate-fruit fondue for dessert. Closed Fridays and Saturdays. Reservations advised. Major credit cards accepted. In the *Princess Country Club, Bahamas Princess* (phone: 352-6721). Expensive to moderate.

Stoned Crab – A breezy beachside eatery on the ocean, with the freshest fish and seafood and steaks broiled over hickory charcoal. Very good drinks; live music Wednesdays through Sundays. Reservations advised. Major credit cards accepted. On Taino Beach (phone: 373-1442). Expensive to moderate.

Buccaneer Club – A Swiss-run spot serving European versions of Bahamian dishes: lobster bisque, conch fritters, broiled lobster, Wiener schnitzel. Its lovely beachside setting is well worth the trip to Deadman's Reef, about half an hour from Freeport. Open from 5 PM for dinner only, although frequent beach parties are arranged. Closed Mondays. Reservations advised. Major credit cards accepted. Complimentary pickup from hotels at 5 and 7 PM — the former is suggested to catch the sunset. Deadman's Reef (phone: 352-5748 or 348-3794). Moderate.

Marcella's – Very good Italian victuals at reasonable prices — it's been going strong for 30 years. Reservations necessary. Major credit cards accepted. East Sunrise Rd., near *Churchill Square* (phone: 352-5085). Moderate.

Pier One – A restaurant on stilts and a longtime favorite for Bahamian specialties, seafood, and sunsets on the waterfront. Reservations necessary. Major credit cards accepted. Freeport Harbour (phone: 352-6674). Moderate.

Taino Beach – An ocean-view eatery, it serves cracked conch, shrimp, steaks, and lamb. No reservations. Major credit cards accepted. Taino Beach (phone: 373-4677). Moderate.

Blackbeard's – Cheerful, rustic spot serving seafood, fresh fish, chicken, ribs; burgers and sandwiches for lunch. Reservations necessary. Major credit cards accepted. On Fortune Beach (phone: 373-2960). Inexpensive.

Fat Man's Nephew – The fat man is no more, nor is his eatery at Pinder's Point, but his nephew carries on in this spot, where tourists and locals dine out on conch specialties, chicken and pork dishes, local lobster. Reservations unnecessary. Major credit cards accepted. *Port Lucaya Marketplace* (phone: 373-8520). Inexpensive.

Freddy's Place – Highly commended by savvy Bahamians. All kinds of conch (salad, chowder, cracked, or steamed), grouper, local lobster (the seafood platter samples all three); plus steaks, daily island specials (pea soup and dumplings, short ribs, souse). Closed Sundays. Reservations unnecessary. Major credit cards accepted. At Hunters Village, Pinder's Point (phone: 352-3250). Inexpensive.

Pub on the Mall – As much for fun as for food. British fare includes fish 'n' chips, steak and kidney pie (on Fridays), Bass ale on tap. Low-priced lunch and dinner specials. Reservations unnecessary. Major credit cards accepted. The mall at Ranfurly Circus (phone: 352-5110 or 352-2700). Inexpensive.

Pusser's Country Store and Pub – A fun place to meet at Port Lucaya, with terrace dining, seafood specials, and exotic rum cocktails. Closed Sundays. Reservations advised. Major credit cards accepted. *Port Lucaya Marketplace* (phone: 373-8450). Inexpensive.

Scorpio's – Authentic Bahamian food — cracked conch, spicy conch salad, turtle steaks, daily specials. Open daily for breakfast, lunch, and dinner. Reservations unnecessary. Major credit cards accepted. Downtown at West Mall Dr. and Explorer's Way (phone: 352-6969). Inexpensive.

Other inexpensive eateries include *Basil's* (phone: 352-8424) and the *Country Squire* (phone: 352-7850) for Bahamian food, and several somewhat successful places among the narrow passageways of the *International Bazaar:* The *Japanese Steak House* (phone: 352-9521) and *China Palace* (phone: 352-7661) are truly ethnic, while *Le Rendezvous* (phone: 352-9610) serves French specialties such as le hamburger and (alas) French fries and ice cream cones; *Café Valencia* (phone: 352-8717) does full Spanish deli service (prime ribs and apple pie, too); and *Café Michel's* (phone: 352-2191) has a French-style pizza.

TURKS & CAICOS

"Turks and *what?*" ask friends when you tell them where you're headed. "Aren't you afraid of the Middle East these days?" "Turks and *where?*" queries the airline reservation clerk. "Are you sure we fly there?" "Turks and Caicos?" ponders an old island hand, showing obvious signs of recognition (you brighten). "Are you going there on purpose?"

It doesn't take long to learn that the rest of the world has rarely, if ever, heard of the Turks & Caicos Islands, in spite of the fact that, anchored 575 miles southeast of Miami, they're considerably closer to the US than Puerto Rico or the Virgin Islands. With a map, a motive, and a reasonably powerful magnifying glass (you'll need all three), you too can find the cluster of tiny land dots (the Turks) and, west of them, the tiny archipelago called the Caicos, roughly 30 miles southeast of Mayaguana in the Bahamas and about 90 miles due north of Haiti. Location and landscape (like most of the Bahamas' Family Islands, they're practically cookie-flat, with shining edges of sand and some low green hills for contrast) should make them part of the Bahamas, which, in fact, they were until 1874, when they were transferred to Jamaican jurisdiction. Since 1962, however, when Jamaica declared its independence, the Turks & Caicos have been a British Crown Colony with a governor appointed by the queen and their own elected ministerial government, which was ushered in by constitutional amendment in 1976.

Six of the eight major islands — Grand Turk and Salt Cay; South, Middle (Grand), and North Caicos; and Providenciales, called Provo — and a few of the 40-some mite-size cays are inhabited. But altogether they encompass only 193 square miles of land, plus an almost equal sprawl of fish-haunted tidal banks. They owe their outsize tourist potential (though until recently almost totally unexploited) to 230 miles of beautiful beaches — much of them untouched by human footprint for days at a time — and to vast surrounding rings of live coral reefs and spectacular drop-offs that lure a small, steady stream of divers from all around the world. And to fishing so fine that the bonefishers who've found it hardly even mention it to one another.

What has deterred other tourists? For years accommodations have been extremely limited, with styles ranging from handsomely simple to downright rustic. Air service to the Turks & Caicos is somewhat erratic, with only *Cayman Airways* flying in regularly from the US. Additionally, the government tourist board's small budget has meant limited promotional efforts and no glossy ads to attract overseas travelers.

But if the islands are just being discovered by tourists today, they were discovered by others long ago. Sometime before the 10th century, Lucaya Indians arrived from islands to the south to settle on Middle Caicos. It is possible that their name — transcribed onto Juan de la Cosa's world map, drawn around 1500, as Yucayo — may have been the root from which the word "Caicos" came. Or it may simply be another version of *cayos,* the Spanish word for keys. There is, however, general agreement that the neighboring Turks isles were named for the barrel-shape native cactus whose scarlet top looks like a Turkish fez.

For years, the islands were thought to have been discovered by Europeans in 1515, when Juan Ponce de León stopped by during his fountain-hunting quest. More recent evidence, supported by historians at the University of Florida and the Smithsonian Institution, suggests that Columbus landed here in 1492. Grand Turk, in fact, may actually be the site of Columbus's first landfall in the New World, rather than the island of San Salvador. During the 16th and 17th centuries, some of the region's most notorious pirates — including bloodthirsty Anne Bonney and marauding Mary Read — found the Caicos convenient for concealment and provisioning. It was not until 1678 that respectable white settlers made their appearance. From Bermuda came Lightbournes, Astwoods, and Butterfields, to rake profit from the wealth of sea salt harvestable on the Turks and South Caicos. Despite the depredations of pirates, a short-lived Spanish invasion in 1710, and three French attacks in the course of the subsequent 70 years, the Bermudians kept returning, rebuilding their salt pans, and sustaining a trade that became a staple of Bermuda's economy. About this time, circa 1787, Gardiners, Williamses, Stubbses, and other Loyalists fleeing the American Revolution arrived to establish plantations on the western Caicos, and they brought slavery with them. By the time slavery was abolished, in 1838, most of those Loyalist plantations were no longer in operation; by the second quarter of the 20th century, the introduction of synthetic fibers had made the sisal industry obsolete. And when the British nationalized salt production in 1951, many whites left the islands for good. But after 3 centuries of intermingling and intermarrying, the old names persist among today's Belongers — the nickname by which Turks Islanders and Caicos men and women are known.

Recently, there have been significant changes in the islands' tourist picture. In 1984, *Club Med Turkoise* opened on a 70-acre section of Provo's 12-mile beach, bringing the first major resort to this British Crown Colony. Direct air service by *Cayman Airways* from Miami to Grand Turk or Provo takes an hour and a half; *Bahamasair* flies from Nassau to South Caicos and Provo in roughly the same time; *Turks and Caicos National Airlines* has flights from Nassau and Freeport to Provo and Grand Turk; and other airlines have expressed interest in serving the islands. Provo's airport boasts an 8,500-foot runway for wide-body jets; condominium construction on Provo is bustling; and interest in the colony's tax-free advantages as an offshore investment portends a rising tourist tide.

Does this mean you should immediately stuff your duffel and take flight? The answer is an unqualified yes and no. Definitely no, if you're happy only in 5-star hotels (not all the islands' rooms are air conditioned) and restaurants serving haute cuisine (meals can be good, even delicious when the fish or lobster is fresh and subtly sauced, but because so much food has to be frozen to be imported, Cordon Bleu cooking is the exception, not the rule). No again, if the absence of a social director will send you into a deep depression (except for *Club Med*'s organizers — GOs — there are none), or if bus touring, disco dancing, or acres of shops rate high on your holiday must list. And double all negatives if totally reliable, split-second timing is essential to your vacation peace of mind. Waiters and waitresses, maids, guides, taxis, and airplanes all come and go according to "island time" — always later than advertised, sometimes not at all — and will drive you crazy before you can say digital quartz chronometer.

On the other hand, if your natural vacation pace is a saunter, and if quiet doesn't scare you; if you genuinely enjoy miles of undeveloped beach, uninhabited cays, and some sort of water sport (beachcombing, shelling, paddling, floating, fishing, snorkeling, windsurfing — and especially scuba diving); if you'd rather watch the world pass and trade talk in a waterfront bar than tromp through a museum; if you really mean it when you say you want to get away from it all and rather like beating the crowd to a place that still can be fairly described as unspoiled — the answer is an unqualified yes. However, progress is on the way; so by all means, go discover the Turks & Caicos while there's time.

TURKS & CAICOS AT-A-GLANCE

FROM THE AIR: The Turks & Caicos Islands lie 575 miles southeast of Florida, halfway between Miami and Puerto Rico and 90 miles north of Haiti. About 14,000 people (90 percent of them black) inhabit the islands; of them, just over half live on Grand Turk, Salt Cay, and South Caicos, known collectively as the Salt Islands. The flight from Miami to Grand Turk or Provo takes about an hour and a half; the flight from Nassau to South Caicos or Provo takes about the same amount of time.

SPECIAL PLACES: Though the islands can't accurately be described as lovely — they're generally flat, dry, and covered with stunted pines or scrub — the Turks & Caicos do have some extraordinary beaches, and the turquoise waters that surround them are a diver's paradise. Each island has its own attractions — some modest, some quite spectacular. (For information on touring each of the main islands, see DIRECTIONS.) Grand Turk is the most historic of the islands; weatherbeaten colonial homes line the narrow streets of Cockburn Town, the main settlement on Grand Turk and the colony's capital. Some maintain that Columbus landed on nearby Pillory Beach in 1492. Off the east coast of Grand Turk, only a quarter of a mile offshore, is one of the most extraordinary diving spots in the world: the great wall, where the coastal shelf ends in a 7,000-foot abyss (see *Quintessential Bahamas,* DIVERSIONS). Salt Cay, just 9 miles south of Grand Turk, is another historic spot. Windmills dot the dazzling white salt pans on the island, and tidy Balfour Town has many relics of the island's whaling and salt-raking days.

If the Turks are the place for history, Provo in the Caicos is the place for fun. US investors — the DuPonts and the Roosevelts, among others — took an interest in

154 TURKS & CAICOS / Sources and Resources

Provo a number of years ago, and the island now boasts a couple of world class resorts, including the *Ramada Turquoise Reef* and the *Club Med Turkoise*. The big hotels line one of the most spectacular beaches in the colony, a 12-mile beauty that stretches from Turtle Bay on the north coast to Grace Bay near the eastern tip of the island. There is another good beach at Sapodilla Bay on the south coast, where the bonefishing is rumored to be excellent. (If the locals tell you it's not, pay no heed; it's just to keep the hordes at bay.) Those who find the crowds on Provo too harrying can escape to the well-heeled *Meridian Club* on nearby Pine Cay, a private island where underwater ecology is as fashionable as Ungaro.

The rest of the Caicos chain has its own attractions: bonefishing and bird sanctuaries (North Caicos); limestone caves and Lucaya Indian ruins (Middle Caicos); sailing and diving off deep Cockburn Harbour (South Caicos). Those who really want to get away from it all can hop on a charter and spend the day on one of the uninhabited isles such as West Caicos, where the honey-hued beaches and great dives make you forget that there's nary a bar nor a grill in sight.

SOURCES AND RESOURCES

TOURIST INFORMATION: The Turks & Caicos government has established a toll-free information line (phone: in the US, 800-441-4419). A private information resource, which primarily handles hotel reservations for the *Kiṭtina* hotel on Grand Turk, is the Turks and Caicos Information Center (255 Alhambra Circle, Suite 312, Coral Gables, FL 33134; phone: in the US, 800-548-8462). In addition, several Turks & Caicos hotels have formed a joint reservation service (phone: in the US, 800-282-4753).

The Ministry of Tourism (phone: 62321; fax: 62733) has offices in the back courtyard of the Government Building on Front Street in Cockburn Town, Grand Turk.

Local Coverage – The *Turks & Caicos News,* published weekly on Grand Turk, is the established newspaper, while the *Free Press* made its debut in December 1990. *Times of the Islands* magazine is published quarterly and includes articles about things to do and where to shop, as well as restaurant reviews. The *Turks & Caicos Pocket Guide,* published seasonally, offers the most comprehensive and detailed information for visitors.

TELEPHONE: The area code for the Turks & Caicos is 809-94.

GETTING AROUND: Taxi – One of the best ways to get an initial orientation. Most island cabbies have tours already designed (you can usually see everything of interest for about $30 to $50 on Provo, $20 to $30 on Grand Turk). Ask your hotel to make arrangements. And be sure to agree on a price before you get in and drive off. Since most drivers own their cars, negotiation is possible — especially since the initial asking price will be high, particularly on Provo.

Car Rental – *Provo Rent-A-Car* (phone: 64404) is located at the airport in Provo, while *Budget* has an office downtown (phone: 64079) and a branch at the *Ramada* (phone: 65400). On Grand Turk there is *Warm Car Rental* (phone: 62744) and *C. J.*

Car Rental (phone: 62744). On North Caicos there is *Saunders Rent-A-Car* (radio VHF "Sierra No. 7," Ch. 16). Rates start at about $45 for subcompacts (with 60 to 70 free miles on Provo; unlimited mileage on Grand Turk), plus mandatory insurance of $2.50 a day and a government tax stamp of $10, a onetime charge regardless of rental period. You pay for gas.

Motor Bikes and Dune Buggies – Dune buggies are available on Provo from *Rent-A-Buggy* (phone: 64158), and motor bikes from *Scooter Rental* (phone: 64684). On Grand Turk, *C. J. Car Rental* (phone: 62744) and the *Kittina* hotel (phone: 62232) both rent scooters.

Local Air Services – *TCNA* (phone: 62606 on Grand Turk; 64562 on Provo), the inter-island plane service, makes two circle flights a day from Grand Turk to the outlying islands. Flights usually are fully booked, with standbys waiting, so reserve ahead. *TCNA* also provides service to Nassau and Freeport in the Bahamas; Cap-Haïtien, Haiti; and Puerto Plata, Dominican Republic. There are several air charter services flying between the islands. Based in Provo are *Charles Air Service* (phone: 64352); *Blue Hills Aviation* (phone: 64388); *Flamingo Air Service* (phone: 64938); *Provo Air Charter* (phone: 64296); and *Provo Flying Service* (phone: 64291). On Grand Turk, *Flamingo Air Service* (phone: 62109). On South Caicos, *Caicos Air Service* (phone: 63283).

SPECIAL EVENTS: On Grand Turk, islanders celebrate a *Carnival* that begins the last few days in August and continues into the first week in September. The *Commonwealth Regatta*, also called the *South Caicos Regatta*, is the biggest event in the islands, taking place on South Caicos the last weekend in May. The *Queen's Birthday* is celebrated early in June. The *Turks & Caicos Islands International Billfish Tournament* is held on Provo in July. *Provo Days*, the islands' major festival, is a week-long annual celebration in late July or early August with races, parades, regattas, and a Miss Turks & Caicos beauty pageant. Businesses also are closed on *New Year's Day, Good Friday, Easter Monday, Commonwealth Day* (the second Monday in March), *J. A. G. S. McCartney Memorial Day* (June 6), *Emancipation Day* (early August), *Columbus Day* (the second Monday in October), *International Human Rights Day* (late October), *Christmas,* and *Boxing Day* (December 26).

SHOPPING: It's certainly not spectacular, although there are some excellent boutiques for beach clothing, shell jewelry, and other souvenirs. There are no duty-free shops per se, although liquor is a relative bargain, costing about the same or less as it would in duty-free shops at the Miami airport. Rum from Haiti or the Dominican Republic is a particular bargain. On Provo there are several small shopping centers along Leeward Highway and in the crossroads area known as town, or Downtown, although no one lives there. The *Town Centre Mall* is where you'll find *Scotia Bank, Island Pride Supermarket,* and *Island Photo* (phone: 64686), the only film processor in the islands. Across the road is *Butterfield Square* with *Barclay's Bank* and *Tasty Temptation,* a café and take-out shop featuring real French bread, croissants, and pastry; closed Saturdays and Sundays (phone: 64049). A little east of these two centers is the *Market Place,* which comes alive on Thursdays, market day. Here you'll find *Bamboo Gallery,* featuring fine Caribbean art (phone: 64748), and *Greensleeves,* an arts and crafts supply store that also sells handiwork by local residents (phone: 64147). Just down the road is *The Centre,* which has a couple of souvenir shops, a lot of offices, and a great watering hole called *Hey José* (see *Eating Out*). Elsewhere on Provo, Turtle Cove Landing has a number of shops, including a pharmacy and news shop, while the *Ramada Turquoise Reef* resort at Grace Bay also has a few shops, including a massage parlor and beauty salon. The gift shop at the conch-breeding farm at *Island Sea Centre* has all sorts of conch and other shell jewelry and many books on fish, sea mammals, and shelling (phone: 65330).

Shopping opportunities are more limited on Grand Turk. The *Gallery,* a freestanding shop on the beach side of Duke (commonly called Front) Street between the *Kittina* hotel and *Salt Raker Inn,* has everything from fine art, swimsuits, and T-shirts to such treasures as painted cardboard models of the traditional donkey carts found on the island; locally made jewelry is very reasonably priced. Closed for lunch and on Sundays (phone: 62745). The best collection of T-shirts on Grand Turk is at *Blue Water Divers* (on Front St. near the center of Cockburn Town; phone: 62432). The *Shell Shack* (just off Front St. behind the Treasury Building) features objets d'art fashioned from local seashells by Douglas Gordon, former owner of the *Salt Raker,* while his wife, Angie, supplies the embroidered T-shirts and totes (phone: 62470). *Dot's Gifts* (on Moxey's Folly east of the *Red Salina*) has some souvenirs not found elsewhere on the island, as well as some books and records dealing with Turks & Caicos' history and folk traditions (phone: 62324).

SPORTS: Bird Watching – There are bird and butterfly sanctuaries everywhere, with particularly interesting species at Penniston Cay, and at Gibb and Round Cay, a patch of small islands south and east of Grand Turk. Or observe the wildlife and beautiful scenery of the reefs, cays, and creeks around East Caicos.

Sailboating and Windsurfing – *Dive Provo* at the *Ramada Turquoise Reef* provides lessons at $30 per hour; rentals are $20 an hour, $45 for a half day, $65 all day (phone: 65040). On Grand Turk, the *Kittina* hotel has a complete water sports shop (phone: 62232).

Sea Excursions – Chloe Zimmerman of *Turtle Tours* (phone: 65585) has been serving visitors for more than a dozen years, putting together half- and full-day trips on land, in the air, and on, under, or over the water. Trips include a flight to North Caicos and a guided tour of the island and its crab farm (about $110 per person); a 5-hour sail-swim-picnic trip to uninhabited cays ($60 for adults; $30 for children under 12); and a trip to *Island Sea Centre* to see the conch-breeding farm and *JoJo Dolphin Project* at $20 per adult and $14 per child under 12.

Other excursions on Provo include glass-bottom boat trips for about $15 to $20 per person by *Provo Turtle Divers* (phone: 64232), *Aquascope* (phone: 65040), and *Submarine Adventure* (phone: 64393); and day cruises — prices vary depending upon destination — aboard the *Beluga* (phone: 64544) and the *Tao and Two Fingers* (phone: 64393). *Caicos Express* runs regularly scheduled ferry service from *Leeward Marina* on Provo to Sandy Point on North Caicos with stops at Pine Cay and Parrot Cay. Cost is $15 per person one way (phone: 67111).

Snorkeling and Scuba – Both are so spectacular that they attract underwater buffs from all over the world. The stunning 7,000-foot Turks Island Passage drop-off and the reefs that circle Grand Turk and the Caicos are the reason. Local divers are extremely protective about their undersea fauna and flora; they take the motto of the Provo-based organization *PRIDE* very seriously: "Take only pictures; leave only bubbles." Island dive outfits are excellent; most offer certified instruction and full equipment rental as well as dive trips. You'll find these at *Dolphin Cay Divers* (phone: 67119) on North Caicos; *Porpoise Divers* (phone: 66927) on Salt Cay; *Blue Water Divers* (phone: 62432), *Omega Divers* (phone: 62232), and *Off the Wall Divers* (phone: 62159) on Grand Turk; and *Provo Turtle Divers* (phone: 64232), *Flamingo Divers* (phone: 64193), *Dive Provo* (phone: 65040), and *Provo Aquatic Adventures* (phone: 64455) on Provo. In addition, there are three live-aboard dive boats: *Sea Dancer* (phone: in the US, 800-932-6237) based at *Caicos Marina* on Provo; *Ocean Outback* (phone: 64393) at Grace Bay on Provo; and *Aquanaut* (phone: 62541) on Grand Turk. There is a recompression chamber at *Dr. Euan Menzies Cottage Hospital* on Leeward Highway on Provo (phone: 64242).

Sport Fishing – Marvelous off Grand Turk, Salt Cay, South Caicos, and Provo, and generally very good on all the islands. Boats can be rented for the day through most hotels. Rates vary from about $100 per person for a half day (minimum 4 people) up to about $725 for a boat for a full day (maximum 8 people). Provo has a trim marina with dockage for visiting sport boats. Deep-sea fishing catches include marlin, sailfish, sawfish, wahoo, dolphin, tuna, mackerel, and barracuda. Among the charter operators on Provo are *Sakitumi*, with Captain Bob Collins in charge (phone: 64393), the *Fair Tide* (phone: 64684), and *Sand Dollar* (phone: 64451); on Grand Turk, *Off the Wall Divers* (phone: 62159). If bonefishing is your passion, Captain Barr Gardiner operates *Bonefish Unlimited* on Provo (phone: 64874). For two persons, a half-day trip will run about $125, a full day about $200. On Parrot Cay, call *Parrot Cay Charters* (phone: 64551). Other guides include Albert Musgrave, Earl Forbes, and Lem "Bonefish" Johnson on Provo; Julius Jennings, South Caicos; Dolphus Arthurs, Middle Caicos (*Conch Bar*); and the Talbots on Salt Cay. They communicate mostly by radio, so ask your hotel for help in contacting them.

The Turks & Caicos seem to be following the lead of the Bahamas and the Cayman Islands, which have had success drawing top sport fishers to summer tournaments. The *Turks & Caicos Islands International Billfish Tournament*, held on Provo each July, is a release-format tournament offering cash prizes. For details, write to the tournament organizers (c/o PO Box 350098, Ft. Lauderdale, FL 33335); or call Bill Young at *Turtle Cove Marina* on Provo (phone: 64308).

Swimming and Sunning – It's hard to go wrong on any of the islands' cays in the chain. With some 230 miles of beaches, the real joy of a Turks & Caicos vacation is to find one you like — and it should be an empty one if you're inclined to sunbathe nude or do a little skinny-dipping — and stretch out with book, food, and nothing but time. On the larger islands, a rundown of tried-and-true spots includes Governor's Beach, Grand Turk; the northern coast of Salt Cay; Conch Bar, Middle Caicos; almost any of the coasts on North Caicos; and Grace and Sapodilla bays on Provo.

Tennis – Courts are available at *Prospect of Whitby* on North Caicos and the *Windmills* on Salt Cay. On Provo you'll find courts at *Treasure Beach Villas, Ramada Turquoise Reef, Club Med, Turtle Cove, Erebus Inn, Le Deck,* and the *Ocean Club.*

NIGHTLIFE: Basically, some talk around the hotel bar or other watering hole and a nightcap (or several) is about as exciting as most evenings get, though the entertainment scene is beginning to heat up on Provo. But when there's a dance, everybody's invited — and almost everyone comes. In addition, Grand Turk boasts three discos: *Police Pub, The Lady,* and *Uprising*. Hotels usually stagger music nights to accommodate all patrons, with Tuesday and Sunday nights belonging to the *Salt Raker Inn* on Grand Turk. The *Banana Boat* (at the *Turtle Cove Marina*), an on-again, off-again operation, and *Disco Elite* (on the Airport Rd.) are Provo's favorite after-dark drop-in spots. The *Three Queens* (in Blue Hills) offers a traditional West Indian show 1 or 2 nights a week. (In T&C parlance, a topless nightclub is one without a roof.) The first — and only — gambling casino in the Turks & Caicos is located at the *Ramada Turquoise Reef* hotel; it features table games and slot machines.

BEST ON THE ISLANDS

CHECKING IN: There are only about 1,000 tourist rooms scattered throughout the islands — a third of them at *Club Med*. Most hotels have fewer than 50 rooms, but take pride in the personal service their small size allows them to offer. Many hotels, primarily those on Provo, now have a reservations representative in the United States (phone: 800-282-4753).

In winter, expect to pay $150 or more a night for a room for two, without meals, in a hotel listed as expensive; $90 to $150 in a place we list as moderate; and under $90 in an inexpensive hotel. Some hotels offer a meal plan with breakfast and dinner for an extra $25 to $35 per person per day. There is a 7% tax on hotel room occupancy and a 10% or 15% service charge on room rates and anything charged to the room. Hotels also are free to charge whatever they want for telephone calls, local or long distance. Packages — particularly those run in conjunction with one of the dive operations — can offer a considerable savings on the posted room rates.

There are a number of bed and breakfast accommodations, but not all operate on a year-round basis. There are no government tax or mandatory gratuities on hostelries with fewer than four rooms. Information can be obtained from the tourist board (phone: 62321; in the US, 800-441-4419). All telephone numbers are in the 809-94 area code, unless otherwise indicated.

GRAND TURK

Kittina – Grand Turk's largest (43 rooms and suites) and very likable hotel has long been popular. It's remarkable, too, in that Kit Fenimore, who built it himself, even quarried the stone. Upper-story rooms, with balconies overlooking the courtyard or the sea, are big and airy (not all are air conditioned). Smaller, courtyard rooms downstairs also are pleasant. The 20 deluxe seaside, beachfront suites, all with full kitchens, and 8 rooms are outstanding. There's a good dining room (see *Eating Out*), popular bar, and a dive shop, and beach and sea are only steps away. Front St. (phone: 62232; in the US, 800-KITTINA; fax: 62877). Expensive to moderate.

Gordon's Guest House – Douglas and Angie Gordon, who owned the *Salt Raker Inn* for years, have moved to a new home that includes a guestroom upstairs with a private bath and private entrance. The accommodation is spacious, with ceiling fan, cable TV, twin beds, small refrigerator, and a roomy porch with a table and two comfortable chairs. The *Shell Shack* gift shop is on the premises. Full breakfast included in the room rate. Front St. (phone: 62470). Moderate.

Guanahani Beach – On the beach north of Cockburn Town, this 16-room hotel with 8 two-bedroom apartments also has a pool. It's a simple, isolated place, but the staff is attentive and the location is a bonus for beach lovers. The hotel's restaurant is another plus (see *Eating Out*). Dive packages are available. Pillory Beach (phone: 62135; fax: 61152). Moderate.

Salt Raker Inn – A "deliberately small and informal" 150-year-old Bermuda-style former home, with a flowering garden, it has 9 freshly done up rooms (the 2 upstairs suites in the front of the main house are choice), plus 2 apartments next door. There's an outdoor pub, lounge, and very good dining, both indoors and out (see *Eating Out*). A guest library and reading room are available, along with scuba, snorkeling, and swimming at the beach across the road. Bikes can be rented nearby. A stroll from the center of town. Front St. (phone: 62260). Moderate to inexpensive.

TURKS & CAICOS / Best on the Islands 159

Turks Head Inn – Renovated and reopened in 1991 by Xavier Tonneau as a Bahamian-style country inn in a designated historic building on Front Street. Each of the 7 rooms has a private bath, ceiling fan, a large balcony, and, as much as possible, antique or period-piece furniture. Rooms are air conditioned and cable-equipped. There's also a restaurant and bar on the premises. Front St. (phone: 62466; fax: 62825). Moderate to inexpensive.

Capt. Kirk's Guest House – Management proclaims that this place doesn't accept divers or "wild people" in its 3 neat, clean rooms on Front Street. One room has a double bed, one has twin beds, and one is a single. All are nicely furnished with plenty of drawer space. The one bathroom is shared. Closed from June to December. Front St. (phone: 62227). Inexpensive.

Ocean View – This spartanly furnished establishment, formerly the *Columbus House*, underwent a complete refurbishing in 1991. Additions include a new deck and 10 large rooms (with TV sets and mini-refrigerators in some). New owners Terry and Maria Hopkins, veteran divers, are known for their down-home hospitality. Pond St. (phone: 62517; fax: 61152). Inexpensive.

SALT CAY

Windmills – A re-creation of a colonial plantation by architect S. Guy Lovelace, with 4 suites — 2 on the ground floor and 2 upstairs. Full American Plan with a minimum 3-night stay. The same rates apply year-round. (phone: in the US, 800-822-7715; fax: 66962). Expensive.

Mount Pleasant Guest House – This refurbished historic building, with 3 rooms, caters mostly to divers. Meals are included in room rates (phone: 63927). Moderate.

NORTH CAICOS

Ocean Beach – Located on the gorgeous beach at Whitby, it offers 8 studio, 1- or 2-bedroom condominium units with full kitchens and a commissary on the premises. Pool, scuba, snorkeling, and tennis are available, with deep-sea and bonefishing facilities nearby. Weekly rates available (phone: 67113; fax: 416-336-1232). Expensive to moderate.

Prospect of Whitby – This venerable and elegant resort, on lovely North Beach, boasts 28 rooms with a choice of views, freshwater pool, tennis, scuba, bar, restaurant, and plenty of seclusion and privacy (phone: 67119; fax: 67114). Expensive to moderate.

Pelican Beach – With 6 miles of powder-white beach at its doorstep, this 14-room shoreside retreat offers snorkeling, fishing, boat trips to nearby islands, and flying excursions to the Dominican Republic (the owner is a first-rate pilot). There's an informal bar and a dining room (phone: 67112; fax: 67139). Moderate.

PARROT CAY

Hotel at Parrot Cay – On a small island a stone's throw from North Caicos, it's a 50-room luxury establishment that is the centerpiece of a major resort development. The brand-new property boasts such amenities as cable TV, VCRs, mini-refrigerators, and terraces for all the rooms; 2 restaurants; lighted tennis courts; a beauty salon; a large exercise room; a pool; and a beautiful beach. Most water sports — including scuba, snorkeling, water skiing, and board and Hobie Cat sailing — on premises, plus deep-sea fishing, bonefishing, and day trips to nearby cays and islands. Guests fly into Provo (or, by special arrangement, North Caicos) and are ferried to Parrot Cay (phone: 67000; in the US, 800-729-3524; fax: 67001). Expensive.

PROVO

Nautilus Apartments – One of several small rental condominium properties, with 10 rooms in a combination of 1-bedroom fully furnished villas and larger 2-bedroom units overlooking the Sapodilla Village interior of Provo, which has seen better days. A good location for divers or long-term vacationers. Chalk Bay (phone: 64286; fax: 64069). Expensive.

Ocean Club – This new condominium development on the beach near *Club Med* has 50 studios, 2-, and 3-bedroom units; all are air conditioned, with full kitchens, cable TV, and patios or terraces. There also is a freshwater pool, Jacuzzi, cabaña bar, and lighted tennis courts. Grace Bay (phone: 65880). Expensive.

Ramada Turquoise Reef – This large, modern property on Grace Bay doesn't have a bad room in the place — almost all have ocean and/or pool views (the oceanfront rooms are the most popular). A large pool, 2 restaurants (see *Eating Out*), a poolside bar and grill, and a full dive shop and water sports operation on the premises, plus the first casino in the Turks & Caicos. There also is a tour operator, rental car service, and shops in the lobby. Grace Bay (phone: 65555). Expensive.

Le Deck Beach Club – On Grace Bay, it boasts 26 rooms plus a honeymoon suite in Bermuda-pink buildings. All rooms have ceiling fans, are air conditioned, and are equipped with cable TV. There's also a restaurant and a swimming pool; most water sports available. Grace Bay (phone: 65547; in the US, 800-441-4419; fax: in the US, 800-946-5770). Expensive to moderate.

Erebus – Overlooking Turtle Cove Marina with 30 hilltop rooms, this chalet-style resort has one of the loveliest views on Provo. Rooms are air conditioned and have ceiling fans, plus cable TV. There are 2 swimming pools, lighted tennis courts, a first class fitness center, and a French restaurant (see *Eating Out*) on the premises. Turtle Cove (phone: 64240; fax: 64704). Expensive to moderate.

Turtle Cove – On the water, with 2 suites and 28 standard rooms catering to yachters and divers who make use of the full-service marina at their doorstep. Open-air and indoor meeting spaces are available. Two lighted clay tennis courts, a pool, and 2 restaurants on the premises. Turtle Cove (phone: 64203; fax: 64141). Expensive to moderate.

Club Med Turkoise – This rambling, 70-acre, 298-room retreat on gorgeous Grace Bay beach offers aerobics classes, a 12-station fitness center, plus sailing, snorkeling, water-skiing, 8 tennis courts (4 lighted), picnic cruises, and beach games. There are 2 specialty restaurants, a grill and a pizzeria, plus dancing, shows, and disco. Rates include sports and activities, all meals (beer and wine with lunch and dinner), scuba, and deep-sea and bonefishing. Grace Bay (phone: 65500; in the US, 800-CLUB-MED). Moderate.

Mariner Inn – This charming, small place has one of the islands' most beautiful views; with a little promotion and a pinch of panache, it could become a favorite celebrity hideaway. The rest is waiting. There are 25 good-size rooms, an attractive dining room, and an on-site bakery; all is surrounded by gardens and suffused with a pleasantly private atmosphere. A water sports center, with diving, boardsailing, and sailing facilities, is on the premises. Sapodilla Bay (phone and fax: 64488). Moderate.

Treasure Beach Villas – An attractive apartment alternative on Grace Bay Beach, with 18 beachfront 1- and 2-bedroom combinations that include bath, living/dining room, terrace, and kitchen completely furnished down to the knives, forks, and spoons. The Bight (phone: 64211; fax: 64108). Moderate.

Island Princess – Its 80 small but bright rooms have balconies or patios for enjoying the spectacular beach and sea views. The big lounge is a gathering place for islanders and guests; the food is good and plentiful, with lots of lobster (omelettes at breakfast, salad at lunch, whole for dinner). Though it's getting a little worn around the edges, it's still attractive to families; all water sports easily arranged. Excellent packages. The Bight (phone: 64460; fax: 64666). Moderate to inexpensive.

SOUTH CAICOS

Club Caribe – This beach resort, with 24 air conditioned units, caters to scuba and snorkeling enthusiasts. There are a bar and restaurant on premises, and MAP is available. Cockburn Harbour (phone and fax: 63386). Moderate.

PINE CAY

Meridian Club – On a privately owned island known for quiet exclusivity, but a real community of interest in relaxation, peace, and preserving the natural beauty of the land and sea life rather than social chic. This limited land development has a central clubhouse (bar/lounge, dining room, pool), 22 smartly comfortable adjacent suites and cottage rentals. Ecologically oriented water sports, nature walks, and boat trips are available, along with a fabulous unspoiled beach and protected swimming. The meals are served family-style, and the nighttime dress is informal. It has its own airstrip and air taxi (phone: in New York City, 212-696-4566; in the rest of the US, 800-331-9154; fax: 64128). Expensive.

EATING OUT: Except on Provo, dining is almost exclusively in hotels, where such island specialties as whelk soup, conch chowder, turtle steaks, lobster, and a number of different kinds of fresh fish are featured. Expect to pay over $55 for dinner for two, without drinks or gratuities, in a restaurant we list as expensive; $40 to $55 in a moderate one; and under $40 in an inexpensive place. All telephone numbers are in the 809-94 area code unless otherwise indicated.

GRAND TURK

Sandpiper – The dining room of the *Kittina* hotel specializes in fresh seafood, including lobster, herbed turtle steaks, conch, plus veal chops for landlubbers. Reservations unnecessary. Major credit cards accepted. Front St. (phone: 62232). Expensive to moderate.

Hong Kong – A branch of Bosco Chan's Provo restaurant, it's located at the *Coral Reef* apartments on the east side of the island. The eatery offers slightly sweet variations on familiar Chinese dishes, plus conch and other island-inspired preparations. Reservations unnecessary. Major credit cards accepted. The Ridge (phone: 61256). Moderate.

Salt Raker Inn – Seafood and steaks served alfresco in a tropical garden. Reservations necessary. Major credit cards accepted. Front St. (phone: 62260). Moderate.

Guanahani Beach – In the hotel of the same name, this place strives to offer items not found elsewhere on island menus — stone crab claws and two-claw lobsters — but there also is cracked conch, grouper, chicken, and the best conch chowder you will find anywhere. Reservations usually unnecessary. Major credit cards accepted. Pillory Beach (phone: 62135). Moderate at dinner; inexpensive at lunch.

Regal Begal – On the east side of Red Salina just below North Folly, this dining spot serves island-style chicken (usually stewed or pan fried), spareribs, pork chops, conch, and lobster for both lunch and dinner. No reservations. No credit cards accepted. Hospital St. (phone: 62274). Inexpensive.

162 TURKS & CAICOS / Best on the Islands

PROVO

Portofino – The elegant upstairs room of the *Ramada Turquoise Reef* offers Italian seafood and pasta dishes in a relaxed and leisurely atmosphere. Extensive wine list. Closed Wednesdays. Reservations advised. Major credit cards accepted. Grace Bay (phone: 65555). Expensive.

Erebus – Restaurateur Pierrik's place is open for breakfast, lunch, and dinner. Dinner starters include *terrine de canard,* with main courses traditionally French, such as steak *au poivre,* lobster with garlic butter, and *poisson*-of-the-day, plus some Caribbean specialties. Reggae band on Thursday nights. Closed Sundays at lunch. Reservations advised on weekends and during the season. Major credit cards accepted. Turtle Cove (phone: 64120). Expensive to moderate.

JoJo's – On the water at Turtle Cove, with a bar fashioned out of half a ship's hull. Lunch includes salad, sandwiches, and a plat du jour, nothing over $15. In the evenings, chef Stephen Solbach turns out such specials as grouper in a chardonnay and scallion sauce, veal in chanterelle sauce, and tenderloin steaks prepared in a variety of ways. Let maître d' Vincent Sylvestre know well ahead of time if you're the adventurous type, and he'll have the chef prepare an imaginative and exotic *menu de gustation.* Closed Sundays. Reservations advised on weekends. Major credit cards accepted. Turtle Cove (phone: 64375). Expensive to moderate.

Leeward – Gilley, the owner of the airport snack bar, has expanded his clientele to include boat owners, day-trippers, and area residents at Leeward Going Through — thus his new eatery. The location is wonderful, but the fare is on the pricey side. Breakfast starts at 8 AM; among the lunch offerings are grouper, conch parmesan, and liver and onions. Dinner specials include lobster thermidor, duck, Cornish hen, steaks, and chops. Open until 10 PM. Reservations unnecessary. Major credit cards accepted. Leeward Marina (phone: 65094). Expensive to moderate.

Alfred's Place – This dining spot affords guests a wonderful view of Turtle Cove from the terrace dining room and bar. Popular with locals at happy hour, when warm hors d'oeuvres are usually served. For snacks, there are potato skins and Buffalo chicken wings; for serious diners, lobster and veal entrées. And for the gastronomically intrepid, there is conch sashimi (that is, served raw). For those who prefer their food cooked, the hot roast-beef sandwich (a slab of boneless prime ribs on homemade bread with lettuce, tomato, onion, and grated horseradish) is a bargain at $7. Reservations advised on weekends or when there's entertainment, usually on Tuesdays and Fridays. Major credit cards accepted. Off Leeward Hwy. at Suzie Turn (phone: 64679). Moderate.

Fast Eddie's – Popular with the younger local crowd for its fresh island dishes and homemade bread. Eddie LaPorte works the kitchen himself. There is music on Wednesdays and Saturdays, when reservations may be necessary. No credit cards accepted. Airport Rd. (phone: 64075). Moderate.

Henry's Road Runner – One of the island's better small places, with very good native dishes and the freshest seafood. No reservations except for large groups. No credit cards accepted. In Blue Hills (no phone; VHF radio "Road Runner"). Moderate.

Island Princess – This family-style place with a typical American "diner" menu seats — and feeds — several dozen at a time. No reservations. Major credit cards accepted. The Bight (phone: 64260). Moderate.

Hey José – Transplanted Californians Jeff and Diane Rollings run a friendly, popular spot featuring *chimichangas,* burritos, tacos, and the best salsa this side of Mexico. Also a selection of pizza where they don't skimp on the cheese or toppings. (Sizes from 6-inch for $5 — plus 50¢ per topping — up to 16-inch for $14, with each topping $1.) Wednesday night is barbecue time, with chicken and ribs for $11. A good place to stop when you're "conch-ed" out. Closed on Sundays. No reservations. Major credit cards accepted. In *Atlas House* at *The Centre* on Leeward Hwy. (phone: 64812). Moderate to inexpensive.

Hong Kong – Bosco Chan features Chinese preparations that are somewhat sweeter than those found in New York's or San Francisco's Chinatown, plus some island specials such as sweet and sour lobster and conch with black bean sauce. Open nightly for dinner; Mondays through Saturdays for lunch. Reservations unnecessary. Major credit cards accepted. On Grace Bay Rd. near *Club Med* (phone: 65678). Moderate to inexpensive.

Dora's – Large and friendly, this local eatery offers sandwiches for under $5. Lunch and dinner specials include cracked or creole conch, barbecued pork chops, steamed or fried fish or chicken, and steamed turtle. ("Steamed" here is analogous to "smothered" in Dixie culinary parlance.) There's a seafood buffet Monday evenings; the restaurant stays open as late as 4 or 5 AM on Fridays and Saturdays. Reservations unnecessary, except for large parties. No credit cards accepted. Leeward Hwy. (phone: 64558). Inexpensive.

Yum Yum – A take-out place with a small counter and a couple of tables featuring a wide selection of sandwiches and island platters, plus hand-scooped ice cream for cones and sundaes. No reservations; no credit cards accepted. Near *Town Centre Mall* downtown (phone: 64480). Inexpensive.

DIVERSIONS

For the Experience

Quintessential Bahamas

To Americans, the Bahamas are both foreign and familiar. The two countries share the same language — though the Bahamian "conch accent" is a good deal more lilting than anything you'll hear stateside — and some of the same history. Yet just because Bahamians speak English, and because some of the Bahamian cays bear a strong resemblance to the Florida Keys, visitors shouldn't be misled into thinking that they've never left home. This is very much a nation in its own right, with its own rich folklore, lively music, and centuries-old traditions. Some of the sights and sounds here can't be experienced anywhere else. Here are a few that shouldn't be missed.

JUNKANOO: No matter how tired you are, no matter what a late riser you may be, there's one night when visitors to the islands simply have to stay awake until the break of dawn: the night of *Boxing Day,* that ever-so-British day-after-*Christmas* holiday that is synonymous with the junkanoo in the Bahamas. The junkanoo is not the national bird, or a rum-and-pineapple concoction served in Nassau's bars, or a fish that George Bush comes to catch when he's vacationing on Bimini. It's a costumed dance-and-music happening — and a national passion. And if there is one cultural tradition that's synonymous with the Bahamas, this is it.

Ask a group of Bahamians about the origins of the name junkanoo and you'll get a dozen answers. The most popular — and probably least credible — version is that the name is a corruption of John Canoe, an African prince enslaved on a plantation in the American South who fled to the Bahamas sometime during early colonial days. The name doesn't really matter — it's the music that counts. Even tourists who would rather die than be dragged to a dance floor will find their feet tapping when they hear the junkanoo beat.

The music starts early — at 3 o'clock in the morning, more or less — on *Boxing Day* and a week or so later on *New Year's Day.* It begins with a blast from a conch-shell horn or a brass trombone or a big plastic foghorn — whatever is at hand. Then the drums join in. They're African drums made of wood and tanned goatskin, and their rhythm is infectiously wild. Once the drums start, the dancers follow: hundreds of them, all dressed in fantastic multicolored costumes fluttering with crêpe-paper fringe. Some may come dressed like Christopher Columbus, or like the Puritan colonists who sailed here in the 17th century, or like Lucaya Indians or astronauts or giant spiders or the Greek muses. Each dancer belongs to a clan — they used to be called gangs, until the word went out of fashion — and each clan represents a neighborhood. As they jive their way down the street, the dancers "scrap" and "rush" at each other, as if they were fighting a stylized street battle, like the Sharks and the Jets in *West Side Story.* The sparring is all in good fun. Though the dance was once linked, rightly or wrongly, to hooliganism or social protest, today it's perfectly proper and respectable; even government ministers join in. Not to say that it's staid. It's one of the craziest and most colorful extravaganzas in the Bahamas, a sort of *Mardi Gras, Carnival,* and *Macy's* parade rolled into one.

Each dancer makes his own costume, and glueing on the crêpe-paper fringe takes patience and a practiced hand. Months of planning go into a the spectacle, which lasts only a few hours. But as one dancer — Jackson Burnside, a Nassau architect and member of the *Saxon Superstars,* the redoubtable junkanoo clan — says, "It's not the dance itself that matters, it's the process." Junkanoo symbolizes freedom — freedom from everyday drudgery, slavery, colonial masters, and colonial governments — and freedom is an evanescent thing. When the dance is done, the costumes are discarded, and the ritual awaits the following year.

GRACIOUS GRAYCLIFF, NASSAU: There are plenty of elegant places tucked away in quiet corners of the Bahamas — places like Lyford Cay and Windermere Island. But if there is one place that epitomizes Bahamian grace and style, it's this exquisite Nassau hotel. The 18th-century mansion in which it is housed was built by Captain John Howard Graysmith, who, according to local lore, made a fortune plundering ships along the Spanish Main. The mansion stands near the spot where the First Anglican Church of Nassau was erected under the auspices of Governor Nicholas Trott, who later resigned in disgrace after he was discovered to be on the payroll of several privateers. During Prohibition days, the mansion was converted into a hotel run by Miss Polly Leach, allegedly a close friend of Al Capone's. In 1966 the property was bought by Lord Dudley, the third Earl of Staffordshire, who soon swept the house clean of any lingering cobwebs of scandal. The household became known for its elegant soirees, and Lord Mountbatten and Lord Beaverbrook, Sir Winston Churchill, and the Duke and Duchess of Kent were entertained here in fine style.

The same high-toned atmosphere prevails today. The decor is Empire and Victorian; prints of London and of English royalty hang on the pale pastel walls, and Persian rugs warm the polished wooden floorboards. The small pool is hemmed in by a dense thicket of palms and ferns. The rooms — there are only 12, plus a handful of cottages and suites — are furnished with imported antiques. The mood is discreet and genteel, like something you'd find in a private club in Kensington or Chelsea.

Even if the hotel were a shambles, which it is not, guests would still come for the food. *Graycliff* has one of the few first class restaurants in the Bahamas. Owner Enrico Garzaroli has spent years refining the hotel's menu, and his efforts have paid off handsomely. Some of the specialties are continental, but most of the dishes have a Bahamian twist. Visitors won't find ordinary guava duff or peas 'n' rice here, though. The dishes are lighter and more deftly sauced and spiced than many traditional local specialties. The grouper is seasoned with shallots and Dijon mustard; the cracked conch is served with cream and tiny shrimp; the guava duff is light and airy, like an English trifle, and is drizzled with champagne zabaglione. The restaurant's wine cellar is wide-ranging and well stocked: Garzaroli has collected more than 175,000 bottles, among them a 1790 malvasia, a 1779 Verdelho, and a 1970 Château Mouton-Rothschild with a label designed by Marc Chagall (phone: 809-322-2796).

SPORT FISHING ON BIMINI: Let's face it: If Bimini didn't have fish, few people would bother to come here. It's a one-track-minded place: monomaniacal fishermen talking monotonously about marlin — or wahoo or tuna or barracuda. All this sounds pretty boring, unless you love to fish.

If Hemingway hadn't fallen in love with the place, even anglers might have passed it by. Fortunately, Hemingway immortalized it in *Islands in the Stream,* in his articles in *Esquire,* and — indirectly — in *The Old Man and the Sea,* whose hero (or antihero) is a big blue marlin. The whole island is suffused with the writer's mystique. It isn't just the bars on Bimini that are reminiscent of Hemingway, though the *Compleat Angler* enshrines his spirit pretty well. It's the sport itself. Hemingway turned fishing into a sort of moral combat — an elemental struggle matched only by a bullfight or war or the battle with the Great White Page with No Words on It. It's not a minor skirmish, after all, that pits a fisherman against a creature 4 or 5 times his size that can streak through the water at 60 miles an hour and smash through a ship's hull in a couple of seconds.

And there aren't just marlin here. Some game fish are temporary visitors, like the tuna, which glide past Bimini on their tours along the Gulf Stream. Sailfish can be found here year-round; white marlin abound in the late winter and spring, and larger blue marlin are most plentiful from mid-June to mid-August. But anglers never know exactly where and when a school of game fish will show up — that's part of the fun. The big fish change their feeding grounds from year to year. As Hemingway wrote in August 1934: "This year, there were many small marlin taken off Miami, and the big ones appeared off Bimini just across the Gulf Stream several months before they run into Cuba."

East of the Gulf Stream, in the waters of the Great Bahamas Bank, swim the mackerel, amberjack, wahoo, dolphin fish, and barracuda, as well as tasty eating fish like grouper and snapper. Bonefish teem in the flats just offshore. (Tourists who manage to catch a bonefish shouldn't attempt to make a meal of it on the beach, unless they have a native to cook it. The bones must be expertly cracked before the fish can be filleted — not an easy task for a neophyte.) Eating your catch is secondary, though. It's the struggle that counts — and the stories you collect. Spend a week or two off Bimini and you'll have plenty, even if you can't recount them as well as Papa did.

THE ISLAND(S) OF DISCOVERY: While no one is sure exactly where in the New World Christopher Columbus first stepped ashore, natives of several Bahamian isles have laid claim to the honor. Historians have disqualified one candidate — Cat Island — leaving two contenders: San Salvador and Grand Turk. (Although it's small, virtually uninhabited Samana Cay has its supporters, too.) San Salvador and Grand Turk are remarkably similar, and it's easy to see how either one could be "Guanahani," as the Lucaya Indians called the isle where Columbus landed.

Guana means "water" in Arawak, and both San Salvador and Grand Turk have plenty. The interior of San Salvador is flecked with sea-fed ponds and lakes; Grand Turk is, too, although early settlers dammed the pools to create the salt pans that sustained the local economy for many years. Both isles are roughly bean-shaped, which corresponds to the description recorded by the bishop who accompanied Columbus. Treacherous coral reefs lie off the east coast of both islands, while the sheltered leeward shores to the west could have made a perfect spot for a landing. Both isles have a protected harbor large enough to hold "all the fleets of Christendom," as Columbus described it. Archaeologists have unearthed evidence that the two islands were populated by Indian tribes who could have been the natives that Columbus said greeted the ship by "calling us and giving thanks to God."

If in doubt about which island to visit, go to both. You can stand on the eastern shore and imagine what it must have been like for the lookout on the *Pinta* who sighted land that moonlit night of October 12, 1492. You can see the ponds in the interior of the islands, and know what Columbus did not: that the water in them is brackish, not fresh and sweet, as the explorer thought. You can walk along the beaches on the western side of the islands and imagine where the admiral might have rowed ashore to plant the standard of Ferdinand and Isabella. Or you can picture the excitement — probably tinged with fear — that the Lucaya must have felt when they beheld the curious sight: bearded creatures wearing scarlet-and-blue doublets and metal helmets disembarking from a boat larger than any they had ever seen. Cynics can amuse themselves by scouting out the numerous monuments erected on San Salvador that mark the "exact" spot where Columbus landed.

PLAYING THE ODDS: Nassau is Washington, DC, New York, Los Angeles, and Las

Vegas all in one: It's the political capital of the Bahamas, its largest city, its entertainment center — and the home of some of the flashiest casinos in the country. Back in the old days, there were just a few casinos from which to choose; now the field is starting to widen. There's the purple *Crystal Palace* at Cable Beach on New Providence, and the other equally gargantuan old standby, the *Paradise Island* casino. (The atmosphere is the same in both places: hotels the size of cities, theme-park-size restaurants, extravagant stage shows and revues, and gaming rooms as cavernous as the grotto on Andros where Henry Morgan buried his trove of jewels and doubloons.) On Grand Bahama, there's the *Princess* casino, whose Moorish decor matches Donald Trump's *Taj Mahal* in style and (questionable) taste; and the *Lucayan Beach,* the favored destination of most Florida junkets. And on Provo, in the Turks & Caicos, the *Ramada Turquoise Reef* has opened a casino, the first ever in that chain of islands — complete with rolls of the dice and slots.

Most of the big casinos offer all the usual diversions: slot machines, blackjack, roulette, craps, wheels of fortune, and baccarat, where the monied few gamble away their fortunes. The casino on Paradise Island — at 30,000 square feet — is not only the world's largest offshore casino, but also one of the world's largest, period. There's no sand, and not a bit of ocean glare; there's nothing, really, to remind you that you are in the Bahamas except the soothing lilt of the dealers, which seems to have an analgesic effect on heavy losers.

VISIT A LOYALIST TOWN: Perhaps no place better embodies the colonial spirit on the islands than Harbour Island. "Briland" — the natives elide the first syllable — is a quaint little town on a small isle of the same name located just off the northern tip of Eleuthera. The main settlement is officially known as Dunmore Town, after John Murray, the fourth Earl of Dunmore, a Governor of the Bahamas who built a summer home here in the 1780s. The earl came to the islands after serving as royal governor of the Virginia colony, where his astounding arrogance made him a target of Patrick Henry's vituperative spleen. He behaved no better in the Bahamas, where he so besmirched his reputation with rumors of nepotism, womanizing, and greed that the residents of straitlaced Harbour Island refused to call their town by his name.

The Brilanders still have reason to be proud. Their town is one of the oldest in the Bahamas, and its residents earned a reputation early on for perseverence and patriotism. Many of the island's early settlers arrived during the late 17th and early 18th centuries from New Providence, where life was frequently disrupted by attacks by pirates and Spanish galleons. The colonists of Harbour Island managed to carve out a life for themselves, surviving storms and epidemics, until a large contingent of Tories landed here soon after the American Revolution. The Loyalists injected new life into the town. They launched a building boom, refurbishing churches like Anglican St. John's and erecting many of the tidy clapboard houses that still line the streets in the old parts of town.

If you stroll down the quiet, tree-lined lanes of Harbour Island, you can see evidence of the island's past at almost every turn. The narrow lanes were plotted by the Earl of Dunmore in 1791. (The earl wasn't motivated by civic duty; he planned to charge rent on the 190 lots carved from portions of his estate.) The bluff called Barracks Hill, near the town's cricket grounds, is named for the barracks that the earl built for the troops who patrolled his estate. Some of the cannon that guarded the earl's property now stand in the yards of various private homes — ramble around and see how many you can find. There are many historic churches, including St. John's — its bell tower was added in the 1860s — and the magnificent Wesley Methodist church at the corner of Dunmore Street and Chapel Road, which was erected in the 1840s. Virtually all the early colonial buildings in town were damaged in the Great Bahama Hurricane of 1866, but many were later rebuilt. Tourism boomed after World War II, and many old buildings were refurbished and new ones added — tastefully and unobtrusively, for the most part. The town is more prosperous now than it was in the days when the locals relied on shipbuilding and sugar refining. But the place isn't grand enough to put on airs, and the locals aren't so besieged by tourists as to be unfriendly. Go now, before everybody else discovers the place (see *Eleuthera,* in DIRECTIONS).

STROLL ALONG A PINK BEACH: If you go to Harbour Island off Eleuthera, don't spend too long dallying in town. There's another attraction that shouldn't be missed: the perfect rose-tinted beach on the eastern strand. The beach stretches the length of the island, roughly 3 miles in all, and although it's lined with guesthouses and hotels, it still manages to conserve a sense of peace and quiet. This is a morning beach; the sun soon chases the slight chill that lingers from the night, and tiny sand creatures scurry to escape the tide. The waves are slight, for the coral reef just offshore bears the brunt of the ocean's force, and there are good places to snorkel nearby. Islanders have pretty much scoured the beach of shells, but it's a wonderful place for a stroll or for a leisurely morning of soaking up the sun.

Pirates and sailors dragged their boats ashore here in colonial times; "Calico Jack" Rackham, one of the most notorious freebooters in the Bahamas, called here from time to time, and pirate Charles Vane, the sworn enemy of Governor Woodes Rogers, hid out here for a while in the early 18th century. Visitors who walk up the beach today will find nothing of the kind — just the small *Coral Sands* hotel and the elegant *Pink Sands Club* at the northern end, which is so quiet and unobtrusive that it is a certified Audubon Society bird sanctuary.

STAY ON A PRIVATE ISLAND: So you're bored with baccarat? Tired of the big-town bustle of Freeport and Nassau? Fed up with lackadaisical island time, slow ferries, bumpy roads, and mosquitoes? Treat yourself: Fly to the *Windermere Island Club,* off Eleuthera. The resort, on an emerald-green slip of an isle 5 miles long and a hairbreadth wide, is linked to the mainland by a causeway; it's 18 miles from the airport at Rock Sound. Visitors can stay in a suite in the clubhouse, a cottage by the pool, or one of 18 villas hidden in the groves of coconut palms. Guests can sail, windsurf, water-ski, snorkel, or stalk bonefish in the shallows near the shore (the hotel provides all equipment, including fishing tackle). They can also play tennis or relax by the pools or the two pristine private beaches. Twice a week, a boat ferries patrons across placid Savannah Sound to West Beach on mainland Eleuthera for a barbecue; the grilled spiny lobster they serve is as succulent as you'll find anywhere. Non-guests can stop by and sip tea on the terrace overlooking the beach. Don't stare at the royals — Prince Charles and Princess Di have been guests — or if you do, don your Armani *occhiali di sole* first (phone: 809-332-6003; in the US, 800-237-1236).

A BAY STREET SHOPPING SPREE: Situated on one of the best deepwater ports in the Bahamas, Nassau has always been a place where goods changed hands. In colonial times, privateers came here to sell their booty. English ships brought Chinese tea and chintz to wealthy Nassau merchants, and returned laden with New England woolens and Southern cotton. Boats still bring in cargo from the Family Islands: hand-plaited palmetto mats, spiny lobster, and pineapples from Eleuthera, sweet white onions from Exuma, tomatoes from Long Island — the Bahamian Long Island, that is — sweet-scented cascarilla bark, Sea Island cotton, and the dense and resinous wood of the lignum vitae tree. Mail boats chug back from Potter's Cay in Nassau Harbour to the Family Islands, laden with tinned food, manufactured goods, and visitors who don't mind a long, desultory passage.

Bay Street is the town's main commercial artery, as it has been since early colonial days, when the Anglican church controlled the town's markets. Not so long ago, the wealthy merchants who sold their goods here — the "Bay Street Boys" — were the *éminences grises* of the colonial government. The political pressure they brought to bear was so great that the black majority wasn't granted the vote until 1962.

But on to shopping. The Bahamian government recently did away with customs duty

172 DIVERSIONS / Quintessential Bahamas

on many items and has encouraged retailers to cut their prices accordingly. As a result, shoppers can buy duty-free china, jewelry, perfume, cameras, leather goods, watches, liquor, and many other goods for 10% to 50% less than they would pay in the US. (There is also the government-sponsored Bahamas Treasure Card, which provides additional discounts for visitors from the United States.) Some goods sold here are unavailable in North America; all have special status under US Customs allowances. Fortify yourself with a good lunch and take a long stroll down Bay Street, stopping in at *John Bull* for cameras and calypso records (phone: 809-322-3328); the *Nassau Shop* for jewelry and English sweaters (phone: 809-322-8405); *Bernard's* for Wedgwood and Baccarat and Lalique (phone: 809-322-2841); and *Lightbourn's* for a fine selection of French perfume (phone: 809-322-2095). *Cole's of Nassau* has designer swimwear and sports clothes (phone: 809-322-8393); the *Brass and Leather Shop* has Italian belts and wallets (phone: 809-322-3806); and *Linen and Lace* has lovely loungewear (phone: 809-322-4266). If you're feeling bold, stop and try on the clothes in the boutiques of *Fendi* (phone: 809-322-6300) and *Gucci* (phone: 809-325-0561), or if you're the timid sort, just stand outside and "lick the windows," as the French say. Wherever you shop, remember: There is no sales tax.

And last, stop by the giant *Straw Market* opposite Market Street; don't be shy about haggling over the prices. In addition to mats and baskets, there are plenty of local goods to buy in Nassau, from conch jewelry to dolls and jasmine-scented perfume and many fine rums and liqueurs. You can even take back a goatskin goombay drum. Remember to keep made-in-Bahamas goods separate when going through customs, as they get special treatment.

PICNIC ON STOCKING ISLAND: This skinny 5-mile-long island is misnamed: It's much better explored in bare feet. Located near the mouth of Elizabeth Harbour off Great Exuma, it's the perfect place for a lazy afternoon. To get here, jump on a ferry from the dock near the *Peace and Plenty* hotel in George Town. The owners of the hotel bought up most of the island a few years ago and have turned it into a semiprivate reserve for their guests. The ferry is free for those staying at the hotel; for the rest, it's about $5 round trip. The sand on the island's two beaches is as fine and white as sugar — not the coarse tan turbinado sugar that the British love, but the powder-fine, driven-snow American kind. Bring a picnic lunch and a thermos of rum cooler, or stop by the *Beach Club* on the island for a hamburger. On Sundays, the *Beach Club* cooks up a seaside barbecue. Take a walk down the beach and explore the many secluded coves and inlets, or hunt for starfish and sand dollars if the tide is low. Divers can explore the 400-foot-deep blue hole known as Mystery Cave.

DIVE THE WALL OFF GRAND TURK: Imagine leaping from the rim of the Grand Canyon, and you have a sense of what diving off the wall east of Grand Turk Island is like. Barely 300 yards offshore, just a stone's throw from Cockburn Town, is one of the most precipitous drop-offs in the western Atlantic. Divers scoot along the shallow coastal shelf, where the depth is only 50 or 60 feet, and then *whoosh!* the floor drops away, and they're gazing into an abyss more than 7,000 feet deep. Humpback whales skim along this channel — once called Turks Passage, and recently renamed Columbus Passage in honor of the recent quincentennial — on their way to their breeding grounds in the Silver and Mouchoir banks.

The wall itself is a craggy, coral-encrusted cliff riddled with odd formations. There's the Black Forest, a shallow indentation in the rock covered with three species of black coral. At the same depth, about 40 feet, is the Amphitheater, a broad gallery where divers can rest and watch for whales. Near a particularly large coral arch (waggishly called McDonald's), schools of grouper and yellowtail mill about waiting for a handout. By following a series of passageways called The Tunnels, divers emerge from the reef at a depth of 80 or 90 feet. There they see a forest of purple sponges and odd gorgonia, and spadefish and schooling jacks darting through the gin-clear water. Night divers head for the Library, where black coral and a rare nocturnal orange anemone grow, and where octopus and eels undulate through the currents. The seas off Grand Turk are at their best from April to November — provided a hurricane doesn't swoop by.

SAILING TO THE BAHAMAS: Why not? It's perfectly legal, and a good way to adjust to slow-as-molasses island time. The route from Miami to Bimini is the shortest; with favorable winds, a crew can set out at 6 in the morning and be in Alice Town by dinnertime. Sailors can also head from Palm Beach to the West End of Grand Bahama, a route that covers roughly the same distance as the trip from Miami to Bimini. Or they can set sail for Walker's Cay, the northernmost of the inhabited Bahamian isles and one of the best diving spots. Some craft have sailed from Charleston, South Carolina, to Walker's Cay in about 48 hours.

Special Havens

It usually is possible to generalize about US cookie-cutter hotel chains and their motel counterparts with relative safety. A room in a *TraveLodge* in Evansville, Indiana, closely resembles a *TraveLodge* room in Effingham, Illinois, or Emporia, Kansas. Not so in the Bahamas or the Turks & Caicos, where no two big hotels — let alone small inns — are even remotely alike.

Things beyond stateside imagining regularly affect island hotel operation — things like hurricanes (the season for them is roughly August through October), late or non-flying planes (all too often), too much or too little rain (if it isn't one . . .). And the candle you find in the dresser drawer even at the luxurious *Graycliff* is there in case the electricity fails (in local parlance, "generator, he out"), which can happen anywhere — though most blackouts are momentary, rather than extended, events.

What you can look forward to throughout the islands, however, at large hotels and small ones, is a sort of personal attention and one-on-one thoughtfulness that has been forgotten — or has simply never existed — in other parts of the world. The manager usually is accessible — and in a small hotel or guesthouse is probably the owner. Planned activities are less often the rule here; but someone is always available to help with any plans you'd like to make — whether they involve chartering a yacht, packing a picnic lunch, or moving your lounge chair under that pair of palms near the beach. Other nice touches: sincere smiles and "good mornings," staffs that do small favors without waiting around for big tips, fresh flowers in your room as a matter of course, and (oh, most saving grace) a shelf of dog-eared paperbacks left by former guests for the very moment you finish your Agatha Christies.

The two places below are our special favorites. Each has a sense of style and luxury especially compatible with its unique island setting, with an atmosphere, location, and service that make it especially appealing. Both are on the expensive side (i.e., $225 and up a day for two, usually including two meals during the high season).

BIG TIME

COTTON BAY CLUB, Eleuthera: If it's tumult that intrigues you, don't look here. A lovely, quiet oasis on one of the Bahamas' most beautiful islands, this former private playground for the rich and dignified (though now open to the public, it still attracts the likes of President George Bush, Richard Nixon, and Sidney Poitier) is luxury living at its best. Great golf, first-rate tennis, windsurfing, sailing, snorkeling, and one of the finest strands of beach in the Atlantic all blend to create the perfect get-away-from-it-all yet have-everything-at-your-fingertips vacation. Acquisition of the 50-acre Edgar Kaiser estate added a 6-bedroom villa (an excellent luxury facility for corporate meetings, it sleeps up to 12 for $2,500 per day) to the 77-room property; the beautifully landscaped grounds, with hibiscus- and bougainvillea-lined walkways and cottages, a replanted and upgraded golf course, plus chef Wayne Christensen's expertise in the resort's excellent restaurant (be sure to try the chilled hearts of palm soup) are all icing on the cake. Rumor has it that this paradise soon may revert to private club status — so sample it while you can. Information: *Cotton Bay Club,* PO Box 28, Rock Sound, Eleuthera, Bahamas (phone: 809-334-6156; in the US, 800-223-1588; fax: 809-334-6082).

SMALL WONDER

GRAYCLIFF, Nassau: Boasting the only truly top restaurant in the Bahamas, this 12-room Georgian colonial house, a member of the prestigious Relais & Châteaux hotel group, offers guests an elegant Old World setting with such modern-day comforts as a sauna, Jacuzzi, and a fully equipped gym. There is a private beach, and daily dive trips to lush underwater gardens (the gardens on the property are equally lush). To know just how special we think this spot is, see *Quintessential Bahamas,* in this section. Information: *Graycliff,* PO Box N 10246, Nassau, Bahamas (phone: 809-322-2796; fax: 809-326-6110).

Private Islands

At the unique hideaways described here, the boundaries of both the resort and its island are virtually identical. These three total-island resorts are mite-sized, and each consists of a central clubhouse with cottages scattered along a trade wind–cooled ridge or a perfect curve of beach. Accommodations are built along simple (though comfortably luxurious) lines, with very private patios and terraces, and none breaks the 50-room barrier.

To Hilton habitués and Sheraton stoppers, paying $300 to $400 a night for digs that lack room telephones and color TV sets is unthinkable. But to the corporate wheels that need to stop turning, escaping celebrities seeking solitude, and affluent couples and families who wait eagerly to return to these private islands year after year, the absence of such "conveniences" ensures the precise peace they've left home and office to find. Even air conditioning is a sometime thing. Most guests prefer island breezes to ceiling fans, louvered shutters to plate glass windows, and bamboo-fenced outdoor showers to marble bathtubs indoors.

These islands are easy to miss on maps; even when you pinpoint them, they are not all that simple to reach. And their devoted clientele wouldn't have it any other way.

MERIDIAN CLUB, Pine Cay, Turks & Caicos: Barefoot-casual, it offers a gorgeous beach with an array of water sports, boat trips, nature walks, 2 tennis courts, even excursions to Haiti and the Dominican Republic. The central clubhouse has a big, homey lounge, family-style dining, and a pool. There are 12 beachfront rooms and 10 cottages available for rent. Pine Cay, encompassed by the club, is noted for the unspoiled beauty of its land and sea life — no spearfishing is allowed. For international travelers, Pine Cay is most easily accessible from Provo. Information: *Meridian Club,* c/o Resorts Managements, The Carriage House, 201½ E. 29th St., New York, NY 10016 (phone: in New York City, 212-696-4566; elsewhere in the US, 800-331-9154; fax: 809-94-64128).

WALKER'S CAY CLUB, Abacos: Sport fishing was originally the island's biggest attraction (a major billfish tournament is still held here each April), but recently scuba diving has been coming on strong. Once a refuge for rumrunners, the 100-acre cay today offers a 75-slip marina, certified dive instruction, and great underwater scenery, along with all-weather tennis courts and 2 pools. Lunch may be a buffet at the marina; dinner is in the hotel restaurant, where the freshest seafood is a specialty. The hotel is only a 20-minute flight from Freeport, Grand Bahama; there is a daily flight from Ft. Lauderdale, except Tuesdays and Thursdays. Information: *Walker's Cay Club,* 700 SW 34th St., Ft. Lauderdale, FL 33315 (phone: 809-352-5252; in Florida, 305-522-1469; elsewhere in the US, 800-432-2092; fax: 809-359-1414).

WINDERMERE ISLAND CLUB, Eleuthera: A tranquil yet luxurious retreat set on an island just off Eleuthera, this is a favorite of well-heeled folk who come to play tennis on the 6 all-weather courts; fish for everything from marlin to bonefish; or just enjoy the sun, sand, and surf. There are 2 beaches and a pineapple-shape pool. Accommodations range from privately owned villas, which are rented out when the owners are off-island, to large, hotel-style rooms in the main clubhouse. The restaurant is among the best in the islands. Dinner here is a dress-up affair, with men required to wear jackets. It's worth the effort. Information: *Windermere Island Club,* Eleuthera, Bahamas (phone: 809-332-6003; in the US, 800-237-1236).

Natural Wonderlands

To most urban dwellers, the island world is one vast natural wonder — a serendipitous embrace of land, sea, and sun that is wide enough to include anyone who ventures into the area. And they aren't all that wrong. But even in paradise there are superlatives, and the spots below give a special sense of the islands' splendor.

UNEXSO, Grand Bahama: Most of the natural wonderlands to be found in and around the Bahamas sit at depths of 100 feet. Here you can swim in the company of pufferfish and yellowtail — and an occasional whale or two — in some of the clearest waters in the western Atlantic. A haven for scuba and snorkel enthusiasts, these isles offer unparalleled underwater exploration opportunities — and a highly experienced group of people to guide you through the coral reefs. The *Underwater Explorers Society (UNEXSO),* located across from the *Lucayan Beach* hotel, Grand Bahama, affords divers aboveground views of the underwater wonders to be found offshore. Attractions include the *Museum of Underwater Exploration,* which features displays, movies, and multimedia presentations depicting Bahamian dives and deep-sea discoveries, and the "Dolphin Experience," where visitors can swim with six dolphins ($59 per person). *UNEXSO* also offers a unique program that permits divers to snorkel with dolphins in the open ocean. Beginners can learn the basics, or take full-certification courses from a highly qualified staff. And if you want to show off to your friends back home, videotapes of your experiences are also available (phone: 809-373-1250 or 809-373-1244; in the US, 800-992-DIVE).

THE RAMSAR SITE, Turks & Caicos: Protected under the Ramsar Convention, an international treaty, the wetlands on the south side of Middle (Grand), North, and East Caicos are home to thousands of waterbirds and intertidal and shallow-water plant life, and an important nursery area for conch, lobster, and myriad marine species. The protected areas of these islands are fairly inaccessible, and a permit is required to enter some of them. Contact the National Parks Department (phone: 809-322-4830) before setting out on this underwater adventure.

Shopping

Shopping is always a major tourist interest and can easily become a main focus on any Bahamian vacation. Nearly duty-free purchases can be found in the Bahamas: Recently, the Bahamian government abolished the duty, or tax on imports, on china, crystal, cameras, perfume, jewelry, and leather goods, making shopping here more attractive (reductions average 25%) to bargain-conscious buyers. It is important, however, that you have an accurate idea of the US prices of the specific items you are after: Often the so-called duty-free prices represent only a tiny savings over US prices; sometimes the difference is significant. Bring an empty suitcase. There are fine stores and boutiques as well as native markets for browsing. The markets are marvelous places to meet and mingle with local people, absorb atmosphere, tune your ear to the island's patois, bargain for native crafts, and — not incidentally — have a great time.

Remember that market dealing in the islands is done on the spot, and you should feel free to haggle a little for bargaining's sake and the fun of it. Local vendors enjoy a friendly negotiation, and while they will take your money for the price asked, everyone will have a better time engaging in the close, good-natured give-and-take of striking a final price. The Bahamas produce mostly straw and shell work, but there is also a rich choice of fine European and Asian imports and/or colorful native fashions, crafts, and art.

Note: US Customs enforces federal laws that prohibit the entry of articles made from the furs or hides of animals on the endangered species list. Beware of shoes, bags, and belts made of crocodile or certain kinds of lizard, and anything made from tortoiseshell. They'll all be confiscated on your return to the US.

Though not a free port for retail goods, the Bahamas nonetheless offer some excellent buys (especially with the reduction in duty). The best buys throughout the Bahamas include British china, crystal, fabrics, liquor, Scandinavian glass and silverware, Swiss watches, and French perfume. German and Japanese cameras and electronic equipment are offered, but are not always cheaper than at US discount stores. Local offerings feature seashells (especially conch), jewelry, and straw goods like hats, mats, bags, and dolls. Prices for imported china, crystal, perfume, and cameras run 10 to 50% below those in the US. Nassau's major stores and shops are on and around Bay Street (see *Quintessential Bahamas,* in this section); be sure to visit the *Straw Market,* which features native handicrafts — straw hats, baskets, and other good stuff (on Bay St., west of Rawson Square). On Grand Bahama Island there is Freeport's *International Bazaar,* a 10-acre, $3-million shopping complex designed by a Hollywood special effects man to showcase imports from Europe, the Far East, and the Mideast. There's also a straw market. You can mix your own perfume at the *Perfume Factory.* Also on Grand Bahama is the *Port Lucaya Market Place,* a multimillion-dollar center with 85 boutiques, restaurants, and specialty shops.

Casino Countdown

Island gambling takes one of two forms: action or distraction. The presence of junkets (trips organized to deliver high rollers to the tables by the planeload) and several casinos (rather than just one or two) usually indicates serious play. Otherwise, it's lowercase stuff — something to do with your evenings in town besides eating, dancing, or watching another island floor show.

There are now four casinos in operation in the Bahamas: the *Princess* and the *Lucayan Beach*, which, with an assist from golf, keeps Grand Bahama tourism alive; *Paradise Island* casino on Paradise Island; and the casino at the *Crystal Palace* hotel at Cable Beach on New Providence. Most junkets head for Freeport. All four feature the usual games, plus baccarat for big spenders. In addition, there is the first-ever casino in the Turks & Caicos, at the *Ramada Turquoise Reef* resort on Provo.

The minimum bet at the casinos is $2 (except baccarat tables, where the stakes are usually *big*), but this figure tends to rise in the evening (with the designation of certain $5 tables, for example) according to the night, the crowd, and who's in charge. The Bahamas prohibit their own nationals from gambling, but tourists aren't stopped at the door or charged admission. Once inside, there may or may not be drinks (which may or may not be free to players). Minimum age is 18; visitors must present a passport or other photo ID. Hours are 1 PM to 4 AM.

A Shutterbug's View

The Bahamas and the Turks & Caicos offer more photo opportunities than you could exhaust in a lifetime of visits. There's the hustle and bustle of Bay Street shoppers in Nassau; the festive Floridians arriving at the dock in Freeport; the clusters of fishing boats off Bimini and at the yacht haven at Walker's Cay; the surf-kissed beaches throughout the islands; and the simple images provided by islanders going through their daily routines.

Sunsets and sailboats, flowers and flamingos, farmers and fishermen, pomp and circumstance, junkanoo and jump-ups — all the color and excitement the islands have to offer is waiting to be captured on film. Whatever your pleasure — nature photography, portraiture, architectural, or fast-action sports shooting — the diversity of the Bahamas affords a cornucopia of images. Even a beginner can achieve remarkable results with a surprisingly basic set of lenses and filters or a camcorder. Equipment is, in fact, only as valuable as the imagination that puts it into use. (For further information on equipment, see *Cameras and Equipment* in GETTING READY TO GO.)

Don't be afraid to experiment. Use what knowledge you have to explore new possibilities. Because the statue of Christopher Columbus in front of Government House in Nassau has been photographed thousands of times before doesn't make it any less worthy of your attention.

In the Bahamas, as anywhere, spontaneity is one of the keys to good photography. Whether it's a sudden shaft of light bursting through the clouds and hitting the waves breaking on the shore just so, or fishermen unloading their catch as dawn creeps over the piers, don't hesitate to shoot if the moment is right. If photography is indeed capturing a moment and making it timeless, success lies in judging just when a moment worth capturing occurs.

A good picture reveals an eye for detail, whether it's a matter of lighting, of positioning your subject, or of taking the time to frame a picture carefully. The better you grasp the importance of details, the better the results will be photographically.

Patience is often necessary. Don't shoot that sweeping view of the pink beach on Harbour Island if a passing cloud dims the shimmering color of the sand. A brand-new car parked on historic Front Street in Cockburn Town on Grand Turk? Reframe your image to capture only the old Bermudian-style buildings lining the narrow lane. People walking toward a scene that would benefit by their presence? Wait until they're in position before you shoot.

The camera or camcorder provides an opportunity not only to capture the islands' varied and subtle beauty, but to interpret it. What it takes is a sensitivity to the

178 DIVERSIONS / A Shutterbug's View

surroundings, a knowledge of the capabilities of your equipment, and a willingness to see things in new ways.

LANDSCAPES AND SEASCAPES: Nassau's busy downtown, its historic buildings, and its waterfront area are the favored subjects of most visiting photographers. But the island's green spaces, bustling Potter's Cay, and the rest of New Providence provide numerous photo possibilities. East of Nassau, for instance, lies a residential area with many unusual homes, including one built in the shape of a lighthouse. West of town, at Cable Beach and in the heights above, are even more luxurious residences, including the prime minister's home and the former residence of Mrs. Harry Oakes, the widow of the near-legendary financier. On the south shore of New Providence is the tiny community of Adelaide, whose placidness evokes images that have all but disappeared from the rest of the island.

The more pristine — and much less photographed — Turks & Caicos islands offer a range of unusual landscapes: Salt Cay's eerie, chalk-white salinas, dotted with abandoned windmills, provide an almost postapocalyptic image. And if you're on the island in the late winter or early spring, you may be lucky enough to capture on film the spectacle of a giant humpback whale swimming up Columbus Passage to its spawning grounds.

Color and form are the obvious ingredients here, and how you frame your pictures can be as important as getting the proper exposure. Study the shapes, angles, and colors that make up the scene, and create a composition that uses them to best advantage.

Lighting is a vital component of landscapes and seascapes. Take advantage of the richer colors of early morning and late afternoon whenever possible. The overhead light of midday is often harsh and without the shadowing that can add to the drama of a scene. This is when a polarizer is used to best effect. Most polarizers come with a mark on the rotating ring. If you can aim at your subject and point that marker at the sun, the sun's rays are likely to be right for the polarizer to be effective. If not, stick to your skylight filter, underexposing slightly if the scene is particularly bright. Most light meters respond to an overall light balance, with the result that bright areas may appear burned out.

Although a standard 50mm to 55mm lens may work well in some landscape situations, most photographers will benefit from a 20mm to 28mm wide-angle lens. A beach shot from a hotel balcony, for example, is the kind of panorama that fits beautifully into a wide-angle format, allowing not only the overview but also the inclusion in the foreground of people or other points of interest. A flower, for instance, may be used to set off a view of the gardens at the old *Royal Victoria* hotel; people can provide a sense of perspective in a shot of the Paradise Island Bridge.

To isolate specific elements of any scene, use your telephoto lens. Perhaps there's a particular carving on a historic church that would make a lovely shot, or it might be the interplay of light and shadow on a pier lined with boats. The successful use of a telephoto means developing your eye for detail.

PEOPLE: As with taking pictures of people anywhere, there are going to be times in the Bahamas when a camera is an intrusion. Your approach is the key: Consider your own reaction under similar circumstances, and you have an idea as to what would make others comfortable enough to be willing subjects. People are often sensitive to having a camera suddenly pointed at them, and a polite request, while getting you a share of refusals, will also provide a chance to shoot some wonderful portraits that capture the spirit of the islands as surely as the scenery does. For candids, an excellent lens is a zoom telephoto in the 70mm to 210mm range; it allows you to remain unobtrusive while the telephoto lens draws the subject closer. And for portraits, a telephoto can be used effectively as close as 2 or 3 feet.

For authenticity and variety, select a place likely to produce interesting subjects. The *Straw Market* is an obvious place for visitors, but, if it's local color you're after, visit

Potter's Cay, where fishermen and produce growers unload their boats every day and the islanders do their shopping. Or go to the village of Gambier, west of Cable Beach, which is more like a Family Island community than a suburb of Nassau. Take a walk to "Over the Hill," where the less wealthy residents of Nassau live. Aim for shots that tell what's different about the islands. In portraiture, there are several factors to keep in mind. Morning or afternoon light will add richness to skin tones. To avoid harsh facial shadows cast by direct sunlight, shoot where the light is diffused.

SUNSETS: When shooting sunsets, keep in mind that the brightness will distort meter readings. When composing a shot directly into the sun, frame the picture in the viewfinder so that only half of the sun is included. Read the meter, set, and shoot. Whenever there is this kind of unusual lighting, shoot a few frames in half-step increments, both over and under the meter reading. Bracketing, as this is called, can provide a range of images, the best of which may well be other than the one shot at the meter's recommended setting.

Use any lens for sunsets. A wide-angle is good when the sky is filled with color-streaked clouds, when the sun is partially hidden, or when you're close to an object that silhouettes dramatically against the sky.

Telephotos also produce wonderful silhouettes, either with the sun as a backdrop or against the palette of a brilliant sunset sky. Bracket again here. For the best silhouettes, wait 10 to 15 minutes after sunset. Unless using a very fast film, a tripod is recommended.

Red and orange filters are often used to accentuate a sunset's picture potential. Orange will help turn even a gray sky into something approaching a photogenic finale to the day, and can provide particularly beautiful shots linking the sky with the sun reflected in the ocean. If the sunset is already bold in hue, the orange will overwhelm the natural colors. A red filter will produce dramatic, highly unrealistic results.

NIGHT: If you think that picture possibilities end at sunset, you're presuming that night photography is the exclusive domain of the professional. If you've got a tripod, all you'll need is a cable release to attach to your camera to assure a steady exposure (which is often timed in minutes rather than fractions of a second).

For situations such as evening shows outdoors at a hotel or nighttime harbor cruises, a strobe does the trick, but beware: Flash units are often used improperly. You can't take a view of the skyline with a flash. It may reach out as far as 30 feet, but that's it. On the other hand, a flash used too close to a subject may result in overexposure, resulting in a 'blown-out' effect. With most cameras, strobes will work with a maximum shutter speed of 1/125 or 1/150 of a second. If you set the exposure properly and shoot within range, you should come up with pretty sharp results.

CLOSE-UPS: Whether of people or of such objects as flower blossoms, close-ups can add another dimension to your photography. There are a number of shooting options, one of which is to use a 70mm or a 210mm lens at its closest focusable distance. Unless you're working in bright sunlight, a tripod will be worthwhile. If you are very near your subject and there is a good deal of reflective light, it may pay to underexpose a bit in relation to the meter reading.

If you do not have a telephoto lens, you can still shoot close-ups using a set of magnification filters. Filter packs of one-, two-, and three-time magnification are available, converting your lens into a close-up lens. Even better is a special macro lens designed for close-up photography.

The following are some of the islands' truly great pictorial perspectives.

A SHORT PHOTOGRAPHIC TOUR

POTTER'S CAY: There are so many photo possibilities here, with the rows of vendors' stalls fronted by heaps of produce: vivid green limes, bright red tomatoes, brown-skinned onions, multicolored peppers, bright orange carrots, yellow and green bananas, and green-crowned pineapples. The conch sellers are partially hidden from view by the piles of pink-tinged shells that are stacked in front of them; island women fry their conch fritters to a golden brown in vats of bubbling-hot oil; and the jostling crowds of shoppers pick up their daily groceries. Down at the outer piers, the mailboats — even in this modern air age — are still the lifeline to the Family Islands, carrying mail, bulky cargo, and an occasional passenger back and forth. While there is much to capture at eye level, an unusual perspective can be gained by shooting from the Paradise Island Bridge. The south end of the bridge is anchored on Potter's Cay and slowly rises over the harbor to descend again at Paradise Island. There are sidewalks on each side of the bridge's roadway, so no matter what time of day you're shooting, one view or the other will be shadow-free. A zoom lens can be useful for such scenes as an unobstructed close-up of a vendor and customer haggling over prices. (Higher up on the Paradise Island Bridge, you can get some spectacular views of downtown Nassau, the cruise-ship dock, and the *Coral World* observation tower to the west, or Nassau's East End to the east.)

DIXON HILL LIGHTHOUSE, San Salvador: The temptation on San Salvador will be to shoot anything and everything having to do with Christopher Columbus and the Bahamian claim that this was the island on which the Great Navigator first set foot in the New World. But most of the Columbus memorabilia is of recent origin, while the lighthouse is nearly 140 years old. One of the few remaining hand-operated, kerosene-powered lights in the world, it sits 163 feet above high water, has 40,000 candlepower, and a visibility of 19 miles; its light emits a double flash every 25 seconds. Its internal workings — with weights that must be pulled by hand, much like those on an antique grandfather clock — can be photographed, but a strobe or flash is necessary. The lighthouse's observation deck provides views of the island's network of saltwater, sea-fed lakes, connected by channels hacked by hand out of solid limestone.

PREACHER'S CAVE, Eleuthera: A natural photo opportunity if there ever was one. This wide-mouthed cavern has a vaulted roof that soars as high as 100 feet in some places, providing plenty of light (and a bat-free experience for those on the ground). There is also a caretaker who keeps the cave clean, so there is no trash or litter to mar your picture. This is the cave where William Sayles led his band of shipwrecked survivors, the remnants of the Eleutherian Adventurers who settled the islands in the middle of the 17th century. The cave offered the band of devout Puritans shelter and a natural site for religious services. Holes in the cave's roof allow shafts of light to penetrate the interior, enhancing its otherworldly ambience.

THE SALINAS OF GRAND TURK: Grand Turk was settled for one reason: the production of salt. In the 1640s, Bermudian salt rakers established the industry by damming the naturally occurring salt ponds and clearing trees to reduce rainfall and increase evaporation. Salt production ended only about 30 years ago and the vast ponds remain, now crisscrossed by causeways and attractive to waterfowl of all sorts. Shooting photos very early in the morning, with the sun peeping over the hills in the east, reduces the glare that makes midday shooting more difficult. In late afternoon, the sunlight is obstructed by buildings in town, which lies west of the salinas. The morning hours also offer a better chance to lure one or more of the island's roving donkeys, or perhaps a lone stroller or solitary car, into the picture.

JUNKANOO: Whether you are in the islands for the real thing on *Boxing Day* (December 26) or *New Year's Day* or find yourself at one of the mock junkanoos staged for visitors at other times of the year, this is an opportunity to capture a quintessentially Bahamian experience. What *Mardi Gras* is to New Orleans and *Carnival* is to Rio de Janeiro or Trinidad, the junkanoo is to the Bahamas. It also happens to be the one time that islanders don't mind at all if you point your camera at them and snap away. In fact, many of the dancers and revelers will stop and pose for you. The costumes are unbelievably colorful and often elaborate, but the action is often so fast that you have to be prepared to shoot at a moment's notice. You will need a strobe or flash for a nighttime junkanoo (the *Boxing Day* and *New Year's Day* festivities begin about 3 AM). Another problem you may have to cope with are the surging crowds joining in the action; they may be more preoccupied with having fun than with helping you take the perfect picture.

For the Body

Dream Beaches

The Bahamas and the Turks & Caicos have some of the loveliest sand along the western Atlantic. It's true that — thanks to too many appearances on recurrent Most Beautiful lists — a few have been overdiscovered. But Paradise Beach (on the island formerly known as Hog) is as Eden-like as ever — in spite of the crowds it hosts on weekends and cruise ship days — and Grace Bay Beach on Provo is still postcard-perfect (and bustling).

The beaches below are not necessarily the *most* anything. They're simply a few of our favorites. And they happen to be the ones we dream of in the gray of mukluk season, when northern US city streets (and our spirits) are full of slush and we desperately need restoring.

FERNANDEZ BAY, Cat Island: Though it's not the easiest beach to get to, the good news is that once there, you can count on white sand, turquoise blue sea — and solitude. This lovely strand, lined with lacy casuarina trees, is also an ideal place from which to go windsurfing (for instruction and/or rental information, stop at the *Fernandez Bay Village,* a charming inn run by the Armbrister family, or call 809-354-5043).

GRACE BAY, Providenciales: Busy, but still beautiful, this reef-protected beach stretches along Provo's north shore for almost 12 miles. Thirty years ago Grace Bay was a deserted place, but time and progress have brought hotels — a *Club Med,* and the *Ramada Turquoise Reef,* the largest resort in the colony — to its shores. No matter. The sand here is still so fine, it's almost like powder; and when the beach gets too crowded, snorkelers and divers can take to the water and frolic with the fish.

HARBOUR ISLAND, off Eleuthera: Flowering shrubs and coconut palms enhance the scene at this 3-mile pink sand beach along Harbour Island's windward shores. Serving such hotels as the *Dunmore Beach Club* and *Pink Sands,* it's a perfect place for picnicking, snorkeling (although the surf tends to get a little rough here), and swimming.

ROLLEVILLE, Great Exumas: Miles of secluded beach, interrupted only by clusters of coconut palms and a wooden house here and there; the waters here vary in color from pale aqua to deep turquoise. And except for an occasional yacht or fishing boat passing by, this as yet undiscovered strand is all yours.

Best Depths: Snorkeling and Scuba

Because of the excellence of the snorkeling and diving conditions in the Bahamas — rock formations, reefs, wrecks, and spectacularly clear water — most beach hotels rent snorkeling equipment, and there are good dive shops that not only rent equipment but lead diving excursions and provide day-by-day advice on local conditions.

Just about anyone can use a snorkel, mask, and flippers wherever the water is clear —

DIVERSIONS / Snorkeling and Scuba 183

and in the Bahamas, that is almost everywhere. (If you are exploring coral reefs without fins in shallow water, you should wear sneakers or other rubber-soled shoes.)

Scuba diving, using the sophisticated system of high-pressure cylinders full of compressed air and a "demand regulator" that balances air flow with water pressure as the diver changes depths, is something else. Handling everyday procedures and emergencies with equal aplomb takes training and practice. Therefore, though you can buy the gear you need at any dive shop, most shops will refill tanks for and rent equipment only to divers who have earned certification — in "Y" courses, which require 1 or 2 nights a week for about 6 weeks, or about a week of resort instruction, partly in a swimming pool and partly in open water. For information, contact the *National Association of Underwater Instructors* (*NAUI*; PO Box 14650, 4650 Arrow Hwy., Suite F1, Montclair, CA 91763; phone: 714-621-5801); the *Professional Association of Diving Instructors* (*PADI*; 1251 E. Dyer Rd., Suite 100, Santa Ana, CA 92705; phone: 714-540-7234); or your *YMCA*. We've selected some of the islands' best spots:

Andros – The Andros Barrier Reef, the world's third-largest, is the best diving spot; *Small Hope Bay Lodge* (near Fresh Creek; phone: 809-368-2014; in the US, 800-223-6961; fax: 809-368-2015) arranges diving trips and offers both certified dive instruction and underwater photography courses. More experienced divers can explore the reef's deep outside drop-off and blue holes.

Bimini – Although better known for its fishing, the island offers a number of spectacular dive opportunities, including a 15-foot dive through the wreck of the *Sapona*, a huge vessel, built by Henry Ford, that sank off these shores in 1929. Now teeming with grouper, grunts, and snapper, the waters are also home to lobsters, moray eels, and hogfish, who dwell among the 3 miles of coral reef along the Bimini Wall. Tours can be arranged through *Bimini Undersea Adventures* (phone: 809-347-2089; in the US, 800-327-8150).

Eleuthera – Off the northern tip of the island are a number of excellent dive sites, including — for daredevils only — the "Rollercoaster," a thrilling 10-minute plunge along a narrow tidal channel where the current whooshes you along its length and, happily, a boat picks you up at the other end. Less intrepid divers may head for the Devil's Backbone to explore the wreck of a wooden barge from the American Civil War that lies under 15 feet of ocean. There are also good sites for novice divers to view the grouper, angel, trigger, and other tropical fish that ply these waters. Contact *Valentine's Dives* (Harbour Island; phone: 809-333-2309; in the US, 800-662-2255) for further information.

Freeport/Lucaya, Grand Bahama – Probably the best instruction anywhere is offered here at the *Underwater Explorers Society* (*UNEXSO*; phone: 809-373-1250 or 809-373-1244; in the US, 800-992-DIVE), where scuba lessons include simulated reef dives in an 18-foot tank. They also arrange dive trips to such sites as Treasure Reef, the Wall and Black Forest Ledge, the Caves, and *Theo's Wreck*. Also specially arranged dives with dolphins in the open sea, called the "Dolphin Experience," the only program of its kind in the world.

Long Island – In addition to the shallow snorkel dives available around the island, divers shouldn't miss the shark dive offered by the *Stella Maris Inn* and marina (phone: 809-336-2106; in the US, 800-426-0466), a day-long outing during which you get to "meet" (and feed) Caribbean reef sharks, mako, hammerhead, bull — and possibly a barracuda or two.

Nassau, New Providence/Paradise Island – There are numerous reefs, wrecks, and coral strands off these two adjoining islands, and certified instruction and equipment can be obtained at most hotels. *Bahama Divers* (phone: 809-393-5644 or 809-393-1466) offers certified instruction and trips and has concessions at major hotels.

San Salvador – There are more than 50 sites here, most of them on the leeward side of the island. The walls drop from a slope of 40 to 100 feet, and again to 170 feet, revealing turtles, grouper, rays and a few sharks on the descent. Snapshot Reef — named by the underwater photography school affiliated with *Guanahani Divers*, with plenty of photo opportunities (contact the *Riding Rock Inn;* phone: 809-332-2694; in Florida, 305-359-8353; elsewhere in the US, 800-272-1492) — is only 20 feet down.

Turks & Caicos – Extraordinary rings of virtually pristine coral reef and the spectacular 7,000-foot Turks Island Passage drop-off draw divers from literally all over the world to these unspoiled islands. Well-equipped dive shops on Provo include *Provo Turtle Divers* (phone: 809-94-64232), *Flamingo Divers* (phone: 809-94-64193), *Dive Provo* (phone: 809-94-65040), and *Provo Aquatic Adventures* (phone: 809-94-64455), and there are two live-aboard dive boats, *Ocean Outback* (phone: 809-94-64393) and *Sea Dancer* (phone: in the US, 800-932-6237). Dive opportunities on Grand Turk can be arranged through *Blue Water Divers* (phone: 809-94-62432), *Omega Divers* (phone: 809-94-62232), and *Off the Wall Divers* (phone: 809-94-62159), and there is a live-aboard boat, *Aquanut* (phone: 809-94-62541); on Salt Cay, try *Porpoise Divers* (phone: 809-94-66927); on North Caicos, there's Dolphin Cay Divers (phone: 809-94-67119).

Lots of Yachts: Sailing

The waters around the Bahamas are well protected and provide delightful day or overnight journeys. Whether you charter a craft with a full crew and provisions or take out a bareboat and eat what you catch, sailing among the islands of the Bahamas can be an unparalleled experience — the opportunity to explore uninhabited islets, anchor in secluded bays and inlets, and visit dozens of tropical landfalls and at your own pace.

In the Bahamas, every size and style of craft is available, and arrangements can be made through a travel agent, your hotel desk, a specialist like *Nassau Yacht Haven* (phone: 809-393-8173), or any of a half-dozen other firms. Bareboat charters can be arranged through *Bahamas Yachting Services* (phone:809-367-2080; in the US, 800-327-2276) of Marsh Harbour in the Abacos. Eleuthera, the Abacos, and the Exumas offer fine anchorages.

Good boat organizations to know for sailing Bahamian waters are *Lynn Jachney Charters,* which handles crewed yachts (phone: in Massachusetts, 617-639-0787; elsewhere in the US, 800-223-2050); and *Regency International Yacht Charters,* crewed and bareboats (Long Bay Rd., St. Thomas, USVI 00802; phone: 809-776-5950; in the US, 800-524-7676). Crewed-charter specialists include *SailAway Yacht Charter Consultants* (15605 SW 92nd Ave., Miami, FL 33157; phone: in Florida, 305-232-2800; elsewhere in the US, 800-872-9224); *Whitney Yacht Charters* (750 N. Dearborn St., Suite 1411, Chicago, IL 60610; phone: 312-929-8989; elsewhere in the US, 800-223-1426). *Avery's Boathouse* (phone: 809-776-0113) provides both crewed and bareboats.

Be aware that (like hotel rooms) charter prices increase during the winter, decrease in the summer. The off-season is the best time to sail without running up astronomical bills. In peak season, charters can become scarce, and if you want a bareboat or a crewed yacht for a holiday, it should be booked at least 6 months in advance.

Top Tennis

Though the tennis capital of the Atlantic and Caribbean islands is Bermuda (as it has been since the game was imported there from England, making it the place where the first court was laid out in the Western Hemisphere), today there are more than 100 courts throughout the Bahamas — some at hotels, some attached to clubs that allow non-members to play for a fee — that are fine for an occasional game. But serious players and those who want to get serious will find their search limited to those resorts with resident pros, ample numbers of courts, programs of lessons, and lights for night play — such as *Club Med* and the *Ocean Club*, both on Paradise Island.

Since the dimensions of a tennis court don't usually vary and resort courts seem to alternate only between rubberized hard courts and clay-like fast-drying surfaces, other factors distinguish a proper tennis facility from a casual court. For example, how many courts does a resort have in relation to its overall size? This determines how much access you will have to these courts and how much time you will really spend playing.

Similarly, are the courts lighted for nighttime play? It is often unwise to play in the subtropical heat, and this means — especially if you are bent on spending considerable time on the court — that you'll want them available in the cooler evening hours.

Last, does the resort offer tennis packages? A good package will sometimes guarantee court time and reduce court fees where there are any. You will find few true clay courts in the islands, because clay needs time to dry out after a rain, and few hotels are willing to put courts out of action after every summer shower.

If you are really into rackets, these are the resorts to consider:

CLUB MED, PARADISE ISLAND, Bahamas: This *Club Med* enclave was specifically designed and created for tennis and is the best place in the islands for lessons. Facilities include 20 clay-composition courts, 8 lighted; free group lessons with the resident pros; pro shop; closed-circuit TV instruction and ball machine (phone: 363-2640; in the US, 800-258-2633).

COTTON BAY CLUB, Rock Sound, Eleuthera: This small but luxurious resort has only 4 Laykold composition courts, but it offers the renowned pro *Peter Burwash International* tennis program. Weekly or weekend packages include 2 hours of instruction per day and free court time. Resident tennis pro is Eric Thorel. Private lessons, $50; clinics and tournaments weekly (phone: 809-334-6156; in the US, 800-223-1588).

OCEAN CLUB, Paradise Island: One of the best tennis facilities on the island, it has 9 Har-Tru courts (4 lighted). The *Marlboro Tennis Open* is held here annually. Half-hour lessons with top pro John Farrington are $25 (phone: 809-363-3000; in the US, 800-321-3000).

Golf

Despite their essentially flat terrain, the Bahamas offer plenty of first-rate places to set your spikes to more than satisfy most golfers. Within the islands are examples of the course craft of a great many of golf's premier architects. Robert Trent Jones (Sr. and Jr.), Pete Dye, Dick Wilson, Joe Lee, and other greensmakers of equal skill are represented. Their talents, combined with weather that sometimes seems specifically designed for perfect course care, provide layouts that exist in a nearly impossible green richness.

That said, here are our choices of the best in the Bahamas:

COTTON BAY CLUB, Rock Sound, Eleuthera: Rated "one of the world's top 33" by *Golf Magazine,* this par 72, 7,068-yard course designed by Robert Trent Jones, Sr., boasts 129 sand traps and 13 water hazards — not counting the Atlantic Ocean. Arnie Palmer is one of the touring pros who plays here. Sean O'Connor is the director of golf; Carrington Butler is the pro. Greens fees are $40 for 18 holes; $25 for cart. Information: *Cotton Bay Club,* PO Box 28, Rock Sound, Eleuthera, Bahamas (phone: 809-334-6156; in the US, 800-223-1588).

DIVI BAHAMAS BEACH, New Providence: Though this is the newest course on New Providence island, it is by far the best. At the southwestern tip of the island usually called Nassau — though this is in fact only the name of the major metropolis on the island — it occupies high ground that provides a striking view of the area called Tongue of the Ocean.

The course, designed by Joe Lee, is highlighted by four challenging water holes, and again the use of the unusually rolling terrain sets the layout of this 18-hole championship golf course apart from its island counterparts. It is reason enough to spend your stay on New Providence at this hotel, formerly called the *South Ocean Beach.* The greens fee is $27.50 for guests, $40 for non-guests, and a (mandatory) cart is $40. Information: *Divi Bahamas Beach Resort and Country Club,* PO Box N8191, New Providence, Bahamas (phone: 809-362-4391; in the US, 800-367-3484).

PARADISE ISLAND GOLF CLUB, Paradise Island: This picturesque, Dick Wilson–designed par 72 course is surrounded by the Atlantic Ocean and water hazards on three sides. Holes 6 and 7 have been redesigned for greater challenge; the par 3 14th hole, affectionately dubbed "cocoa plum," affords golfers a breathtaking ocean view. Greens fee ranges from $40 to $50; cart (which is mandatory) is $20; club rental is $20 for a full day. Information: *Paradise Island Golf Club,* PO Box N4777, Nassau, Bahamas (phone: 809-363-3925; in the US, 800-722-7466).

Sport Fishing

One of the prime sport fishing grounds in the world, the Bahamas attract enthusiastic anglers from all over. Almost every variety of deep-sea game fish, and many world-record-threatening catches, has been taken in these waters. Most of the fish seem to run during the spring-summer and summer-fall seasons, although there is no off-season on most islands — just better and poorer times to go out. Some of the fish run to deep waters, others lie among the reefs and shallows; but whatever style of fishing suits you — casting, trolling, bottom or reef fishing — a challenge awaits you in the Bahamas.

Some of the game fish that abound in the Bahamas are marlin, sailfish, tuna, wahoo, and mackerel — all deep-sea fish — and great barracuda, pompano, tarpon, and bonefish — all shallow-water fish.

Fish move, and local conditions change from season to season, sometimes subtly but critically. The secret of successful fishing in the best waters is your captain — his knowledge of local waters and his feeling about the prevailing conditions will lead you to the big ones. Be sure to work out all the financial details before shoving off.

Below are some of our suggestions for successful sport fishing:

BAHAMAS: Charter a craft at Bimini, and let the captain take you where they're running. Best deep-sea sites include Walker's Cay (world-record skipjack tuna) or Cat Island (world-record wahoo); take a boat from the town of Current, at the Current Club Dock, to fish North Eleuthera's western coast (world-record dorado) or some special area that only the captain knows. More than 50 world-record catches have been made off the Bahamas. Known as the bonefishing capital of the Western world, the Bahamas are the place where the elusive "ghost of the sea" can be stalked on the flats off Bimini, Eleuthera, and the Exumas.

TURKS & CAICOS: Aficionados who've already tried it hope you won't believe the stories you hear about the incredible bonefishing in the shallows off the Caicos. Privately, they say it's some of the best in the world — especially in the waters that wash the west-lying Caicos Bank. Julius Jennings is one guide to seek out on South Caicos; "Bonefish Lem" Johnson is the man on Provo. For more information, contact the Turks & Caicos Tourist Board (phone: in the US, 800-441-4419).

Hunting

There was a time when all the islands were completely open to hunters and the killing of birds and wild animals was not controlled. Today, many island species are protected, and most hunting is restricted to waterfowl and certain other species of birds on those islands where it is allowed at all. Though the days of the big bang are gone, hunting is still possible in the Bahamas.

Hunting permits are granted to non-Bahamians after a stay of 90 days. Wild boar can be hunted on Andros and the Abacos, and throughout the Bahamas there is open season on most varieties of dove, pheasant, heron, and other birds from September 15 until February 28. The season on mourning doves and several varieties of duck and geese extends through March 31; boar season takes place during the winter months. For more information on hunting, including protected species, and bag limits, contact the Bahamas Ministry of Agriculture and Fisheries (PO Box N3028, Nassau, New Providence, Bahamas; phone: 809-326-5515/6 or 809-322-8064). Check with the nearest Bahamian consulate and also the Commissioner of Police (Royal Bahamas Police Force, PO Box N458, Nassau, New Providence, Bahamas; phone: 809-322-4444 or 809-326-7828) about a gun license and bringing guns with you. They can also help you find a guide who knows the area.

Sunken and Buried Treasure

It's certainly childish, and rather a poor way to try to repay your gambling debts, but who can resist the urge to hunt for buried treasure? The odds of striking it rich are not in your favor — but nor are they at the casinos in Nassau or Freeport. There are plenty of wrecks off the Bahamas to explore. In fact, many of the ships that met their end here may have been sunk deliberately. During the lean years in colonial times, many Bahamian communities made a living by "wrecking" — scavenging goods from ships that foundered on the reefs and shoals offshore. Legend has it that the residents of some towns, like Port Howe on Cat Island, deliberately lured ships aground — and then rowed out to claim their treasure.

There are many kinds of wrecks here: Spanish galleons, sloops that patrolled the

188 DIVERSIONS / Treasures

waters during the American Civil War, freighters, and pleasure boats. For all we know, there might be a sunken US submarine in the 6,000-foot-deep trough east of Andros called the Tongue of the Ocean, where the British and American navies conduct secret maneuvers. Here are a few that are a bit easier to find:

For starters, go to Man-O-War Cay in the Abacos, where the steam-powered sloop USS *Adirondack* lies in the shallows 27 feet below the surface. The ship hit a reef soon after dawn on August 23, 1862, on its way to Nassau, where it was being sent to monitor the activities of the Confederate blockade runner *Alabama*. The crew of the *Adirondack*, fortunately, was saved, and the ship's cargo was divided between the captain and the "wreckers" that rowed over from the Abacos to assist the crew. Divers can investigate 14 of the ship's cannon, some of which lie only 10 feet below the the surface of the water. Nearby, off Green Turtle Cay, lies the wreck of the *San Jacinto,* a Union gunboat that sank on *New Year's Day* in 1865. The ship was chasing a blockade runner when it mistook a light on the cay for the renegade craft and ran aground a reef offshore. Divers can also investigate the hulk of the *Potomac,* which lies in 20 feet of water off Andros; the cement-hulled *Sapona* (built by Henry Ford in World War I), which lies near South Bimini; the remains of the *Frascate,* a steel-hulled freighter that sank off San Salvador Island in 1902; and the *Hydrolab,* an underwater research station abandoned off Grand Bahama about 20 years ago.

Like some of the colonial ships, some of the recent wreckage was sunk deliberately. *Theo's Wreck,* off Grand Bahama, is a 280-foot steel freighter intentionally sunk in 1983. Freeport's *Underwater Explorers Society* uses it for exploratory dives and photo ops. The waters off New Providence are littered with wrecks that were deliberately scuttled to provide backdrops for James Bond movies. The (unintentional) wreck of the *Nuestra Señora de la Maravilla* (which went down on January 4, 1656) is thought to be lying somewhere off Little Bahama Bank. And if you're on the Family Islands, try Morgan's Cave, at the northern tip of Andros (Henry Morgan was one of the most successful pirates in the Caribbean, and his treasure caches have never been found).

None of these sites can compare with Treasure Reef off Grand Bahama, where four divers discovered the wreck of a Spanish galleon in 1962. The wreck lies in shallow water about 3 miles due east of the beach at Port Lucaya. The ruins yielded a fabulous treasure trove: 10,000 silver coins minted by Hernán Cortés in Mexico. Initially valued at $9 million, their worth plunged rapidly once collectors were faced with the prospect of a flooded market. Their value was later pegged at $2 million and then halved once again. Subsequently the Bahamian government enacted a law giving it a 25% stake in all wrecks — and said that it applied retroactively. If that wasn't enough, the four divers soon found themselves embroiled in expensive legal disputes with other claimants to the find. One of the divers, a lad named Jack Slack, summed up the whole frustrating experience in a book entitled *Finders, Losers.* Don't get discouraged, though. There are probably still plenty of treasure troves to be found.

DIRECTIONS

Introduction

Ask someone to describe what springs to mind when you mention "The Bahamas" and you'll probably get something resembling this list. Casinos — the Las Vegas sort, with Greek statuary in the parking lot. Golf courses — the postcard-perfect ones designed by some of the world's best architects. Fish — big fish, marlin most likely, preferably caught on Bimini with a grandnephew of Ernest Hemingway. Decadence, probably of the relatively innocent 1950s variety: rhinestone sunglasses, pool bars, chefs in white tuxedos barbecuing lobster on the beach. Colorful figures: swashbuckling Sir Henry Morgan and gangster Al Capone; tax-evader Robert Vesco and Carlos Lehder Rivas, who until a few years ago ran Norman Cay in the Exumas like his own Colombian drug fiefdom.

Would these descriptions be wrong? Well, no, but they are not quite all there is to the Bahamas and Turks & Caicos. Yes, there are championship golf courses and glitzy casinos and great game fishing. Yes, there are tacky developments and pool bars. But most folks don't know about the 18th-century saltbox houses in the Abacos and on Eleuthera, each painted a different pastel shade; or the grand Georgian homes on Queen Street in Nassau; or the ruined Loyalist plantations on Eleuthera or the old saltworks in the Turks Islands. Nor do many visitors think of spending a Sunday morning in a whitewashed church listening to a rousing revival meeting, or dancing to 1950s-style goombay music or a rake-and-scrape band, or watching a Bahamian quadrille or a junkanoo parade.

Each island in the Bahamas has something special to offer. Anglers go to Bimini, sailors to Abaco and the Exumas, divers to Andros and the exquisite coral gardens off the Abacos. Don't expect to find everything on each of the islands. You won't find a casino on San Salvador, but there's great surfing nearby; and while Grand Turk has little in the way of wildlife aside from a few herds of wild donkeys, it has some of the finest reefs this side of Australia.

Here, then, are a dozen island tours. They first take you to the best-known isles: New Providence (and to its capital, Nassau, and to Paradise Island just offshore) and Grand Bahama. Then they follow a zigzag course through the outlying isles, tacking southwest from Grand Bahama to Bimini; east to the Abacos; south to Andros; east and south to the slender isles of Eleuthera, Cat Island, and the Exumas; and even farther east to tiny San Salvador, where Christopher Columbus *may* have landed in 1492. The tours end in the Turks & Caicos, the British crown colony more than 500 miles east of Florida. Several of our tours describe walks through historic towns like Nassau, Harbour Island just off Eleuthera, George Town in the Exumas, and Cockburn Town on Grand Turk. For those with a good map and time to spare, there are also several driving routes. The hardy may want to follow some of the driving routes by bike, though the Bahamas, on the whole, aren't as bike- and moped-friendly as, say, Bermuda. Along the way, our tours point out old plantations and historic churches, great restaurants (or, on the remote isles, the only eateries open after 2 PM), pineapple farms, and rum factories, and the perfect spots for a variety of activities, from swimming to spelunking to shelling. Finding the best places in the Bahamas can take some patience and perseverance, but the rewards are well worth the effort.

Nassau

Nassau, known as Charles Town until 1695, has attracted a mixed crowd over the years. Puritans settled here in the 17th century, and the Anglican church dominated local politics — and commerce — until well into the 19th century. Freebooters came to Bay Street to sell their stolen goods, Spanish galleons periodically assaulted Nassau's forts, and American revolutionaries captured the town briefly in 1776. Pirates and money-grabbing priests abandoned Nassau long ago, to be replaced by gamblers, camera-toting tourists, and offshore banks. Despite this hurly-burly, the town has remained pleasantly civilized and old-fashioned. Skyscrapers and sprawling developments are strictly controlled, and many of the town's historic forts and government buildings have been given a face-lift. Rambling mansions overlook the harbor on the east side of town, and the pastel Georgian houses that line some shady side streets are more than 200 years old.

There is so much to do and see in Nassau that it's best to have a plan of attack before starting out. For those visitors planning a lunchtime break, keep in mind that most restaurants open between 11 AM and noon and close around 2:30 PM,. When a cruise ship is in port, most restaurants are jammed, so be prepared for a long wait — or pack a picnic basket and head for the Botanic Gardens or Fort Charlotte (see *New Providence* in DIRECTIONS). The walking tour described here, which takes in several picturesque and historic spots, can be completed in a leisurely few hours.

The tour starts in Rawson Square in the center of town, just steps from Prince George Wharf, where the big cruise ships are berthed. The Ministry of Tourism has an information booth on the waterfront (north) side of the square, and to the west is the surrey depot, where horse-and-buggy tours of the city begin. Opposite is the Churchill Building, where the prime minister and some government ministries conduct their affairs. The statue in the square is of Sir Milo Butler, a former grocer who became the country's first governor after the Bahamas won its independence in 1973.

Fronting the south side of Rawson Square is busy Bay Street. Just across it is Parliament Square, which is presided over by a statue of a youthful Queen Victoria. (She's actually thin, and her expression isn't as dour as usual.) The stately building to the queen's right houses more government offices. To her left is the House of Assembly, where the oldest governing body in continuous session in the New World convenes. The Senate — the less powerful legislative branch — meets in the building behind the queen. These modified-Georgian buildings, which date from the late 18th and early 19th centuries, were based on the same plans used to build New Bern, North Carolina's first capital.

Behind the Senate building stands the Supreme Court, where bewigged

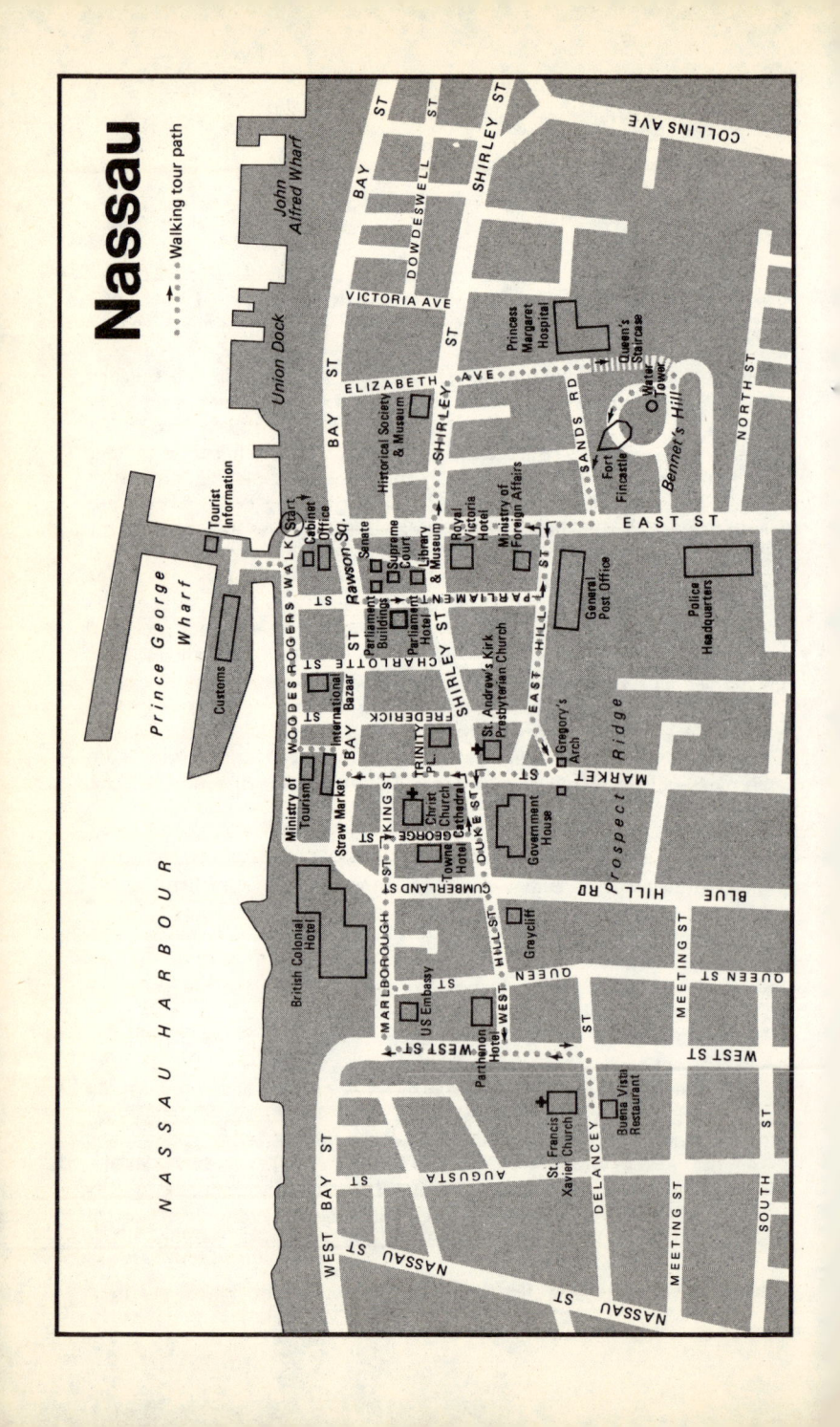

Nassau

••••• Walking tour path

NASSAU HARBOUR

- Union Dock
- John Alfred Wharf
- Prince George Wharf
- Customs
- Tourist Information
- Cabinet Office
- Rawson Sq. (Start)
- Senate
- Supreme Court
- Library & Museum
- Parliament Buildings
- Parliament Hotel
- Royal Victoria Hotel
- Ministry of Foreign Affairs
- Historical Society & Museum
- Princess Margaret Hospital
- Queen's Staircase
- Water Tower
- Fort Fincastle
- Benner's Hill
- General Post Office
- Police Headquarters
- Ministry of Tourism
- Straw Market
- International Bazaar
- St. Andrew's Kirk Presbyterian Church
- Gregory's Arch
- Christ Church Cathedral
- Towne Hotel
- Government House
- Graycliff
- British Colonial Hotel
- US Embassy
- Parthenon Hotel
- St. Francis Xavier Church
- Buena Vista Restaurant

Streets: BAY ST, DOWDESWELL ST, SHIRLEY ST, COLLINS AVE, VICTORIA AVE, ELIZABETH ST, SHIRLEY ST, SANDS RD, NORTH ST, EAST ST, EAST HILL ST, PARLIAMENT ST, CHARLOTTE ST, FREDERICK ST, TRINITY PL, MARKET ST, DUKE ST, KING ST, GEORGE ST, CUMBERLAND ST, MARLBOROUGH ST, HILL ST, WEST ST, QUEEN ST, MEETING ST, WEST BAY ST, NASSAU ST, AUGUSTA ST, DELANCY ST, SOUTH ST, HILL RD, BLUE HILL RD, Prospect Ridge, WOODES ROGERS WALK judges preside. A serene little square separates the courthouse and the *Nassau Public Library and Museum;* in its center stands a cenotaph commemorating the Bahamians who died in both world wars. (A separate plaque honors four members of the Royal Bahamian Defence Forces who were killed in 1980 when their craft was sunk by Cuban MIGs — a traumatic incident that has sunk deeply into the national consciousness.) The library, housed in a yellow octagonal building constructed in the 1790s, was once a jail. History buffs should visit the second floor, which is devoted to Bahamian subjects. There are exhibits of straw plaiting and Bahamian postage stamps and several artifacts, including a *duho,* a low stone bench made by Lucaya Indians. Climb the stairs to the third floor and the verandah, which affords a fine view of the city center.

West of the library, across Parliament Street, is the *Parliament* hotel, built just before World War II. The sandbox trees in front are said to be 2 centuries old. The nearby *Pick-A-Dilly* restaurant (phone: 322-2836) caters to tourists, who come for the daiquiris, and Nassau barristers, who seem to prefer Scotch and sodas and martinis. South of the library, across Shirley Street, stand the remains of the *Royal Victoria,* Nassau's first hotel, completed in 1861. Winter visitors who sailed to Nassau from New York on Samuel Cunard's steamships lodged here in fine style. During the Civil War, Confederate agents and blockade runners conducted their operations from the lobby. The hotel was passed from one proprietor to the next — Florida railroad magnate and developer Henry Flagler owned it for a time — and finally folded in 1971. Its once-lovely gardens, shaded by an old banyan tree, are still open to the public.

Continue down Parliament Street to the post office, where collectors can buy colorful Bahamian stamps. A short walk away is Bennet's Hill, which has a magnificent view of Nassau Harbour. To get there, walk east on East Hill Street and bear left onto East Street, right onto Shirley Street, and straight down to Elizabeth Avenue. On the northwest corner is the *Bahamas Historical Society and Museum* (phone: 322-4231), where historic maps and photographs are on display. (It's generally open for a few days in the middle of the week between 10 AM and 4 PM, but the schedule changes, so call ahead.)

Continue south (away from the harbor) on Elizabeth Avenue to the Queen's Staircase, which leads to Bennet's Hill and an 18th-century fort. The stairway, hewn out of limestone blocks sometime in the late 1830s, has 65 steps — one for each year of Queen Victoria's reign. Don't give up — the view is worth every step. Visitors who can muster the energy should climb the 126-foot tower at the top of the hill, where the view is even better, particularly at twilight, when the town's lights begin to wink on.

Nearby is Fort Fincastle, which was built by Lord Dunmore, a former royal governor of Virginia who came here during the American Revolution. The fort's shape and deck-like ramparts remind some visitors of a Mississippi stern-wheeler. No shot was ever fired in anger from the fort, and it did peacetime duty as a lighthouse until 1816.

Return to the post office, first taking the footpath that leads to Sands Road, bearing right onto East Street and left onto East Hill Street. The 19th-century pink-and-white building on the north side of East Hill houses the Ministry of Foreign Affairs; it was once the home of Lord Beaverbrook, the newspaper tycoon. Nearby is the modern headquarters of the Royal Bank of Canada, built on the site of an old home called "Glenwood Gardens." Woodes Rogers, the 18th-century buccaneer-turned-governor, is reputedly buried in the yard. The grave is said to be marked with a skull and crossbones; don't bother looking for it, though, for the grounds are off limits.

Prospect Ridge, on which you stand, was once the dividing line between Nassau's rich and poor. Most of the town's white population lived along the waterfront, while blacks lived "over the hill." Laborers trudged up the steep hill each night until a tunnel, called Gregory's Arch, was put through in 1850. The poor lived in tumbledown villages like Grant's Town, which was settled in the 1820s by freed slaves; the town is now a middle class neighborhood shaded with palms, casuarinas, and royal poincianas.

Ramble down East Hill Street to Market Street; St. Andrew's Kirk will be to the right. This fine 19th-century Presbyterian church housed the first non-Anglican congregation in the Bahamas. Straight ahead, on a high hill just west of Market Street, is Government House, the official residence of the Governor-General of the Bahamas. (Bahamian governors are mostly figureheads, with the true political power resting in the hands of the prime minister.) The original mansion was destroyed in a hurricane in 1929 and was replaced by this pink-and-white neo-colonial building a few years later. A 12-foot statue of Christopher Columbus stands on the steep flight of steps leading to the main doors. The front gates are usually closed at 5 PM, but you can slip in through the side entrances on Market and Cumberland Streets. On alternate Saturdays, the grounds are open for the spit-and-polish changing-of-the-guard ceremony, which takes place at 10 AM sharp.

Near Government House, where West Hill Street meets Blue Hill Road, is *Graycliff,* one of the special places in the Bahamas. The handsome Georgian building was built in the 1720s by Captain John Howard Graysmith, who made his fortune plundering ships along the Spanish Main. During the American Revolutionary War, it was a mess hall for troops of the West Indian Regiment. Polly Leach, a friend of Al Capone's, ran a hotel here in the 1920s. The house was later bought by Lord and Lady Dudley, who restored it with unimpeachable taste. Twelve rooms of the old house have been renovated for guests — there are suites and cottages as well — and the restaurant is one of the best in the Bahamas (see *Quintessential Bahamas,* in DIVERSIONS). The wall along West Hill Street is built with stones from the oldest church on New Providence, which was destroyed by fire in 1703.

Continue west on West Hill Street; across West Street is the Church of St. Francis Xavier, which was erected in 1886 with funds from the Archdiocese of New York. Just south of the church on Delancey Street, in a charming 19th-century house, is the very good *Buena Vista* restaurant (phone: 322-2811). Lining West Street on the right are the *Parthenon* hotel, a small guesthouse, and the beautiful little Annunciation Greek Orthodox Church. Turn right on Marlborough; walk the short block to Queen Street, and turn right again, which will bring you to the front of the US Embassy. Peer through the dense foliage at the stately old homes that line Queen Street; some are more than 200 years old. The once-elegant *British Colonial* hotel stands near the corner of Queen and Marlborough Streets. Built in 1923, it was run for a time by the near-legendary Nassau entrepreneur Sir Harry Oakes.

Continue east on Marlborough and turn right onto George Street, near Christ Church, an island-Gothic Episcopal cathedral. Though the country hasn't been officially Anglican since 1869, many state ceremonies still take place here. The opening ceremony of the Supreme Court, for example, begins with a procession of robed and bewigged judges and barristers to Christ Church, accompanied by the *Royal Bahamas Police Band.* Farther up George Street, next to the *Towne* hotel, is a curious old mansion named "Georgeside" that is said not to have a single right angle, inside or out. Across the street is an old limestone plantation house.

A left turn onto Duke Street leads to Market Street, just below Gregory Arch. Proceed north, toward the water; the *Straw Market* is dead ahead. On the right side of the street is the huge new Central Bank Building. Across from it are two buildings that were once private homes: "Balcony House," built in the late 18th century, and the somewhat newer "Verandah House." Halfway down the block on the right is Trinity Place, a short street that leads to Trinity Methodist Church, which was put back together in 1869 after a hurricane. Backtrack to Market Street and continue north across Bay Street once again. To the left is "Vendue House," where chattel of all sorts, including slaves, was once put on the block.

At the *Straw Market* on Bay Street, young women will weave you a basket or plait your hair — with beads, if you like — for a dollar or two a strand. The offices of the Bahamas Ministry of Tourism occupy the upper floors of the market. To the north is the waterfront and Woodes Rogers Walk, named for the onetime pirate and former governor.

Stroll east along the walk toward Prince George Wharf, where the passenger liners dock. At the intersection of Charlotte Street is the *Nassau International Bazaar.* Among the shops here is the *Tropical Fine Art Gallery,* where works by watercolorist Darman Stubbs are on display; the gallery is open from 10 AM to 5 PM every day except Sunday. The wharf, where the water taxis chug back and forth from and to Paradise Island, is just a few paces from Rawson Square, where this tour began.

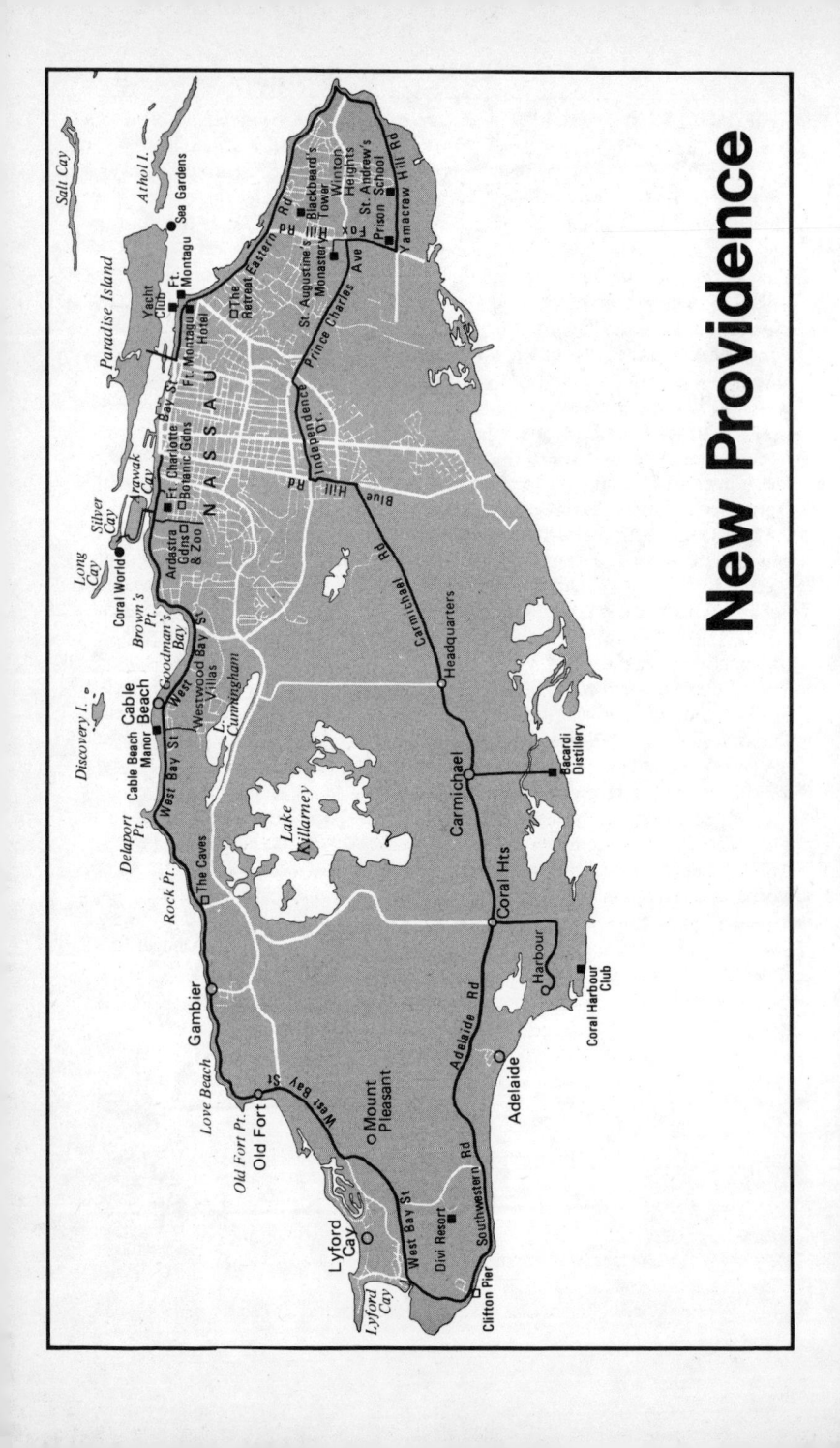

New Providence

New Providence

Two out of every three Bahamians live on New Providence, an almost perfectly symmetrical isle roughly 22 miles long and 7 miles wide. Settled in 1656 by a band of Puritans from Bermuda, it was later chosen as the site of the colony's capital because of its deep natural harbor and abundant freshwater supply. (The island's population, 172,000 at last count, has grown so much in recent years that the government must now import water from Andros.) Most of the settlements are clustered along the coast; the flatlands in the interior are covered with scrub and groves of palmetto and pine. While the capital city of Nassau is the island's main attraction, there are plenty of other places worth seeing.

This tour takes a counterclockwise swing around the island, beginning at Nassau and stopping at some historic forts, grand homes, and quiet beaches along the way. The route merits a leisurely day, whether you go by moped, rental car, or taxi. Celebrity hunters may wish to enlist the services of a guide, as no enterprising local soul has yet published a Hollywood-style star map to the homes of notables.

Just west of Nassau, the shore road — called West Bay Street — bends left and leads to Fort Charlotte, the Ardastra Gardens and Zoo, and the Nassau Botanic Gardens. Fort Charlotte stands atop the hill behind Clifford Park, where the annual *Independence Day* (July 10) festivities are held. Built between 1787 and 1789 to protect Nassau's western harbor, Fort Charlotte was the pet project of the fourth Earl of Dunmore, Governor of the Bahamas. The fort, which soon became known as "Dunmore's Folly," cost about four times the amount budgeted; perhaps this explains why the governor thought it wise to name it after the consort of King George III. The largest of New Providence's many fortifications, it is made of solid limestone buttressed with cedar. It was billed the most impregnable of Nassau's bastions, but the claim was never tested, for it never came under attack. A $1-million restoration was completed several years ago, and it's worth spending an hour or so touring its dungeons, reputed torture chamber, seemingly bottomless well, and drawbridge, which spans the waterless moat. The barricades run about 300 feet along the crest of a hill overlooking the harbor. The fort is open daily, except Sundays, from 9 AM to 4 PM. Admission is free, but expect to pay a tip if you engage one of the free-lance guides who always seem to be loitering around.

Just west of Fort Charlotte, on Chippingham Road, are the Ardastra Gardens and Zoo and the Botanic Gardens. The zoo — the only one in the Bahamas — has a fine display of monkeys, tigers, leopards, kangaroos, and tropical birds. There is also an unusual blue-and-green Bahama parrot, some endangered varieties of iguana, and a very rare hutia, the descendant of a small mammal brought to the islands more than 1,000 years ago by the

Arawak, whose ancestors had come from South America. Children shouldn't miss the trained flamingos, which march briskly through their paces at 11 AM and 4 PM. The Ardastra Gardens and Zoo are open daily from 9 AM to 5 PM; admission is $7.50 for adults, $3.75 for children (phone: 323-5806).

Nearby are the blessedly peaceful Botanic Gardens, which are spread over 18 acres of an old limestone quarry. Lush tropical foliage flourishes alongside succulents that thrive in arid regions of the Bahamas. One garden is planted with shrubs used by "bush doctors" on remote cays. There is also a grotto fashioned out of hundreds of conch shells. Open from 8 AM to 4:30 PM Mondays through Fridays; 9 AM to 4 PM Saturdays and Sundays. Admission is $1 for adults, 50¢ for children (phone: 323-5975).

In the harbor west of Nassau is Silver Cay, site of the vast *Coral World* recreation park. From the Botanic Gardens, take the access road off West Bay Street to the bridge leading to the cay. Here visitors can stand on a glassed-in platform 20 feet below the surface of the sea and watch the fish dart about a large reef. There is also an underwater snorkeling trail, pools with stingrays and sea turtles, and a shark tank. Young children can visit the shallow "petting pool," where they can touch harmless conch, hermit crabs, starfish, and sea cucumbers. *Coral World* is open daily from 9 AM to 6 PM; to 7 PM from April to October. Admission is $14 for adults, $10 for children (phone: 328-1036).

West of the harbor, West Bay Street bends sharply south toward Brown's Point and Goodman's Bay. On the left is the former *Cable Beach Golf Club*, now part of the *Crystal Palace* resort and casino; opposite it is Cable Beach. (An undersea telephone cable, completed in 1892, runs from this beach to Jupiter Beach, Florida.) During the 1930s and 1940s, Cable Beach was crowded with the mansions of the rich and famous; over the years, most have been supplanted by resorts and hotels. The easternmost of these is the *Ambassador Beach* hotel, near the site of "Westbourne," the now-demolished home where American-born entrepreneur Sir Harry Oakes was living at the time of his death in 1943 (his murder is still unsolved). The skyline is dominated by the *Crystal Palace* hotel, which is bedecked with cartoon-bright panels of aqua, purple, and orange. Condominiums and apartments are springing up on the south side of the road across from the beach. One of the shopping centers along this stretch is built on the site of *Hobby Horse Hall,* a thoroughbred racetrack that closed in the late 1970s.

To see one of the island's most exclusive neighborhoods, turn left onto Malcolm Avenue, across from the *Cable Beach Manor.* The area, known as both Westwood Villas and Skyline Drive, was granted by the Crown to Sir Harry Oakes, who moved to the Bahamas in the 1930s. His estate stretched about 7 miles from east to west, past the south shore of Lake Cunningham, the second-largest of the island's saltwater ponds. Oakes's widow lived here, in "Dale House," until her death a few years ago. Nearby, on Ridge Road, is the home of Prime Minister Lynden O. Pindling. Not too far away, at No. 16 Poinciana Street, stands the house where Pindling lived earlier in his career. Many other government officials live here, as do well-heeled Americans, Canadians, and Britons.

On West Bay Street, near the *Cable Beach Inn,* is "Caprice," a former estate that's been carved up into apartments. "La Mouette," the home of legendary Bahamian entertainer Peanuts Taylor, is on the beach side of the road. Farther west is Delaporte Point, where pirates once hid out, according to local legend. Just down the road is "Rock Point," an estate where scenes from the James Bond film *Thunderball* were shot. On the left side of the highway, just before Blake Road, are some caves on what used to be the Oakes estate. Arawak Indians purportedly took refuge in them; some locals say Sir Harry found buried treasure here (like many stories about him, it's probably untrue). Farther down, on the inland side of the road, is the village of Gambier, named for the brothers Gambier. (One was a buccaneer and the other a Governor of the Bahamas — vocations that in the old days weren't all that dissimilar.) The village is traditional and close-knit, more like the settlements in the Family Islands.

Near here the property owned by Oakes ends and the former estate of Harold G. Christie begins. One of the wealthiest of the island's real-estate magnates, Christie was rumored by some to have been involved in Oakes's death. From here, the road parallels Love Beach and skirts by several secluded homes, including one owned by singer Julio Iglesias. Offshore is the Sea Garden, a reef favored by snorkelers.

Next comes the district of Old Fort, where the sand on the beach is as white and fine as sugar. Stately homes block the view, though, and the only way to see the beach is from the water. Near St. Paul's Church the homes begin to thin out until you reach Lyford Cay, which is linked to the main island by a causeway. Harold Christie built a few houses here, but it was Canadian brewing magnate and horse-racing enthusiast E. P. Taylor who turned the cay into an exclusive retreat some 30 years ago. The golf course and beaches here are private, and guards keep celebrity seekers at bay.

At the western tip of the island is Clifton Point; the comfortably bourgeois village of Mount Pleasant is nearby. There are several industries here, including a cement factory; a major power plant; the Commonwealth Brewery, which makes Kalik beer; and Clifton Pier, where oil tankers unload and cruise ships once docked. The beach — which is surprisingly pristine, given its industrial surroundings — is virtually deserted, which may be why a few scenes from *Jaws 3-D* were shot here in 1983.

From here pick up Southwestern Road and head east, parallel to the south shore. Beyond Clifton Pier the road passes the ever-expanding *Divi Bahamas Beach* resort and country club, with its own golf course, condominiums, and beachfront hotel. Visitors who stop for a cold drink — it won't be inexpensive — will have to fend off salespeople peddling vacation homes. Just to the east is a well-marked side road that leads, in half a mile or so, to the tiny town of Adelaide on the beach. The village was founded in 1831 by Sir James Carmichael Smyth, then Governor of the Bahamas, who named it for the consort of King William IV. It was intended as a settlement for Africans liberated from the Portuguese slave ship *Rosa.* Not too many years ago, it had its own courthouse, jail, and primary school, but the town has dwindled as people move to Nassau to look for work. The beach here is narrow, but it does seem to stretch on forever. On most days two or three men sit by the side of the road selling conch shells and coconut-husk gimcracks. One of the men, Allen Albury (he's the one with a ruddy face and white beard), has plenty of stories to tell, and he rents boats to fishermen.

The main road — now called Adelaide Road — continues east to *Coral Harbour*. Begun in the mid-1950s, the development was the darling of Miami banker Lindsey Hopkins, Jr. Hopkins hoped to make it the premier resort on the island — and might have done so, if he hadn't run out of money. Marines from the Royal Bahamas Defense Forces are billeted in the once-grand hotel, and the golf course, designed by George Fazio, shows signs of neglect. Many of the homes that line the canals and slips — designed so that yachts could be moored right by each door — are for sale. The whole place has a forlorn quality, like a Miami suburb of 30 years ago. A couple of businesses have hung on: There's a shop, *Dive Dive Dive,* for scuba enthusiasts, and the *Tiki Bar* on the waterfront, where visitors can dine on barbecued ribs or curried mutton and listen to the jukebox until the early hours of the morning.

From the resort, turn right onto the highway (now called Carmichael Road). A mile or two ahead, past a few tempting fruit stands, is the Bacardi rum distillery. (Tours are available if you call in advance; phone: 362-1412.) Once based in Cuba, Bacardi moved to the Bahamas during the revolution in 1959. At the intersection with Gladstone Road, near the Carmichael Bible Church, stood the town of Headquarters. Founded in 1825, it was the oldest of the communities for liberated slaves established by Governor Smyth. The area east of here is peppered with housing developments built by the government to ease overcrowding in Nassau.

In 5 miles or so, Carmichael Road runs into Blue (formerly Baillou) Hill Road. Continue north — the traffic may be heavy — past A. F. Adderley Senior High School. At the roundabout, go three-quarters of the way around, to Independence Drive. The road becomes Prince Charles Avenue before it reaches Fox Hill Road, where a left turn leads to the St. Augustine Roman Catholic Monastery and College. Built in 1946, this Benedictine abbey was designed by John Hawkes, an architect and Anglican missionary who came to the Bahamas sometime before World War I. Father Jerome, as he was known after his conversion to Catholicism, designed several churches in the islands before retiring to his retreat on Cat Island. The gift shop at the monastery sells goods made by the monks, including freshly baked bread and guava jelly.

A right turn on Fox Hill Road from Prince Charles Avenue leads to the village of Fox Hill, named for Samuel Fox, a slave who became a prosperous landowner after he won his freedom. Several government buildings line the road, including two reformatories and a forbidding prison. Past the prison grounds, turn left onto Yamacraw Hill Road, which passes by St. Andrew's, a 50-year-old Anglican school. As the road sweeps north and west, rounding the tip of the island, the homes that line the north shore become increasingly grand. (Somewhere along here the name of the road changes to Eastern.) There is a mansion on the right side of the road that resembles a lighthouse; it was built by a member of the Solomon clan, a wealthy merchant family.

Some of the stateliest homes stand on a hill in an area known as Winton Heights, where an old plantation once stood. Here visitors can catch an occasional glimpse of the harbor; Athol Island lies just offshore. On a hill on the inland side stands Blackbeard's Tower, a tottery jumble of stones rumored to be the foundations of a tower where the eponymous pirate once watched for ships sailing into the harbor. A narrow unmarked path wedged between two homes — a pink one on the right and a green-and-white one called "Tower Leigh" on the left — leads to the ruins.

Continue west past Brigadoon Estates, site of an eclectic bunch of mansions built around the 1920s by Nassau's elite. A left turn onto Village Road leads to "The Retreat," an 11-acre estate formerly owned by Arthur and Margaret Langlois and now the home of the Bahamas National Trust. The Langloises collected some 200 species of exotic palms, some of which shade the gardens. Guided tours of the house and gardens are conducted between 9 AM and 5 PM Tuesdays and Thursdays; cost is $2 per person. The main road, now called East Bay Street, leads to Fort Montagu, which stands on a bluff overlooking the harbor. Completed in 1744 under the supervision of English military engineer Peter Henry Bruce, the fort was protected by 17 massive cannon. The ordnance appears to have done little good, for the fort was captured in 1776 by an American force led by Ezekiel Hopkins; again in 1782 by the Spanish; and once again the following year by American Loyalist Andrew Deveaux, who retook it from the Spanish. Visitors can roam around the grounds as they wish; there is no admission charge, and there are no guided tours.

Opposite the fort, on the inland side of East Bay Street, stand the remains of the once-magnificent *Fort Montagu* hotel. Built in 1926, it was closed about 20 years ago after a fire. People talk of restoring it, but so far nothing has been done. The bridge to Paradise Island looms off to the north of the hotel; downtown Nassau is about 2 miles to the west. Nearby is the *Waterloo* nightclub; the 60-year-old *Nassau Yacht Club;* the trendy *Ivory Coast* restaurant, which specializes in seafood; a marina; and the *Poop Deck,* a high-spirited bar, where, if you're appropriately exhausted, you can revive yourself after an island tour.

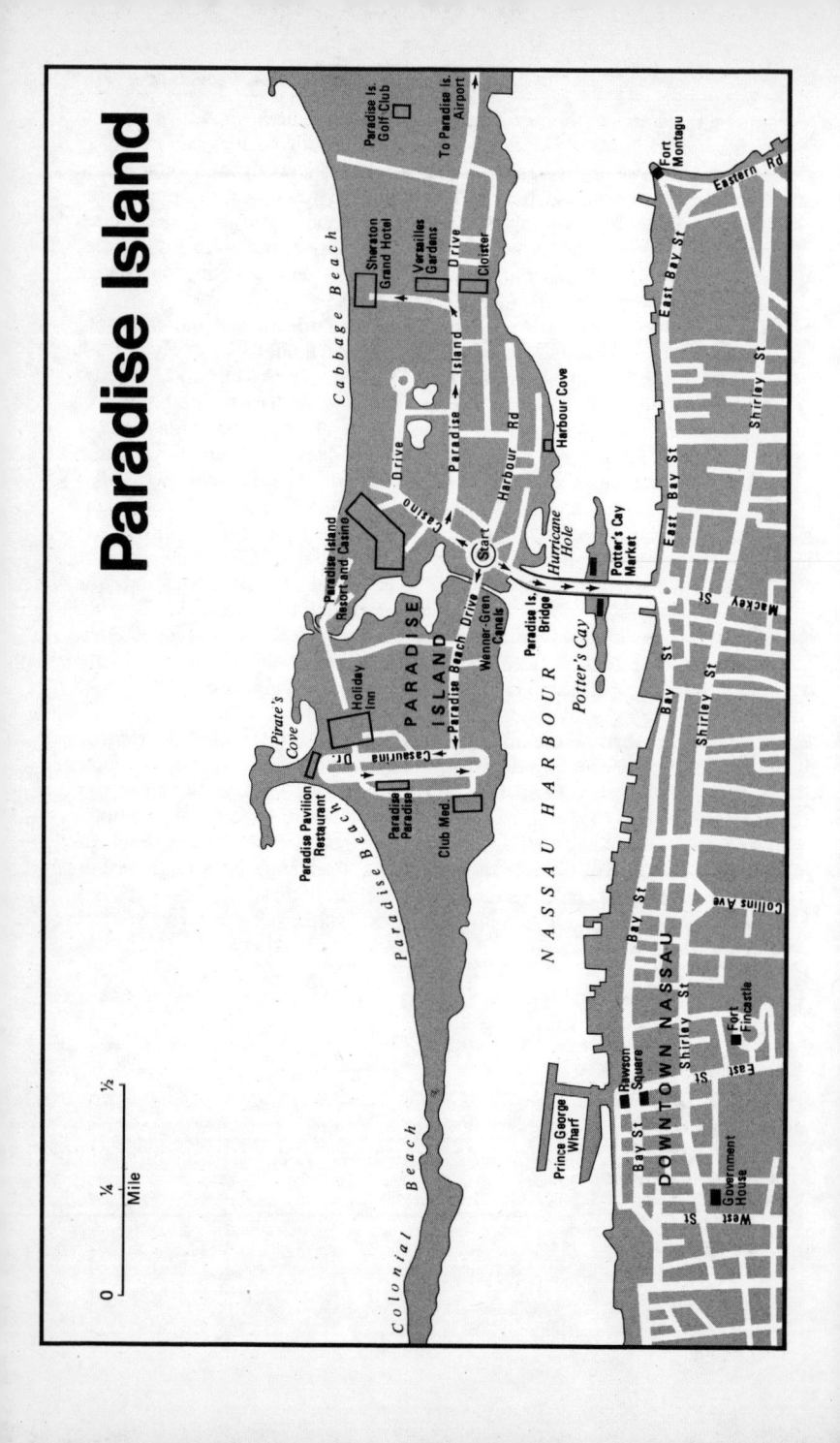

Paradise Island

Paradise Island

Paradise Island, the tiny cay in Nassau Harbour, is proof of the power of advertising. Hog Cay, as it was known until 1959, has been built up, beautified, and marketed so assiduously that it has become a required stop for many tourists. Visitors who like Las Vegas and Atlantic City won't be disappointed. Though the views *from* the island can be magnificent, many of the sights *on* it have a somewhat familiar look. There are no historical landmarks here, and nothing exotic or ethnic, but for visitors who like kitsch, or who are looking for a break from Nassau's bustle, this is the place to come.

Though the island's sights may be faded, its history is colorful indeed. William Sayle, the leader of the of the Eleutherian Adventurers, bought the 685-acre island, which lies just 600 feet offshore, in the mid-17th century. It was he who named it Hog Cay — possibly because he intended to raise pigs there, though it's not clear if he ever did. Forty-odd years later the island was purchased by Bahamian Governor Nicholas Trott for the price of £50, plus an annual rent of a shilling per acre. Trott maintained his claim to the island even after a London court trial and his subsequent removal from office (his ties with several buccaneers had been uncomfortably close).

Little happened on the island until the 1790s, when a French warship, *L'Embuscade,* moored here during its blockade of Nassau Harbour. By the late 19th century, Nassau entrepreneurs had discovered the island's tourist appeal; ferries shuttled wealthy Nassau residents over to pristine Paradise Beach. At some point in the 19th century, American entrepreneur Joseph Lynch (of the brokerage firm Merrill Lynch) bought the island and built a home here.

During the 1930s, the island was sold to Swedish industrialist Axel Wenner-Gren, who moved into Lynch's old house, which he renamed "Shangri-La," and launched several beautification projects. He did so partly as a favor to his friend the Duke of Windsor, Governor of the Bahamas from 1940 to 1945, who was looking for ways to employ poor islanders during the war. Wenner-Gren dug a large lake, which was fed by canals leading to the sea, and hired a landscaper to create a replica of the gardens at Versailles.

In 1959, after Wenner-Gren's death, the island was bought by American multimillionaire Huntington Hartford, heir to the A&P supermarket fortune. Hartford renamed the island and announced plans to turn it into a resort for discriminating clientele. "There will be no automobiles, no roulette wheels, no honky-tonks on Hog Island," Hartford told *The New York Times*. (He was wrong on all counts.) Hartford finished the formal gardens and transplanted a 12th-century French cloister, stone by stone, to his estate. The cloister survives, in a sadly deteriorated state, as do many of the sculptures Hartford collected, including likenesses — of varying quality, and rather uneven taste — of Franklin D. Roosevelt, African explorer David Livingstone, Hercules, Mephistopheles, Faust, and Napoleon and Josephine.

Hartford also spruced up the island's resorts. He built the *Ocean Club,* an 18-hole golf course, the anchorage at Hurricane Hole, and posh riding stables. He also launched a ferry service between the island and downtown Nassau. These ventures, like most of Hartford's projects, generated little profit, and in the late 1960s he sold the island to the Tampa-based Mary Carter Paint Company for about $14 million — considerably less than he reportedly spent refurbishing the island.

It didn't take long for the owners of Mary Carter to realize that tourism was more profitable than paint. The company quickly reorganized, and in its new guise, Resorts International, it built the $2-million Paradise Island Bridge, completed in 1967; promoted gambling at the *Paradise Island* casino; and, after American entertainer/entrepreneur Merv Griffin gained control of the company in the 1980s, built the airport on the eastern end of the island. Resorts International still controls most of the real estate on the island.

It costs 25¢ per pedestrian or bicycle and $2 per car to cross over to Paradise Island from Nassau; the return trip is free. What follows are three short walking tours of the island; each starts at the fountain at the foot of the Paradise Island Bridge.

WALK 1

This tour leads to the beaches on the western strand; it's a leisurely 45-minute round trip. Take Paradise Beach Drive directly across from the fountain; the road crosses one of Axel Wenner-Gren's canals and skirts by the *Club Land D'Or,* a relatively new hotel. Continue down the road past the *Chalk Airline* seaplane terminal. Planes haven't landed here since the Paradise Island airport was built, but the runway is still put to use, in an odd way: The Dobermans and German shepherds that guard the *Paradise Island* resort are trained here, and you may see a couple of canines negotiating an obstacle course on the runway. The airport restaurant, the *Island* (phone: 363-3153), is still open; try the conch fritters and stewed fish.

The road dead-ends at Casuarina Drive, and *Club Med* is straight ahead. From here it's a short walk to the Nassau water taxi dock to the left, and two resort hotels up the road to the right. The drive is lined with stately casaurinas, and a paved footpath runs along the median. Off to the right is the *Pirate's Cove Holiday Inn,* with a conference center, three restaurants, and four bars, including a poolside spot called the *Bonney Anne* that's built like a pirate ship. (Anne Bonney was a pirate — a real swashbuckler, if the stories that have been handed down are credible.) The beach at Pirate's Cove is sheltered and picturesque, but sunbathers take heed: The hotel building casts a shadow on parts of the beach at different times of the day. Across the road is the *Paradise Paradise* resort, with a moderately priced waterside bar and restaurant. The waves here are calm, as they are at the *Club Med* beach a stone's throw away, but neither beach is as attractive as the one at Pirate's Cove.

WALK 2

Our second walk starts from the fountain and leads up Casino Drive, a continuation of the road across the Paradise Island Bridge. It's about a 15-minute stroll to Paradise Island Drive. Turn right, toward the *Ocean Club*, and follow the signs to the swimming pool. There is a fine view of the Versailles Gardens, the cloister, and, in the background, the east end of Nassau (it's so close you can't even see the water separating the two islands). Savor the view, for the gardens have been sadly neglected. If they ever evoked the sense of majestic glory that their namesake does, they certainly don't now. The cloister is somewhat dilapidated, and the draped statue standing in the center has lost its head. The gazebo just beyond the cloister is a good breezy spot to stop for a picnic. There's a broad view of the harbor; notice the boats heading for the market at Potter's Cay, and the planes swooping down for a landing at the Paradise Island Airport just to the east. Also to the east is *Sea Gardens,* an underwater park where *20,000 Leagues Under the Sea* was filmed.

WALK 3

The last walk leads to Potter's Cay, a busy market beneath the Nassau side of the Paradise Island Bridge. (It's no longer a cay, but a finger of land extending into the bay.) The bridge arches high in the center to allow tall ships to glide underneath. Sidewalks run along both sides of the bridge, and the view is equally impressive from both. Directly below, on Paradise Island, are the piers at Hurricane Hole, where deep-sea fishing boats dock in the late afternoon after their daily excursions. To the southwest is the shopping district of downtown Nassau; Prince George Wharf, where passenger liners dock; and, off in the distance, Silver Cay. To the southeast is Fort Montagu and the fine waterfront homes of east Nassau; tiny Athol Island is just offshore.

Potter's Cay is busy, even on Sundays, when many of the stalls are closed. It's open all day, from 8 AM to around 4 PM, and the chefs of the big restaurants in Nassau are rumored to come here early in the day to get their produce. Stalls stocked with fish, conch, and fresh produce — most of it from the Family Islands — stretch in parallel rows underneath the bridge, and vendors — most of them women — sell mangoes, pomegranates, passion fruit, sapodillas, and custard apples, all of which are delicious eaten out of hand. (Some are messier than others, but never mind.) Men and boys sell most of the fish and conch. Conch salads are also well worth a try (see *Island Food and Drink,* in PERSPECTIVES), and if you get hungry while you're waiting for your salad to marinate, try a hot conch fritter or two, or stroll around and look at the baskets and shell gewgaws for sale.

Beyond the stalls are packing houses where seafood is processed for shipment to the US and elsewhere. Several mail boats, the little freighters that are the lifeline of the Family Islands, are moored on the east end of the cay. The boats, which ferry mail between Nassau and the Family Islands, also bring manufactured goods from Nassau to remote islands; they return laden with crates of produce, bales of cotton or fragrant tree bark, and other agricultural products destined for wholesalers in Nassau. The boats also carry passengers to and from the Family Islands at very low fares (be forewarned that the schedules of arrivals and departures are approximate). A cautionary note: Potter's Cay is a fine place to take pictures, but vendors may put up a fuss unless you ask permission to photograph them. If you've just bought something, however, they're far more inclined to pose.

Grand Bahama

Just 55 miles off the coast of Florida, Grand Bahama is the fourth-largest island in the Bahamian chain. Its population has exploded since the twin developments of Freeport and Lucaya were launched here in the 1950s and early 1960s, but for many years it was sparsely settled. Its original inhabitants were the Siboney, a stone-age people from Cuba closely related to the Arawak; they were later displaced by the Lucaya, who migrated to the Bahamas sometime around AD 1000. Many of the Lucaya were carried off as slaves shortly after Columbus landed in the Bahamas in 1492; others were wiped out by war and disease, and Grand Bahama remained virtually uninhabited for the next 300 years, except for a few marauding pirates and a Tory enclave or two.

The Spanish named the island after the phrase *gran bajamar* ("great shallows"), out of respect for the treacherously shallow waters that claimed scores of galleons navigating the Caribbean route. Pirates pillaged many of these wrecks, but they didn't make off with everything. Divers are still discovering vast fortunes here: In 1964, more than $1 million worth of jewels and doubloons were dredged up from a nearby wreck in an area east of Freeport now called Treasure Reef.

The first permanent settlers arrived here during the 19th century. Some were pro-British American Loyalists who had tried their hand at farming cotton and sisal on the Family Islands and had abandoned their farms after the thin soil gave out. Most of the settlers on Grand Bahama made a living diving for sponges, catching spiny lobster and conch, and cutting timber. (Unlike most Bahamian isles, Grand Bahama has an ample supply of fresh water, which accounts for the lush forests — many now thinned by overcutting — in the island's interior.)

During the American Civil War, several settlers abandoned their farms here and moved to Nassau to cash in on the lucrative blockade-running trade. The island's economy picked up during the Prohibition years, when rumrunners found Grand Bahama a convenient conduit for Miami-bound contraband. Lumber companies from the Abacos moved here in the mid-1940s and sold pine to shipbuilders in North and South America. In the early 1980s, Colombian drugs were funneled through here to Miami, but the joint US/Bahamian customs blockade has choked off most of that trade.

Today, tourism is the biggest industry on the island, thanks to a project launched in the mid-1950s by Virginia financier Wallace Groves. In 1955, Groves, who had run a timber concern on the island since the 1940s, made a proposal to the Bahamian government to build a tax-free city — the modern town of Freeport — near the south coast of the island. (A port in name only, it's actually 5 miles inland.) In exchange, Groves was granted exclusive

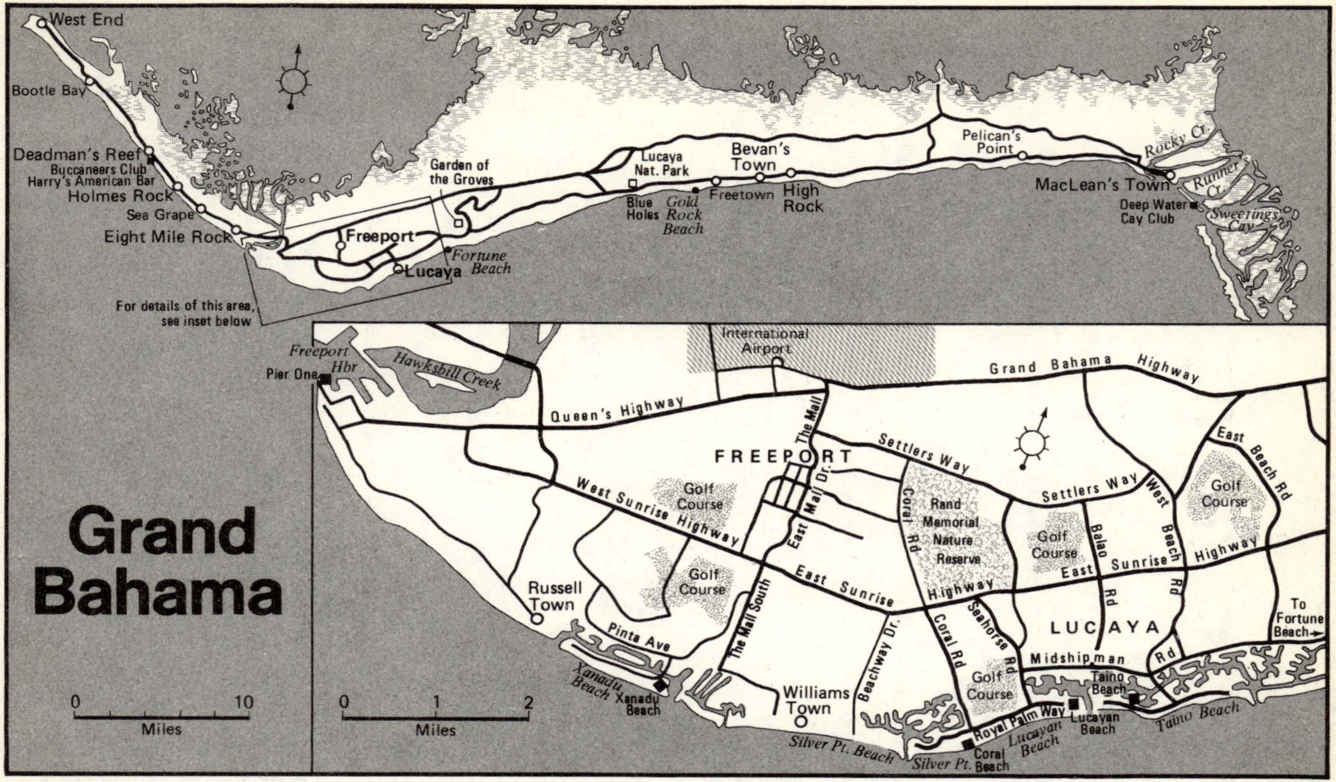
Grand Bahama
West End
Bootle Bay
Deadman's Reef
Buccaneers Club
Harry's American Bar
Holmes Rock
Sea Grape
Eight Mile Rock
Freeport
Lucaya
Fortune Beach
Garden of the Groves
For details of this area, see inset below
Lucaya Nat. Park
Blue Holes
Gold Rock Beach
Freetown
Bevan's Town
High Rock
Pelican's Point
MacLean's Town
Rocky Cr.
Runner's Cr.
Sweetings Cay
Deep Water Cay Club
0
10
Miles
Freeport Hbr
Pier One
Hawksbill Creek
International Airport
Grand Bahama Highway
Queen's Highway
The Mall
FREEPORT
Settlers Way
West Sunrise Highway
East Mall Dr.
East Sunrise Highway
The Mall South
Coral Rd
Rand Memorial Nature Reserve
Golf Course
Balao Rd
West Beach Rd
East Beach Rd
Seahorse Rd
Beachway Dr.
Pinta Ave
Russell Town
Williams Town
Xanadu Beach
Silver Pt. Beach
Coral Beach
Royal Palm Way
Lucayan Beach
Midshipman Rd
LUCAYA
Taino Beach
To Fortune Beach
0
1
2
Miles

development rights and tax exemptions. The complex, built by American firms with Caribbean and Bahamian labor, was initially a failure, for many investors, frustrated by the island's lack of amenities, pulled out. In 1963, in a bid to revive the island's moribund economy, Groves built Lucaya, a large beach resort 5 miles southeast of Freeport. Lucaya's first class hotels, gambling casinos, and golf courses attracted new investors and soon turned Freeport's fortunes around. Between 1963 and 1967, investment in Grand Bahama — and its population — more than trebled. Growth controls were imposed a few years later, however, and since then the island's economy has expanded at a less breakneck pace.

Most people who visit the island make a beeline for the clean white beaches at Lucaya or the glitzy casinos at Freeport. Those who want to take a break from the tourist spots can find plenty of quiet hideaways. The two short cycling tours described here skirt the south shore of the island to the east and west of Lucaya. The shorter of the two driving tours leads to the historic old town of West End; the longer tour, which takes about 2 hours, winds up at some of the old settlements on the eastern end of the island.

While visiting Freeport and Lucaya, it's easiest to get around by bus (they're free here) or taxi, though many of the sights can be seen on foot or by bike. To see the old communities in the east and west of the island, it's best to rent a car, as buses shamble along at a tortoise-slow pace (for car and bike rental and taxi information, see THE ISLANDS chapter).

GRAND BAHAMA BY BIKE

It's easy to cycle in the Freeport/Lucaya area, for the roads are good and the terrain is pancake-flat. To reach lovely Taino Beach, take Seahorse Road out of Lucaya toward Freeport and turn right onto Midshipman Road. Follow it for a mile or so as it skirts the Bell Channel marina, and then turn right again onto West Beach Road. The beach, a broad stretch of fine white sand dotted with palm-frond umbrellas, is just ahead. Nearby is the the *Stoned Crab* (phone: 373-1442), which serves snow and stone crab claws and fresh grilled dolphin fish and wahoo. (Homemade raisin bread comes with each meal.) The *Taino Beach* restaurant (phone: 373-4677) and the *Lobster House* (phone: 373-5101), a good luncheon stop, are just down the road.

To see Fortune Beach, said to be the best on the island, go east on Midshipman Road from Taino Beach for a mile up to the right-hand turnoff to Smith's Point, which leads to the western edge of this 5-mile-long beach. Though it's popular with tourists and locals alike, the beach stretches on so far that visitors are sure to find a secluded spot somewhere. Near the east end of the beach is *Blackbeard's* restaurant (phone: 373-2960), which specializes in crab; try to go at sunset for a cocktail on the terrace. At the east end of the beach, just off Midshipman Road, is Garden of the Groves, a picturesquely contrived 12-acre park with a grotto and a lake, miniature waterfalls, and flocks of flamingos. Next to the park is the *Grand Bahama Museum,* with exhibits of marine life, Lucaya artifacts, and junkanoo costumes. (The gardens are open Tuesdays to Fridays from 10 AM to 5 PM; no admission charge. The museum is open Mondays to Saturdays from 10 AM to 4 PM; closed Wednesdays, Sundays, and holidays. Admission is $2 for adults; $1 for children under 15; phone: 373-5668.)

To see the beaches west of Lucaya, take Seahorse Road to Royal Palm Way. The mansions that line the road have earned it the name "Millionaire's Row." There are two good restaurants along the beachfront: the *Coral Beach* hotel's popular *Sandpiper's Steak House* (no phone), with live country-and-western music, and *La Phoenix* (phone: 373-5700) at the *Silver Sands* hotel, which serves Indian curries and exotic seafood dishes. Continue northwest via Coral Road and East Sunrise Highway to Freeport, 5 miles away. Just 2 miles south of Freeport on Ocean Boulevard, past the 18-hole *D.K. Ludwig's Bahamaia* golf course, is the *Xanadu Beach* hotel. Billionaire Howard Hughes closeted himself on the top floor of the hotel's fortress-like tower for many years before his death in 1976. Once a private club, the hotel has three first-rate restaurants and its own 70-slip marina.

GRAND BAHAMA BY CAR

It's a leisurely 30-mile drive from Freeport or Lucaya to West End, the oldest settlement on the island. The route along the West Sunrise Highway and Queen's Highway meanders through several small towns along the way. On the outskirts of Freeport, half-built concrete block homes line the road, evidence of the real-estate bust that followed independence in 1973, when many jittery investors pulled out of the islands. Past the town, the West Sunrise Highway cuts through stands of skinny second-generation pines, which were planted a few decades ago to replace the dense forests chopped down by lumber companies. Signs are few, and it's easy to get disoriented as you drive past many miles of flat and unvarying green. If you're in a hurry, stick to the main road; the unmarked dirt tracks that branch off from time to time generally lead to small private homes, or an occasional secluded beach. Watch carefully for signs in the small towns that point the way to churches, cafés, and the clear saltwater pools called blue holes.

About halfway between Freeport and Lucaya on the East Sunrise Highway, a road (Beachway Drive) branches off to the left to Williams Town and Russell Town, two early-19th-century settlements. The towns stand on a beautiful stretch of beach near *Pinetree Stables,* where there are good horses and trails down to the beach (closed Mondays; phone: 373-3600). About 3 miles west of Freeport, via the West Sunrise Highway, Queen's Highway, and Harbour Road, is the *Pier One* restaurant, set on stilts overlooking the docks of Freeport Harbor near Hawksbill Creek (phone: 352-6674). Sit by the windows overlooking the harbor and enjoy grilled shark or mahimahi and watch conch fisherman bring in their catch. From here, Queen's Highway continues on to Eight Mile Rock, where wooden bungalows, once brightly painted though now faded to pale pastels, stand close together on the dusty streets. There is a perfume factory here in a former Baptist church where you can watch various tropical scents being concocted. West of town there is a 50-foot-wide "boiling hole," where tidal pressure causes the salt water to bubble like water in a teapot. (Ask a local for directions to the pool, as there are no signs.)

About 5 miles up the road, in the derelict town of Sea Grape, is charming colonial St. Agnes Catholic Church. Continuing past Holmes Rock, the next settlement, Deadman's Reef, has one of the island's best beachside dining spots. The *Buccaneer Club* (phone: 352-5748 or 348-3794) is a good place to sip cocktails at sunset, dance to live music, and dine on fresh seafood. (There's a free bus from the club to Freeport.) Divers can explore the cays just off the reef; bring your own equipment, as there is none for rent here. Back on the main road, just past the ramshackle settlement of Bootle Bay, there is a stone marker on the right marking the fork to West End.

The town of West End is only a shadow of what it was during the glory days of Prohibition, when the population hit 1,700 and the docks were crowded with rum boats ready to make a quick nighttime run over to the coves along Biscayne Bay. Lucaya Indians once lived here in palm-frond huts and caught bonefish off the coast. A generation ago the town was dominated by the *Grand Bahama* hotel, run by the Canadian Jack Tar chain. The huge 450-room resort, called Jack Tar Village by the locals, had its own airport and marina, a 27-hole golf course, and 2,000 acres of tropical gardens. It was shuttered in 1989, and new owners are being sought. Its closing threw many of the locals out of work, and since then the village has sunk into depression. Commerce has dwindled to the town straw market, the small *Harbour* hotel (phone: 346-6432), and a couple of bars. Anglers should bring their rods, for the flats teem with bonefish. To return to Freeport, retrace the route on the Queen's Highway and Sunrise Highway.

If you don't mind a bit of a bumpy ride, there are some fine parks and nature reserves and a few good restaurants on the eastern half of the island. It's a 45-mile drive from Freeport to East End along the Grand Bahama Highway, which gets progressively less grand the farther you get from the city. The road is paved the whole way, but the potholes that crater the surface get bigger as you drive along, so allow a generous 2 hours to reach the remote towns near East End.

Less than 3 miles from Freeport is the Rand Memorial Nature Centre, a 100-acre nature reserve with 130 species of native Bahamian plants, including a dozen varieties of orchids. Several of the plants here were used by the Arawak or the island's colonial settlers. The waxy branches of the candlewood tree may have been used as torches; bunches of springy uniola, a native grass, were gathered to make beds; fibers of the agave plant were spun into thread; and the bright red berries of the psychotria were dried and ground to make a coffee-like beverage. Several varieties of native and migratory birds live here, from tall West Indian flamingos to tiny wood star hummingbirds and parulas (closed Saturdays; phone: 352-5438).

Farther east on East Sunrise Highway, where it intersects with East Beach Drive, are the tropical plant nurseries at the Hydro Flora Gardens, which has a lush collection of tropical ferns, giant sea grapes, and various flowering shrubs (closed Sundays; phone: 352-6052). A white stone marker 10 miles farther on indicates the entrance to Lucaya National Park; the parking lot is to the left, just past the entrance. A nature trail winds through a dense pine forest to two blue holes, which are part of a large network of caverns. (The blue holes are really caves whose roofs have collapsed.) Signs identify various species of trees and plants, as well as some archaeological sites. (Some of the artifacts from Lucaya graves excavated here are on display at the *Grand Bahama Museum,* 8 miles east of Freeport.) A mile-long boardwalk across the road from the car park leads through a tangle of mangroves, ming trees, and wild tamarinds to Gold Rock, a small but lovely beach. Stroll along the dunes by the beach or go for a swim, but be forewarned: The surf can be heavy here.

Just past the park is an American missile-tracking station, also named Gold Rock. The village of Freetown is 5 miles farther on. Opposite the turnoff to the town are two blue holes that are part of another vast network of waterlogged caves. Past the pools is a fork leading to a passable beach. Freetown's somnolent air is briefly dispelled on Sunday mornings, when a loudspeaker attached to the whitewashed Zion Baptist Church broadcasts the sermon throughout the village. Inexpensive native dishes are served at *Deceptions* lounge (no phone) and the *Chickenman's* bar (no phone). Visitors who stop by on a Saturday or Sunday should continue 2 miles east on the main road to the *Bean Sprout,* a cheery beachside spot with good spiny lobster and crab (open weekends only; no phone).

Bevan's Town, 3 miles to the east, has one of the few gas stations in the area; it's just opposite the local diner. The left-hand fork in the road 5 miles farther on leads to an American base built after the Cuban missile crisis. Straight ahead is High Rock, which is dominated by the tall white steeple of the Emmanuel Baptist Church. The *Oceanview* restaurant, run by Ezekiel Pinder — a fine Bahamian name if we ever heard one — serves seafood lunches on a palm-thatch porch overlooking the water (no phone).

The road gets rougher over the next 10 miles and is at its worst near the rusting hulk of the Burma oil depot, which was abandoned some 20 years ago. Overhead floats Fat Albert, a torpedo-shaped barrage balloon built during World War II. Its radar scans the skies for signals from passing Colombian drug runners. About 3 miles past the depot, at the second of two tight bends, a road branches off that leads to a sandbar lapped by clear waters — a secluded spot for a swim. Perhaps the finest beach on the island is 2 miles down the road, at Pelican's Point. The little hotel there, the *Beach Lodge,* is owned by the local minister; the rooms are $50 a night — a bargain by Bahamian standards — and there are fishing boats for hire (no phone).

The road passes another ice-blue saltwater pool at Rocky Creek and deadends at MacLean's Town, which is famous for its annual *Columbus Day* conch-cracking contest (see *Island Food and Drink,* in PERSPECTIVES). It's a short water taxi ride from the town across Runners Creek to the exclusive *Deep Water Cay* club. Bonefish are plentiful in the flats offshore, and the beach is scattered with pretty shells. Snorkelers frequent the reefs off nearby Sweetings Cay, where there are cottages for those who want a respite from the crowds at Lucaya. To return to Freeport, retrace the route along the Grand Bahama Highway.

Bimini

Tiny Bimini, which lies just 50 miles east of Miami, is one of the great game fishing capitals of the world. Immortalized by Ernest Hemingway, who lived here for several years during the 1930s, it still attracts the sporting set: President George Bush still fishes here on occasion, and 1988 Democratic presidential hopeful Gary Hart was forever disgraced after it was learned that he had sailed here from Florida on the *Monkey Business* with model Donna Rice.

Encompassing only 9 square miles, Bimini is actually 2 islands, with a sprinkling of islets and cays thrown in for good measure. Skinny North Bimini is the most developed, while broader South Bimini is largely deserted. A quarter-mile-wide channel separates the two main isles, and a ferry shunts back and forth between them. Despite their occasional brushes with infamy and fame, the islands have retained a homespun quality. The glitz and glamour of Nassau are lacking here, but tourists who are looking for a good quiet spot to dive or fish won't be disappointed.

Arawak Indians were probably the first to settle Bimini, followed in the early 19th century by Seminole slaves fleeing Southern plantations. Spanish explorer Juan Ponce de León, heeding rumors that Bimini possessed fabulous riches, landed here in 1512, but found nothing worth writing home about. During the 17th and 18th centuries, rabble-rousers and miscreants of all stripes found the place appealing. Pirate Henry Morgan had a stronghold here in the late 1600s, and Bahamian sea captains ran supplies from here to the Southern states during the American Civil War. Rumrunners plied a brisk trade between Bimini and southern Florida during Prohibition days, and the many recent plane wrecks off the coast near the airport on North Bimini are testimony to the many failed drug runs between Colombia and Miami.

While some visitors take the sea route to Bimini — several cruise ships call here, and it's 12 hours or so by sailboat from southeast Florida, given favorable winds — most of the tourists who stop here come by plane. Aside from private charters, there is only one way to fly to the island: on *Chalk's* seaplanes from Nassau or Miami. Launched by Floridian Arthur Burns Chalk more than 70 years ago, the charter bills itself as the "oldest continuously operated airline in the world." Al Capone flew to Bimini on *Chalk's,* and so did deposed Cuban dictator Gerardo Machado y Morales, who fled his homeland under a hail of gunfire on a chartered *Chalk's* plane in 1933. The airline, which fell on hard times in the 1980s, was recently rescued by an American from Ft. Lauderdale (phone: in the US, 800-4-CHALKS).

Once on North Bimini, it's impractical to rent a car; the distances are short, and visitors can get everywhere they need to go by walking, cycling, or taking a taxi. The two main settlements on North Bimini — Alice Town and Bailey

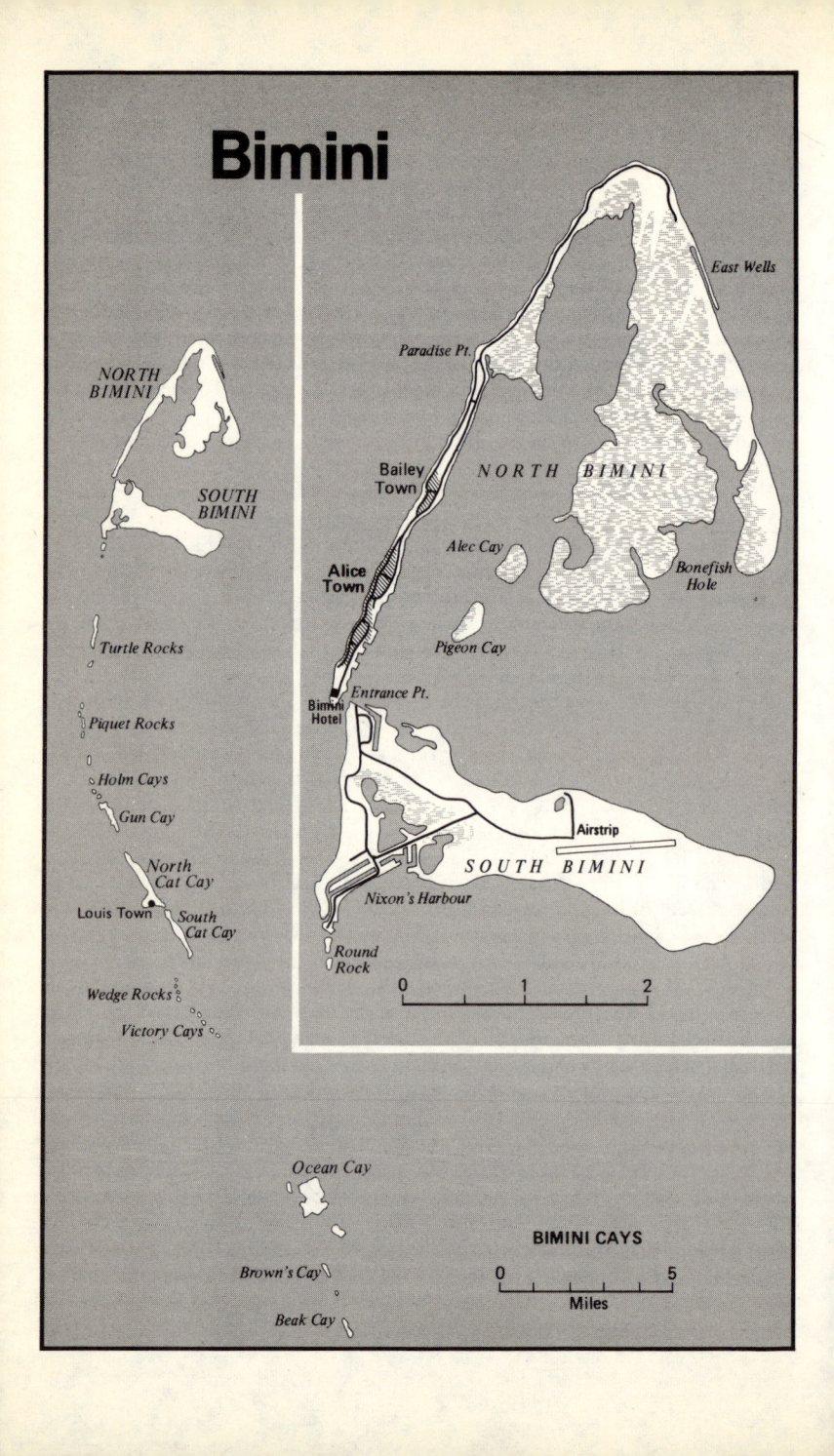

Bimini

NORTH BIMINI

SOUTH BIMINI

Turtle Rocks

Piquet Rocks

Holm Cays

Gun Cay

North Cat Cay
Louis Town
South Cat Cay

Wedge Rocks
Victory Cays

East Wells

Paradise Pt.

Bailey Town

NORTH BIMINI

Alice Town

Alec Cay

Bonefish Hole

Pigeon Cay

Bimini Hotel
Entrance Pt.

Airstrip

SOUTH BIMINI

Nixon's Harbour

Round Rock

0 1 2

Ocean Cay

Brown's Cay

Beak Cay

BIMINI CAYS

0   5
Miles

Town — are only a 10-minute walk apart, and most natives commute by moped or bus. The walking tour described here takes tourists to the main sights in Alice Town; the cycling (or moped, for those who prefer) tour that follows begins at Alice Town and stops at some of the fine beaches to the northeast of town. The tours end with a brief description of some of the sights on South Bimini.

BIMINI WALKS

The tour described here takes an hour or so, depending on how quickly you want to ramble. It's a $7 taxi ride along the King's Highway to the tourist hotels just south of Alice Town; if you're on the island for the day and aren't weighed down with luggage, just head into town on foot. Alice Town is a small, hot, dusty little place, comfortably frayed at the edges and a little tatty. The Mercedes that used to cruise up and down the street here during the prime cocaine-running days of the 1980s have mostly disappeared. There are more bars than shops in Alice Town, just as there are on the rest of Bimini, but the locals, a friendly and patriotic lot, don't seem to mind that in the least.

Just past the airport is the *Star Patio Bar & Disco,* which is painted bright blue with yellow stripes. It's a popular spot for barbecued ribs and chicken and for late-night music. Next door is the rustic *End of the World Sand Bar,* where the walls are obliterated by graffiti and the floors are sprinkled with sand for barefoot dancers. The bar was once a favorite of Adam Clayton Powell, pastor of Harlem's Abyssinian Baptist Church and a member of the US House of Representatives, who fled to Bimini with his mistress in disgrace over tax-fraud charges. Spend time at the bar and you may run across someone who played dominoes here with Powell, who died in 1972.

Across the street is a private home surrounded by a verdant garden shaded by coconut palms. The house is built on the site of the *Bimini Bay Rod and Gun Club,* a hotel and casino destroyed in a hurricane in 1926. Next on the right, past *Brown's* hotel, is the *Fisherman's Paradise* restaurant, which serves breakfast and fresh lunch specials of lobster, grouper, snapper, and conch (no phone). Across the street is *Bimini Undersea Adventures* (phone: 347-2089; in the US, 800-327-8150), which takes divers to wrecks offshore and to the forests of black coral off the Bimini Wall.

Near the center of town stands the imposing limestone Customs Hall, painted white and candy-pink. Badly damaged in a fire in the 1970s, it has since been restored, though the police department, courthouse, and library once housed here have since been moved to other offices. (There is still a customs office in the building.) The small, touristy straw market across the road from Customs Hall sells baskets and trinkets made of shells, and the *Perfume Bar* (no phone) has tropical fragrances from the *Perfume Factory* in Freeport and several imported brands. The path just beyond it to the left leads in a couple of minutes to the island's main beach on the eastern strand. Next on the left is *Captain Bob's Conch Hall of Fame,* where you can chat with owner Bob Smith, one of the island's finest deep-sea fishermen, over your breakfast of boilfish and grits. (In spite of its name, there is no hall of fame here, just some faded photographs of prizewinning catches on the walls; phone: 347-2260.) The Royal Bank of Canada is next door, near *Sawyer's Scooters,* where mopeds rent for $10 an hour — the standard rate. Opposite is the *Red Lion* bar and restaurant (phone: 347-2259), which serves good inexpensive seafood dishes — and can turn rowdy at night.

Up the gentle hill to the left, the highest point on North Bimini, is the *Blue Water Marina,* a small, pleasant hotel whose French windows and doors look out on the sea on both sides of the island. Its popular restaurant serves moderately priced native dishes. The hotel's marina and dockside pool are directly across the street, and fishing and diving tours are available (phone: 347-2166). Next door is the Blue Marlin Cottage, the whitewashed limestone bungalow that Ernest Hemingway built for himself in the mid-1930s. Now a private home, it is said to look much as it did when the author lived here. It stands next to the *Compleat Angler* hotel (phone: 347-2122), where Hemingway lived before the cottage was finished. Now home to Bimini's most famous bar, it's a classic 2-story colonial building surrounded by shady verandahs, with dark varnished wooden floors and wooden paneling inside. Visitors can wander through the rooms and examine the memorabilia on the walls — there are newspaper clippings and pictures of a 785-pound mako shark and a 514-pound tuna that Hemingway caught years ago. Whirring ceiling fans mute the noise from the courtyard bar, where tourists sit around a twisted almond tree drinking Bahama Mamas and munching on conch fritters.

No one leaves Bimini without becoming an expert on Hemingway lore. After a couple of days here, tourists know about the years Hemingway lived on the island (1934 to 1937), the novels he wrote here (*To Have and Have Not* and *Islands in the Stream,* the latter set on Bimini), his notorious bouts of drinking and carousing, the fishing expeditions in which Hemingway used a machine gun to kill sharks attacking his catch, and his famous boxing matches. Several men lost trying to capture Hemingway's $250 boxing purse.

Recent visitors have burnished — or tarnished — the bar's fame. It was here that presidential wannabe Gary Hart posed with Donna Rice, to the delight of the photo editors of the *National Enquirer.* Couples often ask to have their picture taken on the bandstand, where Hart and Rice were photographed. Bimini remains a favorite of Hart's successful rival, George Bush, who comes here to catch blue marlin. (He docks offshore, or at the *Bimini Big Game Fishing Club,* and seldom ventures into Alice Town.)

Just northwest of the *Angler,* past a clutch of tourist shops, is the aforementioned *Bimini Big Game Fishing Club.* Owned by Bacardi, it's the poshest resort on the island (non-guests may stop here for drinks). Separated from the hoi polloi by a concrete wall and a high fence, the hotel is surrounded by coconut palms and flowering shrubs. It's particularly busy in March, April, June, September, and November, when the big fishing tournaments are held here (phone: 347-2391).

For those who can afford it, the game fishing off Bimini is among the finest in the world. Plenty of records have been set here; fishermen have netted 1,800-pound bluefin tuna, and a blue marlin can weigh up to half a ton and can fight on the line for a solid 8 hours or more. Those who can't afford to spend $500 to $700 a day on deep-sea fishing can bonefish in the shallows for less than half that price; the flats here are said to be some of the best in the world. Netting a bonefish is a challenge, for the fish are easily spooked. To catch them, a guide maneuvers a small boat across the flats, cuts the engine, and punts the boat slowly through the water with a long pole, as if it were a Venetian gondola. When a school of bonefish is spotted — they slice the surface of the water with their tails as they dive for shrimp and lobster — the guide inches closer, taking care not to splash the water with the pole. Once within reach, fishermen cast out their lightweight lines baited with juicy shrimp. One cast too close and the whole school turns tail and disappears. When a fish strikes, the battle isn't over, for they fight furiously once they see the boat. The fish make excellent eating, though they're impossible to fillet. Locals "snap" them to align the bones in one direction and then grill them whole. Tourists who are lucky enough to catch one can probably coax a local into cooking it for them. Follow the high road (on the other side of the island) back to Alice Town.

BIMINI BY BIKE

The rest of North Bimini, which is just 2 miles long and a quarter of a mile wide, is explored easily by bike or moped. This tour starts at the *Bimini Big Game Fishing Club;* just opposite is the home of Captain William C. Francis, a.k.a. Bonefish Bill, a lanky man with close-cropped graying hair who can spot a bonefish at 100 yards, despite his age and the glare through his badly scratched sunglasses. Novices who go out fishing with him can expect a stern rebuke if they fail to follow his instructions. Nearby is the *Bimini Breeze* bar and restaurant (no phone), a cool haven that serves seafood and native dishes. West of here the road — still grandiosely named the King's Highway — hugs the coast, passing scattered homes along the way. Fishermen clean and sell their catch along the beachside docks, and women tend the vegetable plots outside their brightly painted wooden homes, or hang laundry from the lines strung along the front porch. The road skirts by the Bimini All-Age School, where you may see kids in maroon-edged gray uniforms playing basketball in the yard.

Farther on, past *Edith's Café* and the power station, is Bailey Town, a quiet native settlement. Small wooden and concrete-block houses stand next to the road. (Skip *Admiral's* hotel, restaurant, and bar, not recommended because it borders the town dump.) The settlement soon comes to an abrupt end, and the road cuts through a forest of slender pines. About a quarter of a mile beyond the town, the road ends at a dock by the entrance to two large private home developments. (There is a private road that continues north and east of here for about 2½ miles to the tip of the island.)

The chief attraction off the northeast shore of the island are curious ruins that some archaeologists say may be the remnants of the lost continent of Atlantis. (It's a farfetched claim, but the site is by any definition mysterious.) The ruins, which lie under 15 feet of water, can't be seen clearly from shore, but tourists can hire a boat and dive or snorkel near the site. Hundreds of stone blocks, each about 4 feet wide and 2 feet deep, are packed together in a sort of causeway that stretches for a hundred yards or so. Archaeologists haven't figured out what the structure was for, but they do know that the blocks are fashioned from a sedimentary rock not native to Bimini.

Nearby are some some secluded coves sheltered by weathered limestone rocks — the perfect place for a picnic and an afternoon swim or snorkel. Hidden among the pines is a small cemetery where some of the headstones are more than 150 years old. Just past the cemetery a road branches off to the right and leads to the east shore road. Take this road to the right, back in the direction of Alice Town, and you will soon come upon two picturesque churches, Our Lady of St. Stephen's and Wesley Methodist. Services are often held during the week at midday, as well as Sunday mornings; they're a welcome retreat from the hot sun, and visitors are welcome. Farther down is the *Blue Water Marina* hotel and the main beach on the island, a wide, steep-sloped swath of white sand that's popular with locals and tourists alike. (It's the same beach that can be reached by the path from the center of Alice Town.)

BIMINI BY BOAT

Though there's not much to see or do here, South Bimini is just a 5-minute ferry ride — and a pleasant one at that — from the main loading dock south of Alice Town. Bring insect repellent: The island, which is covered with a dense carpet of pines and sea grapes, is frequently plagued by mosquitoes. It's virtually deserted except for a few vacation homes, the defunct *South Bimini Yacht Club,* and an airstrip 2 miles to the north. There is a small pool near the airport that is said to alleviate arthritis, but it's a long walk through dense vegetation, and it's tough to find unless you have good directions or a guide. To the south is the hulk of the *Sapona,* a huge concrete ship built by Henry Ford during World War I and wrecked in a storm in 1929. Once moored between Gun and Cat cays, it housed a casino, a private club, and a rumrunners' storehouse. During World War II, it was used in bombing practice, and divers still find fake bombs near the wreck.

On Cat Cay, a gem of an isle 12 miles south of Bimini (reachable only by boat or plane), there is an exclusive private resort, the *Cat Cay Club,* with a good 9-hole golf course, a large marina, a Tudor-style restaurant, and fine beaches (for membership information: in Florida, call 305-858-6856).

The Abacos

This boomerang-shaped archipelago, 130 miles long and roughly 15 miles wide, is just east of Grand Bahama and a quick hop from Miami and Ft. Lauderdale. It's special for many reasons. Nowhere else in the Bahamas is the colonial past as close as it is here on these palm-fringed cays with their pretty New England–style fishing villages. And the gin-clear seas off the coast are said to be among the finest sailing and fishing waters in the world.

Juan Ponce de León called here in 1513 during his search for the Fountain of Youth, but he found nothing more than a few bands of Lucaya Indians. Pirates hid out in the coves along the Abacos coast, for the reefs and shoals offshore were perfect wrecking grounds. More than 500 galleons, many laden with treasure, sank in the waters off the Abacos. (Also referred to as Abaco, the Abacos comprise several islands and cays: Great and Little Abacos, Elbow Cay, Man-O-War Cay, Great Guana Cay, Treasure Cay, Green Turtle Cay, and Walker's Cay.)

Tories from New England, New York, and the Carolinas put down roots here after the American Revolution, and many of the island's 10,000-odd permanent residents trace their ancestry back to them. The Loyalists settled at Carleton, near Treasure Cay in the central Abacos, but their farms soon failed, and the town was razed by a hurricane. In the late 18th century Carleton was abandoned, and the settlers tramped 18 miles south to Elizabeth Harbour. There, with the help of compatriots from Harbour Island near Eleuthera, they founded a farming and fishing community that eventually became Marsh Harbour. Other settlers colonized many of the small cays. Over the years, the Abaconians established a formidable reputation as shipbuilders, and their fast dinghies, smacks, and sloops were prized throughout the western Atlantic. Prosperous and conservative, they remained fiercely loyal to the Crown. Their descendants continued that loyalty by making several attempts to block the Bahamian independence movement in the 1970s. When the plan capsized, they tried to secede and found their own nation. That plan failed, too, and forever divided the loyalties of the natives. Some left the Abacos, but most stayed on.

Marsh Harbour is still the most important settlement in the Abacos, and it's easily reached by the daily *Bahamasair* flights from Nassau. (*American Eagle, USAir Express,* and *Aero Coach* fly to Marsh Harbour as well, and small airstrips serve Treasure and Walker's cays.) Most visitors to the Abacos stop first at Marsh Harbour, spend a day or two seeing the sights and stocking up on provisions, and then take off for the fishing and diving spots on the smaller cays.

Marsh Harbour is at the crook of the bend in the Abacos chain, just opposite aptly named Elbow Cay. From Marsh Harbour Airport, it's a 10-

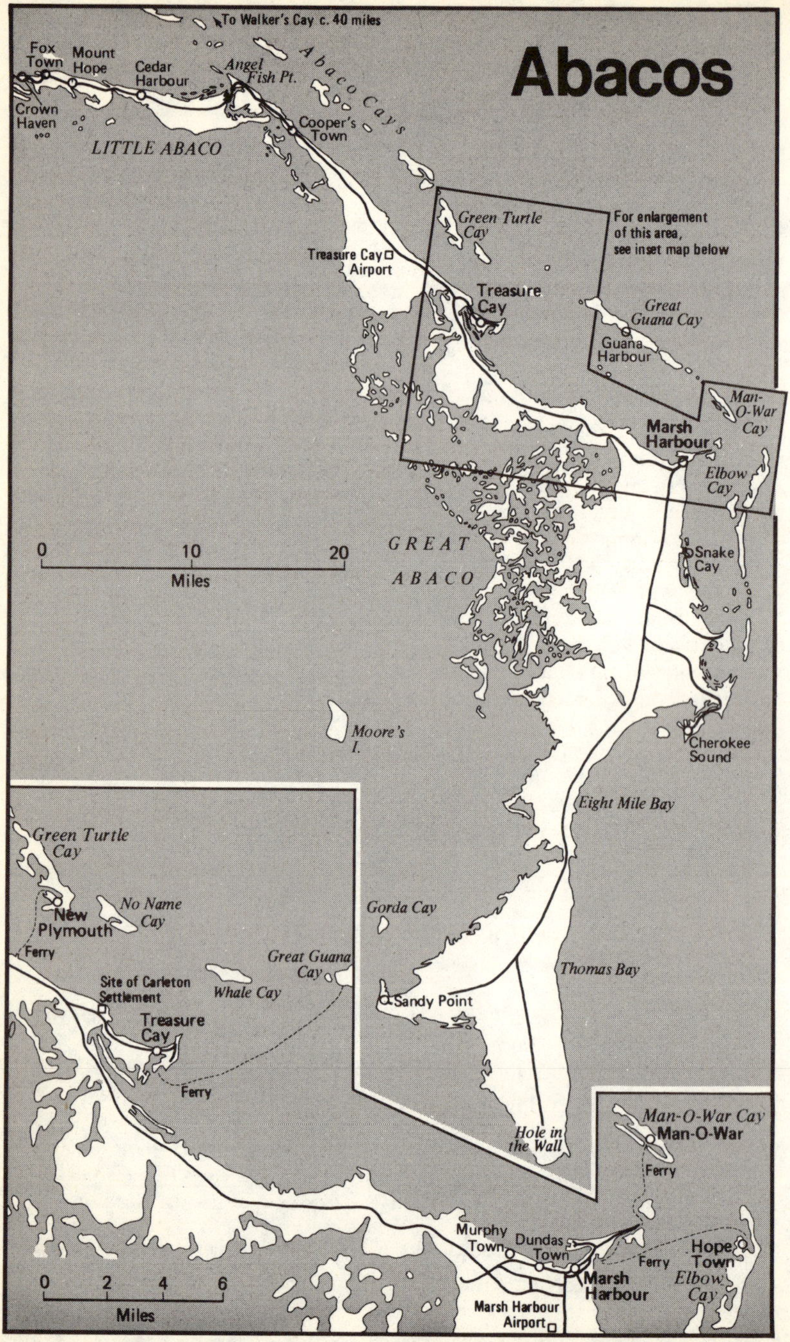

Abacos
To Walker's Cay c. 40 miles
Abaco Cays
Fox Town
Mount Hope
Cedar Harbour
Angel Fish Pt.
Crown Haven
Cooper's Town
LITTLE ABACO
Green Turtle Cay
For enlargement of this area, see inset map below
Treasure Cay Airport
Treasure Cay
Great Guana Cay
Guana Harbour
Man-O-War Cay
Marsh Harbour
Elbow Cay
0 10 20
Miles
GREAT ABACO
Snake Cay
Moore's I.
Cherokee Sound
Eight Mile Bay
Green Turtle Cay
New Plymouth
No Name Cay
Gorda Cay
Ferry
Great Guana Cay
Site of Carleton Settlement
Whale Cay
Thomas Bay
Sandy Point
Treasure Cay
Ferry
Hole in the Wall
Man-O-War Cay
Man-O-War
Ferry
Murphy Town
Dundas Town
Hope Town
Ferry
Marsh Harbour
Elbow Cay
0 2 4 6
Miles
Marsh Harbour Airport

minute drive north to the town proper, which is situated on a broad spit of land on the eastern side of the island. To reach the main harbor, where the old town is, pass the large shopping center, and at the only traffic light on all of the Abacos, make a right turn onto Elizabeth Drive, which leads directly to the wharf.

ABACOS WALKS

About 3,000 people live year-round in Marsh Harbour on Great Abaco, and though it's the third-largest town in the Bahamas, it's hardly a metropolis. Most of the sights around town can be strolled in a leisurely half hour or less. Begin at the old harbor, where hundreds of boats bob up and down in the clear blue water. Here visitors can rent a sloop with crew or without. (The second option is known as "bareboat." Visiting sailors who spend their time drinking beer and polluting nearby fishing boats with smoke from their barbecues are known disparagingly as "bareboaters.")

The waterfront is dominated by the saffron-yellow *Conch Inn,* a sprawling colony of bungalows and cottages with its own 60-slip marina (phone: inn, 367-2800; marina and dive shop, 367-2787). Its bar and dockside restaurant are favorite local gathering spots. *Dive Abaco,* one of the largest scuba and snorkeling centers, is also near the marina (phone: 367-2014 or 367-2787). Nearby are several good restaurants, including *Mangoes* (good bar; phone: 367-2366) and *Wally's,* located in a lovely pink-and-white colonial building — a must for lunch under the patio's striped canvas awning and for the candlelight dinners served every Monday (phone: 367-2074). Bicycles can be rented at the time-share apartments called *Abaco Towns by the Sea.* Nearby *Marsh Harbour Exporters and Importers* sells cleaned frozen fish to tourists heading back home (fileted grouper is $5 a pound; lobster is $10).

There is little development from this point on to the newer harbor on the south side of the spit, about a quarter of a mile away. The southern area, popularly known as Marsh Town, has been developed over the past decade or so, and some claim that the new marina will soon eclipse the old one, but for the moment the older, deepwater harbor is still the better of the two. Marsh Town is dominated by the *Great Abaco Beach* hotel, which has supervised the dredging of the south harbor and vastly expanded the marina. *Seahorse Boat Rentals* on the waterfront rents out boats, bicycles, snorkel gear, and windsurfers (phone: 367-2153), and the cheery clapboard *Bahamian Lights* bar and restaurant is a favorite local venue. The hotel is set back a short distance from the water, surrounded by a grove of coconut palms. For some fine views of the harbor and the cays offshore, follow Harbour Road east for a mile and a half or so, passing the tiny settlements of Pond Bay, Pelican Shores, Fanny Bay, and Upper Cut along the way.

North of Marsh Harbour, it's a pleasant 3-mile walk along Harbour Road to two quaint fishing villages, Dundas Town and Murphy Town. Explore the old clapboard and limestone churches and stop in at *Mother Merle's Fishnet* restaurant (phone: 367-2770) for a bite of broiled lobster or conch salad. On the way back, take a dip in the perfectly clear waters off the small beaches along the strand.

ABACOS BY CAR

Exploring Great Abaco by car requires some grit and patience, for the roads are very bad in spots, and settlements are few and far between. The road that runs the length of Great Abaco was built to transport timber from the northern forests to the lumber mills in the south, and the trucks that rumbled over the highway have taken their toll. (The mills, started by various Bahamian, Cuban, and American companies, shut down completely more than 20 years ago, after most of the Caribbean pine forests in the north had been decimated by overcutting.) Visitors with limited time may be better advised to spend their precious hours on the cays rather than squandering them changing a flat tire on a deserted stretch of highway. Those who do drive are best off heading north, for the road, which is marginally better than it is in the south, leads to some spectacular beaches.

Those who do go north shouldn't get discouraged: The first stretch of road is the worst. The 28 miles between Marsh Harbour and Treasure Cay are unpaved, and the badly corrugated road is hemmed in by stands of young pine with only an occasional wooden house to relieve the monotony. The pines, planted by the lumber companies in areas that were clear-cut years ago, are surrounded by a dense undergrowth of sea grapes, uniola grass, and creeping vines. The drive is worth the discomfort, though, for the beach at Treasure Cay is one of the finest anywhere. The turnoff to the cay, which is linked by causeway to the mainland, is well marked. Coconut palms shade the dazzlingly white beach, which curves in a perfect 3-mile-long arc. Clustered along the beach are the villas and hotels of *Treasure Cay,* one of the finest luxury resorts in the Abacos chain (phone: 367-2570).

The road, mercifully, is paved for the next 25 miles, to the northern end of Little Abaco. Wild horses graze in remote pasturelands near here. Birders should stop now and then and keep an eye out for a West Indian red-bellied woodpecker, whose numbers were drastically reduced when the Abacos' logging operations were in full swing. Though it's no longer on the endangered species list, the bird is still rare. In the late 1980s, several of the birds were caught and banded; if you happen to spot one, note the colors on the band and report them to the Forestry Department. Just off the road a mile north of Treasure Cay, a brass plaque commemorates the spot where the island's early settlers founded the town of Carleton. A mile beyond it is the wharf where the ferries to Green Turtle Cay dock. Treasure Cay Airport is another mile or so to the north; the flights from there to Marsh Harbour take a mere 10 minutes.

Cooper's Town, a flyblown settlement 8 miles farther on, is the last town on Great Abaco. There are good beaches nearby. A causeway links Great and Little Abaco just beyond the town at Angel Fish Point. The next stop, Cedar Harbour, isn't worth more than a glance or two, but the beaches are fine. Mount Hope, 5 miles on, is a slightly larger town, with a drugstore, a grocery, and *B.J.'s* restaurant. The Zion Baptist Church dominates Fox Town, the village 5 miles to the northwest, where there is a police station, a post office, and a good little seafood restaurant. Crown Haven, at the end of the line 2 miles on, has a barbershop, 2 rival churches, and the cheery *Black Room* bar and restaurant. The northern part of Little Abaco, which is reached only by boat, stretches another 10 miles to West End Cay.

South of Marsh Harbour, the road — which is unpaved the entire way — winds by blighted Snake Cay, where a huge lumber mill once stood; Wilson City, another lumber town now fallen on hard times; some large estates where citrus fruits are raised; the fishing village at Cherokee Sound; the superb and desolate beaches at Eight Mile Bay; a small settlement at Sandy Point; and the lighthouse at Hole in the Wall, which was built in 1836 and is one of the oldest in the Bahamas.

CRUISING THE CAYS

Green Turtle Cay, an old Tory stronghold just a few miles from Treasure Cay on Great Abaco, is definitely worth a visit. Water taxis leave from the dock on Treasure Cay at 10:30 AM, 2 PM, and 4 PM, and they leave for Treasure Cay at 8 AM, 9:15 AM, 11:30 AM, 1:30 PM, and 3 PM. It's a 10-minute ride to the island; a round-trip ticket costs $8. On the way, the ferry cruises by New Plymouth Village on the south of the cay, a postcard-perfect fishing town. The ferry stops at New Plymouth after calling at the *Green Turtle Club* and marina a mile farther north (phone: 365-4271; in the US, 800-825-5099).

New Plymouth (pop. 500) is the perfect place for a half-hour walking tour. This jumble of colorful saltbox houses overlooking Black Sound Harbour was settled in 1784. The Loyalists who founded the town established a prosperous boatbuilding industry here. Settlers also made a living catching turtles, diving for sponges, and shipping shark oil and sharkskins to traders in Baltimore and New York. Today the shipyards are closed, and many locals make a living catching lobster and crawfish. More than half of all the lobster exported from the Bahamas is caught in the waters nearby.

Directly opposite the ferry dock is King Street, which is barely 50 yards long. Stop for ice cream at homey *Laura's Kitchen* on King Street, and continue on to bougainvillea-lined Parliament Street, the main thoroughfare. On the left, amid well-tended gardens, is the *Albert Lowe Museum,* named for one of the town's master boatbuilders. Models of several of the ships built by Lowe, who died in 1986, are displayed here, along with contemporary paintings by his son, Alton. The rooms are filled with period furniture (closed on Sundays; phone: 365-4094). To the right down Parliament Street are the library, post office, customs hall, and the pink-and-white Commissioner's Office. On the left is the charming clapboard Methodist church, with a fine old mahogany altar and oil lamps lining the walls.

Farther on to the right is a well-maintained cemetery, and up the small hill past the local school is *Rooster's* bar and restaurant, a rustic spot where you can enjoy simple native cooking, shoot a game of pool, and dance to live music in the evening (no phone). Follow Hill and Bay Streets back to the harbor, near the waterside *Wrecking Tree Bakery.* Directly opposite the bakery is Victoria Street, home of *Miss Emily's Blue Bee* bar, ostensibly the most famous bar in the Bahamas. Its reputation clearly isn't based on its decor, which consists of scruffy T-shirts hanging from the ceiling and walls plastered with business cards (phone: 365-4181). Just down the street is the old jail, which apparently isn't used much, since the door has fallen off. Continue up to Parliament Street, and make a right; then turn left onto Mission Street, passing some weatherbeaten homes; and now make a right onto Crown Street. The *Sea View* restaurant (phone: 365-4141), which serves good Bahamian dishes, is on the short road branching off to the left that leads to the dock and some of the island's best beaches.

Farther down Crown Street is the Gospel Chapel, a canary-yellow church known for its rousing revival meetings. Turn right on Walter Street, which leads back to Parliament Street. Walk down the street past the museum; the bronze busts in the Loyalist Memorial Sculpture Garden were placed there for the island's bicentennial in 1983. Opposite the park, next to the former vacation home of British prime minister Neville Chamberlain, is the *New Plymouth Inn,* the finest hotel in town (phone: 365-4161). Near the end of Parliament Street is the *Ocean Blue Gallery,* where paintings by more than 30 Bahamian artists are on display. From here it is a short walk along Bay Street to the dock, where you can hire a boat and dive for lobster and conch or try your luck fishing for grouper, yellowtail, or triggerfish.

Elbow Cay, just east of Marsh Harbour off Great Abaco, is one of the most visited islands in the Bahamas. The main settlement there, Hope Town, is a colonial fishing village of great charm. The island is reached by a 20-minute water taxi ride from *Albury's Ferry Service* in Marsh Harbour, leaving daily at 10:30 AM and 4 PM; trips from the cay to Marsh Harbour are at 8 AM and 1:30 PM. The round-trip fare is $12 (phone: 365-6010).

Before landing at Hope Town, the ferry calls briefly at the candy-striped lighthouse on the south end of the cay. Built in 1863 (and rebuilt in 1938), it stands 120 feet high, and its kerosene lamp still guides boats far out to sea. Visitors are allowed 10 minutes to scramble up the steep winding staircase to the observation deck to take in the panoramic view of the harbor and snap a photo or two.

The ferry pulls in at the lower public dock at the north end of Hope Town. A left turn just past the Royal Bank of Canada leads to *Uncle B's,* where visitors can rent a bicycle to tour the beaches south of Hope Town. There are two main north-south thoroughfares on the cay: "Up Along," the high road along the central spine of the island; and "Down Along," which parallels the harbor.

East of Up Along are long stretches of secluded beach, ideal for swimming and snorkeling. Along the way, stop in at *Captain Jack's* for a boilfish-and-johnnycake breakfast; at the *Wood Carvings* workshop near the St. James Methodist Church; and at the *Wyannie Malone Museum* (no phone), which is dedicated to the memory of a widow with four children who arrived here around 1793. The museum, housed in a restored colonial building, gives a sense of what life on the island was once like. The rooms are filled with colonial furniture, and visitors can see the faded charts documenting the voyages of the Eleutherian Adventurers, who sailed here from Bermuda during the 17th century; the island's first telephone exchange; an Edison

Talking Machine; old toys; a cistern; and a collection of handwoven linen. Beyond the museum the road passes the *Hope Town Harbour Lodge* hotel (phone: 366-0095), the best place to stay in Hope Town, and ends at the local cemetery.

The harbor road, Down Along — which runs for a mere 200 yards or so — is fronted by colonial saltbox houses overlooking the harbor. There is a handicrafts store, a dive shop, and the post office, commissioner's office, and police station.

Man-O-War Cay, a tiny island barely a quarter of a mile long and as thin as a rail, is the capital of Abaco's modern boatbuilding industry. It's a 20-minute water taxi ride from Albury's Ferry Dock in Marsh Harbour to the cay. Boats leave daily from Great Abaco at 10:30 AM and 4 PM, with trips from the cay at 8 AM and 1:30 PM; the round-trip fare is $12. There are no hotels here, so most people just hop over for a couple of hours. Only 100 or so people live on the island, and the community is as sternly proper as the immaculately maintained clapboard homes surrounded by prim white picket fences. Many natives go to church three times a week — and twice on Sundays. Drinking is outlawed, and local women are barred from wearing shorts or bikinis.

The harbor still bustles with the clamor of shipbuilders at work. Stop by *Dock and Dine* (near Albury's Marina) for grilled grouper and a cool Goombay Smash; *Albury's Sail Loft* has an ample selection of clothes made from sailcloth, and *Joe's Studio* sells nautical gifts. There are pleasant walks north and south of town along the shore, and the beach on the east side of the island offers superb bathing, snorkeling, and diving. Divers can explore the wreck of the Union gunboat USS *Adirondack*, which sank after hitting a reef just 6 months after it was commissioned in 1862, and the nearby wreck of the *San Jacinto*, which ran aground while chasing a blockade runner in 1865.

Walker's Cay, the northernmost of the Abacos isles, is reachable by private boat or chartered aircraft. Ponce de León is said to have landed here in 1513, and the island was later a refuge for criminals of all stripes, from 17th-century pirates to Civil War–era raiders and rumrunners. Tourists have considerably improved its reputation. The island's fine private resort, *Walker's Cay Club* hotel and marina, opened in the 1930s as a fishing club (phone: 352-5252). The dives off the nearby barrier reef are spectacular. Schools of queen triggerfish, Nassau grouper, blue chromis, and wide-eyed squirrelfish dart among the coral and the barnacle-encrusted wrecks offshore. The schools of minnows that live off some of the reefs here are said to be so thick that divers a few feet apart lose temporary sight of each other. Visitors can also tour the tropical fish–breeding farm on the northwest side of the island. Several deep-sea fishing tournaments are held here in the spring and summer.

Great Guana Cay, reached only by private charter boat, is a tiny spot of land lying between Green Turtle and Man-O-War cays. A handful of people live here year-round, and there is nothing much in town aside from a few small shops, a schoolhouse, and an Anglican church. The main attraction is the beach, 7 long miles of white sand fringed with coconut palms. The bonefishing and diving here are excellent.

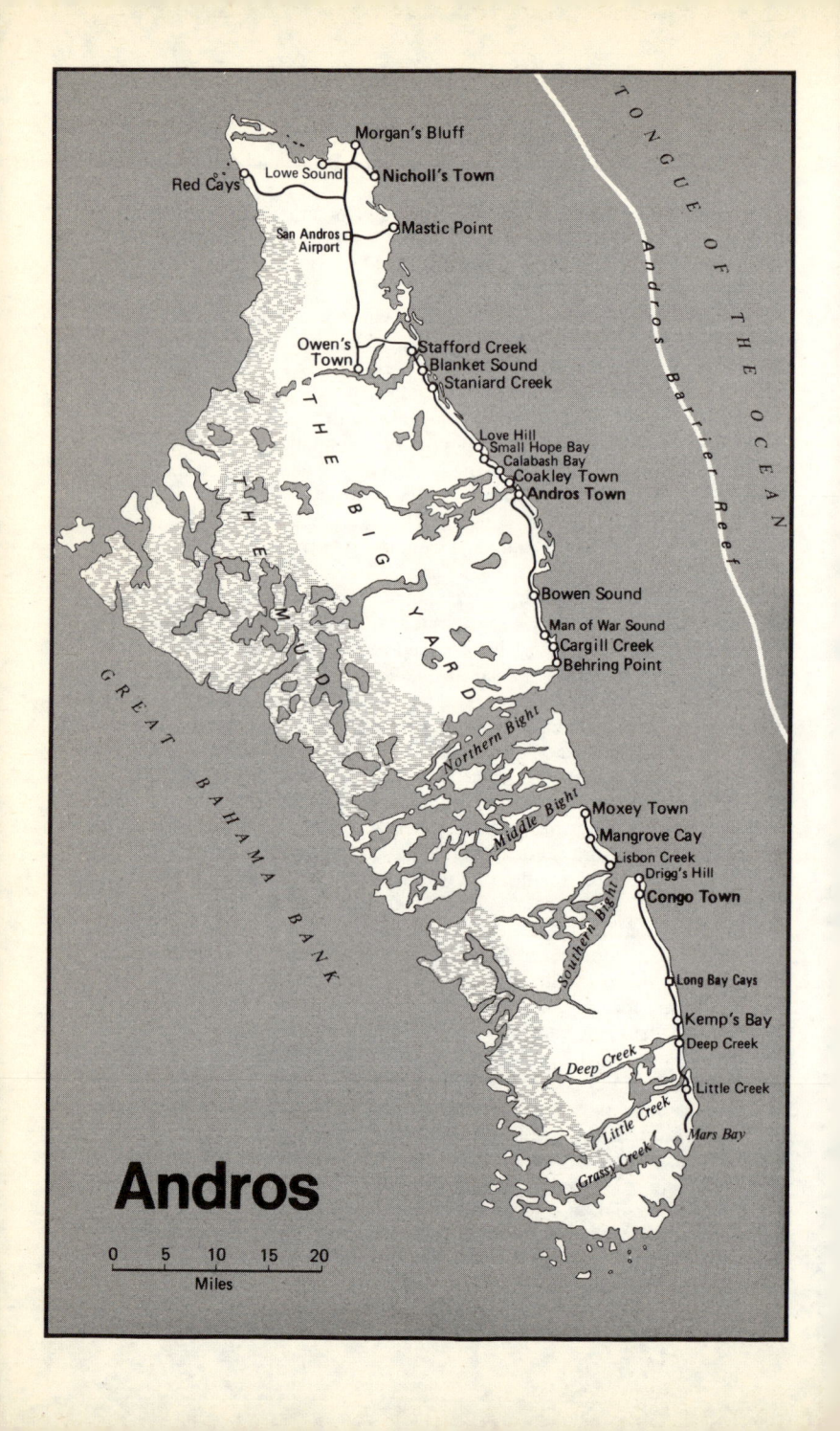

Andros

Andros

The biggest island in the Bahamas — 140 miles long and 40 miles wide — Andros is surprisingly undeveloped, considering its proximity to Nassau and Miami. Much of the interior, known rather vaguely as "The Big Yard," is forested with dense stands of mahogany and pine, and the boggy marshes along the west coast, known straightforwardly as "The Mud," are even more impenetrable. Some of the best sights are offshore. The 120-mile barrier reef just off the east coast is the third-largest in the world and offers some spectacular dives.

Discovered by Columbus in 1492 and christened La Isla del Espíritu Santo (Island of the Holy Spirit), the island was later renamed for Sir Edmund Andros, a Governor of the Dominion of New England. (Modern Bahamians, anxious to repudiate their colonial roots, claim that the island is named after the Aegean isle of Andros.) Stories and legends have lent it a mysterious air. Islanders tell tales of giant octopus-like creatures called *lucas* that attack fishermen and divers. Children are warned to watch out for the *chickarnie*, a mythical red-eyed, three-toed bird said to roost in the dark forests in the interior. Ballads written in colonial times tell of the exploits of pirate Henry Morgan, who is said to have left a vast treasure in a cave off Morgan's Bluff on the northern tip of the island.

Andros has never been easy to explore, for it is broken up by labyrinthine lakes and channels. Water, in fact, is one of the main resources of the island. Unlike most Bahamian isles, Andros has large underground reservoirs of fresh water. These have helped to sustain the large forests on the island, making them less vulnerable to drought. (Timber has been a major export here since colonial times.) Today, Andros supplies Nassau with much of that city's potable water, shipped by barge. The island is also riddled with subterranean limestone caverns filled with seawater. When the roofs of these caves collapse, they expose clear, deep pools called blue holes.

While the interior of the island is largely inaccessible, there are some fine secluded beaches along the eastern strand. Twenty miles offshore lies the Andros barrier reef; the possibilities for diving here are said to be among the best in the world. From the eastern edge of the reef, it's a sheer 6,000-foot drop to a narrow ocean trough called the Tongue of the Ocean. Primitive fish — and submarines from the top-security US naval base on the east coast of Andros — cruise the depths of this 142-mile-long abyss. Cathedrals of elkhorn and staghorn coral tower in the crystal-clear water, where visibility can exceed 200 feet. Reef sharks, moray eels, eagle rays, and shoals of angelfish and friendly grouper feed nearby, and rare black coral clings to the precipice at the eastern edge of the reef. Coral also lines the submerged caverns underneath the island, which can be explored by diving through one of several blue holes.

Sailing can be hazardous off the Andros reef — and on the Great Bahama Bank to the west — but sail fishing is popular here. The bonefishing off Andros is considered by many to be the best in the world, and there are marlin and bluefin tuna off the eastern shore.

Most of the settlements in Andros are strung along the east coast, which is more salubrious than the marshy strands to the west. There are three main towns along the east coast: Nicholl's Town in North Andros, Andros Town in Central Andros, and Congo Town on South Andros (accessible only by boat). Planes fly regularly from Miami and Nassau to these towns, and mail boats call once a week at Nicholl's Town and Andros Town. It's not easy to get around, for rental cars are scarce and most of the roads, while paved, are poorly maintained. Tourists should plan ahead and decide where on the island they want to be based.

Andros Town is perhaps the most convenient spot for divers who want to explore the great reef. Seminole and Arawak Indians once lived in the area, and pirates anchored in the nearby coves during the 17th and 18th centuries. During the mid-1950s, A&P heir Huntington Hartford built the exclusive *Andros Yacht Club* here, with the financial backing of Swedish industrialist Axel Wenner-Gren. In its early years, the resort was enormously successful, but its second owner, American industrialist Louis Reynolds, lost interest in the project after his son and heir was cut to ribbons by a plane propeller. The bank foreclosed on the hotel mortgage, and success passed Andros Town by. The village enjoyed a brief spell of fame in the fall of 1985, when Queen Elizabeth II stopped by for a visit. A few new projects may revive its fortunes. A government-operated resort, the *Lighthouse Yacht Club and Marina*, opened in 1991 (phone: 809-368-2308; in the US, 800-825-5099). And the new super-exclusive — and super-pricey — *Coakley House* is located just across the bay from its parent establishment, the *Small Hope Bay Lodge*, whose diving facilities are available to guests of both hotels (phone for both: 809-368-2014; in the US, 800-223-6961).

For now, the best place to stay in the area is still the homey *Small Hope Bay Lodge,* opened in 1960 by Canadian Dick Birch. It's located 3 miles north of Andros Town on Small Hope Bay, named for pirate Henry Morgan's proverbial claim that there was "small hope" that anyone would find his buried treasure. Dives can be arranged by the hotel — the reefs just off the bay are well worth exploring — and guides can take visitors on a "bush doctor" trek to see the native plants, many of which have medicinal value. More than 50 varieties of orchids bloom in the forests here, and cranes, herons, egrets, and white crown pigeons can be spotted along ponds and creeks. Wild boars and 4-foot-long iguanas live in the forests, as do many kinds of snakes — none of which, thankfully, is poisonous.

South of Andros Town are the villages of Cargill Creek and Behring Point, which both have good hotels, diving facilities, and bonefish flats. The best bonefishing on the island is said to be at Lowe Sound, just west of Nicholl's Town, which has good diving facilities and accommodations (try the *Andros Beach* hotel and villas; phone: 329-2582). Visitors with a taste for luxury can stay at the *Emerald Palms* hotel in Congo Town on South Andros (phone:

329-4661). The beaches here are splendid, but the place is remote: The only way to reach Andros Town and the northern settlements from here is by boat.

ANDROS BY BIKE

The roads are fairly decent around Andros Town, and there is little traffic, so cycling is pleasant. Start from the *Small Hope Bay Lodge,* which has sturdy bikes for rent. South of Small Hope Bay, the road winds up and down the gentle hills along the eastern shore, passing several deserted beaches along the way. At Calabash Bay, a tiny cluster of wooden houses, there is a pretty sickle-shaped beach and *Sampson's Disco and Sunshine Café,* which serves good native dishes. Next is Coakley Town, a tottery old village with a Catholic church and a couple of shops. The graceful mansion on the waterfront, once owned by the Crown, is *Coakley House,* the new diving resort. Next door is the *Landmark* restaurant (phone: 328-2082), with homey pine-paneled rooms, a balcony bar, and excellent Bahamian cooking. Cross the bridge over Fresh Creek into Andros Town; you'll see the flamingo-pink bungalows of the *Lighthouse Yacht Club and Marina* on the left. Nearby is the Androsia factory, where visitors can watch batik cloth being dyed.

ANDROS BY CAR

Andros isn't an automobile-friendly place. New cars here have been known to rust through in 2 years, and most of the locals ride the bus or hitchhike. If you'd like to drive, ask at your hotel, which can usually arrange rental of a local's private car for a day or two. If bumps and ill-marked side roads don't bother you, though, you may want to devote a day or two to exploring the fine beaches and bonefishing flats up and down the east coast.

It's a 28-mile drive along a deserted paved road from Andros Town north to Nicholl's Town. The road, which parallels the water, is surrounded by thick stands of pine. Unmarked tracks ramble off to the east to the villages on the coast. Two miles past Small Hope Bay are the secluded beaches at Love Hill. Snorkelers should stop to explore the coral gardens just offshore. Eight miles farther on is the settlement of Staniard Creek. Turn right onto the wide paved road that leads to the village, cross the bridge, and take the first right and the next left to reach the *Central Andros Inn,* a 2-story, canary-yellow house serving good native dishes (phone: 329-6209). The town has two picturesque churches, the Zion Baptist Church and the Lighthouse Chapel, once brightly painted and now faded to a pale lemon and lime. The beach, which is shaded by coconut palms, is a good place for a swim, or you can hire a boat to go out to the flats and bonefish.

Five miles on is the drowsy hamlet of Blanket Sound. Wooden houses line the town's only street, and there is a short lane that leads to a lovely palm-fringed beach. Not much happens here, but the schoolteacher has rooms for rent, and one of the fishermen will take visitors out in his boat.

Stafford Creek, 5 miles farther on past the Forfar Field Station marine science center, is popular for its good beaches and bonefishing. At the fork

5 miles farther, a left turn leads to the San Andros Airport, which serves Nicholl's Town, and a right turn leads to Mastic Point, a fishing village with a gas station, grocery store, and church. Former British Prime Minister Neville Chamberlain once owned a sisal plantation nearby; wags say that when it failed, locals blamed the mythical *chickarnies*. Stop for a drink and conch fritters at the *Palm Tree* bar (phone: 329-3109) or try a grilled grouper at the *Sabrina Beach Club* overlooking the water (phone: 329-3200). Backtrack to the San Andros Airport to reach the northern tip of the island. The road to Morgan's Bluff skirts by several farms where produce is raised for Nassau markets and an agricultural-research station where drought-resistant crops are being tested. (Informal tours of the station are available.) There is a crossroads 5 miles north of the airport; the road straight ahead leads to the village of Morgan's Bluff. Henry Morgan is said to have hidden his pirate treasure in the cave on the hill overlooking the harbor. (Bring a flashlight if you wish to explore the cave, which opens up into a vast chilly gallery more than 300 feet high.)

A left turn at the crossroads leads to Lowe Sound, a straggly little town only 1 street wide. Coconut palms shade the road, and a dozen jetties jut out into the water, evidence of the thriving local fishing industry. The flats offshore are rumored to be the best bonefishing grounds in the world. *Kevin's* guesthouse (no phone) is comfortable, and *Big Josh* seafood restaurant and lounge next door is a good place for lunch (phone: 329-2517). Fifteen miles west of Lowe Sound, reachable by boat or a bumpy unpaved road, is Red Cays, where a group of mulattoes — the descendants of black and Seminole slaves who escaped from Florida during the early 19th century — live much as their ancestors did, building palm-thatch houses, hunting fish, and practicing old religious rites. The community now earns a living selling straw baskets and mats; visitors can watch demonstrations at the crafts center in Lowe Sound.

A right turn at the crossroads north of the airport leads to Nicholl's Town, the main settlement on North Andros. (To reach the town, take a left off the main road onto an unmarked spur near a rocky bluff.) Seminole Indians once lived near this secluded spot, which is now dominated by the *Andros Beach* hotel and villas, a beachfront hotel with its own dock. The hotel's diving outfit, *Andros Undersea Adventures,* offers tours of the coral gardens offshore (phone: 329-2582; in the US, 800-327-8150). Half a mile down the road, take a left at the whitewashed Mizpah Baptist Church and drive down to the thin, sickle-shape beach. Hard by is *Eva Picaroon's,* where Miss Eva serves some of the finest native dishes on the island in the airy little room on the ground floor of her home (no phone).

South of Andros Town, the road hugs the coast for 25 miles, passing a handful of settlements before reaching the southern end of Central Andros. There is a T-junction just past Andros Town. The road to the left leads to the Atlantic Undersea Test and Evaluation Center (AUTEC), one of several top-secret US/British naval-research centers along the east coast of the island. The road to the right passes through two small settlements, Bowen Sound and Man of War Sound, where the bonefishing is said to be good. A few miles south, at Cargill Creek, there are two first-rate fishing resorts: *Cargill Creek Lodge* (phone: 329-5129) and *Andros Island Bonefishing Club* (for information, contact the *PanAngling Travel Service;* phone: in the US, 312-263-0328). *Cargill Creek Lodge,* the more elegant of the two, also has a dive center. Both have good restaurants that serve lobster, turtle steaks, conch, grouper, chicken, and ribs.

A few miles to the south, at Behring Point, are two more popular fishing lodges: *Charlie's Haven* (phone: 368-4108) and *Nottages Cottages* (phone: 329-5293). This spot, just above Northern Bight — the creek that separates North and Central Andros — is a favorite launching place for bonefishers setting off to explore the labyrinth of creeks and cays to the south. Bonefish weighing 12 pounds or more have been netted in these waters.

South of Behring Point, driving gets more complicated. The settlements of Moxey Town and Mangrove Cay on Central Andros are reachable only by boat or water taxi; the latter cross once in the morning and once in the afternoon. You can park your car right by the dock. Visitors who wish to reach the settlements on South Andros must take a water taxi to Lisbon Creek and a ferry to Drigg's Hill. At Lisbon Creek, snorkelers can explore a network of underwater caverns, and there is a spectacular dive from the blue hole on Linda Cay.

From the ferry stop at Drigg's Hill, take a taxi to Congo Town, the main settlement on South Andros. The road south of Congo Town becomes progressively more isolated — and bumpy — but it's worth the trip, for it leads to Long Bay Cays, possibly the finest coconut-palm beaches on all of Andros. There are good beaches farther south at Kemp's Bay — the hometown of Prime Minister Lynden Pindling's wife, Marguerite — and at Mars Bay, the southernmost settlement, where the road ends.

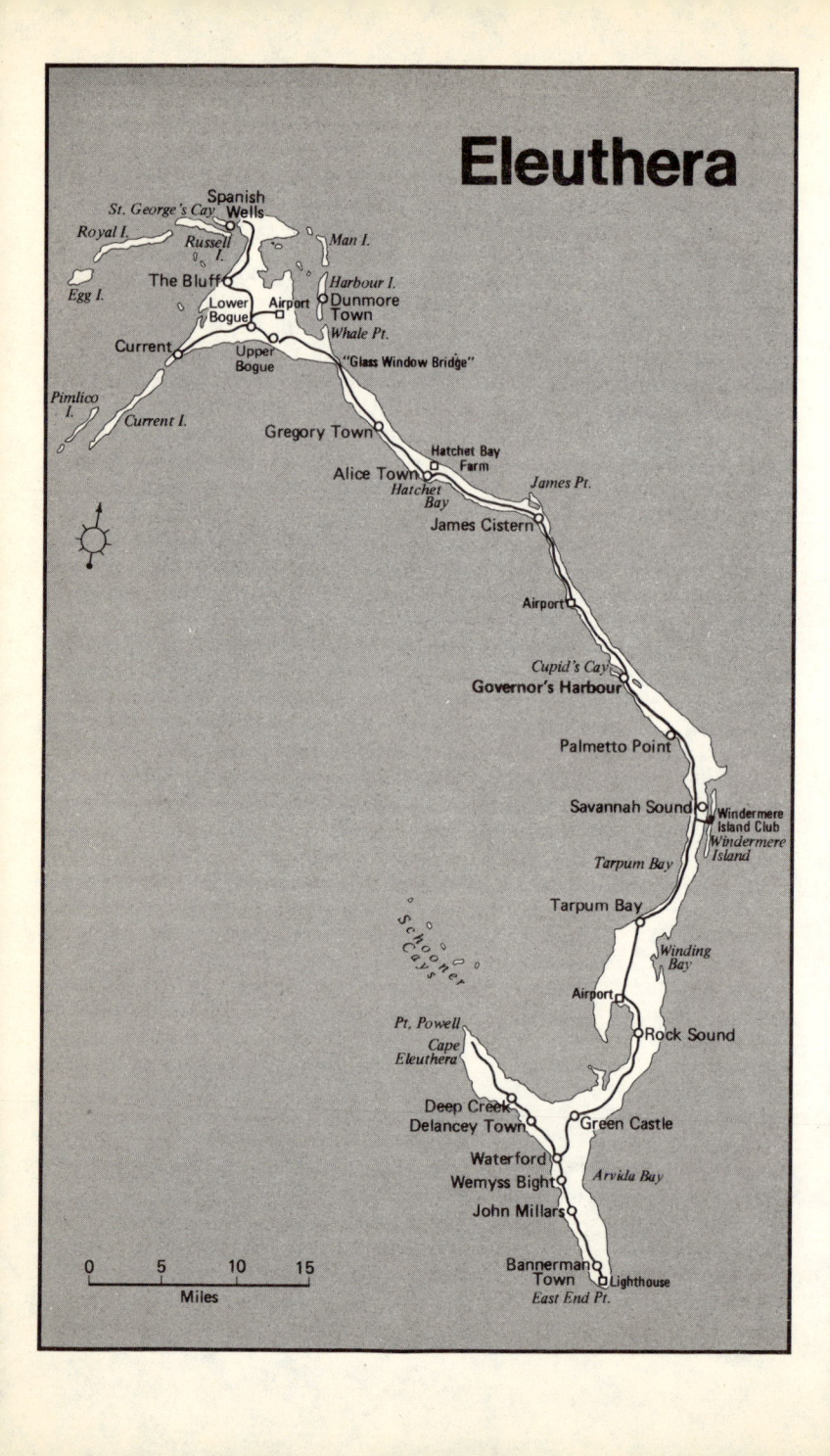

Eleuthera

Eleuthera

About 10,000 people live on ribbon-thin Eleuthera, which is 110 miles long and, in many spots, only about a mile wide. The first permanent European settlement in the Bahamas took root here during the mid-17th century, and the island still has a strong colonial air. Its rolling green hills are dotted with ruined plantations and quaint pastel-hued villages, including Spanish Wells, just offshore, rumored to be the wealthiest town in the Bahamas. There are deliciously deserted beaches here, as well as good offshore surfing and diving.

It's best to explore the island by car, for though the terrain isn't rugged (there are a few rough patches, and a four-wheel-drive vehicle might be a good idea), the distances warrant it. For those who do decide to cycle, a word of caution: Bikes and mopeds aren't permitted on crowded ferries, and you will need a lock if you wish to leave your machine on the docks while island-hopping in the north. Another warning: While plenty of rental cars are available on Eleuthera, rental companies are notorious for leaving very little gas in the tank. Be sure to check the gauge — and the location of the nearest gas station.

Perhaps the best way to see Eleuthera is to start at Governor's Harbour in the center of the island, head south, and then wander back to the historic spots in the north. Founded in 1648, Governor's Harbour is the heart of island life. (It's the technological capital, too, for it has the island's only traffic lights.) The first colonists probably landed near here, on Cupid's Cay just off the western edge of the harbor. The settlers, staunch Puritans from Bermuda, were led by William Sayle, a former governor. They called themselves the Eleutherian Adventurers, after the Greek work for "freedom." After landing on Cupid's Cay, the group argued and split up, and Sayle led a large contingent to the north part of the island, leaving a handful of dissenters behind. A causeway now links Governor's Harbour to the cay, where there is a quaint little community with two landmarks, the stately commissioner's house and the 19th-century St. Patrick's Anglican Church. (That heavenly smell wafting down the street is from *Mamie's Bakery;* don't miss her cinnamon buns.)

Though its beginnings were humble, Governor's Harbour became one of the busiest and wealthiest towns in the islands. Pineapple and citrus fruit were shipped from here to New York, Baltimore, and other ports on the Eastern seaboard during the second half of the 19th century. So sophisticated were its inhabitants that wealthy Nassau matrons came here to see the latest finery from London and New York. The style of those days still survives in the fancifully trimmed Victorian houses that line the side streets.

There is a bank, a few gift shops, and a couple of hotels and guesthouses in and around town, including a *Club Med* on the Atlantic side. The club is built on the site of the first hotel on the island, *French Leave,* which opened in the 1940s. The hotel was said to have been the home of Mauritian Alfred de Marigny, who was accused — and later acquitted — of murdering the near-legendary Nassau millionaire Sir Harry Oakes. The big event of the week is the arrival of the mail boat, which generally chugs in on Friday or Saturday.

Head south out of town on the Queen's Highway; 5 miles down is Palmetto Point, where many wealthy American expatriates live. Just south of town is a sign marking the road that leads west to Ten Bay, where there is a small limestone cave and a beach. The main road leads to Savannah Sound, where the *Windermere Island Club* (phone: 332-6003) is perched on its own cay off the island's eastern side. Prince Charles and Princess Diana stay there from time to time. (Visit the cay, which is linked by a bridge to the mainland, and take tea on the terrace that overlooks the pink beaches; paparazzi will be disappointed, for security is tight when the royals are around.)

It's 7 to 10 miles to the next settlement, the picturesque fishing village of Tarpum Bay. (The name is a corruption of "tarpon," a large fish that abounds in the flats offshore.) Take a stroll along the harbor in the late afternoon and watch the fishermen clean their catch. Several artists — most of them expatriates — work and exhibit here, including Macmillian Hughes and Mal Flanders. Ramble down the streets lined with pastel houses, or climb to the kooky "castle" on the hill. Watch for a sign near the center of town indicating a sharp turn to the left; this leads back to the Queen's Highway, which continues south toward Rock Sound. Less than a mile outside Tarpum Bay, a road branches off to the left toward Winding Bay. The beach and pool at the resort here are reserved for guests, but visitors are welcome to stop for a meal at the restaurant, one of the few on this end of the island.

Just north of Rock Sound there is a small airport on the right where the *Bahamasair, Aero Coach,* and *USAir* flights touch down. The town, which was settled during the early 18th century, has a Bermudian feel, with its narrow streets and prim pastel cottages. The place was originally called Wreck Sound, since most residents made a living by "wrecking" — scavenging cargo from ships that foundered on the rocks and shoals offshore. Today it's home to less than 1,000 residents, many of whom are employed by the government. Few outsiders came here until the early 1940s. One of the first to arrive was Arthur Vining Davis, chairman of the Aluminum Company of America, who built a winter home south of town.

Take a quick stroll through town, stopping in the boutiques along Front Street facing the placid waters of the bay. Just a block up Albury Lane, one of the first cross streets in town, is *Sammy's Place* (phone: 334-2121). Chef/owner Sammy Culmer established his redoubtable reputation at the swanky *Cotton Bay Club.* The food he serves here is homey and unpretentious: Try the conch fritters and peas 'n' rice.

On the southeastern edge of town, past a cemetery on one side of the road and a schoolyard on the other, is a geologic oddity that's worth a brief detour. It's a large blue hole roughly 125 yards wide and at least 100 fathoms — that's 600 feet — deep. The pool is fed by seawater that seeps through the porous limestone bedrock. Visitors can swim here or throw bits of bread to the angelfish and schoolmasters that swim in the clear blue water. Fishing is prohibited, though, and don't try to pry the oysters from the sides of the pool.

South of the blue hole, the road hugs the western shore, and the rocky Schooner Cays seem to float just offshore. Terns and white crown pigeons wheel over the calm water. Just before the small farming community of Green Castle, a road that branches off to the left leads to the *Cotton Bay Club*. The resort, once a private club, was built in the late 1950s by Juan Trippe, the flamboyant founder of the late and lamented *Pan American Airways*. Trippe flew in friends on the "Cotton Bay Special," a 727 Yankee Clipper, to play golf on the 18-hole course designed by Robert Trent Jones, Sr. The large villa on the grounds was once the vacation home of American industrialist Edgar Kaiser.

At Green Castle, a town founded in the 19th century by freed slaves, the island widens and splits into two forks. The road northwest leads by Davis Harbour, where boats are moored in a sheltered cove, and passes through the rustic fishing villages of Waterford, Delancey Town, and Deep Creek. The road meanders on to Point Powell and Cape Eleuthera, where plans for a couple of new resorts are under way. The southeastern route winds through several farming and fishing villages — including Wemyss Bight, John Millars, and Bannerman Town — until it dead-ends at East Point lighthouse at the southern end of the island.

North of Governor's Harbour the road is arrow-straight to the airport, about 10 miles north of town (the airport was built for a US Navy base — now closed — on the eastern side of the island). In 3 or 4 more miles is the small village of James Cistern, named after a 19th-century governor who built a reservoir for Governor's Harbour. A few old traditions still linger in this isolated town; notice the outdoor ovens made from a sand-and-limestone mixture called "tabby." Just past the town the road skirts a series of cliffs on the eastern side, and the views are spectacular.

Huge silos loom in the distance on the way to Alice Town and Hatchet Bay; they are all that remain of a large dairy farm built in the mid-1930s by American Austin Levy. The farm was intended to be self-sufficient: Cattle were fed grain grown on Eleuthera, and their milk was processed here before it was shipped to Nassau. At the height of the farm's activity just after World War II, a refrigerated ship laden with milk, butter, eggs, and poultry made daily trips from here to Nassau. Like most large-scale agricultural schemes in the Bahamas, however, the scheme eventually failed, although the poultry farm survived into the 1980s.

Signs just outside Alice Town point west toward Hatchet Bay Cave, which is worth a side trip. If you don't happen to have a flashlight, a local guide will light the way for a small fee. The steps just past the narrow entrance of the cave were probably carved by farmers who came to gather nitrogen-rich bat guano. The half-mile-deep cave widens into a broad vaulted chamber just 10 or 15 yards from the entrance. Icicle-like stalactites and stalagmites grow here, and hanging from the walls are hundreds of leaf-nosed bats, so-called for the floppy appendages on their snouts.

About 3 miles beyond Alice Town is a fine 5-mile stretch of small beaches on the eastern side of the island. The surfing here is excellent, but the beaches can be tough to reach: Visitors may need a four-wheel-drive vehicle to negotiate the barely visible track (it's a little more than half a mile from the main road to the shore). Halfway along this stretch is Gregory Town, the pineapple capital of Eleuthera. (Tourists who are on the islands in July should stop by for the *Pineapple Festival,* which is celebrated with a regatta and a dance.) Pirates hid out here in the 18th century and kept a lookout for ships from the high cliffs behind the harbor. After the buccaneers cleared out, many Loyalists, or Tories, moved here following the American Revolution. By the beginning of the 20th century, the town looked like a Cornish fishing village. Today, pineapple growers and American and Canadian expatriates live in this picturesque town, and tourists fill the hotels during the winter. Stop by the shop run by the Thompson family, which makes scrumptious pineapple rum.

Five miles past town the island narrows to a sliver just wide enough for a car to drive across. Sailors called the place the Glass Window Bridge, for they could "see through" the island from the rough waters of the Atlantic on one side to the calm blue-green waters of the Great Bahama Bank on the other. American artist Winslow Homer, who spent some time in Eleuthera after the Civil War, captured the scene in a painting.

Beyond the bridge the island widens, and the road meanders through the farming villages of Upper and Lower Bogue. The land here is marshy, or "boguey," as the natives say. The left turn past Lower Bogue leads to the prosperous little town of Current, which overlooks the tranquil waters to the west. Many of the houses here are built on pilings. The townsfolk here are rumored to be the descendants of Lucaya Indians who lived in the Bahamas in pre-Columbian times. More likely their ancestors were English settlers who occasionally intermarried with free blacks, a practice that was discouraged in other settlements.

Back on the main road, you'll soon come to a fork: The right-hand road leads to North Eleuthera Airport and the ferries to Harbour Island; the left leads to the dock for the ferries to Spanish Wells.

The left-hand fork leads first to The Bluff, a fishing village perched by a miniature harbor that was once a settlement for freed slaves. Citrus trees grow in neat rows near the road. Signs past the turnoff to The Bluff point the way to Preacher's Cave. The well-marked track meanders a mile or so to the cave. Inside, the ceiling arches 100 feet overhead, and sunlight filters in through fissures in the roof. It was here, on the lovely stretch of deserted beach that fronts the cave, that the main contingent of Eleutherian Adventurers came ashore in 1648. Since this is the windward side of the island, the water can be choppy, but it's a pleasant place for a picnic.

Back on the main road, it's a short drive to Gene's Bay, where the ferryboats to Spanish Wells dock. The ferries (passengers only; park your car at the dock), which dock at the eastern end of town, cost $4 per person one way; they're skippered by men like Caleb Sawyer and Norell Roberts, descendants of early settlers. It takes just a couple of minutes to reach St. George's Cay and the settlement of Spanish Wells (the latter gets its name from the Spanish galleons that used to take on fresh water here). Most of the residents of this hidebound seafaring town make a living catching spiny lobster; it's a lucrative business, apparently, for Spanish Wells is said to have the highest per capita income of any community in the Bahamas. Notice the not-so-subtle signs of wealth: the large brick homes on the western edge of town, the competing VCR rental shops, and the satellite dishes perched on top of the homes. Red-roofed clapboard houses line the narrow streets in the eastern part of town, and towheaded locals eye visitors cautiously before they nod in greeting. (Note the fine straw hats worn by the men; they can be purchased locally.) It's a reticent, inbred, overwhelmingly white community — and has been for centuries. Before leaving, stop by for a conch sandwich at *La Langousta,* a dockside restaurant run by Walton Pinder and his Brazilian wife.

Hop back on the passenger ferry and then drive 10 minutes or so east on the main road to get to the Harbour Island ferries dock. Unlike Spanish Wells, Harbour Island is a tourist-oriented place, so the ferries that go here are bigger and run more often. It costs $4 per person, one way, to take the 10-minute trip to the dock at Dunmore Town. (The town, like the island on which it is situated, is commonly called Harbour Island.) Guesthouses, hotels, and restaurants line the waterfront, and several more hotels face the magnificent blush-colored beach on the eastern side of the island. Visitors can hail a taxi to take a tour of the island, or they can rent mopeds at the shop on the inland end of the dock.

Harbour Island — or "Briland," as the locals say — was settled more than 300 years ago; it was the original capital of the Bahamas. Ramble slowly down the narrow, tree-lined streets. Some of the homes here are more than 200 years old. A white cottage on Bay Street north of the dock displays a sign proclaiming it a Loyalist house built in 1792. Three fine old churches stand on Dunmore Street: Anglican St. John's; Wesley Methodist, built in 1840; and Catholic St. Benedict's, whose adjoining convent was built in 1922 to house the Sisters of Charity. (For more information on Harbour Island, see *Quintessential Bahamas,* in DIVERSIONS.) From there, head for the beach on the Atlantic side for sun or a dip in the clear blue water, or stroll by one of the newer developments on the island, *Valentine's Yacht Club* and marina on the waterfront (phone: 333-2142 or 333-2080).

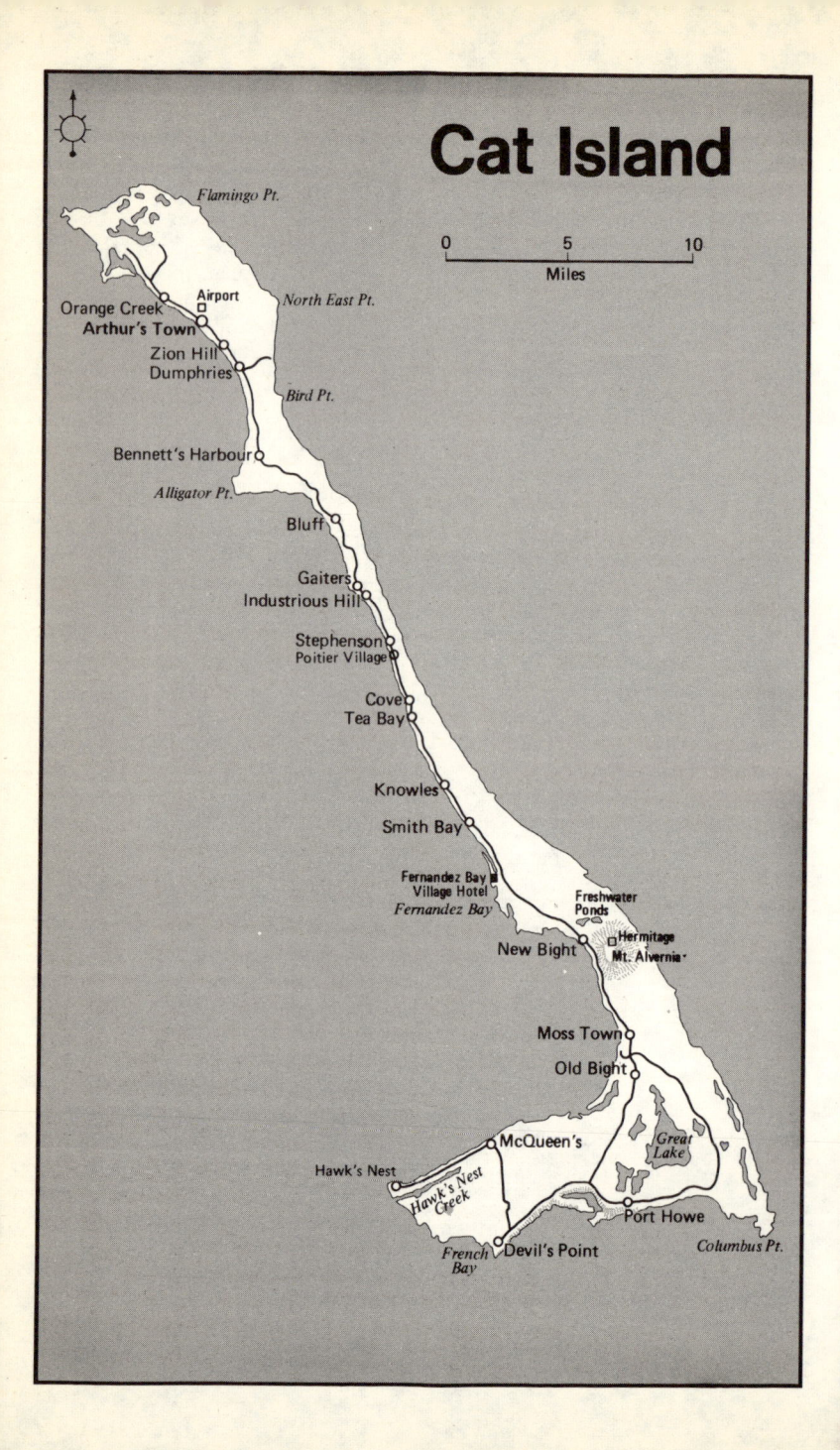

Cat Island

Cat Island

Few tourists — and not even many Bahamians — know much about Cat Island. Don't spread the word: It's one of the loveliest and most unspoiled of the Family Islands. It was named for English sea captain (and pirate, most likely) Arthur Catt, who also lent his name to Arthur's Town, a village at the north end of the island. The isle was known for years as San Salvador, for it was long believed that this was the place where Columbus first landed in the New World. This notion was officially debunked in 1892, when a panel of experts, relying on descriptions from Columbus's long-lost journal and other sources, decided that the *Pinta* had really landed on Watling's Island to the southeast. In 1926, Watling's Island was renamed San Salvador, and Cat Island received its humble new name.

This gossamer-thin isle, 48 miles long and less than a mile wide in places, is fertile by Bahamian standards, and most of its inhabitants farm for a living. Cat Island pineapples and tomatoes are particularly famous; potatoes, melons, peas, and beans are also raised here. The isle once had the reputation of being wild and untamed, for more Arawak Indians lived here than on any island in the Bahamian archipelago when Columbus arrived. The Indians are long gone. There are, however, vestiges of old colonial traditions. Some farmers still clear the land with machetes and till with grub hoes, as they've done for centuries, and women still bake bread in outdoor ovens. Talisman-like "duppies" — bottles or cans filled with earth, hair, and fingernails — protect country homes. (The duppies are a remnant of obeah, the voodoo-like black magic once practiced by slaves and free blacks.) Some of the old folks still know how to dance an English waltz or quadrille, and traditional "rake-and-scrape" bands still play at weddings and parties (see *Music and Dance,* in PERSPECTIVES).

Most visitors land on the island at the little airport in Arthur's Town. (The town's history is recounted in the autobiography of its most famous resident, actor Sidney Poitier.) Only a few hundred people live here, but it's one of the more important settlements on the island. A grassy square stands in the center of town, and there's a school off to one side. To the north, across the harbor, stand the tumbledown remains of the original settlement; nearby is the hot spot of the town's nightlife, *Lovers Boulevard* (no phone), which calls itself a "disco and satellite lounge" because there's a satellite dish on the roof.

It's hard to get lost on Cat Island, for one paved road runs from north to south, and the villages are strung along it like beads on a necklace. Most of the towns line the western shore, where the waters are calmer. The island widens at both ends, and the geography there is slightly more complicated, but it's still easy to find your way around. The best way to see the island is to start at Arthur's Town and head south. Although it's possible to bike or ride a moped, be forewarned that the roads can be rough in spots. Anglers may want to start with a detour to Orange Creek, the only settlement north of Arthur's Town, where the bonefishing in the flats offshore is particularly good.

Just south of Arthur's Town is the tiny community of Zion Hill, where you may see women sitting on their porches plaiting palm fronds. A mile farther south, just beyond the village of Dumphries, is Bennett's Harbour, with its lovely half-mile-long waterfront. One of the island's oldest towns, it was founded in the 1830s by Governor James Carmichael Smyth, who designated it a settlement for blacks freed from slave ships. East of town beyond Thurston Hill is Bird Point, which overlooks the Atlantic (ask for directions; the trail is faint and unmarked). Wrens, blackbirds, egrets, and several kinds of herons nest in the shrubs beside the path; near the shore are some natural salt ponds called salinas, which were worked commercially 50 years ago and later abandoned. (Visitors may still see an islander raking salt here now and then.) Back on the main road, past Alligator Point to the west, is Bluff, a derelict old town that was once a wealthy settlement when cotton was king.

For the next 25 miles or so, the road winds through several small farming villages. Near the Gaiters, huge limestone caves riddle the cliffs on the western shore, but you need a boat to explore them. The women of Industrious Hill are known for their plaiting, while Stephenson is famous for its rooftop ornaments called "prettys." Just below Stephenson is a tiny community called Poitier Village, where almost everyone claims to be related to Sidney Poitier.

The next few communities — Sawyer, Cove, Tea Bay, Bachelor's — are unpretentious little towns where farmers tend their crops of sweet potatoes, onions, and pigeon peas. Next is Knowles, which is big enough to have a gas station and a primary school, the only one in the central part of the island. (High school students travel to Old Bight, the biggest town in these parts, for classes.) Smith Bay is a somewhat larger town with several churches, a clinic, and a government packing house, from which produce is shipped to Nassau. During the busiest months of the year, as many as eight cargo boats set sail from here each week.

Next comes Fernandez Bay, whose fine beach is still relatively undiscovered. On the beach is the *Fernandez Bay Village* hotel, run by the Armbristers, one of the oldest families on the island; it has several villas, a grocery store, a restaurant serving traditional island dishes, and one of Cat Island's few telephones (phone: 354-5043).

The freshwater ponds just east of here are home to the Cat Island turtle, a rare species possibly stranded here at the end of the last Ice Age. (It's also possible that Lucaya Indians brought the turtles here from South America.) Years ago, locals caught the turtles, which they called "peter," with a hook and line baited with fruit. Like the Lucaya, Cat Islanders still prize the turtles for their meat.

Three miles south of Fernandez Bay is New Bight, a large town by island standards; the commissioner's office, police department, and post office are located here. The *Bluebird* restaurant (no phone) on the main road attracts patrons from all over the island.

New Bight is the gateway to the Hermitage, a religious retreat atop Mt. Alvernia. Park the car; the footpath to the retreat begins in the center of town near the commissioner's office. The climb is arduous but short, for the mountain, the highest spot in the Bahamas, is only 206 feet high. (There are no provisions for the handicapped.) The summit affords a panoramic view of the deep blue Atlantic to the east and the calm azure waters to the west. The climb to the chapel, bell tower, and tiny house — all hand-hewn from native rock — is marked by the stations of the cross.

The Hermitage is the handiwork of Father Jerome, born John Hawkes, who came to the Bahamas in 1911 as an Anglican missionary and later converted to Catholicism. An architect by training, he designed and built several churches in the Bahamas, including Anglican St. Paul's and Catholic St. Peter's in Clarence Town on Long Island and the monastery of St. Augustine on New Providence. When he retired in 1939, he was granted permission to build the Alvernia retreat. His grave — he died in 1956 at the age of 80 — is in a cave just below the Hermitage.

Five miles to the south of New Bight, on the way to Old Bight, is the small village of Moss Town, whose name recalls the days when Spanish moss hung from the trees on this part of the island. Here in the south the island broadens to its greatest width: nearly 15 miles. The island's only major crossroads is just north of Old Bight. The left (east) fork skirts Old Bight and a pond called Great Lake and carries on to the historic town of Port Howe. The right (west) fork cuts through the center of Old Bight and heads toward the south shore of the island. From there it meanders west to Devil's Point, McQueen's, and Hawks Nest.

The road to Point Howe skirts by Columbus Point on the southeastern tip of the island. About a mile before Point Howe, a dirt track branches off and leads to the point, but the terrain is rough and last couple of miles must be traversed on foot. It's worth the walk, for the views from the point, where steep cliffs sweep down to the ocean, are spectacular. Back on the main road toward the town of Port Howe, the terrain is open and flat, and pineapple plants flourish in the rich red soil.

Port Howe is hardly a port, for its harbor is fringed with treacherous reefs and shallow waters — by no means a good place for ships to put ashore. Some say that the village's name may have been deliberately misleading. The town's early residents, many of whom made a living by scavenging shipwrecks, apparently decided to increase their business with a little false advertising. Legend says that they hung lanterns from the trees to exaggerate the size of the "port," beckoning hapless sailors to shore.

On the western outskirts of town lie the ruins of an estate built by Colonel Andrew Deveaux, an American Loyalist who fled to the Bahamas during the Revolutionary War. He proved his loyalty to the islands by recapturing Nassau from Spanish invaders in 1783, and was rewarded with a large tract of land here, where he started a cotton plantation; his crops failed, though, and the farm was soon abandoned. The ruins of the outbuildings and once-grand mansion are largely overgrown, but a few brick walls and heavy wooden beams are still visible.

Just west of Port Howe stand the ruins of what was once the 2,000-acre Richman Hill–Newfield plantation. Owned for many years by the Armbrister family, it is now overgrown and crumbling, though visitors can still see the remnants of the slave quarters and the large octagonal house that overlooked the ocean. A few of the walls that surrounded the elaborate gardens still stand, and the once-lovely pools are filled with stagnant water. Locals say that gold and jewels salvaged from nearby shipwrecks are buried here.

Between Port Howe and Devil's Point the road skirts a series of 200-foot cliffs, affording the homes perched near them spectacular views. Five miles offshore is Tartar Bank, where locals fish. For another fine view, continue straight past the turnoff to McQueen's, to reach Devil's Point on the southwestern tip of the island. An old incantation says that here "cork did sink and iron float" — a reference, most likely, to the meeting of the rough Atlantic waters and the calm western seas rather than to a preternatural event.

Follow the main road north to McQueen's, a tradition-bound farming community of palmetto-frond thatch houses where women still make their own baskets and bake in outdoor ovens. Some of the town's residents are members of the Rolle family who came here from Exuma. West of the town is Hawk's Nest Creek, a bird sanctuary where great blue herons nest.

Exumas

This 100-mile-long string of stepping-stone islands and cays is one of the great finds in the Family Islands. The Exumas, 365 in all, are sparsely populated and still largely unsullied by tourism. Only 3,500 people live here year-round — most of them on Great and Little Exuma, the largest islands in the chain. Some of the best sailing waters in the Bahamas are to be found here, and there are fine dives off 5,000-foot-deep Exuma Sound to the east. The shallow pools just offshore, whose colors range from jade to celadon to opal, are superb for bathing and bonefishing.

Lucaya Indians are believed to have lived here before the Spanish carried them off as slaves during the 16th century. In the 17th century, salt rakers came to the Exumas by the hundreds, as did pirates seeking a safe haven for their stolen goods. The islands later became a refuge for a handful of Loyalists fleeing the newly independent United States. Cotton and salt were the main sources of wealth throughout the 18th century, and many slaves were brought here to labor on the plantations and salinas. Eventually, though, both industries failed.

Much of the land here was granted by the Crown in the late 18th century to Lord John Rolle, who according to some accounts gave away his plantations to his slaves after they were freed in 1834. Some say Rolle's gesture was genuinely magnanimous, while cynics claim he had no choice; in any case, the slaves eventually prevailed, and many took Rolle's name. To this day, most of the arable land on the Exumas cannot be sold; instead, it is passed from family to family, many of whom still bear the name Rolle. Islanders still tend their small fruit and vegetable plots and husband their goats and sheep as they have for centuries. Farmers sell their onions, tomatoes, mangoes, avocados, and pineapples to the hotels on the islands, or ship them by mail boat to Nassau. Fishing and tourism are the mainstays of the modern economy.

Many Exuma cays are reachable only by boat or chartered prop plane. Staniel Cay north of Great Exuma has good sailing and fishing; divers can explore the grotto where parts of the James Bond movie *Thunderball* were filmed. (At low tide you can snorkel into the cave.) From there it's a short hop to Sampson Cay, where visitors can stay in one of three villas operated by the *Sampson Cay Colony*. North of Staniel Cay, off the western shore between Conch Cut and Wax Cay Cut, is the Exuma Land and Sea Park, a 200-square-mile reserve — reachable only by boat — where delicate coral gardens grow only a few feet below the surface of the water. Tourists shouldn't plan to visit Norman's Cay, the northernmost in the Exumas chain, unless they want to be arrested by the Royal Bahamian Defence Forces. Once a stronghold of Colombian drug runner Carlos Lehder Rivas, who is now cooling his heels in a US prison, the cay is off-limits to visitors.

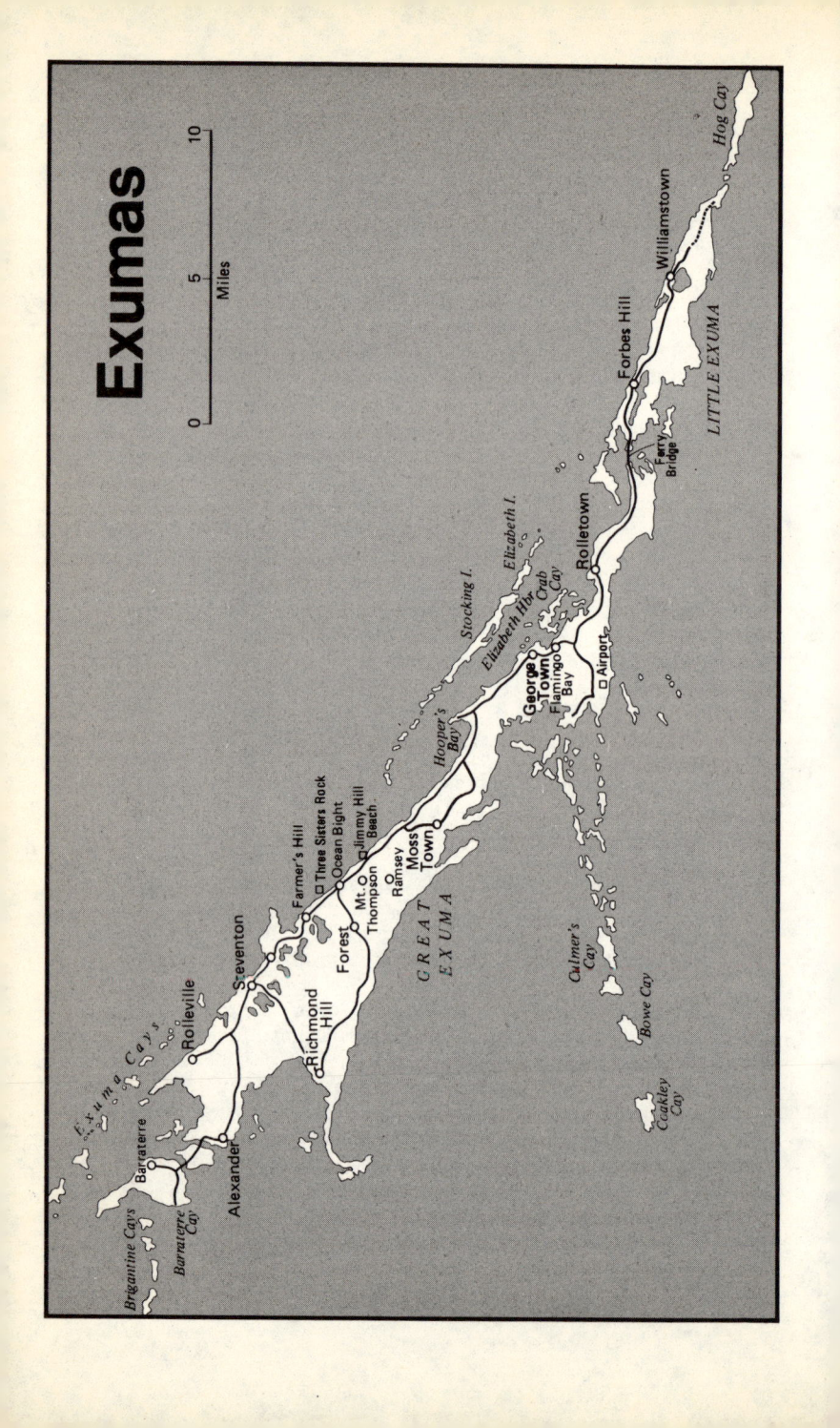

Exumas

George Town, the capital, is hardly a metropolis — 800 people live there year-round — but it's definitely the liveliest spot in the Exumas. Situated on deep Elizabeth Harbour on Great Exuma, it is reachable by *Bahamasair,* which makes daily stops at the airport 9 miles south of town, or by *Aero Coach,* which flies in daily from Miami and Ft. Lauderdale. Tourists with relaxed schedules can reach the Exumas on the *Grand Master,* the mail boat that ferries supplies to the islands; it leaves Nassau each Tuesday and docks in Elizabeth Harbour the following evening. (The boat, which returns to Nassau each Thursday, takes only a limited number of passengers, so inquire well in advance at your hotel.) For three days each April, the harbor here is filled with sloops racing in the *Family Island Regatta,* one of the grand events of the year. Fishing boats from across the islands come here in April, too, to compete for the "Best in the Bahamas" title.

GREAT EXUMA ON FOOT

Small, historic George Town is an ideal place for a leisurely stroll; visitors can see all the main sights in half an hour or so. Start in the center of town on the Queen's Highway at the *Peace and Plenty* hotel (phone: 336-2551), named for the *Peace and Plenty,* the English trading ship that brought Lord Rolle to the Exumas in 1783. The hotel, opened about a decade ago by a grandnephew of Florida railroad/real-estate baron Henry Flagler, is built around the remains of an old sponge warehouse and market. Opposite it is *Minn's Water Sports,* which rents Boston whalers to fishermen.

Up the Queen's Highway to the north is St. Andrew's, a lovely Presbyterian church with a high gabled roof, Norman arch doorways, and smart blue trim. Local theater productions are staged in the church hall next door. You pass one more hotel up the road, the relaxed *Pieces of Eight* (phone: 336-2600) — try its Oriental restaurant — before the town peters out and country begins.

South of *Peace and Plenty* on the Queen's Highway, amid well-tended gardens, is the mint-pink Government Building, modeled after Government House in Nassau. The post office and customs department are inside. Just beyond it, opposite a park and a small straw market set up under a spreading banyan tree, is the *Two Turtles Inn,* a rustic hotel centered around a stone courtyard overlooking the harbor (phone: 336-2545). The staff there will arrange diving tours, and there are bicycles for rent.

Down to the right, near the local supermarket, is the *Town Café* (phone: 336-2194), a delightful Mediterranean-style restaurant with black-and-white decor. It's the best place in town for breakfast, and it serves decent lunches as well. (Insistent visitors may be able to talk the cook into whipping up some grouper stew or peas 'n' rice for dinner.) Farther down on the left is *Gemelli's,* the local pizza hangout, and *Gray's Car Rentals,* the best place on the island to hire a car (phone: 336-2101). Owner Sam Gray also runs *Sam's Place,* a good seafood restaurant a stone's throw away. Sit on the balcony and munch on a conch salad as you watch the boats dock in the harbor (phone: 336-2579). There are a few more shops overlooking nearby Lake Victoria.

After lunch, walk back toward the center of town to *Peace and Plenty,* where the ferries to Stocking Island dock. (They head to the island, which is just a mile offshore, twice a day, at 10 AM and 1 PM.) On the island you can hunt for sand dollars and conch shells on the beach at low tide or relax over a barbecue (weekends only) at the beachside bar and grill. Divers can explore the 400-foot-deep blue hole called Mystery Cave.

GREAT EXUMA BY BIKE

The best cycling route begins at George Town and follows the Queen's Highway along the east coast of Great Exuma north for 8 miles or so to Ocean Bight, stopping at the secluded beaches along the way. About 2 miles north of George Town is the *Peace and Plenty Beach Inn,* a cluster of cottages built right on the beach. A few miles farther on, past *Exuma Straw Work,* which sells local handicrafts, is the turnoff to sheltered Hooper's Bay. Some of the villas here — which are surrounded by well-tended gardens of bougainvillea, pink and yellow hibiscus, birds of paradise, and amaryllis — are available to rent. There are many pleasant beaches along the shore. Two miles on is *Tradewinds,* the last place for several miles with provisions. Nearby, beyond the small village of Ramsey, is Jimmy Hill, famous for its long-deserted beach. There is a picturesque Seventh-Day Adventist church at Mt. Thompson just to the north. Visible from the church is craggy Three Sisters Rock just offshore. The tour ends at the fishing village of Ocean Bight a mile up the road, where visitors can stop for a swim before heading back down the road to George Town.

GREAT EXUMA BY CAR

It's a pleasant half-day drive from George Town to the tip of Great Exuma 30 miles to the northwest. The route along the Queen's Highway winds by the ruins of several old plantations, many of which are still being farmed. There are boats for hire in several of the small fishing villages along the way, and some of the finest beaches on the island are just a few hundred yards from the road. Eight miles north of George Town, a road — Pindling Drive — branches off to Moss Town, a farming village on the west side of the island. Its brightly painted houses contrast with the weatherbeaten hues of its two churches, St. John the Baptist and a small Anglican chapel, which look as if they had survived many a storm. North of the village the road bends east to join the main coastal route.

A few miles on, past another secluded beach, are three of Lord Rolle's old plantations: Farmer's Hill, Poker's Point, and Steventon. Fields of cotton used to blanket the hillsides here until blights and chenille bugs destroyed the crops during the early 19th century. The grand plantation houses are gone, leaving only a scattering of wooden buildings painted in gay hues of green, yellow, and red. The descendants of the slaves who labored here more than a century ago still live nearby, tending their plots of corn and pigeon peas. The taciturnity of the villagers is probably due more to shyness than animosity. If you ask, they'll be glad to point the way to the best beaches.

Rolleville, one of the oldest settlements on the island, is a somnolent village with a few thatch houses and the whitewashed Church of God of Prophecy. Stop by the *Hilltop Tavern* (phone: 345-6006) for a plate of grouper fingers and a chat with the owner, Kermit Rolle, a fine storyteller who knows the island well. The beaches here are well worth the trip.

Past Rolleville, the road turns to dirt, leading after a bumpy mile or so to a perfect crescent beach. The clapboard restaurant nearby is shuttered for the moment — thankfully perhaps, for it means that fewer people stop by to spoil the peace and quiet.

Heading back south, about 5 miles past Rolleville, there is a paved road off to the right that leads to Barraterre, a small cay linked to Great Exuma by a causeway. (The road isn't marked, but you can identify it by the dirt road that runs right alongside it.) This is one of the few spots that can be visited on the marshy western strand. Goats graze on the fields surrounding Alexander, another old settlement founded on the site of an 18th-century cotton plantation. Turn left at the Mt. Sania Baptist Church; the causeway is just ahead, past *Smith's Food Supplies* and the post office. Barraterre is a pretty fishing village with three landmarks: the Baptist Church, *Ryann's Variety Store* (don't miss the straw baskets), and the *Fisherman's Inn* (good barbecue, two rooms for rent, dancing to reggae and calypso at night; phone: 336-5107). The beach is fine for a short stroll, and you can watch the fishermen haul in their daily catch of grouper, conch, and bonefish.

From George Town, the road south to Little Exuma runs for 15 miles along the east coast, passing through several picturesque fishing villages along the way. A half-mile south of George Town is *Flamingo Bay,* a cluster of luxury villas on a high promontory overlooking the clear waters of the sound (phone: 336-2661). There's live music in the evenings at the beachside bar, the *Flamingo.* Just beyond the bay, a wide paved road forks off to the right and leads to the Bahamas Coast Guard rescue station. The barrage balloon that floats a mile above the station is designed to intercept signals from drug-running vessels.

The next settlement, Rolletown, doesn't appear to have changed a whit over the past 50 years. Turn left into the village and right at the top of the hill to find the cemetery, where the tombs of 18th-century settler Captain Alexander McKay and his wife and child lie. McKay immigrated to the Exumas from Scotland in 1789 and was granted 400 acres of farmland by the Crown. His wife and child died in 1792 — the tombs give no explanation for their fate — and McKay died less than a year later. At the bottom of the side road is another small cemetery next to a secluded bathing spot.

The best stop for lunch along this route is the *Blue Hole,* a 2-story clapboard building about 6 miles south of George Town (phone: 345-5014). The restaurant upstairs, which overlooks the bay, serves a wide variety of American and Bahamian dishes. On Friday nights, half the locals on the island crowd into the bar downstairs.

Just to the south, the road crosses Ferry Bridge to Little Exuma Island. Just past the bridge watch for a hand-painted sign on the left proclaiming "Patience Tara, Home of the Shark Lady." (The sign just above it announces that the Tropic of Cancer runs right through her home.) Miss Patience, who is in her 70s, greets visitors with a bone-crushing handshake, strengthened, no doubt, by her years wrestling sharks into her fishing boat. She claims to have caught more than 2,000; the biggest, she says, was an 18-foot tiger shark, and the meanest was a hammerhead that battered her boat to bits. Miss Patience, miraculously, has never been hurt. She still motors out each day to bait and check her lines. When she's not regaling visitors with stories, she's hawking her shark steaks, shark's-tooth necklaces, shell mobiles, ancient green glass bottles, and the seascapes painted by her husband.

Forbes Hill — a clutch of fusty old houses — is the last stop before Williamstown, which is dominated by the tall spire of St. Mary Magdalene Church and the aroma of fried conch from *Gordy's Palace and Disco,* which serves Bahamian dishes in clean, if spartan, surroundings (no phone). The road wanders on past the defunct *Sand Dollar Club* and peters out into a dirt track before reaching the southeastern tip of the island.

San Salvador

This little knob of coralline limestone, about 12 miles long and 6 miles wide, is famous beyond its size. Though the facts are still disputed, most historians believe this is where Christopher Columbus first landed in 1492. Columbus called his first landfall San Salvador, but confusion arose later as to which isle he had actually sighted. Throughout early colonial times, this isle was known as Watling's Island, after a buccaneer who lived here in fine style. During the late 19th century, scholars declared Watling's Island the original San Salvador, based in part on descriptions in Columbus's long-lost journal of his first voyage. In 1926, the island was officially renamed, thanks in large measure to the lobbying of Chrysostom Schreiner, a Benedictine missionary who lived here for many years.

Similar in shape and geography to the isle of Grand Turk, which some historians believe could be the first landfall of Columbus, San Salvador is tiny enough to be seen in a day. Many visitors come to explore the reefs and wall off Riding Rock Point, which has some of the best shallow-water diving spots in the Bahamas. The interior of the island, which is flat and largely unpopulated, is riddled with brackish lakes. Many of the lakes are linked by small canals dug by settlers who found it easier to get around by boat than overland.

It's best to see most of the sights on San Salvador, such as the lighthouse at Dixon Hill and the ruins of the old plantations to the south, by car or moped. The roads are generally well maintained, but in the southeast they can be rutted and tough to negotiate on two wheels. The main road that skirts the perimeter of the island — it's about 35 miles around — is called the Queen's Highway, but neither it nor any of the side roads branching off it is marked. If you're unsure of a turn, don't hesitate to ask for help. Most of the 500 or so people who live here were born on the island and know it as well as native New Yorkers know Manhattan — or better.

Walkers can take several short strolls along the west coast from the *Riding Rock Inn,* the only hotel on the island (call the operator at 332-2694 for more information). It's a 20-minute walk from the inn to Cockburn Town, the island's capital; just head south along the Queen's Highway, past a dive shop and a tiny marina. Heading north on the highway from the hotel, it's a 15-minute walk to the beach at Bonefish Bay, where the swimming is excellent and the bonefishing is not bad, either. On the way, the road skirts by the old *Pan American* building, which was used as a tracking station during the early days of the US space program in the 1960s and is now a school. There is a short marked trail east of the inn across the Queen's Highway to an old observation tower in the interior of the island. The tower overlooks Long Lake, a finger of Great Lake, the largest on the island.

San Salvador

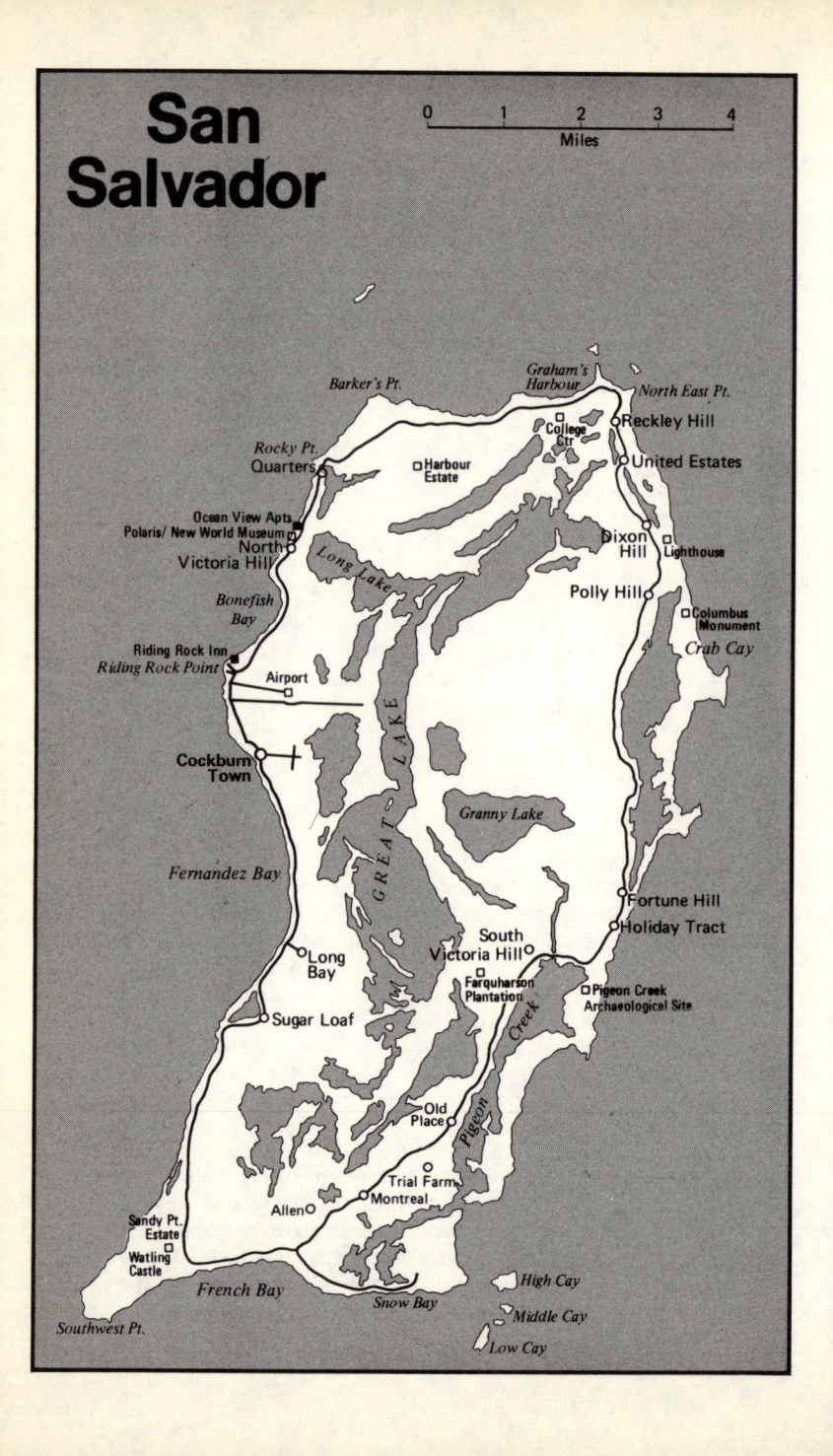

If you choose to drive, head north on the Queen's Highway from the *Riding Rock Inn*. Just past Bonefish Bay is the small community of North Victoria Hill. The large estate on the beach, called "Polaris-by-the-Sea," is owned by Ruth Durlacher Wolper, widow of Hollywood producer David Wolper. On the estate is the *New World Museum* (no phone), which houses pre-Columbian artifacts and a few objects thought to have been left by early Spanish explorers. Many of the artifacts displayed here were found at the Palmetto Grove site on the beach just north of the estate. Next to the museum is *Club Arawak*, a snack bar and occasional nightspot, and nearby are the *Ocean View Apartments* (no phone; call the operator at 332-2694 for more information), the only guest accommodations on the island besides the *Riding Rock Inn*.

Just north of North Victoria Hill and south of Rocky Point is the village of Quarters, where the ruins of the old slave quarters of Harbour Estate, a plantation owned by Loyalist Burton Williams, still stand. The grave of Benedictine missionary Chrysostom Schreiner is somewhere on the property. His coffin reputedly lies directly atop that of Burton Williams — because, it is said, it was too difficult to dig a new grave in the hard rock. Nearby stand the ruins of the *Columbus* hotel, which was built in the 1930s by entrepreneur Sir Harry Oakes and leased to Britain's Royal Air Force during World War II. Just beyond is the Palmetto Grove archaeological site — it's easy to miss, because virtually everything unearthed here has been carted away.

The road rounds the northwest corner of the island and parallels the broad sweep of Graham's Harbour. Some scholars maintain that Columbus was referring to this harbor when he described an anchorage on San Salvador large enough to shelter "all the ships of Christendom." (Take a dip here if you like; the beach is narrow but long, and the water is calm.) Scores of dinghies — or "smack boats," as Bahamians call them — race here every *Discovery Day* (October 12). On the hillside above the harbor stands a former US Navy base that now houses the College Centre for the Finger Lakes (CCFL). Sponsored by schools from upstate New York, the center is a field station for American college students studying everything from marine biology and geology to archaeology. (It says something about the pace of life on San Salvador that the arrival of a new batch of students is a grand event.)

The road rambles on to North East Point and turns south toward Reckley Hill, where descendants of the Pratt family have lived for several generations. The US Coast Guard signal station that stands here was shut down more than 10 years ago. South of Reckley Hill is United Estates, the second-largest town on the island. Known to locals as UE (not to be confused with the US), it's hardly a town at all — just a few houses and chapels scattered on a scrubby plain. Some locals say the village was named sometime in the 19th century by poor blacks imitating the pretentious speech of white foreigners.

Just down the road is Dixon Hill, where one of the world's last kerosene-powered lighthouses stands on a rise 163 feet above the ocean. Built by the British in the second half of the 19th century and remodeled in 1930, the 72-foot-tall lighthouse emits a double flash every 10 seconds; the 400,000-candlepower beam can be seen by ships up to 19 miles out to sea. It's a demanding task to operate: The keeper pumps the kerosene to the giant wick that fuels the lamp every 60 minutes, and pulls the weights that keep the beacon rotating every 2 hours. Marcia, the keeper's daughter, will be glad to give visitors a tour.

The observation deck near the top of the lighthouse commands a fine view of the coast and the saltwater lakes that fleck the interior of the island. To the southeast is the town of Polly Hill, which sprang up around an old plantation. Beyond it is Crab Cay, where, in 1891, the *Chicago Herald* erected a marker commemorating the 400th anniversary of Columbus's voyage to the New World. (The connection seems tenuous, but there *is* a reason: Chicago was the site of the *1892 World's Fair,* which was called the *Columbian Exposition.*) The site the *Herald* picked was probably not where Columbus landed, however. The reefs just offshore are treacherous, and written records seem to show that after Columbus sighted land, he sailed to the western coast to come ashore. Nonetheless, the monument on Crab Cay declares incontrovertibly: "On this spot Christopher Columbus first set foot on the soil of the New World. Erected by the *Chicago Herald,* June 15, 1891." There is no road to the marker, but if the tide is low and the wind calm, you can park by the side of the road and slog across to the cay along East Beach, which fronts the lighthouse. It's a 2-mile trek to the islet, where a small footpath leads from the beach to the worn limestone monument on the point.

Past Polly Hill the Queen's Highway skirts the western shore of a large lake. It's a desolate stretch of land; there are few birds here on the windward side of the island, and vegetation is sparse, except for a scattering of wild cotton and sisal plants and a pomegranate bush here and there. Three miles down are Fortune Hill and Holiday Tract, two modern villages established near old plantation sites. Just south of them, about a mile off the highway on a rough unmarked track, is the archaeological site of Pigeon Creek, which was excavated by students from the CCFL. Their finds, which are displayed at the *San Salvador Museum* in Cockburn Town, show that the spot was occupied by Arawak Indians for several generations.

Past the site the road follows the western shore of Pigeon Creek, which is actually an estuary. In colonial times cargo boats chugged up and down this 4-mile stretch of water, ferrying goods from ports to settlements in the center of the island. One of largest of these was Farquharson Plantation, which lies west of the Queen's Highway near the modern village of South Victoria Hill. The plantation has been carefully excavated, and the objects unearthed, including the estate journal for 1831–32, give a clue about what life here must have been like. The 2,000-acre estate, only a small part of which was arable, was owned by Charles Farquharson, a magistrate for Watling's Island. About 55 slaves worked on the farm during the time the journal was written; of them, just over a dozen labored in the fields, raising cotton, corn, livestock, citrus fruit, and lignum vitae trees. Farquharson purchased flour, cloth, rum, and furniture; the farm was otherwise self-sufficient. Vegetables and pumpkins were raised for the household, and homegrown sage, catnip, and castor beans were used to treat minor ailments. The family subsisted on chickens, turkeys, and bonefish caught in nearby coves, and horses and mules were bred to work in the fields. The journal doesn't describe relations between master and slave, but when Emancipation was proclaimed in 1834, life on the farm must have changed drastically.

Past the plantation, the road winds on through what was once a bustling farm region, where the villages of Old Place, Breezy Hill, Trial Farm, Montreal, and Allen flourished a century ago. (The settlements are now almost entirely abandoned, and there is a ghostly feel to the place.) The road curves west near Blackwood Bay, and just to the left stand the ruins of an old church. Built in the early 20th century, it is called Belmont Church by the locals, for it stands on the ruins of an old estate called Bell Mount. The side road east of the church, which locals call Columbus Landing Road, skirts the south shore of the island and veers north toward the mouth of Pigeon Creek. The view along the coast is breathtaking, and the beach at Snow Bay on the east coast is snowdrift-white and virtually deserted.

Past French Bay, the road turns north, and just to the left is Sandy Point Estate. The pirate John Watling was said to have lived here in the 17th century, and the place was known for years as Watling's Castle. (Despite the pious-sounding name of his ship, the *Most Holy Trinity,* Watling was as ruthless as they came.) Archaeologists claim that the ruins here are the remnants of a plantation built during the early 19th century on land owned by Bud Cade Matthews, who was believed to be a Loyalist who fled during the American Revolution. Unlike many other plantations on the island, Sandy Point prospered. It survived Emancipation and remained a working farm until 1925. In recent years, much of the property has been subdivided for homes and sold. A derelict tower still stands on the estate, and can be reached by the road just west of the dock. Lookouts who manned the tower searched the horizon for ships bringing goods from Nassau. If the ships crashed on the reefs offshore — a welcome event — they were scavenged.

To reach Sandy Point at the southwestern tip of the island, take Sandcliff Road, which branches off the Queen's Highway just north of the plantation. The road curves south to the point and then loops back to rejoin the highway just south of the plantation. Near the point — it's not marked, but it's fairly easy to find — is a limestone cave called Dripping Rock, with an old well inside. Fruit trees — limes, mangoes, and sour oranges — flourish near the shore, and there is a secluded beach just north of the cave.

Heading back north along Queen's Highway, with the calm sea waters off to the west, you'll pass the abandoned settlement of Black Rock before reaching the area known as Sugar Loaf, which takes its name from a rocky outcropping just offshore. The paved road that forks off to the left leads past the abandoned settlement of Strown Landing to the secluded cove at Sugar Loaf Beach.

Two miles farther north, near the tumbledown town of Long Bay, stand two monuments. The larger of the two, a stark, modernistic structure of dark gray stone designed by Mexican architects Pedro Alvarado and Antonio Vilchis, was built in 1968 by the organizers of the Mexico City *Olympic Games.* The ship carrying the *Olympic* flame from Greece to Mexico stopped here, and the monument's torch was lit. The flame is rekindled each *Discovery Day* (October 12) with great fanfare. Just north of the *Olympic* monument stands a cross erected in 1956, flanked by flags of several nations, serving as a tribute to — and a plea for — world unity.

Head toward Cockburn Town, past wild sisal plants that wave in the breeze on the island side of the road: They're the plants with spiky dark green leaves and yellow or white blossoms, which crown stems that shoot up to 25 feet in the air. Two varieties grow here: the smaller silk sisal, used to make bags and baskets; and the larger black or manila sisal, which was woven into rope. The sisal industry flourished here in the late 1890s and early 1900s, but once production picked up in the Philippines after the Spanish-American War, Bahamian growers were wiped out. Also on the right is a small modern cottage belonging to former professional football player Jack "Hacksaw" Reynolds, who played with the *Los Angeles Rams* and the *San Francisco 49ers.*

On the south edge of town, overlooking the shore, is a small Catholic cemetery. A wooden cross commemorates the mass celebrated there on January 25, 1891 — the first on the island since 1492. A larger public cemetery is just to the north. The oldest marked grave belongs to W. Morrah Savage, a lighthouse inspector with the Royal Navy who died in 1885.

Nearby is the public dock, where the mail boat that brings supplies from Nassau calls each week. Across the highway from the dock is First Avenue, the main street of the neatly laid-out Cockburn Town; it's pronounced as one word, *Ko*-burn-town. Named for Sir Francis Cockburn, the Governor of the Bahamas from 1837 to 1844, it's the administrative capital of the island. Most of the sights worth seeing are crowded into the first few blocks of First Avenue.

The San Salvador Public Library stands on one corner of the intersection of First Avenue and Queen's Highway. A pub, the *Ocean View Club,* stands just opposite — stop in for a Kalik beer. On most afternoons, an ancient "straw woman" sits under an almond tree, plaiting her bags and baskets. Across the street in the old telegraph building is the *San Salvador Gift Shop,* run by Iris Fernander, who keeps the key to the *San Salvador Museum.* Nearby is the *Harlem Square Club,* Marcus Jones's spacious bar; with a little prodding, he'll talk about his world travels. Across the street is the *Three Ships* restaurant, run by Jones's wife; aside from the *Riding Rock Inn,* it's the only place on the island where you can get boiled fish and grits for breakfast. (Reservations required for dinner; call the operator at 332-2694 to reach the restaurant.) Next door is Jake Jones's grocery store; up the block, on Carey Street, is St. Augustine's Anglican Church, which was consecrated in 1888.

Along the Queen's Highway north of the dock stand the commissioner's house, the Holy Saviour Catholic Church — Christopher Columbus is immortalized in a ceramic tile imbedded in the stucco façade — and the *San Salvador Museum.* The building that houses the museum, which dates from the mid-19th century, once served as jail, courtroom, and commissioner's office. There are exhibits of Arawak settlements on the island, including artifacts from Palmetto Grove, Pigeon Creek, and Long Bay, and of Columbus's voyage here in 1492. Photographs and mementos from various colonial estates are shown in the second-floor gallery. Admission is $2 per person; groups of under 5 people pay a flat fee of $10. There are no full-time staffers; see Iris Fernander at the gift shop in downtown Cockburn to arrange a visit.

Turks and Caicos

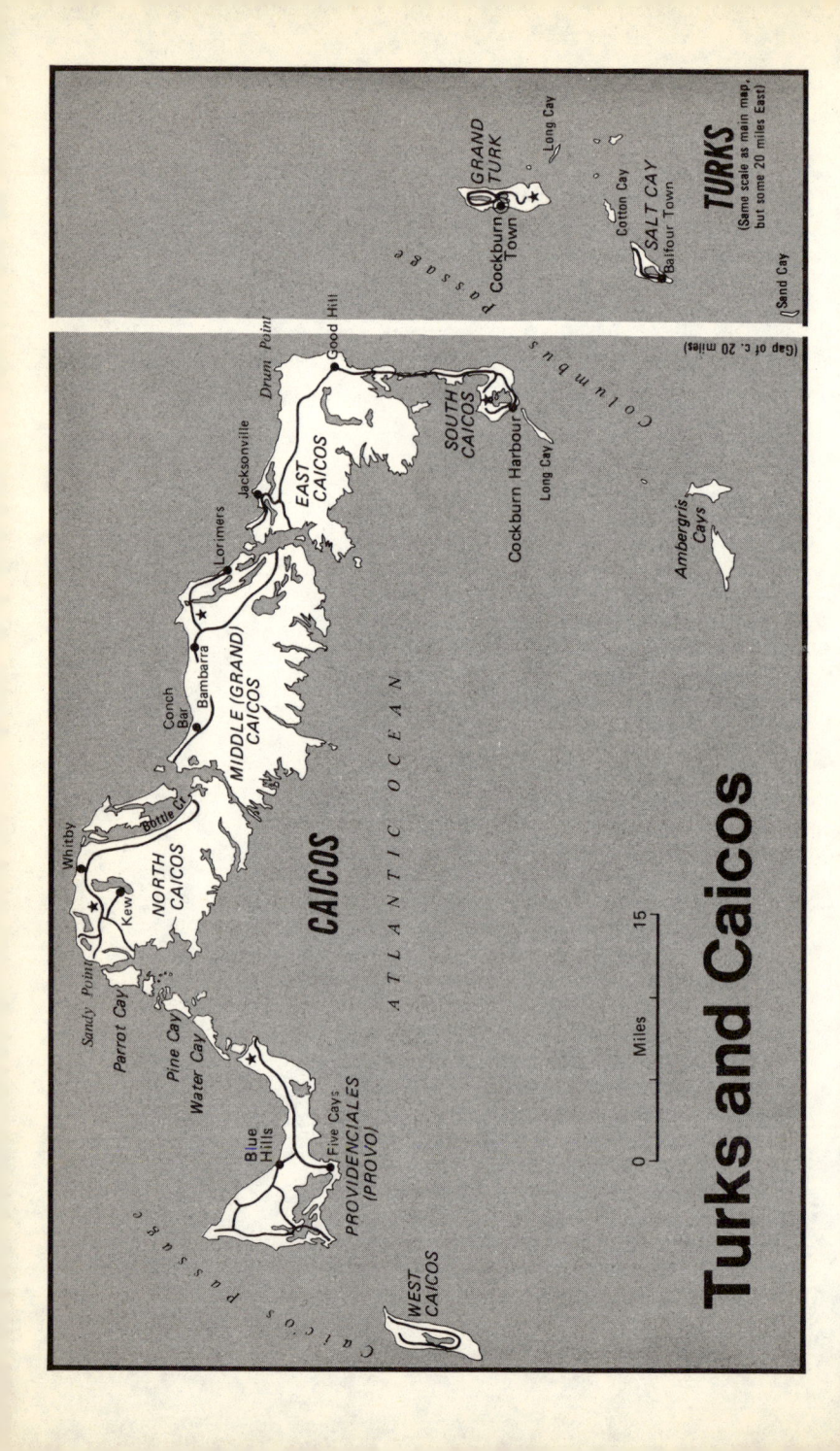

The Turks & Caicos

Of the eight main islands in the Turks & Caicos, six are inhabited: Grand Turk, Salt Cay, South, Middle (Grand), and North Caicos, and Providenciales (commonly shortened to Provo). About 14,000 people live on these islands year-round, half of them on the Salt Islands — Grand Turk, Salt Cay, and South Caicos. Generally, the islands are as flat as the Arizona desert; the highest hill in the entire colony, on Grand Turk, is only 163 feet tall. If you are fond of fog and drizzle, don't come to the Turks & Caicos, where only 26 inches of rain fall, on average, each year. Vegetation is sparse, aside from stands of windswept pine and palmetto and several varieties of cactus, including the red-topped Turk's Head, for which the Turks islands are named. Some of the islands were once forested, but salt rakers cleared the land to make room for their pans. Few crops are grown, except on the Caicos, where the "Belongers," as the islanders are called, raise small plots of corn and pigeon peas.

Until about 30 years ago, salt continued to be the mainstay of the economy; now shellfish — and tourists — are the big moneymakers. Haiti is the big consumer of Turks & Caicos conch, and most of the spiny lobsters caught here end up on American tables. The big hope for the future is tourism. The British government has encouraged the development of the colony's tourist industry, which it hopes will bring the islanders closer to self-sufficiency. Provo, in the Caicos group, is the most developed for tourists, and the building boom in progress there is not unlike the boom on Grand Bahama in the 1950s and early 1960s. With a little luck and some good planning, though, the development in the Turks & Caicos may not spoil the pristine beauty of the place completely. Locals have banded together to protect the reefs that ring the islands, and even on Provo, if you get past the bulldozers and the earth-moving equipment you can still find some lovely secluded spots.

A few words about getting around. From the United States, you can fly into one of the two most populous islands, Grand Turk and Provo. *Cayman Airways* flies from Miami to both islands, and *Turks and Caicos National Airlines* (*TCNA*) brings visitors in from Nassau and Freeport. (*Bahamasair*, in addition, has flights from Nassau to South Caicos and Provo.) *TCNA* flies twice a day from Grand Turk to some of the outlying islands, and there are also several charters that shuttle back and forth among the smaller isles and cays. Visitors can even hop over for the day to one of the uninhabited isles such as West Caicos, where amenities are few but the swimming and diving are great. If you do go to some of the more remote spots, plan carefully. If you're chartering a boat or a plane to one of the unpopulated isles, be very specific about when you want to be picked up. Bring a map and plenty of sunscreen, and carry your own food and water. And make sure someone back at your hotel knows where you're going and when you plan to return.

260 DIRECTIONS / Turks & Caicos

Here, then, are brief descriptions of the six inhabited islands. You can see the major sights on some in a day or less; others deserve a bit more time. We also take you on a walking tour through historic Cockburn Town on Grand Turk and on a driving tour across Provo.

GRAND TURK

Grand Turk's 9 square miles hold some 4,000 of the colony's population; it boasts a high school, a small hospital, international banks, and an airport with a 7,000-foot airstrip. Like most of the Turks & Caicos, the scenery is hardly worth writing home about. The land is flat, dry, and covered with old salinas and scrub. The great treasures are offshore. Submerged coral reefs protect a good deal of the island, and divers have a choice of spectacular wall-diving sites.

Juan Ponce de León paid a call here in 1515, and some historians claim that this is where Columbus first sighted land in 1492. Once the center of the now-defunct salt industry, Grand Turk is the site of the islands' administrative center, and Cockburn Town is its major settlement. The town, a dusty, sleepy little village, has a Bermuda look to it; if you're looking for nightlife, this is definitely *not* the place. Until recently, donkey carts still rattled along the harbor road, which is usually called Front Street (its official name is Duke Street). The donkeys still roam the island, but the carriages that once transported visitors have disappeared. Don't despair: The town is small enough to be explored on foot.

WALKING GRAND TURK

Start at the *Kittina* hotel, the oldest and largest resort on the island, which stands right on the beach at the south end of town. Walk north up Front Street past the *Salt Raker Inn,* a comfy Bermuda-style hostelry where the locals stop for a beer and a snatch of gossip. Just up the road is the *Turks Head Inn,* housed in an 18th-century building that's been designated a historic landmark. In the center of town, up the new red brick sidewalk, is the Victorian-era library. The Cable and Wireless building is on the waterfront; it's cheaper to call long-distance here than from the hotels. Nearby are two banks, plenty of lawyer's offices, and the town's only non-hotel restaurant, the *Poop Deck,* which usually runs out of the daily special by 2 PM.

On the north edge of town is *Blue Water Divers,* where you can rent all the equipment you need, and a historic home, once the *Guinep Lodge,* that now houses the *Turks and Caicos National Museum.* Past the lodge the road doglegs around an old salt pond called North Salina. The road west of the pond leads to the *Guanahani Beach* hotel on near-perfect Pillory Beach, where you can stop for a swim and a rum cooler. Locals maintain that Columbus landed somewhere along this shore in 1492. The town's abandoned icehouse, in operation as recently as the 1940s, is nearby.

Follow the same road back toward town; it soon runs into Pond Street, which runs along the back of town. Nearby are several more salinas, a scattering of pastel-colored homes, and some very old warehouses. Her Majesty's Prison is on Pond Street, and across the salina is the 19th-century Methodist church, one of the oldest in the colony. Colonel Murray Hill, on the eastern side of mile-wide Grand Turk, is the highest point on the island and a favorite rendezvous for lovers. If you prefer, hire a cab (through your hotel) and visit the outlying sights: old St. Thomas Church; Governor's Beach, near his excellency's stately 19th-century home, "Waterloo"; Hawk's Nest anchorage; the lighthouse and the deserted naval station; and the missile-tracking station (John Glenn was debriefed on Grand Turk after his 1962 space mission).

SALT CAY

Nine miles from Grand Turk, accessible by boat and only 5 minutes away by air, this 3½-square-mile island is shaped like a slice of pie pointed south. At the tip, the surf is rough, but the east side is indented with quiet bays and inlets, and the beach that stretches across its wide northern end is as white and peaceful and perfect as a beach can get. Some small hotels have opened up here in the past few years. Windswept and quaint, Balfour Town boasts relics of the island's whaling and salt-raking days. The windmills here haven't operated since 1971, and the abandoned salt flats look like skating rinks melting in the sun. Locals talk of reviving the saltworks to show tourists how they once were run. There is one dive outfit on the island, and the Talbot brothers will be glad to take you fishing. Contact them through the district commissioner's office (phone: 66985). In late winter and early spring, humpback whales swim up the Turks Passage off the west coast on the way to their spawning grounds. They sometimes can be spotted from the beach near the *Windmills* hotel.

SOUTH CAICOS

Some 22 miles west of Grand Turk, across the Turks Islands Passage, South Caicos is anchored behind a sweep of coral reefs that offer an enormous variety of dives. The little town, Cockburn Harbour, is friendly but not much to look at. The only buildings of historic interest are the 18th-century Commissioner's House and the warehouses of the old saltworks. The focal point of the community is Cockburn Harbour, the best natural harbor in the Turks & Caicos. Fishermen bring in their catch of conch and lobster there, and every May the bay is filled with sloops and smacks competing in the *Commonwealth Regatta*. Wild horses graze on the scrub on the eastern part of the island. There is a 7,500-foot airstrip, where the *Bahamasair* flights from Nassau and a steady stream of private craft touches down.

MIDDLE (GRAND) CAICOS

Reached by ferry from North Caicos, Middle (or Grand) Caicos is the largest of the group, though only 400 people live here year-round. The *Eagle's Rest Villas* — two 2-bedroom, 2-bath, air conditioned units with living rooms, fully equipped kitchens, and cable TV (phone: 62142; in the US, 215-255-4640) — and the much more rustic and inexpensive *Taylor's Guest House,* which has 4 rooms (phone: in the US, 305-667-0966), offer the only lodging on the island. The secluded beach near Mudjin Harbour is exceptionally beautiful. There are extraordinary limestone caves along the cliff-edged northern coast; it's worth the trouble to find them, if only to see the reflections of the stalactites and stalagmites in the clear saltwater pools. (Herbert Neat, a.k.a. "Cave Mon," knows the caves like the back of his hand and will, for a small gratuity, gladly take you on a tour.) For more than a decade, groups of American archaeologists have been coming to Middle Caicos to explore the caves and ruins near Bambarra and Lorimers. Bambarra was settled by survivors of the Spanish slave ship *Gambia,* which was shipwrecked offshore in 1842. Most of the slaves were Bombarras from the Niger River Valley in West Africa, hence the town's name. Archaeologists also come to hunt for Lucaya Indian artifacts and to explore the ruins of Loyalist plantations along Benjie Ridge.

NORTH CAICOS

One of the most verdant of the islands, relatively speaking, North Caicos is best known for its 6-mile beach and excellent bonefishing. Its 1,600 permanent residents live in 4 tiny villages: Bottle Creek on its eastern edge, Kew and Whitby in the center, and Sandy Point in the northwest. Near Kew stand the recently excavated ruins of Wade's Green Plantation. On the island's many nature reserves and sanctuaries, visitors can see West Indian whistling ducks, ospreys, grebes, and flocks of flamingos, which look from a distance like billowing pink clouds. At the West Indian Mariculture crab farm between Whitby and Bottle Creek, you can learn how Caribbean king crabs are nurtured from tiny eggs to hefty adults. *Pelican Beach* (phone: 67112), *Prospect of Whitby* (phone: 67119), and *Ocean Beach* condos (phone: 67113) offer fine out-island hideaways for vacationers.

PINE CAY

One of the chain of islets that links North Caicos and Provo, it is quietly notable for the *Meridian Club* (phone: in New York City, 212-696-4566; in the rest of the US, 800-331-9154; fax: 65128), the social center for an enclave of some 20 to 25 homes that occupies the whole 800-acre island. The club is exclusive, but not in a class-conscious sense, though some of its guests may be listed in the *Social Register.* It's special for its devotion to uncomplicated relaxation, and to preserving the peace and beauty of the island. Pine Cay's shimmering 2-mile beach is lovely for sunning, swimming, and strolling, and snorkeling. Visitors can explore several hiking trails and nature walks. Nearby Fort George Cay is worth a visit, and Water Cay and Little Water Cay offer super shelling.

PROVO

Green, hilly Provo is one of the largest of the islands (37½ square miles) and the most sophisticated, from the standpoint of tourism. It lies near the western edge of the Caicos chain, just east of uninhabited West Caicos. About 4,200 people live here year-round, and tourists swell the ranks considerably. The international airport can now accommodate wide-body 747s.

The scenery on Provo isn't remarkable; most of the island is covered with scrub and stunted trees, and there is little in the way of natural beauty, aside from the nature reserve at Crab Pond. The 12-mile-long beach along the north coast near Grace Bay is very fine, though, and it is there that the island's big resorts, including the *Ramada Turquoise Reef* resort and casino and the *Club Med Turkoise,* are located. (The nearby *Sheraton,* under construction for the past 6 or 7 years, was still unfinished at press time.)

Also on the east end, near the slips where the ferry to the North Caicos islands dock, is the *Island Sea Centre* and its conch-breeding farm (phone: 65330). Conch eggs are nurtured in geodesic domes and fed farm-raised algae until they're large enough to be transplanted to seabed nurseries. The research project is sponsored in part by the University of Miami and *PRIDE,* the Provo-based nonprofit organization. Visitors can tour the farm, sample conch dishes at the snack bar, try on conch-shell and coral jewelry, and talk to the folks at *PRIDE,* who, among other things, are studying an extraordinarily amiable bottle-nosed dolphin named JoJo. The center, which was recently renovated and expanded, is open from 9 AM to 5 PM Mondays through Saturdays; tours cost $6 for adults and $3 for children.

DRIVING ON PROVO

Visitors who don't mind dusty, unmarked roads and have some time to kill can rent a car (a four-wheel-drive vehicle is recommended to reach the beaches on the north and west coasts) and visit other spots on the island. The main road, the Leeward Highway, runs east to west along a 100-foot ridge not far from the north shore. Take a map, for few of the roads and settlements are marked. Heading west from the conch farm, past the turnoff to the big resorts on Grace Bay and the settlement of Kingston, is "Richmond Hills," a ruined Loyalist plantation and now an enclave of modern homes. Beyond it is the road to Turtle Cove on the north shore, where the *Erebus Inn* overlooks the blue-green water of the bay (stop by its excellent French restaurant; phone: 64120). The *Turtle Cove* inn, a dive shop, a small shopping center, and *JoJo's* restaurant are nearby.

Back on the main road, in the shopping and commercial development known unimaginatively as *The Centre,* is the lively California-style Mexican restaurant *Hey José.* (If you're tired of burritos, try island-style pizza; phone: 64812.) A little farther down on the right is "Cheshire Hall," another Loyalist plantation that dates from the 1790s. The ruins are more accessible than they are at Richmond Hills, and you can poke around the remaining foundation stones and imagine what the place was like a couple of hundred years ago. About a mile farther on, where five roads converge, is Downtown (not just a geographic name), a soulless place with no houses or sidewalks or historical landmarks but plenty (relatively) of shopping centers, banks, offices, and modest eateries. Once a week, usually on Thursdays, Provo's artisans converge at Market Place east of here to sell their wares.

Fishermen should take the south fork out of Downtown, which leads to the excellent bonefishing flats on Chalk Sound. On the way, the road passes near the South Dock Harbour, where the big freighters dock; the *Mariner Inn* on Sapodilla Hill (some of the rocks up the hill behind the inn are carved with the initials of sailors who were shipwrecked here over the years); and a few secluded beaches.

The road leading directly west from Downtown dead-ends at the airport; the northwest fork from the spaghetti intersection leads to the decent beach at Thompson Cove point on the north coast and wanders through the settlement of Blue Hills, which is said to have been founded by survivors of the wreck of a French ship that was dashed against the reefs here early in the 17th century. Each August, the residents of Blue Hills celebrate *Emancipation Day* with a *Carnival*-like parade. About 3 miles down the road is Wheeland, a small settlement with a couple of restaurants and a lively club called the *Three Queens* (no phone), which offers live entertainment a few times each week. The pavement ends after Wheeland; it's best to have a four-wheel-drive vehicle to reach the beaches on the north and west coasts and the Crab Pond nature reserve in the interior.

INDEX

Index

Abacos, 9, 124, 188, 221–27
  hotels, 140–41
  island resorts, 174–75
  map, 222
  tour of, 221–27
    by car, 224–25
    cruising the cays, 225–27
    walking, 223
Accommodations
  calculating costs, 41–42
  Club Med, 39, 71–72, 185
  couples' resorts, 39, 71
  guesthouses, 68
  hotels, 68
    special havens, 173–74
    See also hotels *entry under name of individual island*
  island resorts, 171, 174–75
  rental homes, 68–71
  traveling with children, 63–64
  vacation apartments, 69–70
Advance purchase excursion fares (APEX), 13–14
Agents
  rental property, 69–71
  travel. *See* Travel agents
Airline clubs, 19
Airplane travel, 11–27
  bartered travel sources, 26
  cancellations due to family emergencies, 77
  charter flights, 20–22
    bookings, 21–22
  with children, 17, 62–63
  consolidators and bucket shops, 23–24
  consumer protection, 20, 26–27
  flight insurance, 48–49
  fly/drive packages, 36
  generic air travel, 25–26
  hints for handicapped travelers, 53–54
  last-minute travel clubs, 25
  scheduled flights, 11–20
    airline clubs, 19–20
    baggage, 18–19
    delays and cancellations, 20
    discounts on, 22–26
    fares, 11–15
    frequent flyers, 15
    getting bumped, 20
    meals, 18, 62–63
    net fares, 23
    reservations, 16
    seating, 16–18
    smoking, 18
    taxes and other fees, 15–16
    tickets, 11
Alcoholic beverages, 79
Andros, 9, 124
  hotels, 142
  map, 228
  sports, 183
  tour of, 229–33
    by bike, 231
    by car, 231–33
Apartments, vacation, 69–70
Automobile insurance, 49

Baggage, 18–19
  personal effects insurance, 46–47
Bahamas, 121–50, 171–72, 176
  general data on, 121–22
  hotels, 135–45
    Abacos, 140–41
    Andros, 142
    Berry Islands, 142
    Bimini, 142–43
    Cat Island, 143
    Eleuthera, 143–44, 171, 173–74, 175
    Exumas, 144–45
    Grand Bahama, 139–40
    Harbour Island, 144
    Long Island, 145
    Nassau-Cable Beach, New Providence, 135–37, 168, 174
    Paradise Island, 137–39
    Rum Cay, 145
    San Salvador, 145
    Western New Providence Island, 139
  island resorts, 171, 174–75, 236
  local transportation, 125–27
  nightlife, 134–35, 169–70, 176–77

268 INDEX

Bahamas (*cont.*)
  places of special interest, 122–24
    outlying islands, 124
  restaurants, 145–50
    Freeport/Lucaya, 149–50
    Nassau, 146–48
    Paradise Island, 148–49
  shopping, 127–30
    Freeport, 129–30, 176
    Nassau, 128–29, 171–72, 176
  special events, 127
  sports, 130–34, 168–69, 182–87
  telephone, 125
  tourist information, 124
  tourist offices, 85
Bankruptcy and/or default insurance, 48
Bareboat chartered boats, traveling by, 31–32
Bartered travel sources, 26
Bay Street, Nassau, 171–72
Beaches, 133, 157, 182
  Eleuthera, 171, 182
  water safety, 75
Berry Islands, 9, 123
  hotels, 142
Biking tours
  Andros, 231
  Bimini, 219–20
  Exumas, 248
  Grand Bahama, 211–12
Bimini, 9, 124, 215–20
  hotels, 142–43
  map, 216
  sports, 168–69, 183
  tour of, 215–20
    by bike, 219–20
    by boat, 220
    walking, 217–19
Boating, 130–31, 220, 225–27
  regattas, 9, 127, 131–32
  See also Charters, boat
Books for travelers, 86–87
Briland, Harbour Island, 170–71, 231
Buried treasure, 187–88
Business hours, 72

Cable Beach, New Providence, hotels, 135–37
Cameras and equipment, 87–88, 177–81
Car, touring by, 32–36
  Abacos tour, 224–25
  Andros tour, 231–33
  Exumas tour, 248–50
  Grand Bahama tour, 212–14
  Great Exuma tour, 248–50
  hints for handicapped travelers, 54–55
  insurance, 49
  Providenciales tour, 263–64
  rentals, 32–36, 125–26, 154–55
    costs, 35–36
    fly/drive packages, 36
    requirements, 34–35
Casinos, 134–35, 169–70, 176–77
Cat Cay, 220
Cat Island, 9, 123, 124, 169, 241–44
  beaches, 182
  hotels, 143
  map, 240
  tour of, 241–44
Charters
  airline, 20–22
  boat, 31–32
    bareboat charters, 31–32
    crewed boats, 31
    sailing to the Bahamas, 173
Children, traveling with, 60–64
  accommodations, 63–64
  getting there and getting around, 17, 62–63
  meals, 63–64
  planning, 60–62
Climate, and clothes, 10
Clothes
  aboard ship, 29
  climate and, 10
Club Med, 39, 71–72, 185
Cockburn Town, Grand Turk, 9, 153–54, 260
Condominiums, 69
Consolidators and bucket shops, 23–24
Consulates. *See* Embassies and consulates
Consumer protection, 20, 26–27
Coral reefs, 111–12
Costs, calculating, 41–42
  rental property discounts and agents, 69–71
  transportation, 11–15, 22–26, 35–36, 41–42
Cottages, 69
Couples' resorts, 39, 71
Craft items, 82, 117
Credit, 65–67
Credit cards, 66–67

INDEX 269

Cricket, 131
Cruise ship, traveling by. *See* Ship, traveling by
Currency, 65–67
Customs and returning to the US, 81–84, 127–28, 171–72, 176

Dance and music, 97–101, 167–68, 180–81
Default and/or bankruptcy insurance, 48
Dixon Hill Lighthouse, San Salvador, 180
Drinking, 79
Drugs
  illegal, 79
  prescription, 76, 79
Duty-free shopping, 81–82, 127–28, 171–72, 176

Electricity, 73
Eleuthera, 9, 124, 235–39
  beaches, 171, 182
  hotels, 143–44, 171, 173–74, 175
  island resorts, 171, 175, 236
  map, 234
  sports, 183, 185–87
  tour of, 235–39
Embassies and consulates
  US in the Bahamas, 77–78
Emergencies
  family, 77
  legal, 77–78
  medical, 75, 78
Entry requirements and documents, 45–46
Excursion fares, 12–15
Exumas, 9, 124
  hotels, 144–45
  map, 246
  tour of, 245–50
    by bike, 248
    by car, 248–50
    walking, 247–48

Family Island
  Regatta, 9, 127, 131
Fauna, 113, 156
Fernandez Bay, Cat Island, 182, 242
Ferry, 156
  Abacos cruises, 225–27
  touring Bimini by, 220
First aid, 74
Fish, 112–13

Fishing. *See* Sport fishing
Flight insurance, 48–49
Flora, 110–11
Fly/drive packages, 36
Folk legends and lore, 115–17
Food and drink
  aboard ship, 29
  island, 105–8, 112–14
  on planes, 18, 62–63
  traveling with children, 63–64
  See also Restaurants
Forbidden imports, 83–84
Freeport/Lucaya, New Providence, 9
  restaurants, 149–50
  shopping, 129–30, 176
  sports, 183
Frequent flyers, 15
Fruits and vegetables, 107–8, 113–14

Gambling. *See* Casinos
George Town, Exumas, 247–49
Golf, 131, 185–86
Goombay, 97, 100–101, 127
Governor's Harbour, Eleuthera, 235–37
Grace Cay, Providenciales, 182
Grand Bahama, 9, 209–14
  hotels, 139–40
  map, 210
  tour of, 209–14
    by bike, 211–12
    by car, 212–14
Grand Turk, 9, 169
  diving off, 172–73
  hotels, 158–159
  restaurants, 161
  tour of, 260–61
Graycliff, Nassau, 136, 168, 174, 196
Great Exuma
  beaches, 182
  bike tours of, 248
  car tours of, 248–50
Guesthouses, 68

Handicapped travelers, hints for, 50–56
  airplane travel, 53–54
  car, touring by, 54–55
  cruise ships, 54
  planning, 50–53
  tours, 55–56
Harbour Island, Eleuthera, 9, 170–71, 182, 239
  hotels, 144

Health care, 74–77
  first aid, 74
  helpful publications, 77
  hints for older travelers, 58–59
  medical aid, 75–77
  personal accident and sickness insurance, 47
  sunburn, 74
  water safety, 75
Hispaniola, 9
History, 91–96
  colonists and privateers, 92–93
  contrabandists, 93–94
  tourism and trade, 94–95
  Turks & Caicos Islands, 95–96
Horseback riding, 131
Hotels, 68
  Bahamas, 135–45
  island resorts, 171, 174–75, 236
  special havens, 173–74
  tipping, 79, 80
  traveling with children, 63–64
  Turks & Caicos, 158–61
  See also Club Med; Couples' resorts; Guesthouses; Rental homes; hotels *entry under name of individual island*
Housekeeping apartments, 69
Houses, rental, 68–71
Hunting, 187

Imports, forbidden, 83–84
Insurance, 46–50
  automobile, 49
  baggage and personal effects, 46–47
  combination policies, 50
  default and/or bankruptcy, 48
  flight, 48–49
  personal accident and sickness, 47
  trip cancellation and interruption, 48
Island food and drink, 105–8, 112–14
Island resorts, 171, 174–75, 236
Island Sea Center, North Caicos, 263
Island tours, 191–264
  Abacos, 221–27
  Andros, 229–33
  Bimini, 215–20
  Cat Island, 241–44
  Eleuthera, 235–39
  Exumas, 245–50
  Grand Bahama, 209–14
  Nassau, 193–97

New Providence, 199–203
Paradise Island, 205–8
San Salvador, 251–57
Turks & Caicos, 259–64

Junkanoo (dance), 97, 98, 100, 102, 121, 134, 167–68, 180–81

Kayaking, 131

Legal aid, 77–78
Long Island, 9, 183
  hotels, 145
Lucaya National Park, Grand Bahama, 213–14

Mail, 72–73
Maps, 4–5
  Abacos, 222
  Andros, 228
  Bimini, 216
  Cat Island, 240
  Eleuthera, 234
  Exumas, 246
  Grand Bahama, 210
  Nassau, 194
  New Providence, 198
  Paradise Island, 204
  San Salvador, 252
  Turks & Caicos, 258
Marine life, 111–13
Marsh Harbour, Abacos, 221–23
Medical assistance in the Bahamas, 75–77
  See also Health care
Middle (Grand) Caicos, 9, 151, 154
  tour of, 261–62
Money, 65, 67
  See also Credit cards; Traveler's checks
Music and dance, 97–101, 167–68, 180–81

Nassau, New Providence/Paradise Island, 9, 193–97
  casinos, 169–70, 176–77
  hotels, 135–39, 168, 174
  map, 194
  restaurants, 146–49
  shopping, 128–29, 171–72, 176
  sports, 183
  tour of, 193–97
Natural wonderlands, 175
New Providence, 9, 199–203
  map, 198

sports, 186
tour of, 199–203
Newsletters for travelers, 87
Nightlife
  Bahamas, 134–35, 169–70, 176–77
  Turks & Caicos, 157, 177
North Caicos, 9, 151, 154
  hotels, 159
  tour of, 262

Off-season travel, 9–10
Older travelers, hints for, 58–60
  discounts and packages, 59–60
  health, 58–59
  planning, 58

Package tours, 36–40
  for handicapped travelers, 55–56
  for older travelers, 59–60
  for single travelers, 57
  sample tours to the Bahamas, 39–40
  sea excursions, 156
Paradise Island, 205–8
  hotels, 137–39
  map, 204
  restaurants, 148–49
  sports, 183, 185, 186
  tour of, 205–8
Parrot Cay, Caicos, hotels, 159
Passport, 45–46
People-to-People Programme, 123–24
Personal accident and sickness insurance, 47
Photography, 87–88, 177–81
Pine Cay, Caicos, 9
  hotels, 161, 174
  tour of, 262
Planning the trip, 42–44
  books and newsletters, 86–87
  hints for handicapped travelers, 50–53
  hints for older travelers, 58
  hints for traveling with children, 60–62
Potter's Cay, Caicos, 179–80
Preacher's Cove, Eleuthera, 180
PRIDE (Foundation to Protect Reefs and Islands from Degradation and Exploitation), North Caicos, 156, 263
Providenciales ("Provo"), Caicos, 9, 151–52, 153–54
  beaches, 182
  hotels, 160–61
  restaurants, 162–63
  tour of, 263–64

Ramsar site, Turks & Caicos, 175
Rand Memorial Nature Center, Grand Bahama, 213
Regattas, 9, 127, 131–32
Religion
  heritage, 102–4
  services, 80–81
Rental homes, 68–71
Restaurants
  Bahamas, 145–50
  tipping, 79–80
  Turks & Caicos, 161–63
  See also restaurants entry under name of individual island
Rolleville, Great Exuma, 182, 249
Rum Cay, hotels, 145

Sailing, 130–31, 156, 184
  regattas, 127, 131–32
  to the Bahamas, 173
Salinas, Grand Turk, 180
Salt Cay, 9
  hotels, 159
  tour of, 261
Samana Cay, 169
San Salvador, 9, 123, 124, 169, 251–57
  hotels, 145
  map, 252
  sports, 183–84
  tour of, 251–57
Scuba diving, 123, 132–33, 156–57, 169, 175, 182–84
  coral reefs, 111–12
  natural wonderlands, 175
  off Grand Turk, 172–73
  sunken and buried treasure, 187–88
  water safety, 75
Sea excursions, 126, 156
Shellfish, 112–13
Shelling, 132
Ship, traveling by, 27–31
  cabins, 28
  cruise lines and ships to the Bahamas, 27, 30–31
  dress, 29
  facilities and activities, 28–29
  hints for handicapped travelers, 54

INDEX

Ship (cont.)
  meals, 29
  sanitation, 29–30
  shore excursions, 28–29
  tipping, 29
  with children, 63
  See also Charters, boat
Shipwrecks, sunken and buried treasure, 187–88
Shopping, 127–30, 176
  Bahamas, 128–30, 171–72, 176
  craft items, 82, 117
  duty-free, 81–82, 127–28, 171–72, 176
  Turks & Caicos, 155–56
Sickness and personal accident insurance, 47
Single travelers, hints for, 56–57
Snorkeling, 132–33, 156–57, 175, 182–84
  coral reefs, 111–12
  natural wonderlands, 175
  off Grand Turk, 172–73
  sunken and buried treasure, 187–88
  water safety, 75
South Caicos, 9, 153, 154, 261
  hotels, 161
  tour of, 261
Spanish Wells, 9, 133, 238–39
Special events
  Bahamas, 127
  Turks & Caicos, 155
Spectator sports, 133
Sport fishing, 112–13, 133, 157, 168–69, 186–87
Sports. See sports *entry under name of individual island*; *names of sports*
Stocking Island, off Great Exuma, 133–34, 172, 247–48
Sunburn, 74
Sunken and buried treasure, 187–88

Telephone, 73, 125, 154
Tennis, 134, 157, 185
Time, 72
Tipping, 79–80
  aboard ship, 29
Tourist offices
  the Bahamas, 85
  Turks & Caicos, 85–86
  See also tourist information *entry under name of individual island*

Tours
  island. See Island tours
  package. See Package tours
  sea excursions, 126, 156
Transportation
  calculating costs, 11–15, 22–26, 35–36, 41–42
  local
    Bahamas, 125–27
    Turks & Caicos, 154–55
  See also Airplane travel; Car, touring by; Charters, boat; Ship, traveling by; local transportation *entry under name of individual island*
Travel agents, 16, 22–24, 38–39, 44–45
  for handicapped travelers, 55–56
  for older travelers, 59–60
Travel clubs, 25
Traveler's checks, 65–66
Treasure hunting spots, 187–88
Treasure Reef, off Grand Bahama, 188
Trip cancellation and interruption insurance, 48
Turks & Caicos, 9, 151–63, 259–64
  general data on, 151–53
  history, 95–96
  hotels, 158–61
    Grand Turk, 158–159
    North Caicos, 159
    Parrot Cay, 159
    Pine Cay, 161, 174
    Providenciales, 160–61
    Salt Cay, 159
    South Caicos, 161
  island resorts, 174
  local transportation, 154–55
  map, 258
  nightlife, 157, 177
  places of special interest, 153–54, 175
  restaurants, 161–63
    Grand Turk, 161
    Provo, 162–63
  shopping, 155–56
  special events, 155
  sports, 156–57, 184, 187
  telephone, 154
  tourist information, 154
  tourist offices, 85–86
  tours of, 259–64
    Grand Turk, 260–61
    Middle (Grand) Caicos, 261–62

North Caicos, 262
Pine Cay, 262
Providenciales, 263–64
Salt Cay, 261
South Caicos, 261

Underwater Explorers Society (UNEXSO), Grand Bahama, 123, 132, 183
US embassies and consulates, 77–78

Walking tours
 of Abacos, 223
 of Bimini, 217–19
 of the Exumas, 247–48
 of Grand Turk, 260–61
 of Great Exuma, 247–48
 of Paradise Island, 206–8
Water safety, 75
Water skiing, 134
Weather report, worldwide, 10
 See also Climate
Western New Providence Island, hotels, 139
Windermere Island Club, off Eleuthera, 143, 171, 175, 236
Windsurfing, 134, 156
Wonderlands, natural, 175

Yachts, 184